SACRAMENTO NORTHERN

Ira L. Swett

with

Vernon J. Sappers

Thomas R. Bold

Harre Demoro

Addison H. Laflin, Jr.

INTERURBANS SPECIAL 26

Contents

(Authors listed in parentheses; where no author listed,
chapter is a symposium or direct quote)

PHOTO CREDITS: We are indebted to the following collectors
for the many rare photos published herein:

AA-AH: Art Alter Photo from Al Haij Collection
AA-BB: Art Alter Photo from Bill Billings Collection
AEB: Alfred E. Barker
AL: Addison H. Laflin, Jr.
BS: Bob Stein
CS: Charles Smallwood
DLO: Donald L. Olsen
ECH: Erle C. Hanson
HD: Harre Demoro
JCW: J. C. Whittaker
LLS: Louis L. Stein, Jr.
LS: Lorin Silleman
Magna: Ira L. Swett
RB: Randolph Brandt
RD: Ralph Demoro
TRB: Thomas R. Bold
VDB: Victor DuBrutz
VS: Vernon J. Sappers
WCW: Wilbur C. Whittaker
WP: Western Pacific RR.

INTERURBAN PRESS
P.O. Box 6444 • Glendale, CA 91205

ISBN 0-916374-47-5

First Printing: September 1962
Second Printing: January 1971
Third Printing: September 1981

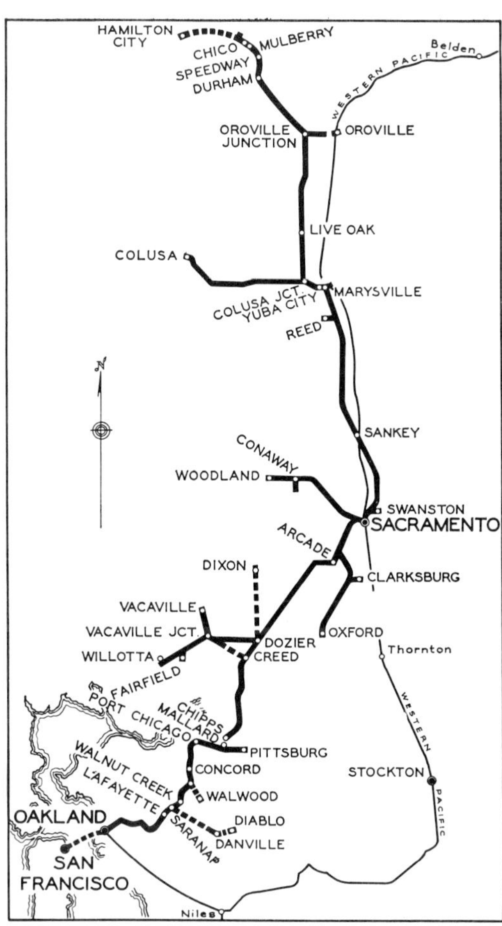

(Western Pacific)

FOREWORD

The more you think about it, the more the interurban world lost when Sacramento Northern abandoned passenger service. Think it over: One ride--- 183 miles long, world's longest interurban--- brought you more diverse operation than you could buy anywhere else in the U.S. ---probably in the world.

Let's consider the features encountered south from Chico: Miles of flat, high speed, third rail running; city street operation in towns; a bit of running on the main line of a steam railroad; a spectacular entrance via bridge and pierced levee into California's capital city, with an impressive interurban Union Station and train yard; more street running and another major bridge, then high speed over the delta country, including long trestles and a drawbridge; a one-in-a-million interurban car ferry, complete with lunch room, crossing almost a mile of sometimes choppy bay; back country running with two steam railroads to race if you were lucky; winding climbs up the mountains and down again--- with a long tunnel in the middle; street operation into Oakland and changing from pole trolley to pantagraph; mingling with the constant stream of orange Key Route trains out to the Pier Terminal; then the final thrill: a ferry boat ride across the bay, ending at San Francisco's world famed Ferry Building (succeeded in later years by the direct rail entry via the longest bridge in the nation and a new interurban terminal in the heart of the city).

All this for the price of one ticket!

Sacramento Northern was all the above, plus more: parlor-dining cars on speedy name trains; little streetcars jouncing along quiet streets; heavy freights on heavy rail; branch lines, each a miniature world of its own; Birneys jogging patiently across hot miles of valley floor en route to or from the shops at Chico; and there a big, old fashioned carbarn and shop building---in a most unlikely place. What a wonderful interurban was SN!

Special 26 is the direct outgrowth of our Special 9, published in 1949 and long out of print. We expected to do better this time around and succeeded too well: because of space limitations set by the announced price, Special 26 will not be our total coverage coverage of SN; Special 32 will be "The Sacramento Northern All Time Roster & Pictorial," and will, with Special 26, comprise exhaustive coverage of a most worthy subject.

Special 26 is three books, just as SN was three railroads: Book I covers The North End---the old Northern Electric and its successor, Sacramento Northern Railroad; Book II deals with The South End---the Oakland, Antioch & Eastern and its successor, the San Francisco-Sacramento Railroad; Book III begins where the first two leave off---the 1928 end-to-end merger and the subsequent history of the unified North and South Ends under the new master company, the Sacramento Northern Railway.

Many helped in the production of Special 26 and they are recognized on another page, but Mr. Vernon J. Sappers of Oakland stands out especially; Mr. Sappers went the extra mile in answering hundreds of questions and in making available rare photographs and other memorabilia of the vanished Sacramento Northern interurbans. We would like to dedicate Special 26 to him.

September 1, 1962   Ira L. Swett

Two views of Tres Vias in Northern Electric days. Above, a 1909 view; Chico is straight ahead, Oroville is to the right, and Sacramento is to left.   Note the attractive little garden in foreground. (CS)

Below, a closeup of the transfer platforms at Tres Vias in the early years.   The big light orange cars were posed, but it does provide a busy scene.   And look at that sharp curve!   (LLS)

SECTION I

THE NORTH END

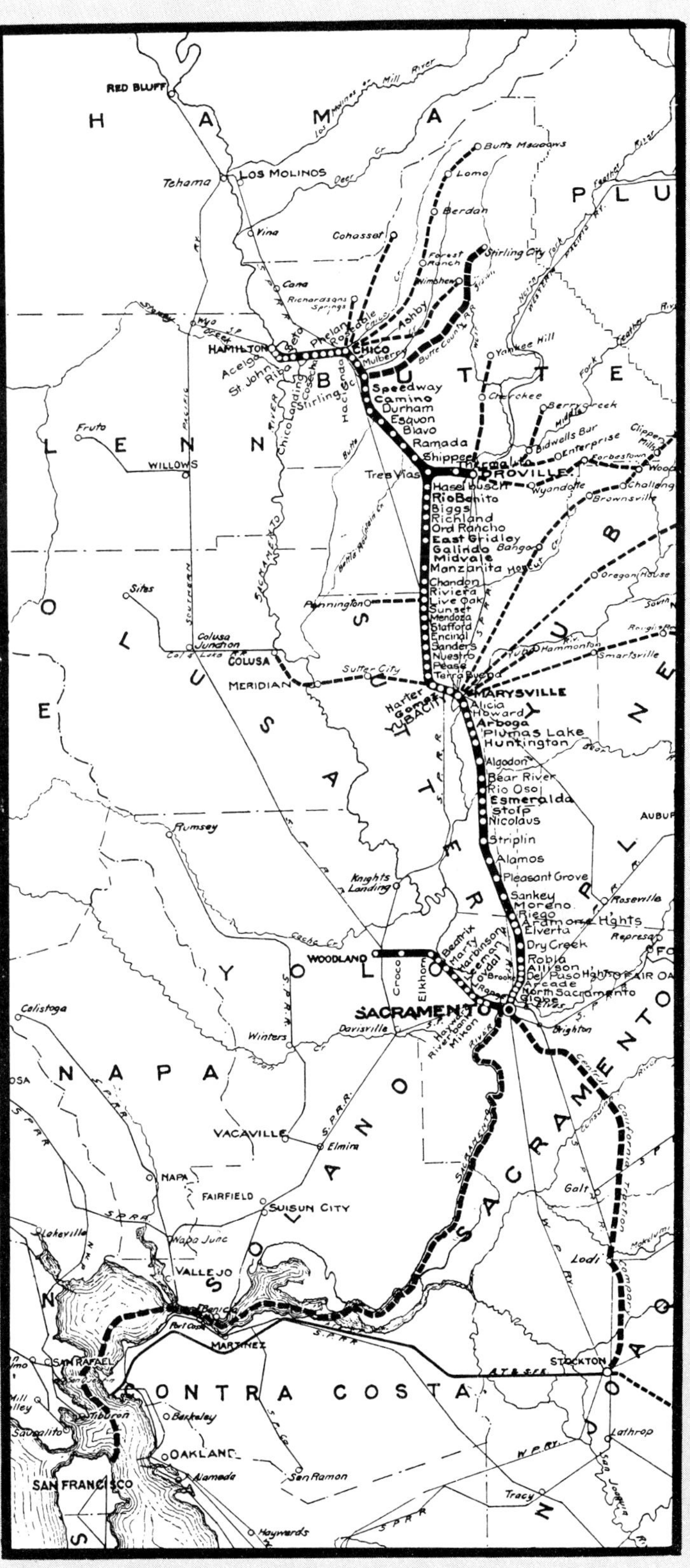

Above, northbound train (car 130) departing North Sacramento, date unknown. Note combination light & semaphore on pole, operated by prospective passengers to flag trains. (CS)

Below, East Nicolaus was a busy spot when this photo was taken circa 1909. Station is in distance, while substation is at left; awnings were familiar sights on NE, what with that blazing sunshine day after day. (LLS)

Introduction

(The following are excerpts from the April 23, 1910 issue of "Journal of Electricity, Power & Gas" which featured "The Northern Electric Railway" by Mr. Rudolph W. Van Norden. These excerpts give an excellent account of the NE as it was in its early years.)

As the tourist descends from his train in Sacramento he is handed a timetable and his eye is attracted to the reminder below a copious list of trains: "a. stands for A.M., p. stands for P.M., and Northern Electric stands for development of the Sacramento Valley." Now he knows the full story and when he boards the spic and span electric train, whose very color breathes California romance in its reflection of the Golden Poppy, to be whisked by miles of fertile lands and to pass through towns where prosperity is evinced on every hand, he marvels at the work already done, the enormous possibilities for the future, and then he fells like making a profound obeisance to the train when he leaves it for its share in making this development possible.

The Sacramento Valley has a length of about 200 miles and a width averaging 50 miles. The Sacramento River passes through its entire length from north to south and divides it about equally. The land adjoining the river on both sides is, as a rule, low and fairly flat and as it recedes from the river gradually rises and becomes more undulating until the foothills of the Sierra Nevada on the east and the more precipitous mountains of the Coast Range on the west are reached.

The one exception is furnished by the "Marysville Buttes," a jagged group of volcanic peaks which appear to have been forced out of the depths of the earth into the very center of the valley.

The land throughout the valley has always been known to be fertile, but the bottom lands along the river are particularly so. The cultivation of hops, wheat, olives, sugar beets, oranges, deciduous fruits pointed a reason for the rapid growth in population and wealth that might be expected with the advent of rapid and convenient transportation.

It was the late Mr. Henry Butters who believed in the county and the people and saw that the establishment of a modern railroad, affording swift means of transportation between the towns and through country having high potential values, would be the means of inducing a rapid but healthy growth and be the nucleus of a great system surrounded and fed by a great country.

It is no easy matter to inaugurate a new railroad through a more or less undeveloped territory. The start was made at Chico and under the engineering direction of Mr. J. B. Robinson, a veteran railroad engineer, and Mr. J. Paulding Edwards, the electrical and mechanical engineer, to whose skill and ingenuity the system now owes its well designed and successfully operating equipment, a road 24.8 miles long was built to Oroville. There was no direct means of transportation between these cities except by stage, and the first section of this system seemed justified by these conditions.

The first car was run from Chico to Oroville on April 25, 1906. The success of this piece of railroad was an inspiration to spur on the work of further construction, and on December 2, 1906 the line was completed to Marysville, an additional distance of 30 miles and regular operation was commenced.

There was in Marysville a primitive street railway system, its diminutive cars being hauled by mules. This was purchased, the road relaid with heavy rails and made standard gauge and extensions made to give a first class local service throughout the city and between it and Yuba City, across the Feather River.

A local system was also purchased in Chico, and in Oroville a loop was built and a local service between that town and Thermalito was inaugurated.

During 1907 construction was continued between Marysville and Sacramento and on September 1st of that year regular service was commenced. Sacramento, while not literally the head of navigation is practically so. There are several lines of steamers which tie up at this point; the possibility of making the road an outlet for a large freight transportation business having steamer connection with the Bay Cities was apparent. Aside from a passenger terminal in the heart of the business section, a branch to a freight terminal on the water front was built. This then gave a clear line of railroad reaching 122 miles up the Sacramento Valley.

On the west of Chico and adjacent to the Sacramento River is a large section devoted to sugar beets with a sugar factory at Hamilton. A line was therefore built due west from Chico to the river; after crossing the river this line follows the west side to Hamilton, 11 miles.

It is now proposed to continue the main line north from Chico 41.7 miles to the city of Red Bluff. Surveys for this work have been made and much has been done toward the completion of this extension.

Another extension is in the course of construction.

This leaves the main line 4.4 miles north of Marysville and will extend due west to Meridian and after crossing the river will proceed northward to Colusa. This branch will be 22 miles long and traverses a wonderfully fertile but more or less undeveloped country.

The Northern Electric has a total of 122 miles not counting the local street railway systems which have a total of 17 miles of track; when the extensions now under way are complete this will be increased to 193.5 miles.

The road between the present terminals, Chico on the north and Sacramento on the south, lies practically north and south on a generally straight line. That section of road into Oroville is treated as a branch; it joins the through line at Tres Vias and runs east for 5.5 miles to Oroville. Except for that section where the foothills are approached nearing Tres Vias and the Oroville Branch, the road is essentially level; the maximum grades at the points mentioned do not exceed one percent. Rail is of 60 lb. A.S.C.E. standard profile. Sawn cross ties from the hearts of pine and fir timber were laid throughout the system, and was supplied by The Diamond Match Company from its forests in the nearby Sierra Madre mountains.

Throughout the system a high class of track construction is in evidence; embankments show a careful study of conditions. Except for about ten miles on the Sacramento end, the track is thoroughly stone ballasted. Rock for this purpose has for the most part been hauled from tailing pits of gold dredgers at Oroville. From Chico to Yuba City the road passes through a number of towns---Durham, Live Oak, Gridley and Biggs---which are rapidly becoming populated. There are few curves and these are of long radius, while there are long tangents, the longest being 15 miles.

The right of way is from 80 to 100 feet in width and is completely fenced with cattle guards at crossings.

Being a single track system, it is necessary to pay great attention to meeting points of trains. There are sidings at all principal stations, but additional sidings at the proper points have been provided for this purpose. A telephone is located at each siding connected to the dispatcher. At Live Oak the line crosses the Southern Pacific; here an interlocking tower has been placed with an attendant constantly on duty.

From Yuba City the road crosses the Feather River on a steel truss bridge into the city of Marysville. This bridge is owned jointly by the railroad and the counties of Yuba and Sutter, and supports a roadway as well as track. The road enters Sacramento after crossing the American River. This it does on a composite Howe truss bridge. In entering Sacramento it is necessary to go through a levee. Wing levees are built to allow this entrance. Within the city the road has a double track and passes through a number of streets until the passenger terminal at 8th & J Sts. is reached. There is a wye provided here to enable the turning of cars or trains. A branch line has been constructed to a freight terminal at the city wharf on the Sacramento River. This line practically circles the city, as it was impossible to secure a franchise to operate freight trains through the streets. This branch is 5.7 miles long and its construction throughout is equal in quality to the high standard maintained by the system. The freight depot is a commodious structure of sufficient size to handle the cars and business for some time to come; it takes up a large part of a block east of the wharves. Tracks are so arranged that cars may be shunted directly on the wharf and loaded to or from the steamer.

The question of the method of supplying electricity to operate trains received a great deal of consideration. For long distance interurban work, both trolley and third rail have their advocates. Engineers in charge of this work were strongly in favor of the third rail and it was adopted. Through cities and towns a trolley is used; cars are therefore equipped with both poles and shoes. An ingenious device

cuts out electrical connection to the shoe when the trolley is in use.

Standard forms are used for switches and crossovers, passing tracks, etc. This is important, as the position of the various arrangements for the third rail must be accurate. A very simple device is used on switches to disconnect the third rail when the switch is not in use. An insulating wood block is inserted in a break in the third rail; fastened to the rail at either end of the break and extending sideways in a horizontal direction are two hook-shaped receptacles. An iron rod with a wooden handle at one end is laid on these projections in such a way that it fits into the hook of each. This closes the circuit. When the siding is not in use, the bar is simply pulled out.

The third rail is 60 lb. steel, having the standard A.S.C.E. profile. It is mounted on a special insulator designed by the engineer of the road. This consists of a treated maple block fitted to a malleable cast iron base and supporting a cast iron top to which the rail is fastened. Insulators are placed on every fifth tie (which is 18 inches longer than the others) for this purpose. Loss by current leakage from the third rail is remarkably small, being one half ampere per mile under the most severe conditions of weather. Track rails are bonded with two No. 0000 and the electric rail with two 400,000 cir. mil. soldered bonds.

At road crossings where there would be an interruption in the third rail, a heavily insulated cable was laid beneath the crossing; this was found to give trouble and it was changed to an overhead cable supported by two poles.

A number of types of passenger stations have been adopted. A new depot at Thermalito built of cobble stones is of a very neat and artistic design. Shelter stations are constructed to a standard design; they are equipped with a manually operated semaphore which when in a horizontal position lights a series of five lamps for night use.

Located at Mulberry, a suburb of Chico, are the car houses, the repair shop, the car building shop and the administrative offices. Here also is the office of the chief train dispatcher as well as a substation.

The car houses are conveniently placed, facing the county road on which the main line operates. The building is a concrete and timber structure, 140 by 140 feet, covered with corrugated iron; it contains eight tracks, all of which connect with the main line. Within the building there are pits throughout the length of two tracks adjacent to the machine shop so that temporary or permanent repairs may be made at any time to coaches or locomotives. Doors at the rear of four tracks allow cars to pass through to the car shop, which is located directly in the rear of and a short distance from the car barn. On the right as one enters, incorporated as a part of the car house building, is the substation. Behind this is a machine shop, equipped with all machines necessary for car repair work. Next to these shops is the air brake department, and in the rear is a forge shop with six forges and one 300-lb. hammer. To the left and at the rear of the car house is the armature and electric repair department. Armature repairing is perhaps the most important of the various classes of repair work on an electric railway system.

Passing from the car house to the car shop, one finds a well constructed corrugated iron building. It is equipped for the erecting and finishing of cars. A woodshop with machinery to turn out all the work from the heavy frames to the inlaid hardwood finish is at one end; at the other is the paint shop. Many of the later cars of this company have been built in this shop and a minute examination evinces the care and thoroughness exhibited in their construction and a finish it would be impossible to get on cars purchased on the open market.

The freight locomotives are a development of the company, each being built with special conditions of operation in view. Locomotives have the same motors as passenger cars but are geared for 25 mph. There is a device installed which consists of a switch that throws all four motors in series; this is for starting heavy loads. After the train is started, the switch is thrown back again, thus restoring the regular connection between the controller and the motors.

Designs for passenger coaches and locomotives having steel framework and covering have been made; none of the former have as yet been constructed, but one of the latter has been built and is proving to be highly satisfactory.

The Westinghouse electro-pneumatic control system has been adopted for all interurban cars and trains. It has now been in operation on the Northern Electric lines for the past three years and has given complete satisfaction.

With an electric railroad the question of a power supply is paramount. One of the features which made this project feasible was the abundant supply of low priced electrical energy generated by hydraulic power in the nearby mountains which was available at all points on this system. The question of expensive steam generating plants did not enter into the problem and it was not even necessary to parallel the road with a high tension distributing line, although this has been partially done. Power is supplied by Pacific Gas & Electric Company which owns and furnishes the transformers and high tension apparatus necessary for use at the substations. All other substation equipment, including the buildings themselves, are owned by the NE. There are three standard types of substations in use, which have been designed and built by the engineers of the company. These are distributed so as to energize about ten miles of road each. There are at present nine stations, although provision has been made for ten and they are numbered accordingly. The equipment throughout is similar, both in the type and size of the motor-generator sets and style of switchboard.

Current is supplied from the transmission lines at 60,000 volts AC, 60 cycles; it is supplied to the motors at 2,000 volts. Motor-generators consist of a Westinghouse type CCL induction motor rated at 580 hp direct connected to a Westinghouse 6 pole 600 volt generator of 400 kw.

Substations are: No. 1, located at Mulberry; No. 2 is 9.4 miles from Mulberry; No. 3 is at Tres Vias and supplies power for the Oroville Branch as well as the main line; No. 4 is at Gridley, No. 5 is a portable consisting of two box cars---one containing transformers, the other the substation proper; No. 6 is at Marysville; there is no No. 7 as yet, and the gap between Marysville and Nicolaus where No. 8 is located is 16 miles. No. 9 is another portable and is located midway between Nicolaus and Sacramento. At Sacramento, power is supplied by the PG&E substation at 6th & H Sts. The total capacity of the substations is 5,200 kw..

During the average day there is run a total of 1500 car miles on the system. As a rule all trains consist of two or more cars. The first is a combination baggage and smoking car, and the second is a passenger car. If more than two cars are used, a trailer passenger car is placed in the center of the train. For short runs where one car is adequate, a combination baggage-smoking-passenger car is used. Through trains are operated at intervals of about 2-1/2 hours throughout the day and evening. Running time from Sacramento to Chico is three hours. All trains are manned by a motorman, conductor and one brakeman.

A private telegraph and telephone system extends the length of the road, the poles being placed three feet from the western edge of the right of way. The road is operated in accordance with Standard American Railway Practice Rules, train order forms 19 and 31 being used. Operating offices including that of the chief dispatcher are located at Mulberry (Chico). Stations having telegraph operators are at Durham, Tres Vias, Thermalito, Live Oak, Oroville, Yuba City, Marysville, Nicolaus and Sacramento. Train orders are issued at these points.

Throughout the day and early evening the road is given over entirely to passenger traffic. Between midnight and six A.M. all freight transportation is accomplished. Were it not for this arrangement, the fast and frequent passenger schedules could not be maintained without seriously inconveniencing freight traffic which is rapidly increasing in importance.

The Northern Electric Company has the distinction of being a thoroughly California corporation; it was founded and is owned and operated by Californians. The executive offices are at San Francisco; the President is Mr. E. R. Lilienthal; Mr. Louis Sloss is Vice-president, and Mr. Norman Logan is Secretary.

The actual operation of the system is under the supervision of the General Manager & Purchasing Agent, Mr. A. D. Schindler, whose office is in San Francisco and who is responsible for the admirable results obtained. He has an admirable assistant in Mr. Melville Dozier, whose headquarters are at Mulberry. Mr. J. P. Edwards is the electrical and mechanical engineer and to him is due the design and construction of the various electrical and mechanical features.

This is a system of which all Californians may feel proud.

The Northern Electric Railway
Owns private right-of-way the whole length
of the Sacramento Valley, besides the
very valuable franchises for street railways
in the cities and towns through which it
runs

The Northern Electric Railway
Covers a wonderful field
An empire in extent
Endowed with all the natural resources man
requires
Rich soil, perfect climate
Water, Timber, Minerals
Villages, towns, cities
The road is also to be built
To Red Bluff and Redding
Colusa, Woodland and Fairoaks
Thus giving service to those
Growing centers of activity
And the country surrounding them
With the varied productions
Of farm, mine and timber land

The bonds are in denominations
Of $100, $500 and $1000
To run 3 years
At 7% interest per annum
Payable twice a year
Interest Coupons attached

The First Subscriber

Mr. Jas. C. Gray, Treasurer of the Ophir
Hardware Company of Oroville, was the
first subscriber to the debenture bonds of the
Northern Electric Railway Company. He
writes:

"I have invested $15,000 in the first issue
of Northern Electric Bonds, and now send
$5,000 for the present issue.

"I am only sorry that I am not able to
invest more.

"The Northern Electric Company and its
management have my full sympathy and
confidence and I wish them all success in
their great undertaking."

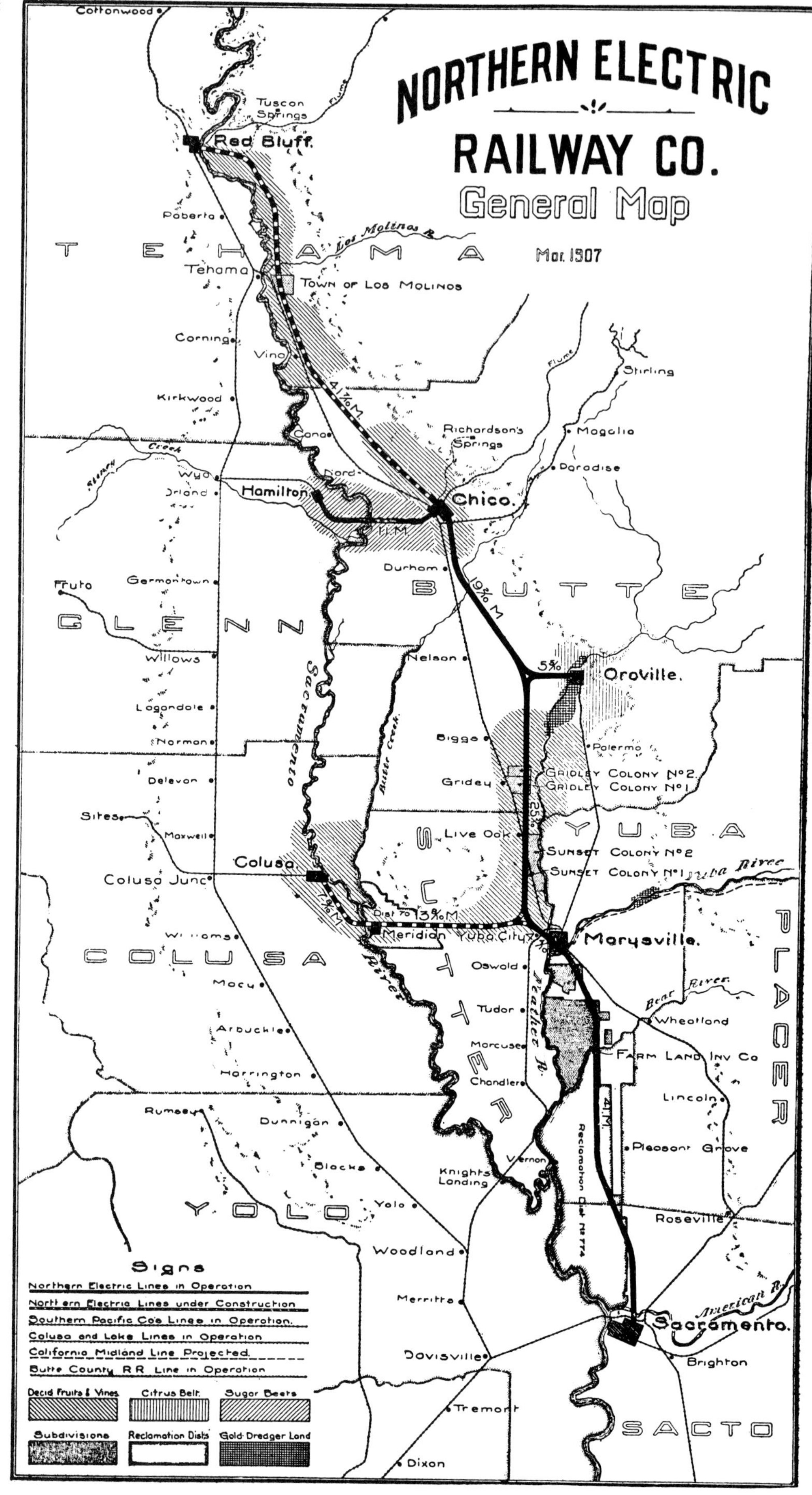

Back page of Northern Electric 1907 prospectus carried this map. (AL)

Chapter 1

North End History

While the first of the companies to make up today's Sacramento Northern Railway was "The Marysville & Yuba City Street Railroad Company" which began to run its mule cars between Marysville and Yuba City via the old covered bridge over the Feather River, August 17, 1889, the real birthplace of the Sacramento Northern was Alta Vista, the huge mansion which Henry A. Butters built in Piedmont upon his return to California in 1895. One June evening in 1905 Mr. Butters, David S. Edwards, Alpheus W. Clement, Charles A. Rose and Adolph Loessel met in the library of the yellow hued Victorian house to draw up the Articles of Incorporation of The Northern Electric Company which was to build the main line of the present day Sacramento Northern between Chico and Sacramento.

Henry A. Butters, father of the Northern Electric, was thinking in terms of provinces, not acreage. He had made a vast fortune in South African mining and now his interests turned toward the great Sacramento Valley where he envisaged a traction empire that would link the growing interior of California with San Francisco Bay. Only the year before---1904---Butters, with his great love of horses, had taken the coveted Blue Ribbon for four-in-hand driving in Burlingame, California's most famed prize for this type of horsemanship.

Born in Haverhill, Massachusetts, on September 20, 1850, Henry A. Butters came to California as a boy of 14. He attended the old College of California which became today's University of California. He was to become connected with Bancroft & Co., one of the largest publishing houses in San Francisco and whose collection was the basis for the famed Bancroft Library of the University of California. He then became identified with the early development of the life insurance business on the Pacific Coast, but Butters made his first big step towards a fortune in 1878 when he went to Leadville, Colorado, where he engaged in mining operations. He was joined there by his brother, Mr. Charles Butters, who became a famous mining engineer and a partner in Butters' very successful mining venture in Africa.

In 1890 Butters, in association with such greats as Cecil Rhodes (of Rhodes Scholarship fame) and John Hays Hammond (a famous mining engineer much sought after as a speaker at Democratic Party national conventions) and the house of Werner, Belt & Co., promoted and built the first electric railway in South Africa at Capetown. This company, Butters' first venture in the electric railway field, was so successful that it branched out and built the first electric street railways in Geneva, Switzerland, Lisbon, Portugal, Valparaiso, Chile, and Mexico City.

Mr. Butters returned to California briefly in 1891 to marry Mrs. Lucy Sactella whose grandfather, Mr. Samuel Woodworth, wrote "The Old Oaken Bucket." It was the third marriage for the new Mrs. Butters---two sons of her first marriage, David S. Edwards and J. Paulding Edwards, were to be associated with Butters in the Northern Electric, and Butters adopted the two girls of Mrs. Butters' second marriage. A son, Henry A. Butters, Jr., was born in San Francisco on April 28, 1892.

While building the Geneva, Switzerland, electric tramways, the Butters family lived at the Beau Rivage, Geneva, in the very same rooms where Emperor Franz Joseph's consort, the Empress of Austria, had just taken her life. The Mexico City venture was to provide the funds for the Northern Electric. Upon his return to California in 1895 Butters had looked into the possibility of purchasing the Los Angeles Railway, but the great Central Valley beckoned and provided him more of a challenge---restless man of vision that he was.

The early 1900s saw many electric railway promotions under way in California, so it was but natural that Mr. Butters should turn his energies in that direction. Even before he came upon the scene, The Shasta Southern Railway had projected a line from Hamilton City down the Sacramento Valley through Colusa to Suisun Bay.

So it was that on June 14, 1905, the Articles of Incorporation of The Northern Electric Company were filed with George T. Knox, Commissioner of Deeds for the State of Nevada, in San Francisco. The incorporation was made under the Nevada general corporation law; the articles gave The Northern Electric Company the power to do almost everything within the United States except in the State of Nevada, and its term was perpetual.

The total authorized capital stock of the Northern Electric was $3,000,000---divided into 30,000 shares with a par value of $100 each. At the time of the filing of the Articles of Incorporation, only $1,000 of this amount had been subscribed by the original stockholders: Henry A. Butters (6 shares), David S. Edwards (1 share), Alpheus W. Clement (1 share), Charles A. Rose (1 share) and Adolph Loessel (1 share)---and none of this amount had been paid into the treasury.

On March 22, 1906, just before the Northern Electric began to operate regular service between Chico and Oroville, The Board of Directors was increased from five to seven; shareholders at that time were Henry A. Butters (9,996 shares) while E. R. Lilenthal, J. Downey Harvey, Louis Sloss and Adolph Loessel held one share each. Henry A. Butters was president,

Construction days on the Northern Electric: Above, engine 1000 with pile driver near Marysville, 1907. (LLS)
Below, a Northern Electric steam locomotive on the newly ballasted track in 1907, probably just south of Tres
Vias. The "deadly third rail" is mighty near that man on the engine. (LLS)

while David S. Edwards was secretary.

The first electric operation on what is today's Sacramento Northern began on January 1, 1905, when The Chico Electric Ry. Co. began service with two double-truck open-bench motor cars which were numbered 50 and 51. These were soon supplemented by four small hand-braked single-truck California-type streetcars which came from The United Railroads of San Francisco.

The Chico Electric Railway Company's Articles of Incorporation were filed in San Francisco on August 12, 1904. This corporation's aims were somewhat less ambitious than those of The Northern Electric Company. The Chico Electric Railway was chartered for a term of fifty years and its capital stock was to be $250,000 in the gold coin of The United States of America, divided into 2,500 shares of $100 par value each. At the time of the filing of the articles of incorporation, $5,000 of this amount had been subscribed by the following persons: Charles W. Waller, 42 shares ($4,200); Leon J. de Sabla, 5 shares ($500); and Harold P. Pitts, L. C. Ralston and D. Howard Foote, 1 share ($100) each.

Chico's largest industry, The Diamond Match Company, was behind The Chico Electric Railway, whose first substation was at the match company's factory. The first substation operator was Bob Durham whose father gave his name to the town of Durham, first important station on The Sacramento Northern south of Chico.

It is interesting to note that the Gould interests which were pushing the construction of The Western Pacific Railroad (which later took over the successor Sacramento Northern) owned The Diamond Match Company at this time.

The Chico Electric Railway Company's charter called for the construction of but 4.5 miles of track within the City of Chico. Its line was not to be used by interurban trains except for that portion on Main St. from Fifth St. to The Northern Electric's depot at First & Main Streets. At the time The Chico Electric Railway was built, Chico and Oroville---the two largest cities of Butte County---were connected only by stage coach. One of the lines of The Chico Electric Railway terminated at the livery stable where rigs were hired to take jurors from Chico to Oroville, the county seat. The old stage fare was five dollars, so it can be seen that the first line of The Northern Electric was to serve a very important function.

Construction of The Northern Electric was started in October, 1905, at Oroville; by January 29, 1906, rails had been laid to a new covered bridge over the Feather River at Oroville. Late in 1905 the Northern Electric acquired The Chico Electric Railway Company and on March 10, 1906, Henry A. Butters bought 250 acres adjacent to its car barns for shops and yards.

Then called "Chapmantown," the shops location became better known as "Mulberry," where The Chico Electric Railway's car line terminated at the rear of the shops. At this time the substation was moved from The Diamond Match Company location to the Northern Electric shops and all electric railway operations in Chico were centered at this location.

The Northern Electric's main line was built from the shops at Mulberry along Park Avenue and Main Street to the NE depot at First & Main, which was to be the northern terminus for NE and successor Sacramento Northern interurban trains until the end of regular service, October 31, 1941.

The line from Chico to Oroville was constructed to steam road standards of the day and was electrified by direct suspension overhead trolley, supported by cross spans and brackets. The NE's first superintendent was Frank J. Ross, who had been the very popular manager of The Sacramento Street Railway system of what was to become The Pacific Gas & Electric Company. On April 11, 1906, Henry A. Butters, Frank J. Ross, and other NE officials made the first run between Chico and Oroville in Niles-built car 100. The first electric service between Chico and Oroville was performed by "Old Maude," a motorized flat car which had been fitted up as a construction locomotive and which began operation early in 1906. Charley Clark was the first motorman and Bob Black was the first conductor.

Plans for a gala celebration of the formal opening of the Oroville line were dampened by the San Francisco Earthquake of April 18, 1906---an event which cast a shadow over all California electric railway projects at the time. However the Northern Electric did formally inaugurate passenger service between Chico and Oroville on April 25, 1906---and the days of the horse drawn stagecoach were over. In keeping with the time, Butters built another mansion---his wonderful summer home, "Los Nogales," at Chico; he thus divided his time between "Alta Vista" at Piedmont and "Los Nogales" at Chico during the dawn of Northern Electric.

While construction was taking place on the Chico-Oroville line, Northern Electric was seeking a franchise through Marysville. At that time both the California Midland and the Western Pacific were also seeking to enter Marysville. Altho the carrying of Western Pacific construction workers accounted for most of the passenger traffic on the then-operating Chico to Oroville line, relations between Northern Electric and Western Pacific were often strained; Butters even held up his Marysville franchise application until he could ascertain the exact location of the Western Pacific's Marysville depot.

The California Midland was to have been a 1200-volt third rail line and was projected to reach Auburn and Nevada City. John Martin, its promoter, had been responsible for the first third-rail electric railroad in California---the electrified suburban service of The North Shore Railroad (now Northwestern Pacific) out of Sausalito, and it was thought that Butters and Martin were working together.

On January 18, 1906, considerable surprise was created when Butters objected to Martin's application for a franchise on E Street in Marysville for the California Midland. By February 23, 1906, Butters and Martin came to an agreement on a franchise by which the Northern Electric and California Midland were to share trackage in Marysville.

A member of the Marysville Board of Trustees, Peter J. Delay, voted against giving the franchise to Martin for E and 8th Streets; during the extended franchise negotiations in Marysville, Trustee Delay had to face an election. Despite the fact that his opponent campaigned with the slogan "No progress with Delay," and had the backing of the electric railway interests, Delay won the election. The electric railroads nevertheless received the franchises they desired. Years later, Peter J. Delay was to write a history of the Yuba City-Marysville area in which the mention of the Northern Electric was confined to two printed lines.

The 1906 San Francisco Fire ended all hopes for the California Midland, but construction continued on the Northern Electric, although slowed. To enter Marysville, NE purchased The Marysville & Yuba City Street Railroad Company. This company operated a 3'6" gauge horse car line between the two cities and crossed the Feather River on the old covered bridge. This bridge was hardly adequate to handle the big interurbans, so construction of the new line into Sacramento was held up until the bridge could be replaced with a new structure of steel.

To build the new bridge at this point, NE first built a temporary bridge of piling which was used by the first electric trains between Yuba City and Marysville. This bridge used a third rail to convey power; its function was to facilitate the handling of materials for the new permanent span. A major flood in 1907 badly damaged the temporary bridge as well as the permanent span---and thus NE had its first taste of what was to be a continuing and expensive problem---washouts due to floods which tended to decrease NE's earning capacity.

The new NE bridge over the Feather River was to serve until December 25, 1955, when its approaches were washed out in the great flood of that year which also flooded Yuba City.

NE rebuilt The Marysville & Yuba City Street Railroad Company's narrow gauge horse car line as a standard gauge

The Northern Electric-California Transportation Company's transfer sheds, Sacramento, in the early years. The steamer, "Pride of the River," is tied up at the wharf. (LLS)

Below, car 129 is seen turning onto X St. from Front St., Sacramento, about 1909, on an inspection trip. (LLS)

THE STEAMER SPECIAL: When NE was completed between Chico and Sacramento in September, 1907, the new interurban had no connections to San Francisco except for the Southern Pacific and the river steamers of the SP and California Transportation Company. Since the SP was naturally hostile and chose to fight NE by greatly improving its own train service between Chico and Oakland, NE arranged with California Transportation to inaugurate a train-steamer service between Chico and San Francisco. To hold up its end of the bargain, NE operated a train called "The Steamer Special" which made direct connections with the river steamers which provided overnight service between Sacramento and San Francisco. In 1915, The Steamer Special (Train No. 17) left Chico at 3:15 PM and arrived at Front & M Sts. at the dock at 6:30 PM. Arriving boat passengers in the morning found the Chico-bound Steamer Special awaiting them, leaving at 7:40 AM and pulling in at Chico at 11:20 AM. Train No. 17 usually consisted of a motor and trailer. In pre-auto days, river steamers did a big business, and Cal Transportation was in direct competition with SP's Netherlands Route stern wheel steamers.

electric line. The new electric streetcar tracks followed the same route as did the horse cars; this line ran along Second Street in Yuba City (then the main part of town and where the Sutter County Courthouse is still located), thence over the Feather River Bridge via Fifth, D, Second, C and Sixth Streets to the Southern Pacific Depot in Marysville. For some time, the Northern Electric used the old Marysville horsecar barn on C Street at Second for the electric cars. In Yuba City, the streetcar line was extended along B and Plumas Streets to Bridge Street where the Sacramento Northern Yuba City station is now located. Except for the new bridge and Fifth and D Streets in Marysville, interurban cars followed a different route than the streetcars.

The displaced horsecar bodies of The Marysville & Yuba City Street Railroad were used as way stations on the Northern Electric interurban line, while the light displaced rail was used as third rail at the Chico Shops until de-electrified years later.

Vice President E. S. Dimmock of the Northern Electric and Superintendent Frank Ross did not get on well together. On June 11, 1906, Dimmock was hurt in a wreck on the new line at Durham. This second wreck on the new line may have led to some changes in management that took place a month later (on July 11, 1906) when A. D. Schindler was made General Manager and Dimmock became General Superintendent. Frank Ross then acted as special representative for the Northern Electric at Sacramento and may have played a leading role in obtaining for the NE franchises that it desired but which were opposed by such influential Sacramento forces as the Real Estate Board and "The Sacramento Bee." It is interesting to note that the tracks of the Sacramento Northern in Sacramento follow exactly the same routes as asked for in the original franchise application by Henry A. Butters.

A. D. Schindler came to the Northern Electric from the Pacific Electric and the PE influence made itself felt early. The Niles-built cars 100 and 101 which opened regular service on the Chico-Oroville line were equipped with the pneumatic trolley base which for many years was almost a trademark of the Pacific Electric. 1906, however, was the year in which the third rail gained much favor in electric traction and some of the financial interests behind the Northern Electric had been interested earlier in the North Shore, the pioneer third rail line in California.

Northern Electric's first electrical & mechanical engineer, J. Paulding Edwards, was ever ready to experiment. The line built from Oroville and Marysville Junction was laid with third rail; at first, NE used the suspended link type shoe (still used on the Chicago Elevated) but changed early to the Potter shoe. The success of the third rail on the line to Marysville (which opened for regular service on December 3, 1906) led to its general adoption, so that three years later the original line between Thermalito and Speedway was changed to third rail, resulting in the resignation of the entire section gang along the affected trackage.

The building up of the Northern Electric made larger administrative and maintenance facilities imperative, and as a result the company erected the shop building, and office building at Chico; thus the center of street railway operations in that city shifted from the Diamond Match Company's plant to Mulberry. These buildings served the Sacramento Northern until 1950. The Chico substation was first placed in one of the bays of the shop building but was moved into another building in 1920. While on this subject, it is well to mention that the Northern Electric was the first large electric railway enterprise in California to rely exclusively on purchased power, and the 60,000-volt 60-cycle AC transmission set a world's record for the time. Power was purchased from The Valley Counties Power Company at first under an agreement made on March 26, 1906. The Pacific Gas & Electric Company succeeded this company and supplied both NE and its successor, Sacramento Northern.

On December 18, 1906, the Northern Electric was enjoined from laying tracks in Marysville by the Western Pacific, whose tracks reached Marysville at the same time. January 12, 1907, saw the famous battle of the Bee Farm; the NE had laid its tracks in Marysville despite the Western Pacific and began to grade its line between Marysville and Sacramento. On the other side of the Yuba River was a tract of land known as the Bee Farm---and here the forces of the two new railroads had to cross each other's route.

The Western Pacific put down tracks where it was to cross the NE's right of way. On January 12, 1907, the NE sent a force of a hundred men to the Bee Farm and tore up all of the newly laid Western Pacific track.

On Saturday, July 20, 1907, the first Northern Electric train reached Sacramento from Marysville. This first train was hauled by a Northern Electric steam locomotive. Some months were to go by before the third rail was to be put down and while this was being done, NE offered steam freight service between Marysville and Sacramento.

On September 7, 1907, Northern Electric's first electric train reached Sacramento with W. W. Nelson at the controls. Thus the NE's main line was completed in time for the State Fair of 1907. It was not until October, 1907, that the NE underpass under the Southern Pacific main line at B Street, Sacramento, was completed. The Sacramento Bee, never too friendly towards the Northern Electric, printed a photo of this work in progress and in the caption pointed to the NE yard beyond, saying that was where the deadly third rail began. The crossing of the Western Pacific at Globe presented no problem since NE did reach that point ahead of the new steam line.

The Northern Electric did encounter opposition in the matter of franchises for its tracks in Sacramento. The Real Estate Board and the home owners along the route opposed the freight line along C, 30th, X and Front Streets. The first franchise application for the passenger line along C, 16th, Eye and 7th to 8th & K Streets did not contemplate streetcar service, but on August 7, 1906, Butters amended his application to include local streetcar service. The Bee had urged that NE enter Sacramento over the Sacramento Electric, Gas & Railway Company (later PG&E) tracks on D and E and 7th to J Street. On September 4, 1907, the Bee headed its account of the granting of the X Street franchise to NE with: "The Public Be Damned." After NE began regular passenger service, the Bee was very careful to point out every time when NE let a train stand overnight on Eye Street between 8th and 7th (the original Sacramento city trackage included a wye at 8th and Eye).

On September 12, 1907, just three days after the first Northern Electric electrically-operated train reached Sacramento, the first train was run over NE's Hamilton line from Chico to Hamilton City. Like the first train into Sacramento, the first Hamilton train was hauled by steam power. The opening of this branch had been delayed by non-arrival of the pontoon for the temporary pontoon bridge over the Sacramento River at Chico Landing.

The Hamilton City Branch had been built primarily to supply J. B. Hamilton's beet sugar factory with sugar beets. In building the Hamilton Branch, NE purchased the Shasta Southern, which had projected its line from Red Bluff south through Hamilton City and Colusa to San Francisco Bay. As early as March 19, 1906, the Shasta Southern dug up Colusa's Main Street between Fifth and Sixth Streets and laid two rails to hold a franchise. The only other trackage constructed by the Shasta Southern was about a mile of track at Monroeville which became a part of the Hamilton City branch. While the Shasta Southern did have electric interurban dreams, it was chiefly to be a sugar beet carrier.

October 31, 1907, saw the Hamilton City Branch formally opened with an electric train carrying Chamber of Commerce officials from Chico to inspect the new sugar factory at Hamilton City. Unlike the Sacramento main line, the Hamilton City line used overhead trolley and regular passenger service service was performed by streetcars of the Los Angeles type. The famed pontoon bridge itself did feature third rail. Trains were run from Chico to Hamilton City but six months of the year---during the sugar season from July first to January first, when there was no navigation on the Sacramento River. As river boats operated from January first to July first, the pontoon bridge could not then be used. A fund was set up for the construction of a permanent drawbridge but this money was used for other purposes. Due to lack of business, the Hamilton Branch suspended operations in 1913.

Now that the Northern Electric Company had completed its main line, it turned its attention to branch line construction. On September 19, 1907, The Northern Electric Railway Company was incorporated under the laws of the State of California to take over both The Shasta Southern Railway Company and The Northern Electric Company. The new Northern Electric Railway Company was chartered for a period of fifty years and its Articles of Incorporation spelled out the railway line to be built. The articles called for the construction of a line from Chico to Redding by way of Red Bluff (76 miles); a line from Sacramento to Folsom (20 miles); a line from Sacramento to Woodland, Colusa, and Hamilton (108 miles); and a line from Colusa to Yuba City (26 miles). Had The Northern Electric Railway Company been able to carry out its aims it would have had two main lines up the Sacramento Valley connected by intermediate branches between Colusa and Yuba City, and Hamilton City and Chico. Of these ambitious plans, only the Sacramento-Woodland line and the Colusa-Yuba City line were to be built, and they were built by separate corporations organized for the purpose.

The Northern Electric Railway Company was capitalized for $25,000,000 and the capital stock was divided into 250,000 shares of a par value each of $100. Of these, 100,000 shares were designated as "preferred capital stock" and 150,000 shares were to be designated "common capital stock." Of this capital stock, $339,000 for 3,390 shares of preferred capital stock was actually subscribed. This amounted to $1,000 per mile of the 339 miles of railroad that The Northern Electric Company was to acquire or build. The several incorporators of The Northern Electric Company and the amount of stock they each subscribed were:

R. Augustus Bray	3,360	($ 336,000)
Alan W. Maginis	5	($500)
Curtis Hillyer	5	($500)
Francis V. VanDeinse	5	($500)
Martin L. Washburn	5	($500)
Charles Elsey	5	($500)

Of this amount, 10%, or $ 33,900 was actually paid into the treasury of Northern Electric. It is interesting to note that the organization meetings of The Northern Electric Railway Company took place in San Francisco's famous Montgomery Block.

To build the freight line encircling Sacramento, The Sacramento Terminal Company was incorporated September 16, 1908. The Articles of Incorporation described the line to be built from a point on The Northern Electric Railway in Sacramento near C St. and between 18th and 19th Sts. to run easterly upon C. St. to 31st St., thence on 31st St. to X St. and on X St. to Front St., thence on Front St. to M St., west on M St. across the Sacramento River and in a general westerly direction to the town of Broderick in Solano County. This trackage was built and today most of it is still intact as part of today's Sacramento Northern belt line in Sacramento.

The Sacramento Terminal Company's charter also called for an additional line from 31st St. west between L and X Streets to and across the Sacramento River to Broderick, but this additional line was not built.

Henry A. Butters was not to live to see the Northern Electric branches constructed. On October 26, 1908, Mr. Butters passed away at the home of his mother, Mrs. Sarah Butters, 2646 Telegraph Ave., Berkeley. The NE had not only taken his finances but also his home and his health. A solemn requiem mass was said for him at the Church of St. Francis de Sales (now St. Francis de Sales Cathedral) in Oakland on Wednesday morning, October 28, 1908. Honorary pallbearers were prominent in NE: E. R. Lilienthal, E. J. DeSabla, Louis Sloss, A. D. Schindler, Ferdinand Reis, Charles W. Slack, A. M. Seymour, George W. Mc Niel Jr., Charles G. Wingate, and Charles Tarpey. Henry A. Butters was buried in Oakland's St. Mary's Cemetery, not far from his great mansion, Alta Vista, where Northern Electric had been born.

Mr. E. R. Lilienthal succeeded Mr. Butters as NE's President. The Sloss-Lilienthal interests were now in complete control of NE, and the first thing they did was to see about a San Francisco connection. On October 20, 1909, they incorporated the company which they intended to be the instrument in getting the big orange NE cars to the San Francisco Bay area: The Vallejo & Northern Railroad Co. Incorporators of the V&N were Thomas T. C. Gregory, William Pierce, John W. Bauman, and Ernest D. Holley, all of Suisun, California; and Winfield R. Madden, of Dixon, California.

The Vallejo & Northern was proposed to build from Vallejo to Sacramento via Napa Junction, Jamison Canyon, Cordelia, Fairfield, Cement, and directly to Broderick. A branch was intended from Fairfield to Suisun, plus branches from the main line to Vacaville and to Woodland. V&N's main line was to have been 62 miles long. Except for that portion of the main line from Vacaville Junction to Willota, the Vacaville Branch and the Suisun Branch, none of the trackage projected by the V&N was built.

However, grading was done in Vallejo and to the north of that town, and this was later taken over by another electric interurban railway company, The San Francisco, Napa & Calistoga Railway, for its new line out of Vallejo, in 1920.

Under the aegis of the V&N, however, other NE lines were constructed, all ultimately intended to tie in to the grand V&N design. The Woodland Branch was constructed as a V&N undertaking, as was a new local line in Sacramento, intended to be the V&N's entry into that city. This line ran from Front & M, via M, 8th, I, 19th to J Sts. For this service a California car of the Los Angeles Standard type was purchased, painted green, and lettered "Vallejo & Northern No. 1." Crews assigned to this line, the only railway service actually operated in the name of V&N, wore V&N badges.

Next came the Woodland Branch. On July 20, 1911, The Sacramento & Woodland Railroad Company was incorporated with the following incorporators: Thomas T. C. Gregory, William Pierce, Council J. Goodell, George A. Posey, and Irving H. Smith. This company was originally capitalized at $1,000,000 and of this amount, $17,000 was subscribed.

The building of the Woodland Branch took place concurrently with the construction of the M St. Bridge across the Sacramento River. The great bridge was built jointly by NE and V&N, and these companies agreed to lease the highway portion of the structure to the Counties of Sacramento and Yolo until December 15, 1917, at which time the twin roadways were to be turned over to the counties for use as long as the railroad used the bridge.

NE's attempt to cross the Southern Pacific's tracks on Front St. at M St. met with spirited opposition; the SP put down on that intersection everything from old lathes and locomotives to anything else lying around its Sacramento Shops. However, NE eventually won out and the crossing was installed.

Despite the SP opposition encountered in Sacramento, the first piece of rolling stock to enter Woodland on NE rails was a Southern Pacific handcar whose passengers included Woodland's Mayor J. R. Mitchell, John Tillottson (first NE warehouseman at Woodland), Claude A. King (NE's first Woodland agent), and D. L. Carter, SP section foreman. In connection with the construction of the Woodland Line, NE was later to sue SP for tearing out the interchange track at Mikon, thus disrupting deliveries of ballast for the new branch.

On July 4, 1912, the first interurban train ran between Sacramento and Woodland. A 25¢ roundtrip fare was charged and a seven-car train ran all day; this train consisted of locomotive 1010 and six coaches and, because the wyes had not yet been installed, two motormen were necessary.

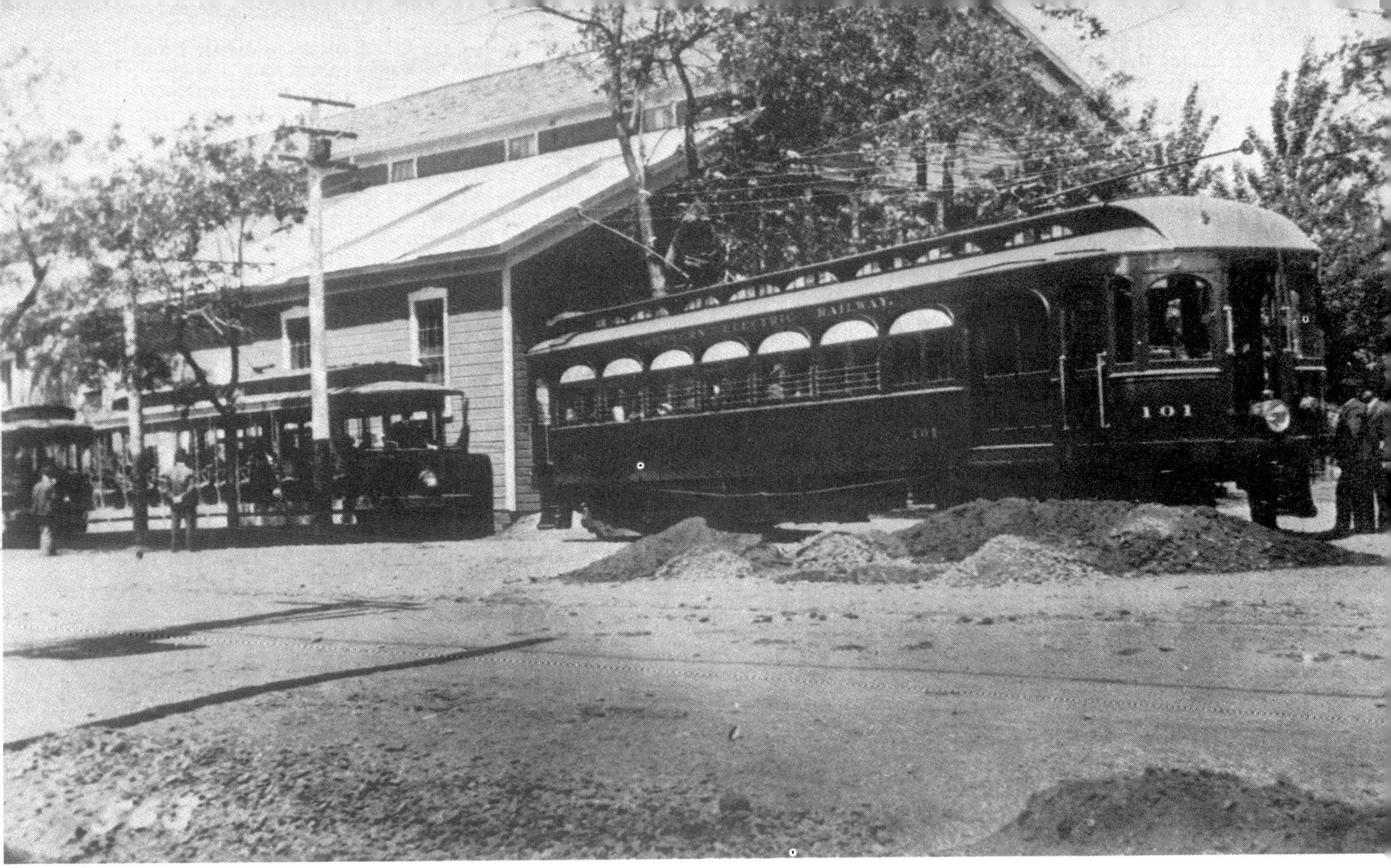

Opening day of **service** on Northern Electric, with motor 101 **ready** to **leave** Chico Depot for Oroville on April 25th, 1906.   Open **streetcars 50 and** 51 carried the overflow of passengers to Oroville.   Motor 100 was the first car,   with 101 following.   Note P. E. pneumatic **trolley bases and** lack of pilot on the 101.   (VS)

Left: The over-head trolley has almost disappear-ed and the third rail has taken over. The scene is near Tres Vias looking toward Chico. When NE decided to aban-don overhead trolley wire for third rail pickup, the entire section gang here resigned en masse.   (LLS)

In one direction the train operated as an MU train; in the other, the 1010 hauled the cars dead. A total of 860 persons rode this inaugural train. The official opening of the Woodland Branch took place on July 15, 1912, without any ceremonies.

Next came the Colusa Branch, running from NE's Marysville Station to the town of Colusa; 20.2 miles long from its junction with the main line at Heyman (Colusa Jct.). On April 29, 1910, The Northern Electric Railway Company-Marysville & Colusa Branch was incorporated; incorporators were Charles H. Hammon, Leon J. DeSabla, Samuel Lilienthal, George E. Springer and Herbert W. Furlong. This new company was incorporated for $1,500,000.

As early as March 19, 1906, the Shasta Southern had dug up Colusa's Main St. between 5th and 6th Streets and laid a couple of rails to hold its franchise. NE itself applied for a franchise in Colusa on January 7, 1907, which was granted but expired because NE did not begin work within ninety days.

Not until 1911 did the interurban construction spotlight again focus on Colusa. A major obstacle was the Sacramento River, which this branch would cross at Meridian. On January 3, 1912 NE entered into an agreement with Colusa County whereby both would participate in a joint rail & highway structure. The Meridian bridge turned out to be a major facility: 436 feet of span with a clear width of drawspan of 150 feet; foundations were of solid concrete placed on bedrock fifty feet below the riverbed by pneumatic caissons. The bridge cost in all $260,000.

April 1, 1913, saw the first NE train cross the brand new Meridian Bridge. The first work train reached Colusa on May 14, 1913. Regular passenger service began on Monday, June 16, 1913, and the first schedule called for nine daily roundtrips. In 1915 the worst floods in the history of the Sacramento Valley caused the undermining of one of the Meridian Bridge's concrete piers and a motorboat was pressed into service to ferry passengers across; not until October 15, 1915 was electric railway service restored.

A feature of the Colusa Branch was the balloon track at the end of this branch just west of the end of Market St. As originally built, this loop used a third rail for power, later changed to overhead trolley. With the completion of the Colusa Branch, NE reached its greatest extent.

In 1913 two short extensions were constructed in the Sacramento area: the Globe-Swanston Line, and the Sacramento West Side Line; both were streetcar lines.

The Sacramento Eastern was incorporated on November 28, 1911, to build the Swanston Line. While its Articles of Incorporation called for it to go from Sacramento to Folsom via Sycamore, its true destination was probably Swanston, as the line was subsidized by the North Sacramento Land Company---which firm made up the deficits incurred by the passenger service until 1933; by that time this line had developed enough freight business to keep it in use, but passenger service was then discontinued because no further subsidies were forthcoming from the land company.

The West Sacramento line was built under similar circumstances. In 1913 the ambitions of NE received their most serious setback when the Oakland, Antioch & Eastern built its line on a direct route between Oakland and Sacramento. The coming of this line knocked out all hope for completing the Vallejo & Northern, although that project died hard and was not abandoned until NE itself was forced into receivership in 1914.

The tension that existed between NE and OA&E in regards to the V&N can best be illustrated by recounting the following true incident:

Just before the OA&E opened regular service from Sacramento to Oakland, NE was building its streetcar line from Broderick to Headquarters (now West Gate). This line paralleled the track of the OA&E for some distance and NE found its rival's track to be a convenient means of getting its work trains out along the new streetcar line to deliver rails and other construction material. J. B. Rowray, NE Superintendent, ordered an NE work train to proceed upon OA&E's line under the cover of night. When the NE train stopped to unload its rails, it was surprised by the glare of a powerful headlight bearing down upon it from the direction of Oakland. The NE crew, of course, realized they had absolutely no right to be on a foreign company's rails without permission. A hiss of air signalled the emergency application of its brakes by the OA&E train (which consisted of a combination passenger motor and the big business car of the president of the Burlington Railroad) and it stopped with a jerk just short of the standing NE work train.

Riding on the front end of the OA&E special train was Harry A. Mitchell, OA&E's General Manager, who jumped down quickly and landed running. "Where's Nelson? Where's Nelson?" he yelled, but he sought in vain, for Mr. Nelson was not there---he had taken refuge in the bridge tender's shanty of the then new M St. Bridge to await further developments. After a few minutes' wait while the work train finished dumping its rails, both trains proceeded to Sacramento. Such was the state of electric railway construction in California in the days just before the State Railroad Commission undertook to regulate every last detail of operation.

Many years later, Harry A. Mitchell, who retired as President of The Sacramento Northern Railway---said in a talk to a Bay Area Electric Railroad Association banquet in San Francisco's Palace Hotel:

"We (OA&E) did the Northern Electric a favor in reaching Sacramento in the way we did at the time we did. Had Northern Electric completed the Vallejo & Northern it would have been handicapped with a round about route between Sacramento and San Francisco which would have been a constant drain on the Northern Electric and the successor Sacramento Northern finances."

Mr. Mitchell further remarked that the successor consolidated company would have been burdened with track it did not need. The eventual (1928) consolidation of the NE's successor, Sacramento Northern Railroad---and the OA&E's successor---San Francisco-Sacramento Railroad---was to be the completion of Henry A. Butters' fondest dream: reaching San Francisco with an electric railway.

Thus in 1913 the Northern Electric was to reach its final stage of operation; its original promoters were to make no further extensions. In 1913, NE had the longest third rail line in the United States. Perhaps this would be the best time to look back upon the company's operating methods.

The original Chico-Oroville Line was operated with single cars making three daily roundtrips. The first freight carried was five bags of prunes between Chico and Oroville on the platform of the 701---"Old Maude"---and passenger business remained all important in those early days. Sundays saw the open bench streetcars 50 and 51 running between Chico and Oroville, giving a roundtrip ride for fifty cents, the longest open bench ride ever given in California. It took one hour for 50 and 51 to make the 25 mile run, but the big Niles passenger motors 100 and 101 with their PE pneumatic trolley bases covered the distance in fifty minutes, although charging twice as much.

When NE reached ninety miles south to Sacramento in 1907, the company found itself short of rolling stock and California type car 21 was often used on the Oroville Line.

The originally contemplated schedule from Chico had local trains to Sacramento running at 5:30 AM, 7:30, 9:30, 11:30, 1:30 PM, 3:30, 5:30, 7:30 and 11:20. Express trains were to leave Chico at 10:03 AM, 12:03 PM, 4:03, 6:03, 10:03 and 12:33 AM. However, this newspaper published schedule was never put into effect; only the locals were run when the new line opened to Sacramento.

Southern Pacific sought to meet NE's competition by reducing its fare to $2.65 one way to Sacramento and $5.10 to San Francisco. In addition, SP assigned a parlor car complete with porter to its San Francisco-Chico train.

The first full scale excursion to be run by NE was a four-car special from Chico to Sacramento on Thursday, the 12th of September, 1907, with two hundred representative citizens of Chico on board. When this train arrived at 8th & J Sts., Sacramento, at 11:00 AM, its passengers marched through the Sacramento streets in celebration of the opening of interurban service between Chico and Sacramento. This special was operated by NE instead of by SP because SP had insisted on a guarantee of one hundred fares at one-third rate whereas NE ran the special at a one-and-a-third rate with return permitted on any date.

For almost every event of major importance in the Sacramento Valley NE was ready to run special trains. Mr. A. D. Schindler, General Manager of NE, jotted down every one of these movements in a little notebook he carried, with special emphasis on their earnings.

Hardly had NE been opened for service when rumors began to go the rounds that it was to be sold to the Western Pacific. Headlines in the Chico "Enterprise" on September 19, 1907 read: "Western Pacific Will Absorb The Northern Electric Road." Other newspapers, including the Sacramento "Bee," speculated at this same time upon WP's taking over the interurban company because the WP, then building its main line, had planned no feeders---and also because Henry A. Butters had pointed out the value of NE to the citizens of Red Bluff as a connecting link in a transcontinental railroad when he sought a franchise there.

The typical early day NE train consisted of a combination motor car pulling a passenger trailer. Except for Sundays and days of unusually heavy travel, the multiple unit train in its strict sense was rare on the Northern Electric.

Like all new lines, NE was troubled by wrecks in its early years. Live Oak seems to have been outstanding as a place where NE trains came to grief frequently. The first one to occur there was on September 3, 1907 when No. 23 met No. 22 head-on at a heavily wooded curve at 5:30 PM. Several passengers were hurt---none seriously---and the motormen were described as "acting coolly in the face of danger." Motorman Conrad and Conductor Black were cut by flying glass, while Motorman Fenwick and Conductor Dillingham escaped with nary a scratch.

A more serious crash, however, took place at Live Oak on November 2, 1907 when an electric car from Marysville, due to arrive at Live Oak at 5:46 AM, crashed into a freight train which had left Chico at 1:40 AM. A difference of five minutes in the watches of Freight Conductor Dolan and Passenger Conductor Hawthorne was noted, and Superintendent Dimmock said that Dolan should have gone into the Live Oak siding. One of the passengers, a George Butsner, was reading a Greek language newspaper at the time and it was no Greek to him when the lights went out at Live Oak, for he knew that there the car changed from third rail to trolley. Just when he expected the lights to go back on, there was a terrific crash. Motor 101 was almost totally wrecked and freight motor 1002 was described as being a total loss. Passenger Motorman E. O. Nidiffer suffered a broken leg and internal injuries and was to succumb to these injuries two days later.

While these first mentioned wrecks could be attributed to the Operating Department, the first derailment near Sacramento was due to the newness of the track. On October 14th, 1907, a two-car train was ditched after crossing the American River Trestle. Traffic was tied up until ten o'clock that evening as an SP wrecking crew put the electric train back on the rails.

To train the relatively new train crews in their duties, W. W. Nelson was promoted to Traveling Motorman. In carrying out his duties, Mr. Nelson carried a front end riding permit which stated that no talking with the motorman was permitted! In those days, riding on the head end of an NE train was strictly prohibited.

Mr. Nelson was shortly thereafter promoted to Traveling Conductor after the first holder of this position overlooked a meet order and headed his train into the face of an opposing train. The flat nature of the land traversed by the NE enabled the motormen to see each other in plenty of time to stop.

In the first years of the Northern Electric, riding for the sake of riding was extremely popular. NE made a specialty of "Poppy Excursions," running to Riego where the golden blooms grew in profusion. On Saturdays, car 200 was placed on the head end of the regular train and then was cut off at Riego, to return later in the day at the head end of a Sacramento-bound train. A 25¢ roundtrip ticket was sold to poppy pickers. Sundays saw special trains operated to Riego and one bright, sunny Sunday morning Mr. Nelson noted that Governor (later Senator) Hiram Johnson was aboard the train; realizing that the front end was sacred but also vulnerable to the laws of hospitality, Mr. Nelson suggested to Mr. Rowray that a front end pass be made out for the Governor. A motorman's toolbox was up-ended, and it was from this informal seat that California's leading citizen viewed the poppies from his orange-hued train. Governor Johnson, who was responsible for California's present Public Utilities Commission (then the Railroad Commission) is said to have enjoyed his ride very much.

Northern Electric had a major setback in 1914 when it was forced into receivership. This event marked the end of the Sloss-Lilienthal regime, but the Receiver, Mr. John B. Coghlan, and General Manager W. A. McGovern, continued work improving the line and its operations. All officers of the old Northern Electric were put out except Superintendent Rowray who had come to the NE from Pacific Electric in 1912 and W. W. Nelson who became Trainmaster.

In August 1913 the OA&E had completed its line between Oakland and Sacramento, and NE thereafter had a rail connection between its lines and the San Francisco Bay area. At first no through cars were run; it was not until 1915 that NE completed its first parlor car to provide through service between Chico and Oakland.

Before the coming of the OA&E to Sacramento, NE had widely publicized its Sacramento River boat connection with San Francisco. The California Transportation Company, operating the river steamers "Fort Sutter" and "Capital City," and NE had a traffic agreement which bound them to exchange both passengers and freight at the Sacramento wharves. NE ran a name train to connect with these boats for many years; it bore the dash sign, "The Steamer Special." It is interesting to note that the contract between the riverboat company and NE contained clauses permitting the railway to have similar agreements with electric railways, both building and proposed.

While the Northern Electric was very much like an interurban in that it ran electric trains on city streets, its scheduling approached that of the steam railroads of the time. There was just sufficient traffic to warrant trains every hour on the hour.

Wells Fargo & Company had the express contract with NE and handled all express business over its lines, just as it did with the OA&E. This connection continued with both sides' respective successor companies.

No railway mail postoffices ever operated over the Northern Electric and its successors; however, sacked mail was handled from the beginning. From its inception Northern Electric sought to handle interchange freight with steam railroads but it was not until February 17, 1912, that the California Railroad Commission in its Case No. 227 rendered an order to the Northern Electric and the Western Pacific to set up joint rates on freight between points on the NE and San Francisco via WP. Only 30% of NE revenues came from freight at that time.

Physically, NE built its lines to the best steam railroad standards of that day, with 100-foot-wide rights of way outside cities and towns; only in thickly populated areas did its tracks have to traverse paved streets. With the OA&E connection in

1913, NE had an entry into the San Francisco Bay region; no longer did the majority of its passengers transfer to the SP at Sacramento.

However, only parlor car passengers were to ride through Sacramento without physically transferring to cars of the other interurban line. For its parlor car service, NE had rebuilt one of its Niles motors into the palatial and photogenic "Bidwell." As of 1916, "Bidwell" was the parlor car assigned to "The Sacramento Valley Limited," the morning train from Oakland and afternoon train from Chico. For its share of this service, the OA&E provided the parlor car "Sacramento" which was operated on "The Meteor," the evening train from Oakland and the morning train from Chico. Passengers who did not ride in parlor car seats had to change cars in Sacramento at 3rd & M Sts.; it was at this point that parlor cars were switched back and forth between the two companies' lines.

On June 20, 1918, a new company, The Sacramento Northern Railroad Company, was incorporated to take over all properties of the Northern Electric. On July 1, 1918, NE was knocked down to the new company at auction, and at the very same moment a freight motor kicked a cut of cars on the M St. Bridge which ran down the rather steep grade at this point, left the tracks and demolished NE's freight shed at Front & M Sts.

No drastic changes in operation were introduced by the new company except at Chico, where Birney cars 60 and 61 took over as rolling stock on the Chico local lines. SN adopted the famous Pullman Green as its standard color for passenger cars and the traditional Northern Electric orange---not unlike the orange of Butters' great mansion, Alta Vista---thus faded away under a dark green sea.

After the OA&E became The San Francisco-Sacramento Railroad, the Sacramento Northern and the SF-S ("Sacramento Short Line") inaugurated dining car service between Oakland and Chico on October 20, 1921. SN purchased the great car "Alabama" from former PE President Henry E. Huntington for its share of this new service and also had dining facilities installed on the "Bidwell." SF-S made a diner out of its "Sacramento" to run opposite "Alabama."

This dining car service proved to be quite a source of unhappiness to SN President Detrick, as the SF-S under Harry A Mitchell forced all passengers to pay parlor car fares while riding over its lines. Thus Detrick had to pay SF-S to ride his own car.

On December 23, 1921, the Western Pacific took over the Sacramento Northern Railroad. With the acquisition of the electric road, WP announced plans to extend the Vacaville Branch from Willota to Vallejo, and to extend the Woodland Branch to Vacaville via Winters. Such plans recalled in the minds of the old timers the heyday of NE's Vallejo & Northern project.

Changes were effected in Marysville; there SN took over all switching chores for WP. Also in 1925 the old NE bridge over the Yuba River at Marysville was abandoned and SN trains were given trackage rights over the WP bridge at this point. It is interesting to note that at Oliver, where this connection was made, was the very point where the famed "Battle of the Bee Farm" occurred many years before when WP put down two 30-lb. rails across the NE right of way in a vain effort to prevent the interurban company's reaching Sacramento.

1923 saw substation equipment replaced with more modern machines with automatic operation, except at Oroville. This modernization, which was carried out under the direction of Electrical Engineer W. H. Evans, accounted for the continued use of electric power on SN when passenger service ended.

Besides purchasing new freight motors, SN rebuilt its California type streetcars for use on its Elverta and Swanston suburban services. On August 23, 1923, Birneys came to the Sacramento streetcar line; the cars were obtained second hand from The San Diego Electric Railway Company.

Main line passenger operation continued under SN in about the same pattern it had when NE operated the system; although trains were dark green, still the motor-trailer set predominated; the trailers had no controls, hence could not be operated on the head ends of trains, and so SN trains still had to be wyed at terminals.

Biggest and most ambitious project of the SN was the construction in Sacramento of the Union Passenger Station at 11th & I Streets. It was the building of this imposing edifice which led to the eventual consolidation of the SN and the SF-S, for SN's parent, WP, advanced funds to the SF-S so it could pay its share of the cost of the major terminal. Also participating was the Central California Traction Company, operators of the interurban electric railway between Sacramento and Stockton.

SN also constructed attractive new stations in Chico and Marysville, as well.

SN was to rename two important and historic junctions: Tres Vias lost its colorful Spanish name and became prosaic Oroville Junction. Heyman became Colusa Junction; Heyman had been named after a San Francisco investor in the old NE, who responded with alacrity when a group of NE officials offered to name a station after him if he would buy their lunch.

First interests behind the Northern Electric aside from Henry A. Butters were men closely identified with the Pacific Gas & Electric Company, such as De Sabla and Lilienthal. In California, however, the power interests tended to keep out of the electric railway business. Thus, when the Northern Electric and the Sacramento Northern needed assistance, a steam railroad was at hand---the Western Pacific. It was also Western Pacific which was to merge California's two longest electric railways into one to make The Sacramento Northern Railway by far the longest interurban line in the United States.

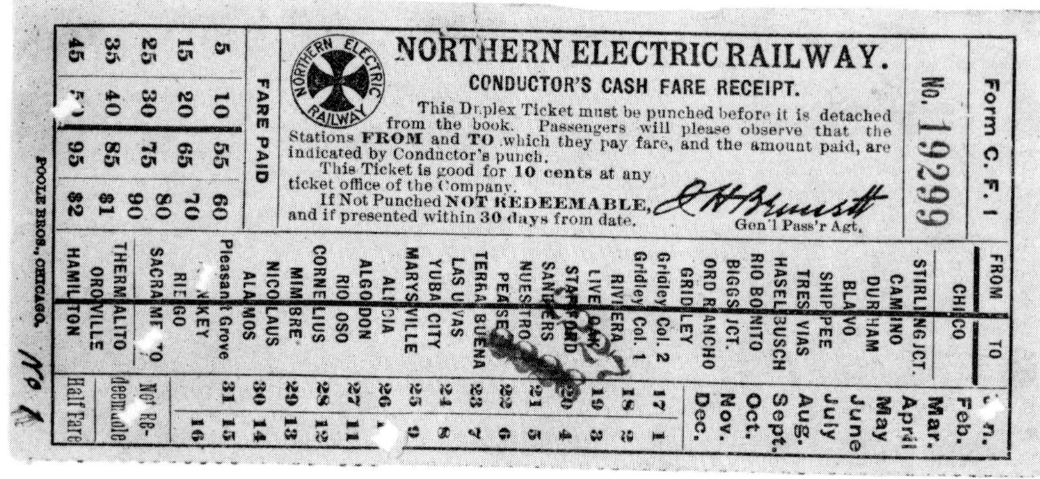

NORTHERN ELECTRIC RAILWAY.

CONDUCTOR'S CASH FARE RECEIPT.

This Duplex Ticket must be punched before it is detached from the book. Passengers will please observe that the Stations FROM and TO which they pay fare, and the amount paid, are indicated by Conductor's punch.

This Ticket is good for 10 cents at any ticket office of the Company.

If Not Punched NOT REDEEMABLE, and if presented within 30 days from date.

Gen'l Pass'r Agt.

Form C. F. 1

No. 19299

FARE PAID: 5 10 15 20 25 30 35 40 45 50 55 60 65 70 75 80 85 90 95 $1 $2 81 82

POOLE BROS., CHICAGO.

FROM CHICO TO — STIRLING JCT., CAMINO, DURHAM, BLAVO, SHIPPEE, TRES VIAS, HASEL BUSCH, RIO BONITO, BIGGS JCT., ORD RANCHO, GRIDLEY, Gridley Col. 2, Gridley Col. 1, RIVIERA, LIVE OAK, STANFORD, NUESTRO, SANDERS, PEASE, TERRA BUENA, LAS UVAS, YUBA CITY, MARYSVILLE, ALICIA, ALGODON, RIO OSO, CORNELIUS, MIMBRE, NICOLAUS, ALAMOS, Pleasant Grove, NKEY, RIEGO, SACRAM'O TO, THERMALITO, OROVILLE, THERMALITO, HAMILTON

Jan. Feb. Mar. April May June July Aug. Sept. Oct. Nov. Dec.

Half Fare — Not Redeemable

(TRB)

Chapter 2

I.C.C. Evaluation

(Ed.: The following information has been compiled from Valuation Docket No. 1193
of the Interstate Commerce Commission, dated September 19, 1933.)

CHICO ELECTRIC RAILWAY COMPANY

Incorporated in California on August 15, 1904 and controlled by the Northern Electric Company on August 1, 1905, the date of sale, through ownership of all of the capital stock. The property on date of sale consisted of 5.14 miles of tracks in the city of Chico, all of which trackage had been acquired by construction prior to 1905.

Capital stock: $250,000 par value, shares $100, classified as common.

Northern Electric Co. abandoned the greater part of this company's trackage and the remainder was reconstructed and included in mileage shown as constructed by NE. The accounts of NE do not record the retirement of property of this company.

NORTHERN ELECTRIC COMPANY

Incorporated in Nevada on June 14, 1905. Its records and results of operations closed on November 30, 1907 and its property was sold and transferred to The Northern Electric Railway Company as of December 2, 1907, this corporation remaining inactive thereafter.

The Northern Electric Company controlled through stock ownership The Marysville & Yuba City Street Rail Road Company and The Shasta Southern Railway Company. The property of NE was operated by its own organization from successive dates of acquisitions of portions of its line to date of sale. It also operated the property of The Marysville & Yuba City Street Rail Road Company from 1906 to date of sale.

The owned mileage amounted to 113.23 miles and consisted of a single track main line from Chico to Sacramento, and branches from Oroville Jct. to Oroville and Chico to Hamilton, and street car tracks in Chico. The 108.10 miles owned by NE on the date of its sale to NE Ry. had been acquired by construction during the period 1905 to 1907. This company also acquired from The Chico Electric Railway Company 5.14 miles of street car line in the city of Chico. It also acquired from The Marysville & Yuba City Street Rail Road Company 3.20 miles of road between Marysville and Yuba City. The greater part of the mileage in the city of Chico was abandoned, and the remainder, together with the 3.20 miles between Marysville and Yuba City was reconstructed by this company and the mileage included in the 108.10 miles shown as constructed by this company.

Trackage constructed by this company:
    Chico, via Oroville Jct., to Sacramento, 1905-07-------------------- 90.50 miles
    Oroville Jct. to Oroville, 1906-07--------------------------------- 5.50 "
    Chico to Hamilton, 1907 --- 12.10 "

Capital stock: $6,000,000 with common shares par value $100 each.

MARYSVILLE & YUBA CITY STREET RAIL ROAD COMPANY

Incorporated in California on April 17, 1889. It was controlled by The Northern Electric Company on July 12, 1906, the date of sale, through ownership of capital stock.

During 1880 this company constructed 3.20 miles of road between Marysville and Yuba City, designed for horse drawn vehicles. This mileage was rebuilt for electric operation during 1905-07 by NE.

Capitalization: $50,000---common shares, $100 each.

In 1906 the Marysville-south segment of NE was operated temporarily by steam locomotives hauling interurban trains. Here locomotive 3 prepares to leave Marysville with 220 and 127, as motor 202 (later "Bidwell") completes transferring its passengers and baggage from Chico and points en route. (RD)

A bucolic scene at NE's Oroville Depot, about 1906; motor 101 is featured. (RD)

REDDING & RED BLUFF RAILWAY COMPANY

Incorporated in California February 23, 1906 to construct a railroad from Chico to Redding.

This company had acquired some right-of-way and surveys had been made, but no completed property was owned on date of sale, July 1906, to The Shasta Southern Railway Company.

Authorized capital stock was $800,000; how much, if any, was issued is not shown by records.

SHASTA SOUTHERN RAILWAY COMPANY

Incorporated in California on July 17, 1906 to acquire the railroad of The Redding & Red Bluff Railroad Company. This company did acquire the uncompleted property formerly owned by The Redding & Red Bluff Railway Company, the extent of which is not known, and constructed about 4 miles of road between Hamilton and Monroeville in 1907. The extent of the operations and by whom are not indicated in available records. The records of The Northern Electric Railway Company, the successor, indicate that during 1907 it expended $172,108.21 in the construction of the property of this company.

Capitalization: $4,000,000 par value, shares $100 each, of which $15,000 was issued.

This company was sold on January 18, 1907 to The Northern Electric Railway Company.

NORTHERN ELECTRIC RAILWAY COMPANY

Incorporated in California on September 19, 1907. This company took over the property of The Northern Electric Company on December 2, 1907. In addition, it operated under lease the properties of the following:

    The Sacramento & Woodland Railroad Company, 17 miles, after ------------- July 13, 1912
    NE Ry. Co., Marysville and Colusa Branch, 22.39 miles, from -------------- June 2, 1913
    The Sacramento Terminal Company, 5.73 miles, from -------------------- May 15, 1909
    The West Side Railroad, 0.498 miles, from---------------------------- 1912
                    Total miles leased: 45.618

The railroad operated by this company was a single track, standard gauge electrically operated road, aggregating about 159.818 miles. The owned mileage amounted to about 114.20 miles, and was acquired partly by purchase and partly by construction.

Trackage constructed by this company:
    Willeta to Vacaville, 1913-14--------------------------- 14.90
    Globe to Swanston, 1914-15--------------------------- 1.50   16.40
Less retirements, about 1917:
    Chico to Hamilton------------------------------------- 12.10
    Hamilton to Monroeville------------------------------- 4.00   16.10

                                        Net Increase: 0.30

Capitalization: $25,000,000 par value, shares $100 each, of which $10,000,000 was preferred and $15,000,000, was common.

This company on December 2, 1907 purchased the property formerly owned and controlled by The Northern Electric Company for $5,000,000 stock issued in exchange for $6,000,000 par value of NE Co. stock, assumed the outstanding funded debt, and transferred the current asset and liability accounts to its books.

This company purchased the property formerly owned by The Vallejo & Northern Railroad Company in December 1912, for which it issued $1,000,000 par value of funded debt.

It purchased the property formerly owned by The Shasta Southern Railway Company, date not of record, and transferred to its road-and-equipment account an amount representing construction advances of The Northern Electric Company to The Shasta Southern Railway Company: $169,708.21.

Funds for construction and additions and betterments were obtained through issuance of funded debt and advances received from affiliated companies.

From October 5, 1914 to June 30, 1918 this company's property was operated by a receiver appointed by The United States District Court who also operated during this period this company's leased properties. This company was controlled on June 28, 1918, the date of sale, by The Sloss Securities Company thru ownership of a majority of its capital stock. On the other hand, this company then controlled The Sacramento & Woodland Railroad Company and The Northern Realty Company, the latter being a noncarrier corporation.

The property of The Northern Electric Railway Company, together with the properties of its leased companies except the property of The West Side Railroad, were sold June 28, 1918, and on July 1, 1918 the property was released by the receiver to The Sacramento Northern Railroad.

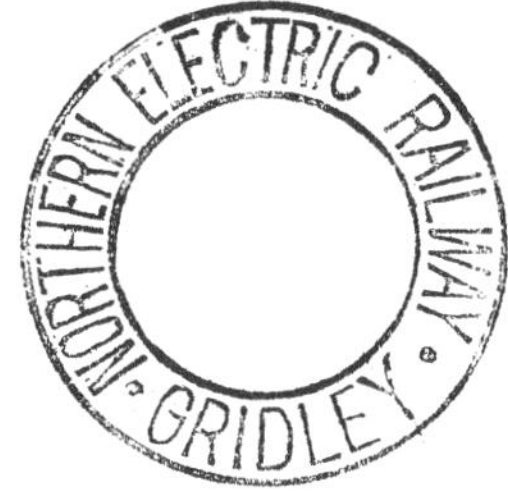

1912 was a good year for Northern Electric, and it proceeded to beat its drum throughout the west. In the magazines, newspapers, and anywhere else possible, NE took its message of low priced land and convenient, thrifty transportation to prospective settlers. Above, a full page ad from a magazine (Woods), and right, an enticing ad published in "Sunset Magazine." (Magna)

Left, the 1912 NE emblem featured river steamers as well as interurbans.

REAL ESTATE—California

SUTTER COUNTY LAND SYNDICATE, NORTHERN Electric Railway Lands.—Get a home at Terra Buena, Sutter County, on the Northern Electric Railway, four miles from Marysville. This Subdivision is of 5 and 10-acre tracts of the best land in the Sacramento Valley at $125.00 per acre. $25.00 per acre cash, balance in four equal annual payments. Good school, store and depot on tract. No irrigation required to get most satisfactory returns from this land. The best Thompson Seedless grapes in this state grow here and have made over $100.00 per acre net profit for the past five years. For particulars about this tract and also about our alfalfa and dairy lands on the Sacramento River, address Sutter County Land Syndicate, 410 ½ Third St.. Marysville, Cal., or 310 Sansome St., San Francisco, or P. W. Lytle, Agent, Terra Buena, Cal.

MAYWOOD COLONY, in the SACRAMENTO VAL-

VALLEJO & NORTHERN RAILWAY COMPANY

Incorporated in California on November 8, 1906.   Capitalization: $2,500,000 par value, common shares $100 each.

This company owned no completed road at the time its property was conveyed to The Vallejo & Northern Railroad Company in January, 1910; records of the latter company show that $164,550.91 was expended by this company for construction, the extent of which is not indicated in available records.

VALLEJO & NORTHERN RAILROAD COMPANY

Incorporated in California on October 20, 1909, to build a railroad between Sacramento and Vallejo.

This company acquired from The Vallejo & Northern Railway Company by purchase in January, 1910, an uncompleted road, the extent of which is unknown. It acquired by construction 1.8 miles of road in the city of Sacramento during 1911 and 1912. It acquired the uncompleted property of the V&N Ry. by assuming a liability for advances amounting to $163,343.63. It also began construction of a road north of Suisun.

At the time of this company's sale to The Northern Electric Railway Company on December 31, 1912, it had not placed any of its property in operation. It owned no equipment as of the date of sale, but its investment in road, including land, was stated in its books as being $309,870.32.

THE SACRAMENTO TERMINAL COMPANY

Incorporated in California on September 17, 1908.   Its authorized capital stock was $250,000 par value, with common shares at $100 each.

This company owned a single track, standard gauge electrically operated railroad within the city of Sacramento about 5.73 miles in length, of which 2.67 miles was owned jointly with The Central California Traction Company. This trackage was constructed for this company in 1909 and 1910 by The Northern Electric Railway Company.   This company owned no equipment.

This company was controlled by interests affiliated with The Northern Electric Railway Company on June 28, 1918, when it was sold to The Sacramento Northern Railroad.

NORTHERN ELECTRIC RAILWAY COMPANY, MARYSVILLE & COLUSA BRANCH

Incorporated in California on May 6, 1910 with authorized capital stock of $1,500,000 par value, its common stock selling at $100 each at par.

This company built a single track, standard gauge electrically operated railroad extending from Heyman to Colusa, about 22.39 miles; construction took place between December 1911 and June 1913.

This property was operated under lease by The Northern Electric Railway Company, for which it received 50% of the net income as its compensation.

A combination railway and highway bridge on this line was partially paid for by the counties of Colusa and Sutter, this company receiving from them $186,861.67.   This bridge was at Meridian.

The investment in road, including land (no equipment being owned) on June 30, 1918, is stated in the books as $1,144,990.96.

On June 30, 1918, the property of this company was taken over by The Sacramento Northern RR. Co.

SACRAMENTO & WOODLAND RAILROAD COMPANY

Incorporated in California on July 20, 1911; its authorized capital stock was $1,000,000 par value, common shares $100 each.

This railroad owned a single track, standard gauge electrically operated railroad, extending from the Sacramento River near Sacramento to Woodland, about 17 miles. This line was constructed between September 1911 and July 1912.

The property was operated by The Northern Electric Railway Company and its receiver from date of completion in July, 1912, to June 30, 1918.

The investment in road, including land (no equipment being owned) on June 30, 1918 was stated to be $920,626.74.

This company was acquired on June 28, 1918 by The Sacramento Northern Railroad Company.

<u>SACRAMENTO & EASTERN RAILWAY COMPANY</u>

Incorporated in California on November 28, 1911 with an authorized capital stock of $1,000,000 but there is no record to show whether or not any was issued.

This company owned no road when its rights and franchises were conveyed to The Northern Electric Railway Company about February, 1913---the exact date not of record.

<u>SACRAMENTO-FOLSOM ELECTRIC RAILWAY COMPANY</u>

Incorporated in California on May 9, 1911 to build a railway between Sacramento and Folsom, about 23 miles. Authorized capital stock was $1,000,000 par value, shares $100 each, classified as common. There is no record of any issuance of stock.

This company owned no road when its rights and franchises were conveyed to The Northern Electric Ry. Co. on February 26, 1913.

<u>SACRAMENTO NORTHERN RAILROAD</u>

Incorporated in California on June 20, 1918. It was organized to acquire and operate all the properties owned by Northern Electric Railway Company, Sacramento Terminal Company, Sacramento & Woodland Railroad Company, and Northern Electric Railway Company, Marysville & Colusa Branch, all of which had been purchased at foreclosure sale, April 18, 1918, by sundry individuals acting as a reorganization committee. The property acquired was conveyed by deed dated June 28, 1918, and surrendered by the receivers July 1, 1918. From the latter date to November 4, 1925, the date of sale, it was operated by its own organization.

The Sacramento Northern Railroad is controlled by The Western Pacific Railroad Company through ownership of all of the outstanding capital stock, authorized July 8, 1925 by the I.C.C.

The railroad operated by this company at the time of its sale was a single track, standard gauge electrically operated railroad about 160.78 miles in length. The wholly owned mileage amounted to 156.26 miles extending from Sacramento to Chico, together with several branches. The jointly owned mileage consisted of 3.06 miles in and around the city of Sacramento.

The mileage operated under lease at date of sale comprised that of the West Side Railroad Company, in West Sacramento, 0.50 mile, and 0.96 mile owned by The Western Pacific Railroad Company.

The properties of the companies hereinbefore named were acquired under the "Northern Electric Reorganization Agreement," dated July 1, 1915, and modification thereof, referred to as "The Amended Northern Electric Reorganization Agreement," dated March 31, 1917, which provided for the reorganization of the company and the issuance of its securities in the acquisition of the properties named and for other purposes.

The authorized capital stock is $5,200,000 par value, shares $100 each, of which $2,340,000 par value is classified as common, $1,902,200 par value as first preferred, and $957,800 as second preferred.

The par value of capital stock and long term securities issued by The Sacramento Northern Railroad in acquiring the properties of the hereinbefore named companies in the reorganization of 1918 was about $30,000,000 less than the par value of the actually outstanding securities of those companies at the date of reorganization. The S.N. RR. Co. took over the companies for $ 9,713,202.02.

The Sacramento Northern Railroad Company was sold to The Sacramento Northern Railway Company on November 4, 1925.

<u>SACRAMENTO NORTHERN RAILWAY COMPANY</u>

Incorporated in California on August 29, 1921 to construct, purchase, lease, own and operate railroads in California and to purchase the property owned by The Sacramento Northern Railroad Company. This company was organized on September 1, 1921. The property of the S.N. RR. Co. was acquired by this company on November 4, 1925.

The wholly owned road is 157.044 miles, extending from Chico to Sacramento with various branch lines; 2.720 miles jointly owned and used at Sacramento; 1.235 miles jointly owned but not used, Napa Jct. to Vallejo; and 0.256 mile jointly owned at Sacramento; all of which aggregates 161.255 miles---all purchased from the S.N. RR. Co. on November 4, 1925.

Of the 14 corporations which comprise the line of corporate succession culminating in the carrier as at present constituted, The Sacramento-Folsom Electric Railway Company and The Sacramento & Eastern Railway Company did not construct or improve any property.

Of the 12 other corporations, The Redding & Red Bluff Railway Company, The Vallejo & Northern Railway Company each acquired some property, the extent of which is not indicated in the records obtained, and The Sacramento Northern Railroad improved property completed by others. The Chico Electric Ry. Co. and The Marysville & Yuba City Street Rail Road Company each constructed certain property which was later reconstructed by another company and the mileage is shown as constructed by that company.

The data with respect to the miles of road constructed by the 7 remaining corporations, the years in which the various portions of the line were constructed, and the manner in which the carrier acquired the property are indicated in the following table:

Constructed by Sacramento Northern RR. Co. ---		
Napa Jct. to Vallejo, 1919 and 1920		1.235
Jointly owned with SF, Napa & Calistoga RR.		
Constructed by Northern Electric Ry. Co. ---		
Willeta-Vacaville, 1913-14	14.90	
Globe-Swanston, 1914-15	1.50	
	16.40	
Less retirements, about 1917---		
Chico-Hamilton	12.10	
Hamilton-Monroeville	4.00	
	16.10	0.300
Constructed by Northern Electric Co. ---		
Chico-Sacramento, 1905-07		90.500
Oroville Jct.-Oroville, 1905		5.500
Chico-Hamilton, 1907		12.100
Constructed by the Shasta Southern Ry. Co. ---		
Hamilton-Monroeville, about 1907		4.000
Constructed by The Vallejo & Northern RR. Co., in City of Sacramento, 1911-12, and construction of road north of Suisun begun but completed by NE Ry.		1.800
Constructed by The Vallejo & Northern Ry. Co., certain construction prior to January, 1910, the extent of which is not indicated in records reviewed		------
Constructed by The Northern Electric Ry. Co., Marysville & Colusa Branch,---		
Colusa Jct.-Colusa, 1912-13		22.390
Constructed by The Sacramento & Woodland Ry. Co. ---		
Sacramento-Woodland, 1911-12		17.000
Constructed by The Sacramento Terminal Co. in City of Sacramento, 1909-10, of which 2.70 miles are owned jointly with Central California Traction Co.		5.730
Total recorded as of date of valuation		160.555

CORPORATE HISTORY, SACRAMENTO NORTHERN RAILWAY COMPANY:

The carrier was incorporated August 29, 1921, under general laws of California to construct, purchase, lease, own and operate railroads in California and to purchase the property owned by The Sacramento Northern Railroad Company. The date of its organization was September 1, 1921. The property of The Sacramento Northern Railroad Company was acquired by the carrier November 4, 1925, under authority dated July 8, 1925, 99 I.C.C. 382.

The names of the corporations, the respective dates of incorporation, and for each predecessor the date and manner of succession follow:

1. SACRAMENTO NORTHERN RAILWAY, August 29, 1921.

2. SACRAMENTO NORTHERN RAILROAD, June 20, 1918; sold November 4, 1925, to 1.

3. NORTHERN ELECTRIC RAILWAY COMPANY, September 19, 1907; sold at foreclosure sale on April 16, 1918, and acquired by 2 from reorganization committee June 28, 1918.

4. NORTHERN ELECTRIC COMPANY, June 14, 1905 (Nevada); sold to 3 on December 2, 1907.

5. CHICO ELECTRIC RAILWAY COMPANY, August 15, 1904; sold to 4 on August 1, 1905.

6. MARYSVILLE & YUBA CITY STREET RAIL ROAD COMPANY, April 17, 1889; sold to 4 on July 12, 1906.

7. SHASTA SOUTHERN RAILWAY COMPANY, July 17, 1906; sold to 3 January 18, 1907.

8. REDDING & RED BLUFF RAILWAY COMPANY, February 23, 1906; sold to 7 July, 1906.

9. VALLEJO & NORTHERN RAILROAD COMPANY, October 20, 1909; sold to 3 Decembdr 31, 1912.

10. VALLEJO & NORTHERN RAILWAY COMPANY, November 8, 1906; sold to 9 January, 1910.

11. SACRAMENTO-FOLSOM ELECTRIC RAILWAY COMPANY, May 9, 1911; sold to 3 about February, 1913.

12. SACRAMENTO & EASTERN RAILWAY COMPANY, November 28, 1911; sold to 3 about February, 1913.

13. NORTHERN ELECTRIC RY. CO., MARYSVILLE & COLUSA BRANCH, May 6, 1910; sold at foreclosure April 16, 1918 and acquired by 2 from reorganization committee June 28, 1918.

14. SACRAMENTO & WOODLAND RAILROAD COMPANY, July 20, 1911; sold at foreclosure on April 16, 1918 and acquired by 2 from reorganization committee on June 28, 1918.

15. SACRAMENTO TERMINAL COMPANY, September 17, 1908; sold at foreclosure April 16, 1918 and acquired by 2 from reorganization committee June 28, 1918.

PROPERTY WHOLLY OWNED BUT NOT USED:

This property consists of certain grading and right of way at Vallejo, used exclusively by The San Francisco, Napa & Calistoga Railway. Estimated cost: $110,884.

PROPERTY JOINTLY OWNED BUT NOT USED:

This property consists of the carrier's portion of 1.235 miles of main track between Napa Jct. and Vallejo and 0.560 mile of other tracks, owned jointly with but used exclusively by The San Francisco, Napa & Calistoga Railway. Estimated cost, $38,922. This includes the cost of one locomotive.

ORIGINAL COST TO DATE:

SACRAMENTO NORTHERN RAILWAY COMPANY	$ 513,632.59
SACRAMENTO NORTHERN RAILROAD COMPANY	1,336,749.68
NORTHERN ELECTRIC RAILWAY COMPANY	3,941,020.81
NORTHERN ELECTRIC COMPANY	4,678,603.61
SHASTA SOUTHERN RAILWAY COMPANY	172,108.21
VALLEJO & NORTHERN RAILROAD COMPANY	647,164.23
VALLEJO & NORTHERN RAILWAY COMPANY	164,550.91
NORTHERN ELECTRIC RY., MARYSVILLE & COLUSA	937,429.61
SACRAMENTO & WOODLAND RAILROAD COMPANY	870,475.46
SACRAMENTO TERMINAL COMPANY	237,417.97
TOTAL:	$13,499,153.08

The above figures represent the outlays by the respective companies, as shown by their individual road and equipment accounts, for the construction and improvement of the entire property.

THE WEST SIDE RAILROAD (LESSOR COMPANY):

The West Side Railroad is a California corporation, having its principal office at San Francisco. It is controlled by the SN Railway through ownership of its entire outstanding capital stock. West Side records are incomplete and cover only theperiod from January 1913 (subsequent to construction) to May 31, 1921. The property of the West Side has always been operated by the SN or its predecessors.

The West Side was incorporated on August 31, 1911 to construct a railroad from Sacramento to Rio Vista, about 35 miles. The road, all owned, of 1.009 miles in West Sacramento, was acquired by construction. Of this, 0.400 mile was built in 1912 and 0.609 mile in 1921. Available data indicates that the SN Railroad advanced funds for the construction of a part of this company's railroad. The company has not kept any income accounts. No rental is recorded as received. The investment of the West Side in land and road (no equipment being owned) is stated in its books on date of evaluation to be $111,701.78.

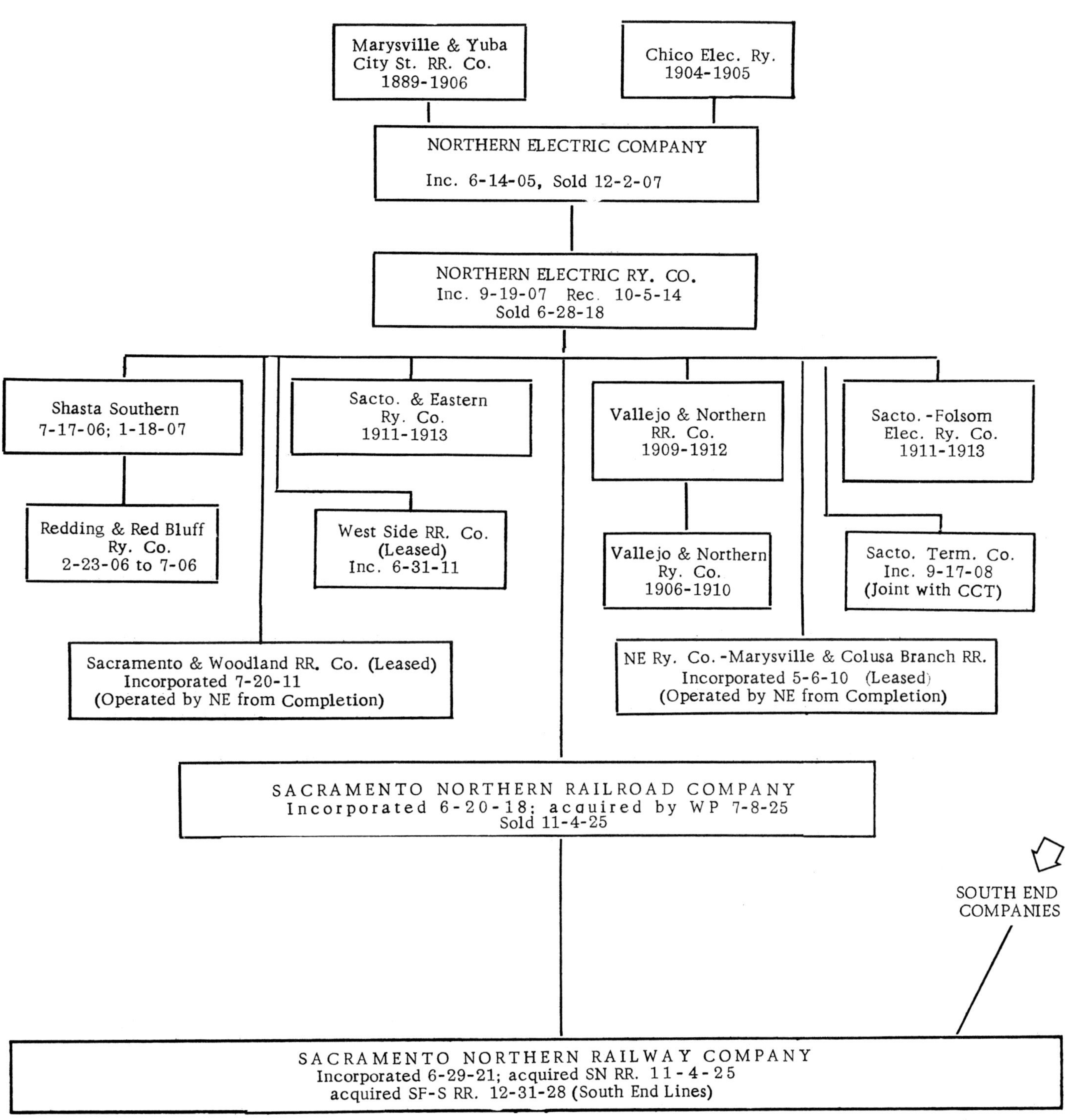

FAMILY TREE, NORTH END LINES

Note: The West Side Railroad Company was purchased by Western Pacific in 1925; it has always been operated by SN and predecessor companies.

Note: The Sacramento Terminal Company is and has always been owned jointly by SN & predecessors and Central California Traction Company.

This corporate diagram by Harre W. Demoro.

Northern Electric's impressive Chico passenger depot was a local landmark for many years.   It was succeeded by a stucco structure in the mid-Twenties.   The above photo, taken about 1908, shows the original structure at its best. (CS)

The Sacramento Union Station, located at 12th and H Sts. This view, taken from Terminal Way, shows the front of the structure with the names of the three interurban companies---SF-S, SN, CCT---carved in the rectangles between the pillars.   The small building at right housed the barber shop and restaurant, while the open area at left was used by Railway Express Agency and baggage room.   Today this building houses a supermarket. (VS)

Chapter 3

Facilities

In this chapter are considered the more important items included in the physical plant of Northern Electric--- stations, bridges, substations, etc.

(Above) Shipping scene on the busy Sacramento waterfront about 1914. Looming over all is NE's big steel bridge. In those days the river was navigable for 300 miles by small craft, and ocean going ships could steam up to Sacramento, 120 miles inland. Tonnage then had an annual value of $50 millions. In all, the Sacramento River flowed through 450 miles of some of the west's most beautiful scenery. (Magna)

(Right) Northern Electric's large substation at Tres Vias (Oroville Jct.), as it appeared in 1910.
(VS)

Chico

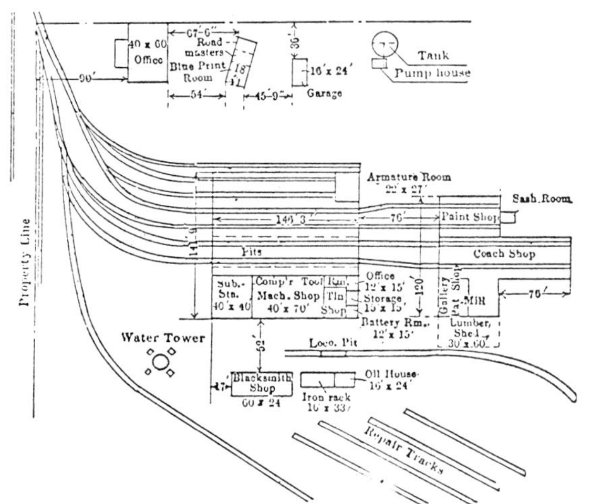

The Mulberry Shops at Chico were well equipped and gave NE and SN an excellent car maintenance facility. The general arrangement of tracks and buildings on the shop tract is shown at left. The main building was approximately square and contained four through tracks and two stub tracks. Two of the through tracks were built with inspection pits of sufficient length to hold three cars each. The car shed section was divided into three bays, and the machine shop, substation and store room occupied the fourth bay adjoining. Each bay had a peak roof with a monitor skylight along the ridge. The building had a wood frame and its sides and roof were covered with corrugated galvanized iron. Due to the mild climate, no doors were provided at either end of the car shed.

The paint shop, wood mill and carpenter shop were in a separate building in the rear of the main shop building, and the blacksmith shop was also in a detached building, 60 ft. x 24 ft., at one side of the main building. Two 1.5 ton air hoists were provided in the machine shop to serve the larger tools. Among equipment provided were the following: larger tools. The shops usually employed about 50 men in NE days, caring for 28 passenger cars, 300 freight cars and 6 locomotives. Fire protection consisted of water and sand pails and a number of hydrants connected to an elevated storage tank near the main building. Much light repair work was done on the outside repair tracks, shown on the plan.

Mulberry Shops, Chico, was the key equipment maintenance and car building facility of NE-SN from the beginning until 1952, when its duties were taken over by Western Pacific's shops in Sacramento.

Top: Interior of carbarn with cars of all types pictured; a 1908 view. (Magna)

Left: The "backyard" was a maze of third rail in early days.

Engineering Offices, Northern Electric Railway, Chico, 1908. (LLS)

<u>GENERAL SPECIFICATIONS: NORTHERN ELECTRIC RY.</u>

(From C. G. Young Report, 1911)

RIGHT OF WAY: Width, 40-100 ft., average 80; line entirely on private way except when necessary to use public streets in passing through municipalities.

WIDTH OF ROADBED: 16 ft. on fills; 18 ft. in cuts.

TRACKS: Standard gauge; 60, 72 and 73 lb. rail of A.S.C.E. section. Ties 6x8x8, partially plated.

TRESTLES: Standard steam road construction of sufficient strength to carry heaviest steam road equipment.

BRIDGES; Partly in steel; combination steel and timber; and all timber.

MAXIMUM GRADIENT: On main line, except where necessary to follow grades of streets in larger cities, .5 to 100 feet, average about .2 maximum; on branches, 1 ft. to 100 ft.

MAXIMUM CURVATURE: On main line, exclusive of cities, established at 4 degrees; 2 degrees used wherever possible excepting on first construction between Oroville and Chico on which a few 6 degree curves were used. About 95% of line is on tangent. Line equipped with third rail system except on streets of cities where overhead trolley is necessary.

Physical track connections at Sacramento with SP, WP and CCT. At Marysville with California Midland and thru it with SP, also with WP. At Chico with Butte County RR and through it with SP. At Oroville with WP.

The company has traffic connection at Sacramento with steamers of California Transportation Co. for San Francisco for both passengers and freight; transfer is made through the Sacramento Terminal directly at the wharf.

EQUIPMENT: PASSENGER:
    30 interurban cars (15 with motors)
    11 combination open and city cars.

EQUIPMENT: FREIGHT:
25	30,000 lb.	capacity flat cars
4	40,000 lb.	capacity flat cars
163	80,000 lb.	capacity flat cars (M.C.B.)
11	40,000 lb.	capacity box cars
3	50,000 lb.	capacity box cars
100	80,000 lb.	capacity box cars
50	80,000 lb.	capacity Rodgers ballast cars

1	Construction motor
4	Freight motors
1	Tower car, 40,000 lbs. capacity
1	Water tank car, 30,000 lbs. capacity
1	Dump car, 40,000 lbs. capacity
1	Plow

SUBSTATIONS:
No. 1 ---	Mulberry	2 - 400 KW (PG&E)
No. 2 ---	Esquon	1 - 400 KW
No. 3 ---	Tres Vias	2 - 400 KW
No. 4 ---	Boga	1 - 400 KW
No. 5 ---	Encinal	1 - 400 KW (Portable)
No. 6 ---	Marysville	2 - 400 KW (PG&E)
No. 8 ---	Nicolaus	2 - 400 KW
No. 9 ---	Riego	1 - 400 KW (Portable)

(Pencilled notation: New subs: Stohlman & Elkhorn)

All above machines are standard type Westinghouse, known as two bearing motor generator sets, composed of one 400 KW 600 v. DC multipolar compound wound engine type generator, speed approximately 500 rpm, mounted on common base and shaft and direct connected to one 3-phase 2200 volt 60 cycle induction motor, complete with motor starting panel and field rheostat.

<u>CHANGES IN ABOVE SPECIFICATIONS, VALLEJO & NORTHERN:</u>

The following changes have been made in the above specifications for the construction of the Marysville & Colusa Branch and the Sacramento & Woodland, and will be adopted for the Vallejo & Northern:

RIGHT OF WAY: All 100 ft. wide.
WIDTH OF ROADBED: 18 ft. on fills, 20 ft. in cuts.
BRIDGES: All steel.
MAXIMUM GRADIENT: 1-1/2% at Jamison Canyon.
MAXIMUM CURVATURE: 3-1/2% on V&N.
PASSENGER EQUIPMENT: Will be all steel.

Northern Electric's original depot in Sacramento at 8th & J Streets was as seen above in a 1907 view. (RB)
This building was later remodeled in modified Mission style, as seen below. (AEB)

(LLS)

NORTHERN ELECTRIC STATIONS

NE's General Manager A. D. Schindler brought more than the pneumatic trolley base with him from the Pacific Electric; these cobblestone stations bear more than a coincidental resemblance to PE's Glendale Depot. Among towns having cobblestone stations on NE were Thermalito (left) and Pleasant Grove (bottom); the East Gridley station (center) was of more traditional architecture; the bus connected NE patrons with Gridley.

It is noted of Pleasant Grove that if there was no business there, trains would coast through the half mile of overhead trolley wire between stretches of third rail without bothering to raise trolleys.

(LLS)

(WP)

SACRAMENTO RIVER DRAWBRIDGE

The big drawbridge over which OA&E and Woodland trains gained access to Sacramento was a major facility and merits our attention.

The Sacramento River at Sacramento has raised its bed many feet above its original level due to constant silting and deposits of mining debris carried down from hydraulic mining of the early days. Thus engineers were forced to go down much further than ordinarily necessary to gain a sound foundation for the piers.

The NE Bridge was constructed in 1911 by the interurban company and the counties of Sacramento and Yolo; it bore a single track and twin roadways and pedestrian walks.

In all, the bridge had five piers---two embedded in the levee at either end and three in the stream, the middle pier bearing the draw span. These piers raised themselves 40 feet above the river bed and went down 60 feet below it. It was necessary to use heavy timber caissons, sealed air tight and sunk by their own weight as excavating proceeded. Air pressure within was 45 lbs. to the square inch which prevented water and sand from falling into the hole under the shield. Excavated material was carried in a 6 inch pipe up through the top of the caisson and discharged onto a barge. One man remained at the bottom during excavating to direct material into the hose and prevent rocks clogging it. When concrete nearly filled the hole, the caisson was raised nearly to the bed of the river and sheet piling was driven to enable completion of the job.

Pile bulkheads were driven up and down the river on either side of the center foundation; on these the draw span was erected and they were retained to act as buffers against floating debris.

There were two fixed spans, each 125 feet long, and the center draw span, 400 feet long. The single track passed through the bridge, which had a clear width of 16 feet. Loading for the railway portion was Cooper's E-40.

The operator's house was placed over the center of the draw; it was a reinforced concrete structure, 12 feet square, with 4 inch walls. Leading up to this house was a cast iron stairway from the railway part of the bridge. Inside the operator's house were placed 20 signal levers, five of which were reserved for possible future use. The other 15 operated the interlocking signals and gates whenever the draw was opened or closed. Two double pole knife switches controlled (1) the bridge motors, and (2) the jack motors. Between was an interlocking device preventing conflicting movements--- when one was open, the other had to be closed. Various other switches controlled the bridge lights, circuit breakers, a jack testing device, etc. Two interurban type controllers were mounted on the floor in front of the main panel and controlled the speed of the two sets of motors.

The draw was operated by two 60 HP DC motors, set directly beneath the track at the center of the draw and which were back geared to a vertical countershaft, a spur gear on this countershaft engaging a stationary gear rack mounted on the pier structure. A high concrete wall protected these motors from damage by high water. Ends of the draw rested on cast iron plates which rested on the tops of the two adjacent piers. Ends of the draw span were made to rest upon the plates by means of 6 inch vertical screw jacks which, by pressing on the plates, raised the ends of the draw span slightly. The jacks were operated by 15 HP DC 500-volt motors. While turning the jacks they also shot two rail bolts into sockets close beside each rail end of the fixed spans; these locked the draw against any lateral motion and formed a continuation of the rails from the fixed spans to the draw span.

The bridge motors were operated by railway current, supplied from the Sacramento side; this current was also carried across the river in a single conductor submarine cable. This cable was brought up the pier at the east end of the draw

Head-on view of the great Northern Electric bridge over the Sacramento River at Sacramento. This was largest, most costly span on the interurban system.   (Magna)

span to a switch box and was then taken to the center pier, where there were two switch boxes, and thence to the west pier where there was one switch box, and then to the western shore. This enabled the cutting out of any section of cable in case of damage or break, using the electric rail as the conductor for that section. Power for operating the bridge was tapped from the cable at the center pier. A motor driven centrifugal pump delivering 600 gallons of water a minute at a pressure of 100 lbs. per square inch was mounted on the draw span; this was for fire protection. Armored telephone cable was also carried across on the bridge and this had a loop to the center pier, enabling the operator to talk to any place on the line.

This bridge served well from 1912 to 1935, when it was replaced by the present Tower Bridge, over which the SN still operates. The Tower Bridge, a $994,000 vertical lift span, was opened on December 15, 1935. Built by the State Department of Public Works, the city and county of Sacramento and the Federal government, the Tower Bridge is 737 feet long, has a 52 foot roadway, two sidewalks, and a 13 foot center roadway for SN's single track line. Construction work on the Tower Bridge began in July, 1934, and necessitated building a $90,000 temporary detour trestle for SN trains. This was located about 75 feet north of the old bridge. The Tower Bridge consists of both steel and concrete spans. The central lift span is a 209 foot truss supported by two vertical towers 160 feet high. When lifted, the lift span is 100 feet above high water and a horizontal clearance of 172 feet between fenders. The weight of the lift span is 2,300,000 pounds, counterbalanced by steel frames filled with concrete.

This 1911 photo shows NE's M St. Bridge under construction. Its dominance of the scene can best be appreciated by comparing its size with the Southern Pacific river steamer "Modoc," seen in channel to extreme right. (LLS)

NE's "other" bridge at Sacramento carried the big green electric trains safely above the sometimes turbulent waters of the American River. (LLS)

Severe floods in 1907 destroyed Northern Electric's covered bridge at Marysville.   These photos show steps in
meeting this problem.   Above, wreckage of the covered bridge and the new bridge under construction. (AL)
Below, the new bridge completed; note that it was much higher and on a slightly different alignment than
the old bridge, a portion of which still stands at the left.   (LLS)

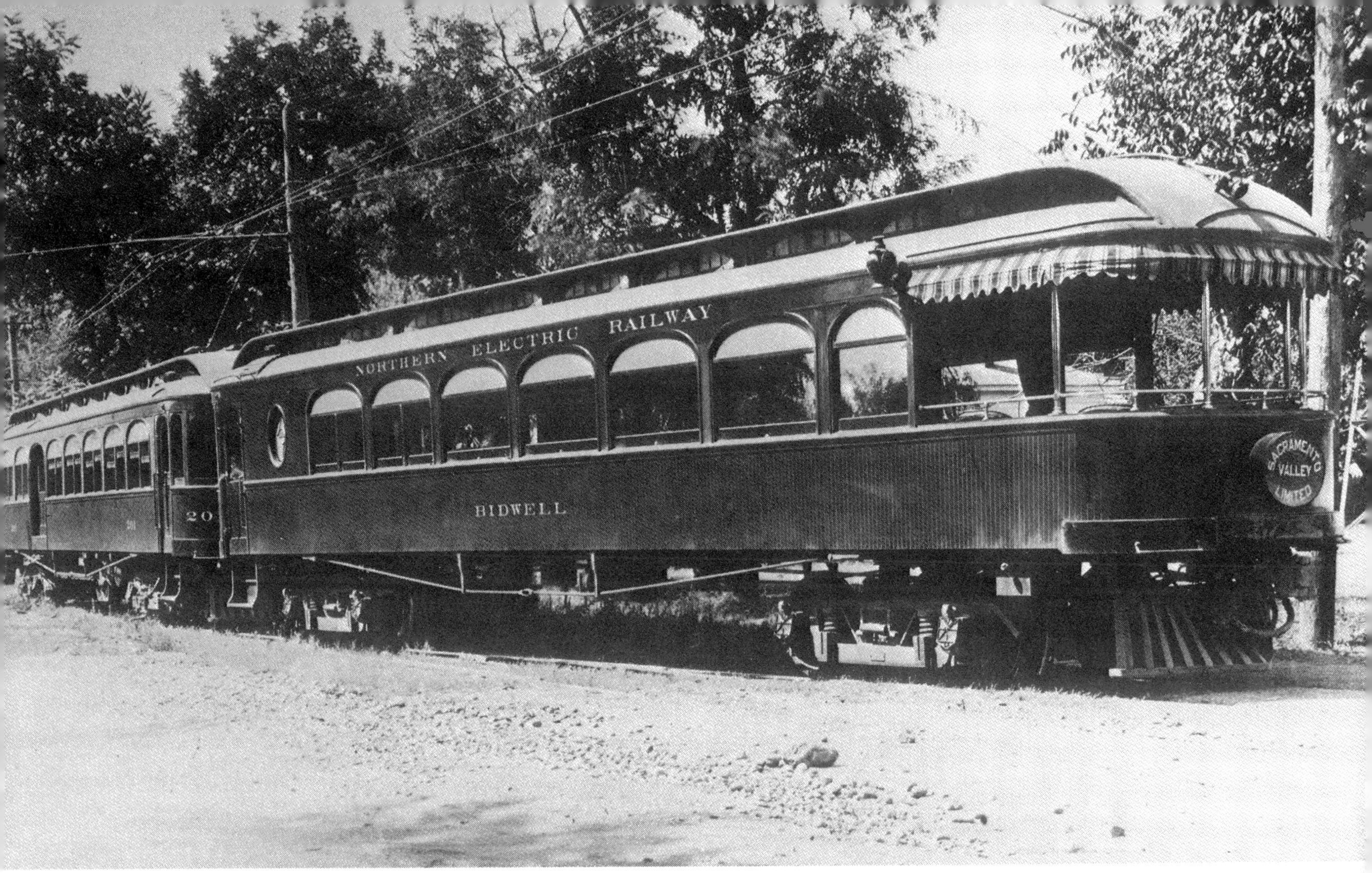

The North End's most palatial car was "Bidwell," a rebuild in Chico's Mulberry Shops of damaged Niles car 202. This 1915 view shows "Bidwell" in its first public appearance. (Magna)

This photo, taken circa 1919, depicts the transition period between the respective regimes of Northern Electric and Sacramento Northern Railroad. Motor 1030 bears the SN name, caboose 623 is NE. (RB)

Chapter 4

Operation

The first timecard of the Northern Electric was the size of an ordinary business card, according to Mr. W. W. Nelson who became NE's first trainmaster. As the line was extended, timetables became more extended and detailed. Southern Pacific timetables served as models.

Almost from its inception NE was operated according to steam railroad rules. E. J. Dimmock, first general superintendent, had had only steam road experience, while A. D. Schindler, General Manager, who came to NE from Pacific Electric, was better known to Northern Californians as the man who built The San Joaquin Valley Railroad (now Santa Fe's line to the San Francisco Bay area).

At first the dispatcher was located in the office building at Mulberry Shops, Chico. His office was connected to the stations along the line by both telegraph and telephone. Train orders were telegraphed and operators handed them up to train crews. In the earliest days, NE motormen encountered no signals whatsoever, as trains were governed exclusively by timetable and train order. Form 19 and Form 31 orders were used, along with the customary clearances. Crews had to register their trains at certain specified points.

The Northern Electric was later to have interlocking plants at the Southern Pacific crossings at Live Oak, Mikon, and Woodland. After a freight motor knocked streetcar 21 off the trestle approach to the Feather River bridge at Marysville at 7:14 AM, November 17, 1912, block signals were installed at this point. NE also had streetcar type trolley operated block signals at several single track curves in Sacramento as well as on the single track on Park Ave., Chico, between Mulberry and Ashby Junction. When the drawbridges at Sacramento and Meridian went into operation they were equipped with signals that were operated by the bridge tenders. Aside from these places, there were no signals on the Northern Electric except the train order signals at the train order stations.

When the Woodland Branch went into operation the NE moved the dispatcher's office to Sacramento. Telegraph dispatching ended at that time and from then on orders were transmitted by telephone. NE schedules never approached the "every hour on the hour" basis so common to interurbans. The main line trains usually consisted of two cars, usually a combination motor and the other a passenger trailer. The crew was composed of a conductor, a motorman and a brakeman. Schedule speeds approached 35 miles per hour so that fast running was required on the private right of way, for NE trains had to run through the streets of all important towns en route.

NE trains were equipped with the air communicating signals generally used by steam railroad passenger trains and the usual steam railroad code was used. For instance, the conductor used three blasts of the communicating whistle to tell the motorman to stop the train at the next station instead of the "one bell" so common to most electric railways. While the NE stations and sidings were equipped with phones, trainmen generally received their orders from the operators rather than directly over the phone as was usually the case with interurbans. However, provision was made for crews to take phone orders when operators were not in attendance.

In 1925 the SN gave up its Yuba River Bridge at Marysville in favor of the Western Pacific's bridge. This joint track of WP-SN was protected by block signals. At this time, the SN freight trains ran over the long siding in front of the WP passenger station to the end of the siding at WP's Yuba River Bridge at which point they entered the WP main track across the bridge proper to Oliver, the site of the famed Battle of the Bee Farm, where they again entered SN's own line. Prior to this, the SN freights had operated via 5th and Orange Sts., Marysville, and thence by the Northern Electric Yuba River Bridge.

Employees' timetables listed all meeting times in bold type. In this chapter are reproduced two such timetables, one of December 18, 1910 (No. 22) and one of March 30, 1914 (No. 29). Not only the schedules but the special rules and instructions should prove interesting reading. Both are loaned through the courtesy of The Bay Area Electric Railroad Association.

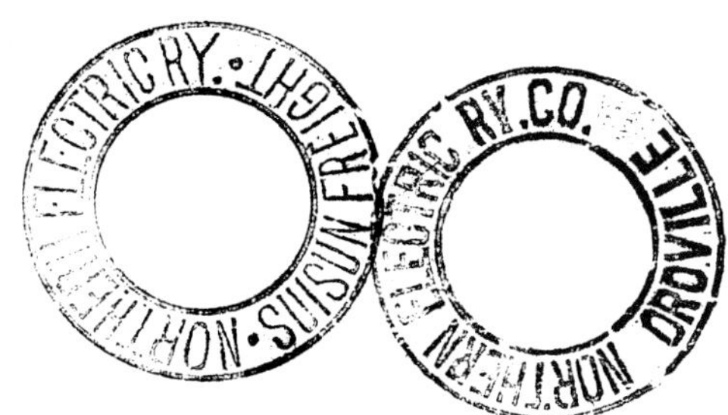

NORTHERN ELECTRIC RAILWAY COMPANY

TIME TABLE

22

To Take Effect Dec. 18, 1910, at 12:01 A. M.

PACIFIC STANDARD TIME (120th MERIDIAN)

For the government and information of employees only, and not intended for the use of the public.
The Company reserves the right to vary from this time table as
circumstances may require.

A. D. SCHINDLER,
General Manager

MELVILLE DOZIER, Jr.,
Asst. General Manager.

CHICO AND MARYSVILLE

Time Table No. 22 — December 18, 1910.

READ DOWN — South Bound   North Bound — READ UP

South Bound: trains under FIRST CLASS are 15, 13, 11, 9, 7, 5, 3, 1 (Passenger, Lv. Daily / Ar. Daily); THIRD CLASS is 81 (Freight). North Bound: FIRST CLASS trains 2, 4, 6, 8, 10, 12, 14, 16 (Passenger, Ar. Daily / Lv. Daily); THIRD CLASS is 82 (Freight).

81 Frt	15	13	11	9	7	5	3	1	Cap. of Sidings (freight cars)	Dist. from Chico	STATIONS	Dist. from Sacramento	Tel. & Tel. Sta.	2	4	6	8	10	12	14	16	82 Frt
	11.45pm	8.30pm	5.45pm	3.45pm	1.30pm	10.30am	8.30am	6.30am	10	0.00	**CHICO**	90.53	T-P	8.20am	10.50am	12.45pm	2.45pm	5.00pm	7.00pm	9.00pm	11.30pm	
											0.17											
										0.17	CHICO, MAIN ST., BET. 3D AND 4TH	90.36										
											0.34											
										0.51	CHICO, MAIN & 9th, B.C.R.R. Crossing	90.02										
											0.51											
	f 11.50	f 8.34	f 5.50	f 3.50	f 1.35	f 10.35	f 8.35	f 6.35		1.02	ASHBY JUNCTION	89.51		8.15	f 10.45	f 12.40	f 2.40	f 4.56	f 6.56	f 8.56	f 11.25	
											0.24										
6.55pm[12]	f 11.51	f 8.35	f 5.51	f 3.51	f 1.36	f 10.36	f 8.36	f 6.36	300	1.26	MULBERRY	89.27	T-P	8.14	f 10.44	f 12.39	2.39	4.55	6.55[81]	8.55	f 11.24	4.30am
											1.07										
										2.33	STIRLING JCT., B.C.R.R. Crossing	88.20										
											0.38										
7.36	f 11.55pm	f 8.38	f 5.55	f 3.55	f 1.40	f 10.40[4]	f 8.40	f 6.40	14	2.71	SPEEDWAY	87.82	P	8.10	f 10.40[5]	f 12.36	f 2.36	4.52	6.52	8.52	f 11.20	4.24
											1.54										
										4.25	CAMINO	86.28	P									
											2.66										
7.52	f 12.01am	8.45[14]	6.02	4.02	f 1.47	f 10.48	f 8.48	f 6.47	14 (Spur)	6.91	**DURHAM**	83.62	P	8.04	f 10.31	f 12.29	2.29	4.45	f 6.45	8.45[13]	f 11.13	4.18
											3.15										
8.02	f 12.05	8.50	6.07	4.07	f 1.52	f 10.53	f 8.53	f 6.51	4 (Spur)	10.06	ESQUON	80.47	P	8.00	f 10.26	f 12.25	2.25	4.40	f 6.40	8.40	f 11.08	4.11
											3.22										
8.09	f 12.09	8.54	6.11	4.11	f 1.56	f 10.57	f 8.57	f 6.55	10 (Spur)	13.28	BLAVO	77.25	P	7.56	f 10.22	f 12.21	2.21	4.36	f 6.36	8.36	f 11.04	4.03
											1.72										
8.19	f 12.11	8.57	6.14	4.14	f 1.59	f 11.00	f 9.00	f 6.58	23	15.00	RAMADA	75.53	P	7.54	f 10.19	f 12.19	2.18	4.33	f 6.33	8.34	f 11.01	3.56
											1.39										
8.32[14]	f 12.13	8.59	6.16	4.16	f 2.01	f 11.02	f 9.02	f 7.00	10 (Spur)	16.39	SHIPPEE	74.14	P	7.52	f 10.17	f 12.16	2.15	4.30	6.30	8.32[81]	f 10.59	3.52
											2.91										
8.40	12.17am	9.04	6.21[12]	4.21[16]	2.06[8]	11.07	9.07	7.05	14	19.30	**TRES VIAS**	71.23	T-P	7.49am	10.13	12.12	2.11[7]	4.26[9]	6.26[11]	8.29	10.55	3.45
10.15	Ar Daily	9.07	6.24	4.24	2.09	11.10	9.10	7.08						Lv. Daily	10.10	12.09	2.09	4.24	6.24	8.27	10.52	2.30
											4.17										
10.25		f 9.13	f 6.30	f 4.30	f 2.15	f 11.16	f 9.16	f 7.14	4 (Spur)	23.47	HASELBUSCH	67.06	P		f 10.03	f 12.02pm	f 2.02	4.17	6.17	8.21	f 10.46	2.16
											1.46										
10.44[16]		f 9.16	f 6.32	f 4.33	f 2.18	f 11.19	f 9.19	f 7.17	28 (Spurs)	24.93	RIO BONITO	65.60	P		f 10.00	f 11.59am	1.59	4.14	6.14	8.19	f 10.44[81]	2.12
											0.89										
										25.82	BIGGS	64.71										
											1.24										
10.51		f 9.20	f 6.35	f 4.36	f 2.22	f 11.22	f 9.22	f 7.20	4 (Spur)	27.06	RICHLAND	63.47	P		f 9.56	f 11.56	f 1.55	4.10	f 6.10	8.16	f 10.41	2.06
											1.33										
10.56		f 9.22	f 6.37	f 4.38	f 2.24	f 11.24	f 9.24	f 7.22	8 (Spur)	28.39	ORD RANCHO	62.14	P		f 9.54	f 11.54	f 1.53	4.08	f 6.08	8.14	f 10.39	2.02
											1.19										
										29.58	GRIDLEY	60.95										
											0.25										
11.05		9.24	6.40	4.41	2.27	11.27	9.27	7.25	38	29.83	BOGA	60.70	P		9.51	11.51	1.50	4.05	6.05	8.11	10.36	1.55
											0.63										
										30.46	GALINDO	60.07										
											0.58										
11.10		9.26	6.42	4.43	2.29	11.29	9.29	7.27	9 (Spur)	31.04	MIDVALE	59.49			9.49	11.49	1.48	4.03	6.03	8.09	10.34	1.52
											0.55										
11.14		f 9.27	f 6.43	f 4.44	f 2.30	f 11.30	f 9.30	f 7.28	10 (Spur)	31.59	MANZANITA	58.94	P		9.48	f 11.48	1.47	4.02	6.02	8.08	f 10.33	1.49
											1.36										
11.18		f 9.29	f 6.45	f 4.46	f 2.32	f 11.32	f 9.32	f 7.30	7 (Spur)	32.95	CHANDON	57.58	P		9.46	f 11.46	1.45	4.00	6.00	8.06	f 10.31	1.44
											0.89										
11.21		f 9.31	f 6.47	f 4.48	f 2.34	f 11.34	f 9.34	f 7.32	5 (Spur)	33.84	RIVIERA	56.69			9.44	f 11.44	1.43	3.58	5.58	8.05	f 10.30	1.40
											1.21										
										35.05	TORRES, S.P.R.R. Crossing	55.48										
											0.69										
11.31		f 9.34	f 6.51	f 4.52	f 2.38	f 11.38	f 9.38	f 7.36	8 (Spur)	35.74	**LIVE OAK**	54.79	T-P		f 9.40	f 11.40	f 1.39	3.54	5.54	8.01	f 10.26	1.30
											0.20										
11.33		9.35	6.52	4.53	2.39	11.39[6]	9.39[4]	7.37	24	35.94	MACETA	54.59			9.39[3]	11.39[5]	1.38	3.53	5.53	8.00	10.25	1.24
											0.48										
										36.42	BIHLMAN	54.11										
											0.98										
										37.40	SUNSET	53.13										
											1.08										
11.41		9.39	6.56	4.57	2.43	11.43	9.43	7.41	12	38.48	MENDOZA	52.05	P		9.35	11.35	1.34	3.49	5.49	7.56	10.21	1.18
											0.56										
11.51		f 9.40	f 6.57	f 4.58	f 2.44	f 11.44	f 9.44	f 7.42	6 (Spur)	39.04	STAFFORD	51.49			f 9.34	f 11.34	1.33	3.48	5.48	7.55	f 10.20	1.15
											0.56										
11.55pm		f 9.41	f 6.58	f 4.59	f 2.45	f 11.45	f 9.45	f 7.43	4 (Spur)	39.60	ENCINAL	50.93	P		f 9.33	f 11.33	1.32	3.47	5.47	7.54	f 10.19	1.10
											1.01										
										40.61	SANDERS	49.92										
											1.25										
12.01am		f 9.45	f 7.02	f 5.03	f 2.49	f 11.49	f 9.49	f 7.47	5 (Spur)	41.86	NUESTRO	48.67	P		f 9.29	f 11.29	1.28	3.43	5.43	7.51	f 10.16	1.05
											1.13										
										42.99	PEASE	47.54										
											1.11										
12.13		f 9.48	f 7.05	f 5.07	f 2.53	f 11.54	f 9.54	f 7.52	9 (Spur)	44.10	TERRA BUENA	46.43	P		f 9.25	f 11.25	1.24	3.39	5.39	7.47	f 10.12	12.55
											0.66										
										44.76	LAS UVAS	45.77										
											2.30										
12.50[82]		s 9.52	s 7.09	s 5.12	s 2.59	s 11.59am	s 10.00	s 7.58	65	47.06	**YUBA CITY**	43.47	T-P		s 9.19	s 11.19	s 1.19	s 3.34	s 5.34	s 7.43	s 10.08	12.50[81]
											0.18										
										47.24	YUBA CITY, S.P.R.R. Crossing	43.29										
											0.29										
										47.53	YUBA CITY, 2nd ST.	43.00										
											0.52										
										48.05	MARYSVILLE, W.P.R.R. Depot	42.48										
											0.43										
										48.48	MARYSVILLE, 5th & E STS.	42.05										
											0.32										
1.30am		10.02pm[16]	7.19pm	5.21pm[12]	3.09pm	12.10pm	10.10am	8.08am	50	48.80	**MARYSVILLE**	41.73	T-P		9.09am	11.09am	1.09pm	3.24pm	5.24pm[9]	7.34pm	9.58pm[13]	12.10am

Southbound, foot of columns: Ar. Daily. Northbound, foot of columns: Lv. Daily.

Southbound trains have absolute right over all northbound trains of the same or inferior class.

Trains 9 and 12, and Trains 13 and 16 meet on the double track between Marysville and Yuba City.

MARYSVILLE AND SACRAMENTO

READ DOWN — South Bound | Time Table No. 22, December 18, 1910. | North Bound — **READ UP**

Southbound columns 81, 13, 11, 9, 7, 5, 3, 1 are FIRST CLASS (81 = THIRD CLASS Freight; 13–1 = Passenger), all "Lv. Daily". Northbound columns 4, 6, 8, 10, 12, 14, 16, 82 are FIRST CLASS (4–16 = Passenger; 82 = THIRD CLASS Freight), "Ar. Daily". In the STATIONS column the small number after each station name is the distance to the next station. "f" marks a flag stop.

81 Freight	13	11	9	7	5	3	1	Cap. of Sidings (freight cars)	Dist. from Chico	STATIONS	Dist. from Sacto	Tel. & Tel.	4	6	8	10	12	14	16	82 Freight
1.40am	**10.04**pm[16]	7.21pm	**5.23**pm[12]	3.11pm	12.12pm	10.12am	8.10am	50	48.80	**MARYSVILLE** (0.23)	41.73	T-P	9.07am	11.07am	1.07pm	3.22pm	**5.22**pm[9]	7.32pm	**9.56**pm[13]	11.20pm
									49.03	MARYSVILLE W.P.R.R. Crossing (0.25)	41.50									
									49.28	OLIVER W.P.R.R. Crossing (2.01)	41.25									
1.50	f 10.10	**7.26**[14]	f 5.28	f **3.16**[10]	f 12.17	f 10.17	f 8.16	18	51.29	ALICIA (2.50)	39.24	P	f 9.00	f 11.00	f 1.00	f **3.16**[7]	5.16	f **7.26**[11]	f 9.50	11.08
1.55	f 10.14	7.30	f 5.33	f 3.21	f 12.22	f 10.22	f 8.21	3 (Spur)	53.79	HOWARD (1.35)	36.74	P	f 8.56	f 10.56	f 12.56	f 3.11	5.11	f 7.21	f 9.46	10.58
									55.14	OSTROM (1.57)	35.39									
2.04	f 10.18	7.34	5.38	f 3.26	f 12.26	f 10.26	8.26	7	56.71	PLUMAS LAKE (1.27)	33.82	P	f 8.51	f 10.51	f 12.51	f 3.06	5.06	f 7.17	f 9.42	10.48
									57.98	SERICO (1.51)	32.55									
2.10	f 10.22	f 7.38	f 5.43	f 3.31	f 12.31	f 10.31	f 8.31	12 (Spur)	59.49	ALGODON (1.06)	31.04	P	f 8.46	f 10.46	f 12.46	f 3.01	5.01	f 7.13	f 9.38	10.40
									60.55	BEAR RIVER (0.95)	29.98									
2.17	f 10.25	7.41	5.46	f 3.34	f 12.34	f 10.34	f 8.34	7 (Spur)	61.50	RIO OSO (1.25)	29.03	P	8.42	f 10.42	f 12.42	f 2.57	4.57	f 7.10	f 9.35	10.35
									62.75	ESMERALDA (1.25)	27.78	P								
2.27	f **10.28**[82]	f 7.44	5.50	3.38	f **12.38**[8]	f **10.38**[6]	f **8.38**[4]	12 (Spur)	64.00	STOLP (1.16)	26.53	P	**8.38**[1]	f **10.38**[3]	f **12.38**[5]	f 2.53	4.53	f 7.06	f 9.31	**10.28**[13]
2.32	f 10.30	7.46	5.52	3.40	f 12.40	f 10.40	f 8.40	42	65.16	**NICOLAUS** (2.84)	25.37	T-P	f 8.35	f 10.35	f 12.35	f 2.50	4.50	f 7.04	f 9.29	10.20
									68.00	STRIPLIN (1.55)	22.53									
2.40	f 10.36	7.53	5.59	3.47	f 12.47	f 10.47	f 8.47	8 (Spur)	69.55	ALAMOS (1.64)	20.98	P	8.29	f 10.29	f 12.29	f 2.44	4.44	f 6.57	f 9.23	10.05
2.45	f 10.39	7.56	6.02	3.51	f 12.51	f 10.51	8.51	43	71.19	PLEASANT GROVE (3.27)	19.34	P	8.25	f 10.25	f 12.25	f 2.40	4.40	f 6.54	f 9.20	10.00
2.50	f 10.44	8.01	6.07	3.56	f 12.56	f 10.56	8.56	7 (Spur)	74.46	SANKEY (0.48)	16.07	P	8.20	f 10.20	f 12.20	f 2.35	4.35	f 6.49	f 9.15	9.50
									74.94	MORENO W.P.R.R. Crossing (1.68)	15.59									
3.00	f 10.48	8.05	6.11	4.00	f 12.59	f 11.00	9.00	10 (Spur)	76.62	RIEGO (3.14)	13.91	P	f 8.16	f 10.16	f 12.16	f 2.31	4.31	f 6.46	f 9.12	9.45
3.05	f 10.53	8.10	6.16	4.05	1.05	f 11.05	f 9.05	7 (Spur)	79.76	ELVERTA (1.49)	10.77	P	8.11	f 10.11	f 12.11	f 2.26	4.26	f 6.42	f 9.08	9.40
3.11	f 10.56	8.13	6.19	4.08	1.08	f 11.08	f 9.08	8 (Spur)	81.25	DRY CREEK (1.94)	9.28	P	8.08	f 10.08	f 12.08	f 2.23	4.23	f 6.39	f 9.05	9.25
									83.19	ROBLA (1.77)	7.34									
3.17	f 11.02	8.20	6.25	**4.15**[12]	1.15	f 11.15	f 9.15	7 (Spur)	84.96	DEL PASO HEIGHTS (0.83)	5.57	P	8.01	f 10.01	f 12.01pm	f 2.16	**4.15**[7]	6.32	8.59	9.20
									85.79	ARCADE (1.11)	4.74									
3.21	f 11.04	8.23	**6.28**[14]	4.18	1.18	f 11.18	f 9.18	7 (Spur)	86.90	NORTH SACRAMENTO (0.73)	3.63	P	f 7.57	f 9.57	f 11.57am	f 2.12	4.11	**6.28**[9]	8.55	9.10
									87.63	VEGAS W.P.R.R. Crossing (0.96)	2.90									
3.30	11.07	8.27	6.32	4.22	1.22	11.22	9.22		88.59	HAGGIN (0.78)	1.94	P	7.53	9.53	11.53	2.08	4.08	6.23	8.52	9.00
3.35am								150	89.37	SACRAMENTO 17th ST. (0.40)	1.16	P								**8.55**pm[16]
									89.77	SACTO G ST. ST. Ry. Crossing (0.38)	0.76									
									90.15	SACRAMENTO 12th ST. (0.38)	0.38									
	11.15pm	8.35pm	6.40pm	4.30pm	1.30pm	11.30am	9.30am		90.53	**SACRAMENTO**	0.00	T-P	7.45am	9.45am	11.45am	2.00pm	4.00pm	6.15pm	8.45pm	
Ar. Daily	Ar. Daily	Ar. Daily	Ar. Daily	Ar. Daily	Ar. Daily	Ar. Daily	Ar. Daily						Lv. Daily	Lv. Daily	Lv. Daily	Lv. Daily	Lv. Daily	Lv. Daily	Lv. Daily	Lv. Daily

Southbound Trains have absolute Right over all Northbound Trains of the same or inferior class.

Trains 9 and 12, and Trains 13 and 16 meet on the double track between Marysville and Yuba City.

OROVILLE AND TRES VIAS

South Bound

READ DOWN (FROM OROVILLE) — Time Table No. 22, December 18, 1910.

	THIRD CLASS		SECOND CLASS						FIRST CLASS												Capacity of Sidings in Freight cars.	Distance from Oroville.	STATIONS
Train	93[82]	91[81]	61	59	57	55	53	51	43[16]	41[13]	39[14]	37[11/12]	35[9/10]	33[7/8]	31[6]	29[5]	27[4]	25[3]	23[2]	21[1]			
Type	Freight	Freight	Passenger	Passenger	Passenger	Passenger	Passenger	Passenger	Passenger	Passenger	Passenger	Passenger	Passenger	Passenger	Passenger	Passenger	Passenger	Passenger	Passenger	Passenger			
	Lv. Daily	Lv. Daily	Lv. Daily	Lv. Daily	Lv. Daily	Lv. Daily	Lv. Daily	Lv. Daily	Lv. Daily	Lv. Daily	Lv. Daily	Lv. Daily	Lv. Daily	Lv. Daily	Lv. Daily	Lv. Daily	Lv. Daily	Lv. Daily	Lv. Daily	Lv. Daily			
OROVILLE	3.15am	9.45pm	9.48pm	7.00pm	5.00pm	2.45pm	1.00pm	7.35am	10.32pm	8.45pm	8.07pm	6.00pm	4.00pm	1.45pm	11.51am	10.47am	9.50am	8.47am	7.30am	6.45am	16	0.00	OROVILLE
OROVILLE, UNION HOTEL			f	f	f	f	f	f	f	f	f	f	f	f	f	f	f	f	f	f		0.18	−0.18−
OROVILLE, POST OFFICE			f	f	f	f	f	f	f	f	f	f	f	f	f	f	f	f	f	f		0.30	−0.12−
OROVILLE, Pine and Mtgy Sts.			f	f	f	f	f	f	f	f	f	f	f	f	f	f	f	f	f	f		0.45	−0.15−
OROVILLE, 2nd and Mtgy Sts.			f	f	f	f	f	f	f	f	f	f	f	f	f	f	f	f	f	f		0.68	−0.23−
OROVILLE BOSTON MCH. SHOPS			f	f	f	f	f	f	f	f	f	f	f	f	f	f	f	f	f	f	10	0.93	−0.25−
OROVILLE MARYSVILLE ROAD	3.25	9.50	f 9.56	f 7.08	f 5.08	f 2.53	f 1.08	f 7.43	f 10.40	f 8.53	f 8.15	f 6.08	f 4.08	f 1.53	f 11.59am	f 10.55	f 9.58	f 8.55	f 7.38	f 6.53	28	1.26	−0.33−
THERMALITO	3.30	9.55	10.00pm	7.12pm	5.12pm	2.57pm	1.12pm	7.47am	f 10.44	f 8.57[92]	f 8.19	f 6.12	f 4.12	f 1.57	f 12.03pm	f 10.59	f 10.02	f 8.59	f 7.42	f 6.57	26	2.48	−1.22−
TRES VIAS	3.40am	10.10pm	Ar. Daily	Ar. Daily	Ar. Daily	Ar. Daily	Ar. Daily	Ar. Daily	10.50pm	9.03pm	8.25pm	6.18pm	4.18pm	2.03pm	12.09pm	11.05am	10.08am	9.05am	7.48am	7.03am	14	5.74	−3.26−
	Ar. Daily	Ar. Daily							Ar. Daily	Ar. Daily	Ar. Daily	Ar. Daily	Ar. Daily	Ar. Daily	Ar. Daily	Ar. Daily	Ar. Daily	Ar. Daily	Ar. Daily	Ar. Daily			TRES VIAS

North Bound

Time Table No. 22, December 18, 1910 — North Bound (TO OROVILLE) — READ UP

STATIONS	Distance from Tres Vias.	Telephone and Telegraph Stations.	22[1]	24[3]	26[4]	28[5]	30[6]	32[7/8]	34[9/10]	36[11/12]	38[14]	40[13]	42[16]	44[15]	52	54	56	58	60	62	92[81]	94[82]
			FIRST CLASS												SECOND CLASS						THIRD CLASS	
Type			Passenger	Passenger	Passenger	Passenger	Passenger	Passenger	Passenger	Passenger	Passenger	Passenger	Passenger	Passenger	Passenger	Passenger	Passenger	Passenger	Passenger	Passenger	Freight	Freight
			Ar. Daily	Ar. Daily	Ar. Daily	Ar. Daily	Ar. Daily	Ar. Daily	Ar. Daily	Ar. Daily	Ar. Daily	Ar. Daily	Ar. Daily	Ar. Daily	Ar. Daily	Ar. Daily	Ar. Daily	Ar. Daily	Ar. Daily	Ar. Daily	Ar. Daily	Ar. Daily
OROVILLE	5.38	T-P	7.26am	9.28am	10.31am	11.28am	12.30pm	2.29pm	4.44pm	6.44pm	8.45pm	9.22pm	11.12pm	12.34am	8.00am	1.25pm	3.10pm	5.25pm	7.25pm	10.13pm	9.15pm	3.00am
OROVILLE, 2nd Ave. and High St (−0.42−)	4.96		f	f	f	f	f	f	f	f	f	f	f	f								
OROVILLE, Marysville Road (−0.48−)	4.48	P	f 7.20	f 9.22	f 10.25	f 11.22	f 12.24	f 2.23	f 4.38	f 6.38	f 8.39	f 9.16	f 11.06	f 12.28	f 7.52	f 1.17	f 3.02	f 5.17	7.17	f 10.05	9.05	2.50
THERMALITO (−1.22−)	3.26	T-P	f 7.16	f 9.18	f 10.21	f 11.18	f 12.20	f 2.19	f 4.34	f 6.34	f 8.35	f 9.12	f 11.02	f 12.24	7.48am	1.13pm	2.58pm	5.13pm	7.13pm	10.01pm	8.57[41]	2.45
TRES VIAS (−3.26−)	0.00	T-P	7.10am	9.12am	10.15am	11.12am	12.14pm	2.13pm	4.28pm	6.28pm	8.30pm	9.08pm	10.56pm	12.18am	Lv. Daily	Lv. Daily	Lv. Daily	Lv. Daily	Lv. Daily	Lv. Daily	8.45pm	2.35am
			Lv. Daily	Lv. Daily	Lv. Daily	Lv. Daily	Lv. Daily	Lv. Daily	Lv. Daily	Lv. Daily	Lv. Daily	Lv. Daily	Lv. Daily	Lv. Daily							Lv. Daily	Lv. Daily

Southbound Trains have absolute Right over all Northbound Trains of the same or inferior class.

All second class trains will use Montgomery and Myers streets in both directions between Oroville and Marysville Road.

Northbound second class trains will observe same flag stops as south bound second class trains.

SPECIAL RULES AND REGULATIONS

s.—Regular stop.

f.—Stop on signal.

T.—Telegraph stations.

P.—Telephone stations.

All trains must come to a full stop at Railroad and Street Car Grade Crossings, except when crossing Ninth Street at Main Street, and when crossing West Fourth Street at Ashby Junction, Chico.

In addition to trains coming to full stop at all Railroad Grade Crossings, all trains must be flagged over the S. P. R. R. at Chico,—Butte Co. R. R. at Stirling Junction,—and S. P. R. R. at Yuba City by conductor or flagman.

All trains must be controlled by towerman's signals at S. P. R. R. Crossing at Torres.

Bulletin Stations:—Chico, Tres Vias, Oroville, Marysville and Sacramento.

Registering Stations:—Chico, Mulberry, Tres Vias, Thermalito, Oroville, Marysville, 17th Street and Sacramento.

All trains must get clearance cards before leaving registering stations except at Mulberry, Thermalito, and 17th Street.

Freight trains will *not* register at Chico and Sacramento.

Freight trains must get clearance from Dispatcher before leaving Mulberry and 17th Street.

Freight trains must not go south of Fifteenth and D Streets in Sacramento.

Freight trains will not carry passengers.

Bold face type denotes meeting point of trains.

Where only one time is shown it denotes leaving time.

Note particularly trains *from Oroville* to Tres Vias and Thermalito are southbound, and trains *to Oroville* from Tres Vias and Thermalito are northbound.

Freight trains between Marysville Road and Oroville will take High Street track both north and southbound.

The Chico yards include all tracks north of point 600 feet south of south switch at Mulberry, and north of point 600 feet south of Rosedale.

Oroville yards include all tracks in Oroville north of the north end of the north trestle approach of the Feather River Bridge.

The limits of Tres Vias yards extend 600 feet south of south switch, 600 feet north of north switch and 600 feet north of north switch on Oroville branch.

The limits of Marysville and Yuba City yards extend from 600 feet north of north switch in Yuba City to the south end of the Yuba River Bridge just north of Oliver.

Insofar as concerns the operation of trains and the determination of their rights, Marysville and Yuba City yards will be considered as one yard.

The Sacramento yards include all tracks south of the north end of American River Bridge.

When running within limits of yards as designated on Time Table, all trains must be run under full control and be prepared to stop within the limit of vision.

Single tracks between Ashby Junction and Mulberry, and between the S. P. crossing in Yuba City and the south end of Feather River bridge in Marysville, and between D Street and I Street on Fifteenth Street in Sacramento, are protected by block signals which will be operated as per bulletin.

The tracks between the north end of the Cooper Tract in Yuba City and Second and F Streets in Marysville, and the track between Haggin and Eighth and J Streets, Sacramento, are operated as double tracks. All trains must use right hand track.

Derailing switches are located at S. P. R. R., (Sperry Flour Mill) in Chico, on Packing House Spur in Thermalito, on Valley Contracting Co. Spur in Oroville, on High line in Oroville, on W. P. R. R. transfer track at east end of Feather River Bridge in Marysville, on Passing Track at Third and Orange Streets in Marysville, and on Siding just north of Subway in Sacramento, and must be thrown by all trains using those tracks.

By ordinances the rate of speed of trains is limited to twelve (12) miles per hour within the limits of Chico, Marysville and Sacramento, and ten (10) miles per hour within the limits of Oroville.

Spring switches are placed at the following points:

Chico: House track and three legs of Y at First and Main Streets, Second and Main Streets, three legs of Y at Fifth and Main Streets, Fifth and Broadway Streets and Ninth and Main Streets.

Mulberry: Both ends of passing track.

Tres Vias: Three legs of little Y.

Oroville: Marysville Road and High Street.

Yuba City: All main line switches in Yuba City.

Marysville: Both ends of double track on Fifth and D Streets, three legs of Y at Second and D Streets, both ends of double track on Second Street, and Orange and Second Streets.

Sacramento: Both ends of double track between American River Bridge and Fifteenth and D Streets, and three legs of Y at 8th and I Streets.

The above spring switches may be run through by passenger trains (without throwing) at a speed not to exceed six (6) miles per hour.

All trains must reduce speed to six (6) miles per hour when passing over spring switches within yard limits.

Freight trains, construction trains and yard motors must throw ALL switches.

Standard Clocks are located at Dispatcher's Office in Mulberry and at passenger Depots in Chico, Oroville, Marysville and Sacramento.

CHIEF DISPATCHER - - - **G. A. ROGERS**		
Train Dispatchers - - - - { A. J. LEBOURVEAU B. F. HAINER J. J. BLANEY		
Inspector - - - - - W. W. NELSON		

Company Watch Inspectors:

Chief Watch Inspector, C. A. DREISS - 418 Broadway, Chico

Sub. Watch Inspector -	KLUNE & FLOBERG	528 K Street, Sacramento
Sub. Watch Inspector -	PETER ENGEL -	220 D Street, Marysville
Sub. Watch Inspector -	O. W. HALSTEAD	320 Myers St., Oroville

Company Surgeons:

Chief Surgeon - **D. H. MOULTON, M. D.** -		Chico
Assistant Surgeon - F. L. ATKINSON, M. D.	- - -	Sacramento
Assistant Surgeon - DAVID POWELL, M. D.	- - -	Marysville
Assistant Surgeon - H. A. MOREL, M. D.	- - - -	Oroville
Assistant Surgeon - JAMES CAMPBELL, M. D.	- - -	Hamilton

Interurban 104 and a Niles trailer on D St., Marysville, circa 1908. (LLS)

The 201 on the trestle at Marysville back in 1907. (CS)

NORTHERN ELECTRIC RAILWAY COMPANY
SACRAMENTO AND WOODLAND RAILROAD CO.

TIME TABLE

To Take Effect Monday, March 30, 1914 at 12:01 A. M.

PACIFIC STANDARD TIME (120th MERIDIAN)

For the government and information of employees only, and not intended for the use of the public. The Companies reserve the right to vary from this time table as circumstances may require.

A. D. SCHINDLER,
General Manager.

J. B. ROWRAY,
Superintendent.

CHICO AND MARYSVILLE — South Bound

Time Table No. 29 — MARCH 30, 1914

SECOND CLASS: 151. FIRST CLASS: 113, 21, 19, 17, 15, 13, 11, 9, 7.

151	113	21	19	17	15	13	11	9	7	Capacity of Sidings in freight cars	Distance from Chico	STATIONS
Way Freight	Marysville Passenger	Sacram'nto Woodland Passenger	Sacram'nto Woodland Passenger	Steamer Special	Sacram'nto Woodland Passenger	Sacram'nto Woodland Passenger	Sacram'nto Woodland Passenger	Sacram'nto Woodland Passenger	Bay Cities Limited			
Lv. Daily	Lv. Sat. & Sun. Only	Lv. Daily	Lv. Daily	Lv. Daily	Lv. Daily	Lv. Daily	Lv. Daily	Lv. Daily	Lv. Daily			
		8.15pm	6.00pm	4.00pm	2.30pm	11.35am	3.55am	7.05am	6.20am	10	0.00	CHICO 1.02
		f 8.19	f 6.04	4.04	f 2.34	f11.40	f 8.59	f 7.10	6.25		1.02	ASHBY JUNCTION 0.24
7.20pm		8.20	6.05	4.05	2.35[12]	11.41	9.00[4]	7.11	6.26	300	1.26	MULBERRY 1.07
		f	f	f	f	f	f				2.33	STIRLING JCT. B.C. R.R. Cross. 0.38
7.30		f 8.24	f 6.09	4.07	f 2.39	f11.44	f 9.04	f 7.15	6.28	14	2.71	SPEEDWAY 4.20
7.50		s 8.31	s 6.16	f 4.13	s 2.46	s 11.52[10]	s 9.11	s 7.22	f 6.34	19 (Spurs)	6.91	DURHAM 3.15
8.00		f 8.36	f 6.21	4.17	f 2.51	f11.58am	f 9.15	f 7.26	6.38	6 (Spur)	10.06	ESQUON 3.22
8.10		f 8.40	f 6.25	4.21	f 2.55	f12.02pm	f 9.19	f 7.30	6.42	10 (Spur)	13.28	BLAVO 1.72
8.20		f 8.43	f 6.28	4.23	f 2.58	f12.04	f 9.22	f 7.33	6.44	23	15.00	RAMADA 1.39
8.30		f 8.45	f 6.30	4.25	f 3.00	f12.07	f 9.24	f 7.35	6.46	10 (Spur)	16.39	SHIPPEE 2.91
8.45[18]		8.50[18]	6.35[16]	4.28[14]	3.05	12.12	9.30[8]	7.40	6.50			
9.25[21]		8.52	6.37	4.29	3.07	12.14	9.32	7.42	6.52	14	19.30	TRES VIAS 2.89
9.40		f 8.56	f 6.41	4.32	f 3.11	f12.18	f 9.36	f 7.46	6.55	10 (Spur)	22.19	FEATHER RIVER 1.28
9.55[20]		f 8.58	f 6.43	4.34	f 3.13	f12.20	f 9.38	f 7.48	6.57	4 (Spur)	23.47	HASELBUSCH 1.46
10.15		f 9.01	f 6.46	4.36	f 3.16	f12.23	f 9.41	f 7.51	6.59	28 (Spurs)	24.93	RIO BONITO 2.13
10.25		f 9.04	f 6.50	4.39	f 3.20	f12.27	f 9.44	f 7.55	7.02	4 (Spur)	27.06	RICHLAND 1.33
10.35		f 9.06	f 6.53	4.41	f 3.22	f12.29	f 9.47	f 7.57	7.04	8 (Spur)	28.39	ORD RANCHO 1.19
10.55		f 9.08	f 6.56	f 4.43	f 3.25	f12.32	f 9.50	f 8.00	f 7.06	50	29.58	EAST GRIDLEY 1.46
11.20		9.10	6.58	4.45	3.27	12.34	9.52	8.03	7.08	10 (Spur)	31.04	MIDVALE 0.55
11.25		f 9.11	f 7.00	4.43	f 3.28	f12.35	f 9.53	8.04	7.09	10 (Spur)	31.59	MANZANITA 1.36
11.30		f 9.13	f 7.02	4.47	f 3.30	f12.38	f 9.56	8.06[4]	7.11	12 (Spur)	32.95	CHANDON 0.89
11.35		f 9.15	f 7.03	4.48	f 3.31	f12.40	f 9.58	8.08	7.12	5 (Spur)	33.84	RIVIERA 1.21
											35.05	TORRES, S.P.R.R. Cross. 0.69
11.45		f 9.19	f 7.07	f 4.50	f 3.35	f12.45	f10.04	f 8.12	f 7.14	8 (Spur)	35.74	LIVE OAK 0.20
11.50pm		9.20	7.08	4.51	3.36	12.46	10.05	8.13	7.15	24	35.94	MACETA 1.94
12.01am		9.23	7.11	4.53	3.39	12.49	10.09	8.16	7.17	6 (Spur)	37.88	THOMPSON 0.60
12.10		9.24	7.12	4.54	3.40	12.50	10.10	8.17	7.18	12	38.48	MENDOZA 0.56
12.20		f 9.25	f 7.13	4.55	3.41	f12.51	f10.11	f 8.18	7.19	6 (Spur)	39.04	STAFFORD 0.56
12.30		f 9.26	f 7.14	4.56	3.42	f12.52	f10.12	f 8.19	7.20	4 (Spur)	39.60	ENCINAL 1.01
12.40		f 9.29[20]	f 7.16	4.57	3.45[14]	f12.53	f10.14	f 8.21	7.21	9 (Spur)	40.61	SANDERS 1.25
12.50		f 9.31	f 7.18	4.59	3.48	f12.55	f10.16	f 8.24	7.23	5 (Spur)	41.86	NUESTRO 2.24
1.05		f 9.35	f 7.21	5.02	f 3.52	f12.59	f10.20	f 8.28	7.26	9 (Spur)	44.10	TIERRA BUENA 0.50
		9.36	7.22	5.03	3.53	1.00	10.21	8.30	7.27			
1.10	11.06pm	9.37	7.23	5.04	3.55	1.02	10.23	8.32	7.29		44.60	HEYMAN 2.46
1.20[152]	f11.10	s 9.40	s 7.27	f 5.07	s 4.00	s 1.06[12]	s10.28	s 8.37	7.33[4]	65	47.06	YUBA CITY 0.18
		f	f	f	f	f	f	f	f		47.24	S. P. R. R. Crossing 1.56
1.45am	11.20pm	9.49pm	7.36pm	5.15pm	4.10pm	1.16pm	10.38am[10]	8.47am[8]	7.42am	50	48.80	MARYSVILLE
Ar. Daily	Ar. Sat. & Sun. Only	Ar. Daily	Ar. Daily	Ar. Daily	Ar. Daily	Ar. Daily	Ar. Daily	Ar. Daily	Ar. Daily			

Southbound trains have absolute right over all northbound trains of the same or inferior class.

Time Table No. 29 MARCH 30, 1914 STATIONS	Distance from Woodland	Telephone Stations, Office Hours and Station Numbers	4 Chico Passenger Ar. Daily	8 Steamer Special Ar. Daily	10 Chico Sacram'nto Passenger Ar. Daily	12 Chico Sacram'nto Passenger Ar. Daily	14 Chico Sacram'nto Passenger Ar. Daily	16 Chico Sacram'nto Passenger Ar. Daily	18 Chico Sacram'nto Passenger Ar. Daily	20 Bay Cities Limited Ar. Daily	114 Colusa Passenger Ar. Sat. & Sun. Only	152 Way Freight Ar. Daily
CHICO — 1.02 —	108.46	5.50a-8.30p P. 91	9.05am	10.05am	12.10pm	2.40pm	5.05pm	7.15pm	9.30pm	10.35pm		
ASHBY JUNCTION — 0.24 —	107.44		f 9.01	10.00	f12.04	f 2.36	f 5.01	f 7.11	f 9.26	10.30		
MULBERRY — 1.07 —	107.20	24 Hours P. 89	**9.00**[11]	9.59	12.03pm	**2.35**[15]	5.00	7.10	9.25	10.29		6.20am
STIRLING JCT. B. C. R. R. Cross. — 0.38 —	106.13		f		f	f	f	f	f			
SPEEDWAY — 4.20 —	105.75	P.	f 8.55	9.56	f11.59am	f 2.30	f 4.55	f 7.05	f 9.20	10.26		6.15
DURHAM — 3.15 —	101.55	6.05a-7.00p P. 84	s 8.48	9.49	s **11.52**[13]	s 2.22	s 4.48	s 6.58	s 9.13	f10.20		6.10
ESQUON — 3.22 —	98.40	P. 80	f 8.43	9.44	f11.46	f 2.17	f 4.43	f 6.53	f 9.08	10.15		5.50
BLAVO — 1.72 —	95.18	P. 77	f 8.39	9.40	f11.41	f 2.13	f 4.39	f 6.49	f 9.04	10.11		5.45
RAMADA — 1.39 —	93.46	P. 76	f 8.37	9.38	f11.38	f 2.11	f 4.36	f 6.46	f 9.02	10.09		5.40
SHIPPEE — 2.91 —	92.07	P. 74	f 8.34	9.36	f11.36	f 2.08	f 4.33	f 6.43	f 8.59	10.07		5.35
TRES VIAS	89.16	6.50a-12.50a P. 71	8.30	**9.33**[11]	11.31	2.04	**4.28**[17]	**6.38**[19]	**8.54**[21] [151]	10.04		5.25
— 2.89 —			8.28	**9.32**	11.29	2.02	**4.26**	**6.35**	**8.52**	10.02		5.10
FEATHER RIVER — 1.28 —	86.27	P. 68	f 8.24	9.29	f11.25	f 1.56	f 4.21	f 6.30	f 8.47	9.57		4.50
HASELBUSCH — 1.46 —	84.99	P. 67	f 8.22	9.27	f11.23	f 1.53	f 4.19	f 6.28	f 8.45	**9.55**[151]		4.40
RIO BONITO — 2.13 —	83.53	P. 66	f 8.19	9.25	f11.20	f 1.50	f 4.16	f 6.25	f 8.42	9.53		4.30
RICHLAND — 1.33 —	81.40	P. 63	f 8.16	9.22	f11.17	f 1.47	f 4.13	f 6.22	f 8.39	9.50		4.20
ORO RANCHO — 1.19 —	80.07	P. 62	f 8.14	9.20	f11.15	f 1.45	f 4.11	f 6.20	f 8.37	9.48		4.10
EAST GRIDLEY — 1.46 —	78.88	6.35a-7.00p P. 61	f 8.11	f 9.18	f11.12	f 1.43	f 4.08	f 6.17	f 8.34	f 9.46		3.50
MIDVALE — 0.55 —	77.42	P.	8.09	9.16	11.10	1.40	4.05	6.14	8.31	9.44		3.30
MANZANITA — 1.36 —	76.87	P. 59	f 8.08	9.15	f11.09	f 1.39	f 4.04	f 6.13	f 8.30	9.43		3.15
CHANDON — 0.89 —	75.51	P. 58	f **8.06** [9]	9.13	f11.07	f 1.37	f 4.02	f 6.11	f 8.28	9.41		3.05
RIVIERA — 1.21 —	74.62	P. 57	f 8.03	9.12	f11.05	f 1.36	f 3.59	f 6.08	f 8.26	9.40		3.00
TORRES, S.P.R.R. Cross. — 0.69 —	73.41											
LIVE OAK — 0.20 —	72.72	6.45a-7.15p P. 56	f 7.59	f 9.10	f11.00	f 1.31	f 3.55	f 6.04	f 8.22	f 9.37		2.55
MACETA — 1.94 —	72.52		7.58	9.09	10.59	1.30	3.54	6.03	8.21	9.36		2.50
THOMPSON — 0.60 —	70.38	P.	7.55	9.07	10.55	1.26	3.50	5.59	8.17	9.34		2.35
MENDOZA — 0.56 —	69.98	P.	7.54	9.06	10.54	1.25	3.49	5.58	8.16	9.33		2.30
STAFFORD — 0.56 —	69.42	53	f 7.53	9.05	f10.53	f 1.24	f 3.48	f 5.57	f 8.15	9.32		2.20
ENCINAL — 1.01 —	68.86	P. 52	f 7.52	9.04	f10.51	f 1.22	f 3.47	f 5.56	f 8.14	9.31		2.10
SANDERS — 1.25 —	67.85	P. 51	f 7.50	9.03	f10.49	f 1.20	f **3.45**[15]	f 5.54	f 8.12	**9.29**[21]		2.00
NUESTRO — 2.24 —	66.60	P. 50	f 7.47	9.01	f10.46	f 1.18	f 3.43	f 5.52	f 8.10	9.27		1.50
TIERRA BUENA — 0.50 —	64.36	48	f 7.43	8.59	f10.42	f 1.14	f 3.39	f 5.48	f 8.07	9.23		1.35
HEYMAN	63.86	7.20a-7.30p P. 47	7.42	8.58	10.41	1.13	3.38	5.47	8.06	9.22		1.30
— 2.46 —			7.41	8.57	10.39	1.11	3.36	5.45	8.05	9.21	11.44pm	
YUBA CITY — 0.18 —	61.40	7.00a-6.00p P. 45	s **7.38** [7]	8.54	s10.36	s **1.07**[13]	s 3.31	s 5.40	s 8.00	f 9.18	s11.40	**1.20**[151]
S. P. R. R. Crossing — 1.56 —	61.22		f		f	f	f	f	f		f	
MARYSVILLE	59.66	6.30a-3.00a P. 41	7.29am	**8.46**am [9]	**10.27**am [11]	12.57pm	3.21pm	5.30pm	7.50pm	9.10pm	11.30pm	12.45am
			Lv. Daily	Lv. Daily	Lv. Daily	Lv. Daily	Lv. Daily	Lv. Daily	Lv. Daily	Lv. Daily	Lv. Sat. & Sun. Only	Lv. Daily

Southbound trains have absolute right over all northbound trains of the same or inferior class.

MARYSVILLE AND WOODLAND — South Bound

FIRST CLASS · SECOND CLASS (151)

Time Table No. 29 — MARCH 30, 1914

151	21	19	41	17	15	39	13	37	11	9	35	7	5	33	3	31	1	Capacity of Sidings in freight cars	Distance from Chico	STATIONS
Way Freight	Sacram'nto Woodland Passenger	Sacram'nto Woodland Passenger	Woodland Fast Freight	Steamer Special	Sacram'nto Woodland Passenger	Woodland Passenger	Sacram'nto Woodland Passenger	Woodland Passenger	Sacram'nto Woodland Passenger	Sacram'nto Woodland Passenger	Woodland Passenger	Bay Cities Limited	Sacram'nto Passenger	Woodland Passenger	Sacram'nto Passenger	Woodland Passenger	Sacram'nto Passenger			
Lv. Daily	Lv. Daily	Lv. Daily	Lv. Daily Ex. Sun.	Lv. Daily	Lv. Daily	Lv. Daily	Lv. Daily	Lv. Daily	Lv. Daily	Lv. Daily	Lv. Daily	Lv. Daily	Lv. Daily	Lv. Daily	Lv. Daily	Lv. Daily	Lv. Daily			
2.45am	9.51pm	7.38pm		5.16pm	4.12pm		1.18pm		10.40am[10]	8.49am[8]		7.44am	7.00am					50	48.80	MARYSVILLE 0.23
																			49.03	W. P. R. R. Crossing 0.25
																			49.28	OLIVER, W.P.R.R. Cross. 2.01
3.00	f 9.57	f 7.43[18]		5.22[16]	f 4.18		f 1.23		f10.46	f 8.54		7.49	f 7.05					18	51.29	ALICIA 2.50
3.10	f10.01	f 7.48		5.25	f 4.22		f 1.28		f10.51	f 8.59		7.53	f 7.08					3 (Spur)	53.79	HOWARD 1.35
3.15	f10.04	f 7.51		5.27	f 4.25		f 1.31		f10.54	f 9.02		7.55	f 7.10					6 (Spur)	55.14	ARBOGA 1.57
3.20	f10.07	f 7.54		5.30	f 4.29		f 1.34		f10.58	f 9.05		7.58	f 7.13[4]					7	56.71	PLUMAS LAKE 2.78
3.30	f10.11	f 7.59		5.34	f 4.34		f 1.39		f11.02	f 9.10		8.02	f 7.18					12 (Spur)	59.49	ALGODON 2.01
3.35	f10.14	f 8.03		5.37	f 4.38		f 1.43		f11.05	f 9.13		8.05	f 7.22					8 (Spur)	61.50	RIO OSO 2.50
3.45	f10.17	f 8.08		5.40	f 4.42		f 1.48		f11.11	f 9.18		8.08	f 7.26					12 (Spur)	64.00	STOLP 1.16
3.50	f10.19	f 8.11		5.41	f 4.44		f 1.51		f11.13	f 9.21		8.10	f 7.28					42	65.16	NICOLAUS 2.95
4.00	f10.23	f 8.16		5.44	f 4.49[16]		f 1.55		f11.17	f 9.25		8.13	f 7.32					10 (Spur)	68.11	STRIPLIN 1.44
4.05	f 10.25[22]	f 8.20		5.46	f 4.54		f 1.59		f11.20	f 9.28		8.15	f 7.35					8 (Spur)	69.55	CATLETT 1.64
4.15	f 10.28[152]	f 8.23		5.49	f 4.57		f 2.02		f11.23	f 9.31		8.17[8]	f 7.38					43	71.19	PLEASANT GROVE 3.27
4.25	f10.33	f 8.28[20]		5.53	f 5.02		f 2.07		f11.28	f 9.36[10]		8.22	f 7.42					7 (Spur)	74.46	SANKEY 0.48
																			74.94	MORENO W.P.R.R. CROSSING 1.68
4.35	f10.37	f 8.33		5.56	f 5.07		f 2.12		f11.33	f 9.41		8.26	f 7.47					10 (Spur)	76.62	RIEGO 3.14
4.40	f10.42	f 8.37		6.00	f 5.12		2.18[14]		f11.38	f 9.46		8.31	f 7.51				6.11am[2]	7 (Spur)	79.76	ELVERTA 1.49
4.45	f10.45	f 8.40		6.02	f 5.15		2.22		f11.41	f 9.49		8.33	f 7.54				f 6.14	8 (Spur)	81.25	RIO LINDA 1.94
4.50	f10.48	f 8.43		6.05	f 5.18		2.26		f11.45	f 9.53		8.36	8.00[8]				f 6.18	8 (Spur)	83.19	ROBLA 1.77
4.55	f10.52	f 8.46		6.08	f 5.22		2.29		f11.47[12]	f 9.56		8.39	f 8.03		7.35am[6]		f 6.22	7 (Spur)	84.96	DEL PASO 1.94
5.05	f10.54	f 8.49		6.10	f 5.26		2.32		f11.52	f10.00		8.42	f 8.07		f 7.38		f 6.26[4]	7 (Spur)	86.90	NORTH SACRAMENTO 0.73
	f	f		f	f		f		f	f		f	f		f		f		87.63	GLOBE W.P. R.R. Cross. 0.96
5.15am	10.57	8.53		6.13	5.32		2.37		11.57am	10.06		8.47	8.12		7.42[8]		6.29	50	88.59	HAGGIN 0.38
																			88.97	SACRAMENTO, C St. 1.56
	11.05 / 11.30	9.00 / 9.15		6.20[18] / 6.21	5.40[18] / 6.10	5.10pm	2.45[40] / 3.00	1.20pm	12.05pm / 12.20	10.15 / 10.40	9.40am	8.55[10] / 8.56	8.20am	8.00am	7.50am	6.30am	6.37am		90.53	SACRAMENTO 0.69
	11.35	f 9.20	8.00pm	6.25pm	6.15	5.15	3.05	1.25[14]	12.25[38]	10.45	9.45	9.00am		8.05		f 6.35			91.22	Sacramento, Front & M Sts. S.P.R.R.Cros 0.20
	f 11.37	f 9.22	8.05		f 6.17	5.17	3.07	1.27	f12.27	f10.47	9.47			f 8.07		f 6.36		3 (Spur)	91.42	WEST SACRAMENTO 1.52
	11.40	9.24	8.06		6.20	5.20	3.10	1.30	12.30	10.50	9.50			8.10		6.38		8 (Spur)	92.94	MIKON, S.P. R.R. Cross 0.75
	f 11.41	f 9.25[46]	8.07		f 6.22	f 5.22	f 3.12	1.32	f12.32	f10.52	9.52			f 8.12		f 6.40[32]		8 (Spur)	93.69	ROSE ORCHARD 0.46
	f 11.42	f 9.27	8.08		f 6.23	f 5.23	f 3.13	1.33	f12.33	f10.53	9.53			f 8.13		f 6.42		9	94.15	LOVDAL 0.71
	f 11.43	f 9.28	8.10		f 6.24	f 5.24	f 3.14	1.34	f12.34	f10.54	9.54			f 8.14		f 6.43		6 (Spur)	94.86	LEEMAN 0.72
	f 11.44	f 9.29	8.12		f 6.25	f 5.25	f 3.15	1.35	f12.35	f 10.55[12]	9.55			f 8.15		f 6.44		15 (Spur)	95.58	FOURNESS 0.59
	f 11.46	f 9.31	8.15		f 6.27	f 5.27	f 3.17	1.37	f12.37	f10.57	9.57			f 8.17		f 6.45		10 (Spur)	96.17	MARTY 1.63
	f 11.50	f 9.35	8.20		f 6.30	f 5.30	3.20[16]	1.41	f12.41	f11.01	f10.01			f 8.21		f 6.48		12 (Spur)	97.80	BEATRICE 0.75
	f 11.52	f 9.36	8.22		f 6.31	f 5.31	3.22	1.42	f12.42	f11.02	f10.02			f 8.22		f 6.49		7 (Spur)	98.55	VIN 2.49
	f 11.57pm	f 9.41	8.28		f 6.36	f 5.35[18]	f 3.26	1.46	f12.46	f11.06	f10.06			f 8.26		f 6.53		12 (Spurs)	101.04	ELKHORN 4.46
	f 12.05am	f 9.50	8.38		f 6.44	f 5.44	f 3.35	1.55	f 12.55[14]	f11.14	f10.14			f 8.34		f 7.00		7 (Spur)	105.50	HEBRON 2.36
																			107.86	WOODLAND, SPRR Cros 0.60
	12.10am	9.55pm	8.45pm		6.50pm	5.50pm	3.40pm	2.00pm	1.00pm	11.20am	10.20am			8.40am		7.05am		30	108.46	WOODLAND
Ar. Daily	Ar. Daily	Ar. Daily	Ar. Daily Ex. Sun.	Ar. Daily	Ar. Daily	Ar. Daily	Ar. Daily	Ar. Daily	Ar. Daily	Ar. Daily	Ar. Daily	Ar. Daily	Ar. Daily	Ar. Daily	Ar. Daily	Ar. Daily	Ar. Daily			

Southbound trains have absolute right over all northbound trains of the same or inferior class.

Trains No. 2, 4, 6 and 8 have right over trains No. 1 and 3 between Haggin and Elverta.

MARYSVILLE AND WOODLAND

North Bound

Time Table No. 29 — MARCH 30, 1914

FIRST CLASS / SECOND CLASS

Column headers — each train: number, name, and "Ar. Daily" at top / "Lv. Daily" at bottom. Train 152 is SECOND CLASS (Way Freight); all others are FIRST CLASS.

Stations (office hours)	Miles	Dist. from Woodland	Sta. No.	152 Way Freight	22 Marysville Pass.	46 Sacram'nto Pass.	20 Bay Cities *Limited*	44 Sacram'nto Pass.	18 Chico-Marysville Pass.	42 Sacram'nto Pass.	16 Chico-Marysville Pass.	40 Sacram'nto Pass.	14 Chico-Marysville Pass.
MARYSVILLE (6.30a–3.00a)	0.23	59.66	41 P.	12.05am	11.05pm		9.08pm		7.48pm		5.28pm		3.19pm
W. P. R. R. Crossing	0.25	59.43											
OLIVER, W.P.R.R. Cross.	2.01	59.18											
ALICIA	2.50	57.17	39 P.	11.45pm	f10.59		9.03		f7.43[19]		f5.22[17]		f3.11
HOWARD	1.35	54.67	37 P.	11.35	f10.54		8.59		f7.38		f5.17		f3.06
ARBOGA	1.57	53.32	35 P.	11.25	f10.51		8.57		f7.34		f5.13		f3.03
PLUMAS LAKE	2.78	51.75	34 P.	11.15	f10.48		8.53		f7.30		f5.09		f3.00
ALGODON	2.01	48.97	31 P.	11.10	f10.43		8.48		f7.24		f5.03		f2.55
RIO OSO	2.50	46.96	29 P.	11.00	f10.39		8.44		f7.20		f4.59		f2.51
STOLP	1.16	44.46	27 P.	10.55	f10.35		8.41		f7.15		f4.55		f2.46
NICOLAUS (6.30a–7.15p)	2.95	43.30	25 P.	10.50	f10.33		8.40		f7.13		f4.53		f2.44
STRIPLIN	1.44	40.35	23 P.	10.45	f10.29		8.37		f7.09		f4.49[15]		f2.40
CATLETT	1.64	38.91	21 P.	10.35	f10.25[21]		8.35		f7.06		f4.46		f2.37
PLEASANT GROVE	3.27	37.27	19 P.	10.28[21]	f10.21		8.32		f7.03		f4.43		f2.34
SANKEY	0.48	34.00	16 P.	10.21	f10.16		8.28[19]		f6.58		f4.38		f2.29
MORENO, W.P.RR.Cross.	1.68	33.52											
RIEGO	3.14	31.84	14 P.	10.16	f10.11		8.25		f6.53		f4.33		f2.24
ELVERTA	1.49	28.70	11 P.	10.12	f10.07		8.21		f6.48		f4.28		f2.18[13]
RIO LINDA	1.94	27.21	9 P.	10.10	f10.05		8.19		f6.45		f4.25		f2.14
ROBLA	1.77	25.27	7 P.		f10.02		8.15		f6.41		f4.21		f2.11
DEL PASO	1.94	23.50	6 P.	10.02[22]	9.59		8.12		f6.37		f4.17		f2.07
NORTH SACRAMENTO	0.73	21.56	3 P.	9.50	9.56		8.10		f6.32		f4.12		f2.03
GLOBE, W.P.R.R. Cross.	0.96	20.82											
HAGGIN	0.38	19.87	1 P.	9.45	9.53		8.07		f6.27		f4.08		1.58
SACRAMENTO, C St. (5.45a–11.30p)	1.56	19.49	0 P.	9.35pm	9.45pm	9.35pm	8.00	7.40pm	6.20[15]	4.55pm	4.00	2.50pm[13]	1.50
SACRAMENTO	0.69	17.93				9.30	7.55	7.35	6.00[17]	4.50	3.40	2.45	1.30
Sacramento, Front & M Sts. S.P.R.R.Cross.	0.20	17.24	W.1 P.			f9.28	7.50pm	f7.32	f5.55	f4.47	3.35	f2.42	1.25[37]
WEST SACRAMENTO	1.52	17.04				9.26		7.30	f5.52	4.45	f3.32	2.40	f1.22
MIKON, S.P. R.R. Cross	0.75	15.52	P.			f9.25[19]		f7.28	5.50	f4.43	3.30	f2.38	1.20
ROSE ORCHARD	0.46	14.77	W.3 P.			f9.24		f7.27	f5.48	f4.42	f3.28	f2.37	f1.18
LOVDAL	0.71	14.31	W.4 P.			f9.23		f7.26	f5.47	f4.41	f3.27	f2.36	f1.17
LEEMAN	0.72	13.60	W.5 P.			f9.21		f7.24	f5.46	f4.39	f3.26	f2.34	f1.16
FOURNESS	0.59	12.88	W.6 P.			f9.20		f7.23	f5.44	f4.38	f3.24	f2.33	f1.14
MARTY	1.63	12.29	W.7 P.			f9.18		f7.20	f5.43	f4.35	f3.23	f2.30	f1.13
BEATRICE	0.75	10.66	W.8 P.			f9.17		f7.18	f5.40	f4.33	f3.20[13]	f2.28	f1.10
VIN	2.49	9.91	W.9 P.			f9.13		f7.13	f5.39	f4.28	f3.18	f2.23	f1.08
ELKHORN	4.46	7.42	W.11 P.			f9.05		f7.05	f5.35[33]	f4.20	f3.13	f2.15	f1.03
HEBRON	2.36	2.96	W.15 P.						f5.25		f3.05		f12.55[11]
WOODLAND, SPRR Cros	0.60	0.60									f		
WOODLAND (5.45a–7.15p)		0.00	W.18 P.			9.00pm		7.00pm	5.20pm	4.15pm	3.00pm	2.10pm	12.50pm

Stations (office hours)	Miles	Dist. from Woodland	Sta. No.	38 Sacram'nto Pass.	12 Chico-Marysville Pass.	10 Chico-Marysville Pass.	36 Sacram'nto Pass.	8 *Steamer Special*	34 Sacram'nto Pass.	6 Del Paso Pass.	32 Sacram'nto Pass.	4 Chico-Marysville Pass.	2 Elverta Pass.
MARYSVILLE (6.30a–3.00a)	0.23	59.66	41 P.		12.55pm	10.25am		8.45am[9]				7.27am	
W. P. R. R. Crossing	0.25	59.43											
OLIVER, W.P.R.R. Cross.	2.01	59.18											
ALICIA	2.50	57.17	39 P.		f12.49	f10.18		8.41				f7.21	
HOWARD	1.35	54.67	37 P.		f12.44	f10.13		8.38				f7.17	
ARBOGA	1.57	53.32	35 P.		f12.41	f10.10		8.36				f7.15	
PLUMAS LAKE	2.78	51.75	34 P.		f12.38	f10.07		8.34				f7.13[5]	
ALGODON	2.01	48.97	31 P.		f12.33	f10.02		8.31				f7.09	
RIO OSO	2.50	46.96	29 P.		f12.29	f9.58		8.28				f7.06	
STOLP	1.16	44.46	27 P.		f12.25	f9.53		8.25				f7.02	
NICOLAUS (6.30a–7.15p)	2.95	43.30	25 P.		f12.23	f9.51		8.24				f7.00	
STRIPLIN	1.44	40.35	23 P.		f12.19	f9.47		8.21				f6.56	
CATLETT	1.64	38.91	21 P.		f12.16	f9.44		8.19				f6.54	
PLEASANT GROVE	3.27	37.27	19 P.		f12.13	f9.41		8.17[7]				f6.51	
SANKEY	0.48	34.00	16 P.		f12.08	f9.36[9]		8.12				f6.46	
MORENO, W.P.RR.Cross.	1.68	33.52											
RIEGO	3.14	31.84	14 P.		12.03pm	f9.31		8.09				f6.42	
ELVERTA	1.49	28.70	11 P.		f11.58	f9.26		8.05				f6.38	6.08am
RIO LINDA	1.94	27.21	9 P.		f11.55	f9.23		8.03				f6.35	6.04
ROBLA	1.77	25.27	7 P.		f11.51	f9.19		8.00[5]				f6.32	6.01
DEL PASO	1.94	23.50	6 P.		11.47[1]	f9.16		7.57		7.30am[3]		f6.29	5.58
NORTH SACRAMENTO	0.73	21.56	3 P.		f11.43	f9.13		7.55		7.27		f6.26[1]	5.55
GLOBE, W.P.R.R. Cross.	0.96	20.82											
HAGGIN	0.38	19.87	1 P.		11.38	f9.08		7.52[3]		7.23		f6.23	5.51
SACRAMENTO, C St. (5.45a–11.30p)	1.56	19.49	0 P.	12.25pm	11.30	9.00am[7]	9.30am	7.45	7.50am	7.15am	6.50am	6.15am	5.50am
SACRAMENTO	0.69	17.93		12.20[11]	11.10		9.25	7.35	7.45		6.45		
Sacramento, Front & M Sts. S.P.R.R.Cross.	0.20	17.24	W.1 P.	f12.17	11.05		f9.22	7.30am	f7.43		f6.43		
WEST SACRAMENTO	1.52	17.04		12.15	f11.02		9.20		7.41		6.41		
MIKON, S.P. R.R. Cross	0.75	15.52	P.	f12.13	11.00		f9.18		f7.40		f6.40[31]		
ROSE ORCHARD	0.46	14.77	W.3 P.	f12.12	f10.58		f9.17		f7.39		f6.39		
LOVDAL	0.71	14.31	W.4 P.	f12.11	f10.57		f9.16		f7.38		f6.38		
LEEMAN	0.72	13.60	W.5 P.	f12.09[9]	f10.56		f9.14		f7.36		f6.36		
FOURNESS	0.59	12.88	W.6 P.	f12.08	f10.55[9]		f9.13		f7.35		f6.35		
MARTY	1.63	12.29	W.7 P.	f12.05	f10.53		f9.10		f7.33		f6.33		
BEATRICE	0.75	10.66	W.8 P.	f12.03pm	f10.50		f9.08		f7.32		f6.32		
VIN	2.49	9.91	W.9 P.	f11.58am	f10.48		f9.03		f7.28		f6.28		
ELKHORN	4.46	7.42	W.11 P.	f11.50	f10.43		f8.55		f7.21		f6.21		
HEBRON	2.36	2.96	W.15 P.		f10.35								
WOODLAND, SPRR Cros	0.60	0.60											
WOODLAND (5.45a–7.15p)		0.00	W.18 P.	11.45am	10.30am		8.50am		7.15am		6.15am		

Southbound trains have absolute right over all northbound trains of the same or inferior class.

Trains No. 2, 4, 6 and 8 have right over all northbound trains of the same or inferior class.

Trains No. 2, 4, 6 and 8 have right over trains No. 1 and 3 between Haggin and Elverta.

OROVILLE AND TRES VIAS

South Bound — (FROM OROVILLE) — FIRST CLASS — Time Table No. 29, MARCH 30, 1914

STATIONS	Distance from Oroville.	Capacity of Sidings in Freight cars.	51[7] Sacram'nto Passenger	53[9] Sacram'nto Woodland Passenger	55[4] Chico Passenger	57[8/11] Chico Sacram'nto Passenger	59[10] Chico Passenger	61[13] Sacram'nto Woodland Passenger	63[12] Chico Passenger	65[15] Sacram'nto Woodland Passenger	67[14/17] Chico Sacram'nto Passenger	69[16/19] Chico Sacram'nto Passenger	71[18/21] Chico Sacram'nto Passenger	73[20] Chico Passenger
			Lv. Daily	Lv. Daily	Lv. Daily	Lv. Daily	Lv. Daily	Lv. Daily	Lv. Daily	Lv. Daily	Lv. Daily	Lv. Daily	Lv. Daily	Lv. Daily
OROVILLE	0.00	16	6.32am	7.22am	8.10am	9.11am	11.12am	11.54am	1.44pm	2.46pm	4.08pm	6.17pm	8.32pm	9.44pm
OROVILLE MARYSVILLE ROAD	1.26	28	f 6.38	f 7.28	f 8.16	f 9.17	f11.18	f12.01pm	f 1.50	f 2.52	f 4.14	f 6.23	f 8.38	f 9.50
THERMALITO	2.48	26	f 6.42	f 7.32	f 8.20	f 9.21	f11.22	f12.04	f 1.54	f 2.56	f 4.18	f 6.27	f 8.42	f 9.54
TRES VIAS	5.74	14	6.48am	7.38am	8.26am	9.27am	11.28am	12.10pm	2.00pm	3.02pm	4.24pm	6.33pm	8.48pm	10.00pm
			Ar. Daily	Ar. Daily	Ar. Daily	Ar. Daily	Ar. Daily	Ar. Daily	Ar. Daily	Ar. Daily	Ar. Daily	Ar. Daily	Ar. Daily	Ar. Daily

Station distances: OROVILLE 1.26; OROVILLE MARYSVILLE ROAD 1.22; THERMALITO 3.26.

North Bound — (TO OROVILLE) — FIRST CLASS — Time Table No. 29, MARCH 30, 1914

STATIONS	Distance from Tres Vias.	Telephone Stations Office Hours and Station Numbers	52[7] Oroville Passenger	54[9] Oroville Passenger	56[4] Oroville Passenger	58[8/11] Oroville Passenger	60[10] Oroville Passenger	62[13] Oroville Passenger	64[12] Oroville Passenger	66[15] Oroville Passenger	68[14/17] Oroville Passenger	70[16/19] Oroville Passenger	72[18/21] Oroville Passenger	74[20] Oroville Passenger
			Ar. Daily	Ar. Daily	Ar. Daily	Ar. Daily	Ar. Daily	Ar. Daily	Ar. Daily	Ar. Daily	Ar. Daily	Ar. Daily	Ar. Daily	Ar. Daily
OROVILLE	5.38	6.05a-9.45p P. 05	7.09am	7.59am	8.48am	9.50am	11.51am	12.32pm	2.22pm	3.24pm	4.46pm	6.56pm	9.12pm	10.21pm
OROVILLE, Marysville Road	4.48	P. 04	f 7.03	f 7.53	f 8.42	f 9.44	f11.45	f12.26	f 2.16	f 3.18	f 4.40	f 6.50	f 9.06	f10.15
THERMALITO	3.26	6.15a-6.30p P. 03	f 6.59	f 7.49	f 8.38	f 9.40	f11.41	f12.22	f 2.12	f 3.14	f 4.36	f 6.46	f 9.02	f10.11
TRES VIAS	0.00	7.00a-1.00a P. 71	6.53am	7.43am	8.32am	9.34am	11.35am	12.16pm	2.06pm	3.08pm	4.30pm	6.40pm	8.56pm	10.05pm
			Lv. Daily	Lv. Daily	Lv. Daily	Lv. Daily	Lv. Daily	Lv. Daily	Lv. Daily	Lv. Daily	Lv. Daily	Lv. Daily	Lv. Daily	Lv. Daily

Station distances: OROVILLE 0.90; OROVILLE, Marysville Road 1.22; THERMALITO 3.26.

Southbound trains have absolute right over all northbound trains of the same or inferior class.

MARYSVILLE AND COLUSA

113 Marysville Passenger Lv. Sat. & Sun. Only	111 19/20 Marysville Sacram'nto Passenger Lv. Daily	109 16/17 Marysville Sacram'nto Passenger Lv. Daily	107 14/15 Marysville Sacram'nto Passenger Lv. Daily	105 12/13 Marysville Sacram'nto Passenger Lv. Daily	103 10/11 Marysville Sacram'nto Passenger Lv. Daily	101 4/7 Marysville Sacram'nto Passenger Lv. Daily	Capacity of Sidings in Freight Cars	Distance from Colusa	STATIONS (Time Table No. 29, MARCH 30, 1914)	Distance from Heyman	Telephone Stations Office Hours and Station Numbers	102 4/7 Colusa Passenger Ar. Daily	104 10/11 Colusa Passenger Ar. Daily	106 12/13 Colusa Passenger Ar. Daily	108 14/15 Colusa Passenger Ar. Daily	110 16/17 Colusa Passenger Ar. Daily	112 19/20/21 Colusa Passenger Ar. Daily	114 Colusa Passenger Ar. Sat. & Sun. Only
10.30pm	6.40pm	4.20pm	3.10pm	12.15pm	9.40am	6.45am	10	0.00	**COLUSA** — 4.38 —	21.71	6.15a--7.00p P. C21	8.25am	11.23am	1.55pm	4.35pm	6.30pm	10.15pm	12.25am
f10.36	f 6.48	f **4.28** (108)	f 3.18	f12.23	f 9.48	f 6.53	8 (Spur)	4.38	TUTTLE — 2.18 —	17.33	P. C17	f 8.17	f11.15	f 1.47	f **4.28** (109)	f 6.22	f10.07	f12.17
f10.40	f 6.53	f 4.33	f 3.23	f12.28	f 9.53	f 6.58	8 (Spur)	6.56	SYCAMORE — 1.36 —	15.15	P. C15	f 8.12	f11.10	f 1.42	f 4.22	f 6.17	f10.02	f12.12
f10.43	f 6.56	f 4.36	f 3.26	f12.31	f 9.56	f 7.01	24 (Spurs)	7.92	**MERIDIAN** — 1.79 —	13.79	6.30a-7.00p P. C14	f 8.09	f11.07	f 1.39	f 4.19	f 6.14	f 9.59	f12.09
10.45	7.00	4.40	3.30	12.35	10.00	7.05	40	9.71	BEET SPUR — 0.59 —	12.00	P. C12	8.06	f11.04	1.36	4.16	6.11	9.56	12.06
f10.46	f 7.01	f 4.41	f 3.31	f12.36	f10.01	f 7.06	9 (Spur)	10.30	HAGEMAN — 1.32 —	11.41	P. C11	f 8.04	f11.02	f 1.34	f 4.14	f 6.09	f 9.55	f12.05
f10.48	f 7.03	f 4.43	f 3.33	f12.38	f10.03	f 7.08	10 (Spur)	11.62	TARKE — 1.04 —	10.09	P. C10	f 8.02	f11.00	f 1.32	f 4.12	f 6.07	f 9.53	f12.03
f10.50	f 7.05	f 4.45	f 3.35	f12.40	f10.05	f 7.10	18 (Spur)	12.66	**STOHLMANN** — 1.20 —	9.05	P. C9	f 8.00	f10.58	f 1.30	f 4.10	f 6.05	f 9.51	f12.01am
f10.52	f 7.07	f 4.47	f 3.37	f12.42	f10.07	f 7.12	9 (Spur)	13.86	SUMMY — 2.70 —	7.85	P. C8	f 7.58	f10.56	f 1.28	f 4.08	f 6.03	f 9.49	f11.58pm
f10.57	f 7.12	f 4.52	f 3.42	f12.47	f10.12	f 7.17	29	16.56	**SUTTER** — 3.55 —	5.15	6.45a-7.15p P. C5	f 7.53	f10.51	f 1.23	f 4.03	f 5.58	f 9.44	f11.53
f11.02	f 7.17	f 4.57	f 3.47	f12.52	f10.17	f 7.22	8 (Spur)	20.11	ALMENDRA — 1.60 —	1.60	P. C2	f 7.48	f10.46	f 1.18	f 3.58	f 5.53	f 9.39	f11.48
11.05pm	7.20pm	5.00pm	3.50pm	12.55pm	10.20am	7.25am		21.71	**HEYMAN**	0.00	7.20a-7.30p P	7.45am	10.43am	1.15pm	3.55pm	5.50pm	9.36pm	11.45pm
Ar. Sat. & Sun. Only	Ar. Daily	Ar. Daily	Ar. Daily	Ar. Daily	Ar. Daily	Ar. Daily						Lv. Daily	Lv. Daily	Lv. Daily	Lv. Daily	Lv. Daily	Lv. Daily	Lv. Sat. & Sun. Only

South bound trains have absolute right over all north bound trains of the same or inferior class.

SPECIAL RULES AND REGULATIONS

s.—Regular stop.

f.---Stop on signal.

P.—Telephone stations.

All trains must come to a full stop at Railroad and Street Car Grade Crossings not protected by interlocking plants, except when crossing West Fourth Street at Ashby Junction, Chico, and P. G. & E. Ry. Crossings at 31st & J, 28th & X, 21st & X, 10th & X, Front & T, 8th & J, 8th & K and 7th & M Streets, Sacramento.

In addition to trains coming to a full stop at all Railroad Grade Crossings, all trains must be flagged over the Butte Co. R R. at Stirling Junction, S. P. R. R. at Chico, Front & R and Front & N Streets, Sacramento, and at Woodland, by conductor or flagman.

All trains must be controlled by towerman's signals at S. P. R. R. crossings at Torres, 31st and R Streets, and Front and M Streets, Sacramento, and at drawbridges at Sacramento and Meridian.

Bulletin Stations:—Chico, Tres Vias, Oroville, Marysville, Sacramento, Woodland and Colusa.

Registering Stations:—Chico, Mulberry, Tres Vias, Oroville, Marysville, C Street, Sacramento, Woodland, Heyman and Colusa.

All trains must get clearance cards before leaving registering stations, except Mulberry and C Street.

Freight trains will *not* register at Chico and Sacramento.

Freight trains must get clearance from Dispatcher before leaving Mulberry and C Street and Front & M Streets, Sacramento.

Freight trains must not go south of Fifteenth and D Streets in Sacramento.

Freight trains will not carry passengers.

Bold face type denotes meeting or passing point of trains.

Where only one time is shown it denotes leaving time.

Note particularly trains from Oroville to Tres Vias and from Sacramento to Woodland and from Colusa to Heyman are southbound, and trains to Oroville from Tres Vias and to Sacramento from Woodland and from Heyman to Colusa are northbound.

Freight trains between Marysville Road and Oroville will take High Street track both north and southbound.

The Chico yards include all tracks north of Little Chico Creek, and north of point 600 feet south of Rosedale.

The Mulberry yards include all tracks between a point 600 feet south of south switch at Mulberry and Little Chico Creek.

Oroville yards include all tracks in Oroville north of the north end of the north trestle approach of the Feather River Bridge.

The limits of Tres Vias yards extend 600 feet south of south switch, 600 feet north of north switch and 600 feet north of north switch on Oroville branch.

The limits of Marysville and Yuba City yard extend from 600 feet north of north switch in Yuba City to the south end of the Yuba River Bridge just north of Oliver.

Insofar as concerns the operation of trains and the determination of their rights, Marysville and Yuba City yards will be considered as one yard.

The limits of Heyman yard extend 600 feet south of south switch, 600 feet north of north switch and 600 feet north of north switch on Colusa branch.

The limits of Colusa yard include all tracks north of a point 600 feet south of south end of double track.

The Sacramento yards include all tracks between Range and a point 600 feet south of West Sacramento.

The limits of Woodland yard include all tracks south of a point 600 feet north of stock corral spur.

When running within yard limits as designated on Time Table, all trains must be run under full control and be prepared to stop within the limit of vision.

Single tracks between Ashby Junction and Mulberry, between the S. P. crossing in Yuba City and the south end of Feather River bridge in Marysville, between D Street and I Street on Fifteenth, in Sacramento, are protected by block signals which will be operated as per bulletin.

The tracks between the north end of Cooper Tract in Yuba City and Second and F Streets in Marysville, on Market Street, Colusa, between Haggin and Front and M Streets, on X Street between 8th and 31st, on C Street between 19th and 31st in Sacramento, and on Main Street between 1st and 9th Streets in Chico, are operated as double tracks. All trains must use right-hand track.

Derailing switches are located on rip tracks at Mulberry, on Packing House Spur in Thermalito, on Natomas Consolidated Spur in Oroville, on Truckee Lumber Co. Spur in Oroville, on High line in Oroville, on W. P. R. R. transfer track at south end of Feather River Bridge in Marysville, on siding just north of Subway in Sacramento, and must be thrown by all trains using those tracks.

By ordinance the rate of speed of trains is limited to twelve (12) miles per hour within the city limits of Chico, Marysville and Sacramento, ten (10) miles per hour within the city limits of Oroville, and fifteen (15) miles per hour within the city limits of Live Oak.

Spring switches are placed at the following points:

Chico: House track and three legs of Y at First and Main Streets, three legs of Y at 9th and Main Streets, both ends of double track on Main Street, and 9th and Broadway.

Mulberry: Both ends of passing track.

Tres Vias: Three legs of little Y.

Oroville: Marysville Road and High Street.

Heyman: North and south legs of Y on Colusa branch.

Yuba City: All main line switches in Yuba City.

Marysville: Both ends of double track on Fifth and D Streets, three legs of Y at Second and D Streets, both ends of double track on Second Street, Orange and Second Streets, crossover on 5th Street between G and H, 5th and G Streets and 5th and J Streets.

Sacramento: Both ends of double track between American River Bridge and Fifteenth and D Streets, two legs of Y at 8th and I Streets, both ends of double track on I and X Streets, crossover on C Street between 25th and 26th, on 8th Street between J and K and L and M Streets, both ends of double track on C and M Streets, and back-up derailer on northbound track Front and M Streets.

Woodland: Three legs of Y Second and Main Streets, end of double track on South Second Street and at 2nd and Lincoln Streets.

The above spring switches may be run through by passenger trains and freight motors running light (without throwing) at a speed not to exceed six (6) miles per hour.

All trains must reduce speed to six (6) miles per hour when passing over spring switches within yard limits.

Except as above, freight trains, construction trains and yard motors must throw ALL switches.

Standard Clocks are located at Dispatcher's Office in Mulberry and at passenger Depots in Chico, Oroville, Marysville, Colusa, Sacramento and Woodland.

Street cars within yard limits in Sacramento, Marysville and Chico have right over yard motors and deadhead equipment.

When main line passenger trains meet at Tres Vias the south leg of little Wye will be the meeting point unless otherwise specified in train order.

When trains meet at Heyman the south switch of the Wye will be the meeting point unless otherwise specified in train order.

When passenger trains meet at Marysville the meeting point will be on the double track.

All trains except Nos. 7, 8, 17 and 20 will stop on signal at the following stations to take on and discharge passengers:

MAIN LINE.

Chico, Main, bet. 3rd and 4th Sts.,
Chico, 9th and Main Sts.,
Camino,
Yocum's Crossing,
East Biggs,
Galindo,
Bihlman,
Sunset,
Pease,
Harter,
Tharp,
Gomez,
Yuba City, 2nd St.,
Marysville, W. P. R. R. Depot,
Marysville, 5th and D Sts.,
Huntington,

MAIN LINE.

Bear River,
Esmeralda,
Ardmore,
Allison,
Brooke,
Arcade,
Range,
Sacramento, 12th St.,
Riverbank,
Beardslee,
Kiesel,
Haviland,
Target,
Deaner.

COLUSA BRANCH.

Bridge Street,
Cromer Avenue,
Rowena,
Azucar,
Girdner,
Saye,
Humphrey.

OROVILLE BRANCH.

Oroville, Post Office,
Oroville, Pine and Montgomery Sts.,
Oroville, 2nd and Montgomery Sts.,
Oroville, Boston Machine Shops,
Oroville, 2nd Ave. and High St.,
Oroville, 5th Ave. and High St.

LOCATION OF SIDE AND OVERHEAD OBSTRUCTIONS

Chico—Depot, side.
Durham—Stockyard, side.
Shippee—Stockyard, side.
Marysville Road passing track—Rock Crusher, side.
Marysville Garretts Spur—Clark & Henery Warehouse, side.
Marysville Garretts Spur—Garretts Warehouse. side and overhead.
Sacramento—Subway, side and overhead.
Sacramento—31st Street, poles, side.
Sacramento—Front & N—poles, side.
Sacramento—Front & M—Freight Depot. side and overhead.
Hop Tram—One quarter mile south of Lovdal, side.
Woodland—West Valley Lumber Spur, side.
Trainmen will at all times look out for low hanging trolley and span wires.

MOTOR RATING

Motor	Main Line and Colusa Branch	Oroville Branch	Hamilton Branch	"C", "31st", "X" & Front Strs.
701	600 Ms	300 Ms	300 Ms	300 Ms
1000	1200 Ms	800 Ms	600 Ms	800 Ms
1002	1600 Ms	1200 Ms	600 Ms	1200 Ms
1003	1600 Ms	1200 Ms	600 Ms	1200 Ms
1004	1600 Ms	1200 Ms	600 Ms	1200 Ms
1010	2400 Ms	1400 Ms	0 Ms	1400 Ms

LOCATION OF INTERCHANGE TRACKS

Chico—S. P. R. R., 9th & Orange Streets.
    B. C. R. R., Barber.

Oroville—W. P. R. R., High Line.

Marysville—W. P. R. R., South of Feather River Bridge.
    S. P. R. R., Yuba Construction Co. yard.

Sacramento—W. P. R. R., Haggin and 19th & X Streets.
    S. P. R. R., B Street, and Front & X Streets.
    C. C. T. Co., Front & X Streets.
    O. A. & E. R. R., West Sacramento. (Headquarters)

LOCATION OF WYES

Chico—1st & Main Streets.
    9th & Main Streets.
Mulberry—
Tres Vias—
Heyman—

Marysville—2nd & D Streets.
Sacramento—19th & C Streets, 8th & I Streets.
Woodland—2nd & Main Streets.
Colusa—Circle track.
Track scales are located at Yuba City and Hamilton.

Train Master - - - - - - -	**W. W. NELSON**
Train Dispatchers - - - - - - -	G. A. ROGERS B. F. HAINER J. J. BLANEY

Company Watch Inspectors:

Chief Watch Inspector C. A. DREISS.............226 Main St., Chico
Sub. Watch Inspector... PETER ENGEL .... 220 D St., Marysville
Sub. Watch Inspector....O. W. HALSTEAD .... 320 Meyers St., Oroville
Sub. Watch Inspector....G. W. GREEN & SON..... 621 Main St., Woodland
Sub. Watch Inspector... G. W. WACHHORST......718 K St., Sacramento
Sub. Watch Inspector...BAUM & MINASIAN ......Colusa.

Company Surgeons:

Chief Surgeon Dr. D. H. Moulton, Morehead Bldg. Tel. 38-R Chico
Asst. Surgeon....DR. F. L. ATKINSON, Bryte Bldg., Tel 2497-R...Sacramento
Asst. Surgeon....DR. DAVID POWELL, 302 D St., Tel 85 ....Marysville
Asst. Surgeon....DR. F. A. KUSEL, Sangster Bldg., Tel. 302-R....Oroville
Asst. Surgeon....DR. M. P. STANSBURY, Shotover Inn........Hamilton
Asst. Surgeon....DR. F. R. FAIRCHILD, Tel 18 ....Woodland
Asst. Surgeon....DR. W. T. RATHBURN, Tel. 1542............Colusa
Asst. Surgeon....DR. E. V. JACOBS, Tel. 47 (Kent)............Meridian

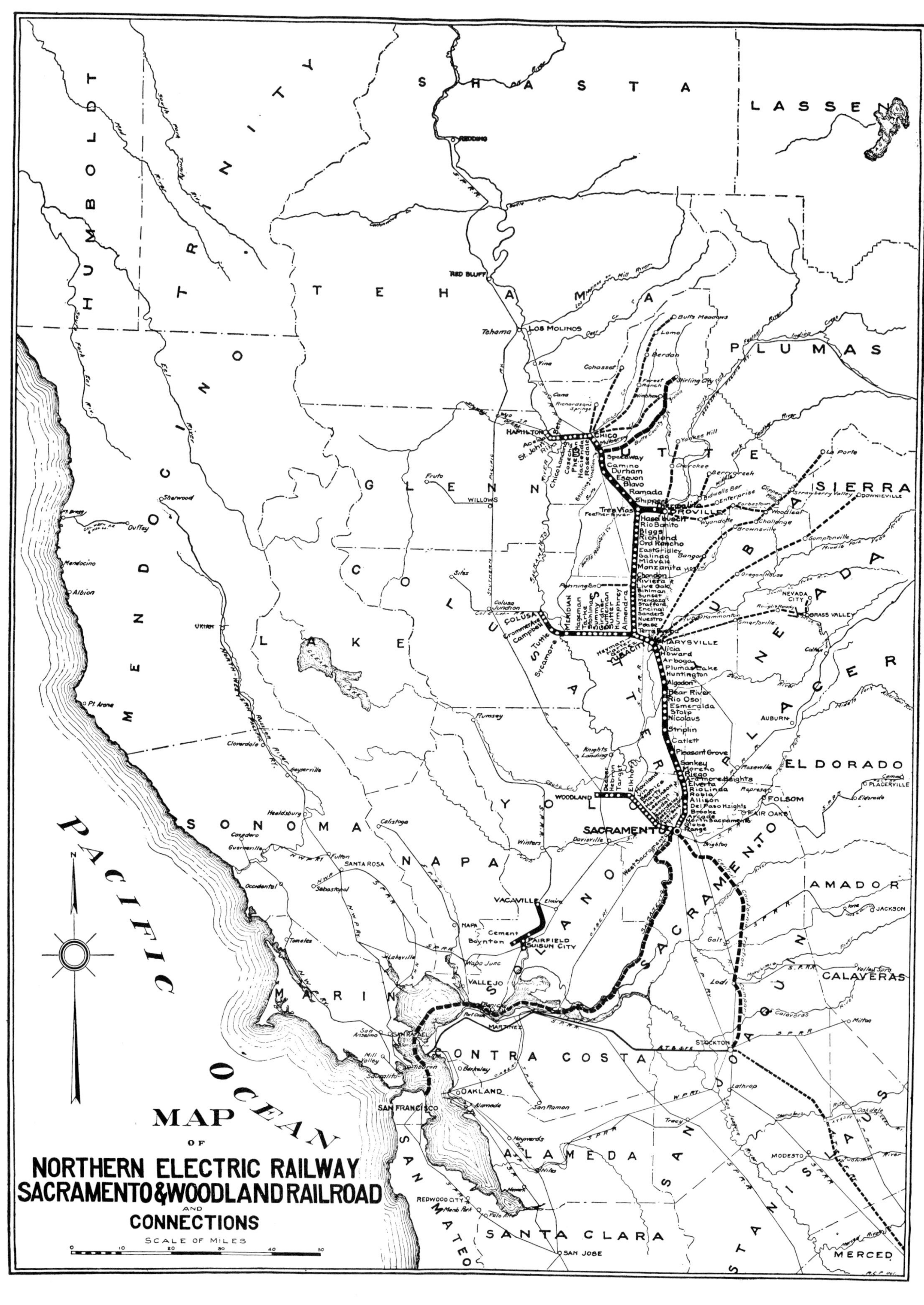
MAP
OF
NORTHERN ELECTRIC RAILWAY
SACRAMENTO & WOODLAND RAILROAD
AND
CONNECTIONS
SCALE OF MILES
0   10   20   30   40   50
PACIFIC OCEAN
HUMBOLDT
TRINITY
SHASTA
LASSEN
TEHAMA
PLUMAS
GLENN
BUTTE
SIERRA
MENDOCINO
COLUSA
YUBA
NEVADA
LAKE
SUTTER
PLACER
ELDORADO
SONOMA
NAPA
YOLO
SACRAMENTO
AMADOR
MARIN
SOLANO
CALAVERAS
CONTRA COSTA
SAN JOAQUIN
ALAMEDA
STANISLAUS
SAN MATEO
SANTA CLARA
MERCED
REDDING
RED BLUFF
LOS MOLINOS
TEHAMA
HAMILTON
CHICO
Speedway
Camino
Durham
Esquon
Biavo
Ramada
Shippee
Stirling City
OROVILLE
Hase Vista
Rio Bonito
Biggs
Richland
Ord Rancho
East Gridley
Galinda
Midvale
Manzanita
Chandon
Riviera
Live Oak
Sohlman
Sunset
Mendoza
Stafford
Encinal
Sanders
Nuestro
Peabe
Tarr
Tres Vias
MARYSVILLE
Alicia
Howard
Arboga
Plumas Lake
Huntington
Algodon
Bear River
Rio Oso
Esmeralda
Stolp
Nicolaus
Striplin
Catlett
Pleasant Grove
Sankey
Oreho
Diego
Elverta
Rio Linda
Robla
Allison
Brooke
Del Paso Hights
Arcade
North Sacramento
Globe
Range
Elmore Heights
WOODLAND
SACRAMENTO
COLUSA
MERIDIAN
Hagaman
Bohinas
Sunny
Coffman
Humphrey
Commercial
Campbell
Tuttle
Sycamore
YUBA CITY
WILLOWS
Sites
Colusa Junction
Pennington
Maxwell
Fruto
Sherwood
Duffey
Mendocino
Albion
Pt Arena
UKIAH
Cloverdale
Geyserville
Healdsburg
Calistoga
Guerneville
SANTA ROSA
Sebastopol
Occidental
Tomales
VACAVILLE
Elmira
NAPA
Cement
Boynton
FAIRFIELD
SUISUN CITY
Winters
Davisville
VALLEJO
San Anselmo
SAN RAFAEL
Mill Valley
Sausalito
Tiburon
Berkeley
OAKLAND
Alameda
SAN FRANCISCO
San Ramon
MARTINEZ
STOCKTON
Lodi
Galt
Brighton
West Sacramento
Lathrop
Tracy
Haywards
REDWOOD CITY
Menlo Park
Palo Alto
SAN JOSE
MODESTO
Milton
JACKSON
PLACERVILLE
Eldorado
FOLSOM
FAIR OAKS
Roseville
AUBURN
GRASS VALLEY
NEVADA CITY
Colfax
DOWNIEVILLE
Comptonville
Challenge
Brownsville
Bangor
La Porte
Cherokee
Berry Creek
Bidwells Bar
Enterprise
Forbestown
Wyandotte
Buffs Meadows
Lomo
Berdan
Cohasset
Vina
Cana
Richardsons Springs
Nord
Yankee Hill
Strawberry Valley
Oregon House
Smartsville
Knights Landing
Elkhorn
PACIFIC
N

Chapter 5

North End Branch Lines

Heyman---later Colusa Jct.---was one of several busy junction points on the Northern Electric system; here, in an early day photo, combo motor 129 in its orange livery stands on the branch awaiting its connection on the main line. But why is that trolley pole raised?   (LLS)

The several branch lines constructed to bolster the service territory of the NE-SN system were invaluable in building up their respective areas. Starting on the north end and coming south, these branches were:

The Hamilton Branch---Chico to Hamilton City
The Oroville Branch---Tres Vias to Oroville
The Colusa Branch---Heyman to Colusa
The Swanston Branch---Globe to Swanston
The Woodland Branch---Sacramento to Woodland
The Suisun-Vacaville Branch---isolated

The above points on the main line were the actual junction points; in service, some branch line trains operated over portions of the main line to reach their destinations---as: Swanston cars operated from Sacramento to Globe on the main line, then switched to the branch line; Colusa trains operated from Heyman to Marysville on the main line. Suisun-Vacaville trains, on the other hand, were separated from the system by many miles; not until a connection was built to the OA&E-SFS main line after the consolidation of 1928 were the Suisun-Vacaville cars able to reach other points on the system without being hauled over Southern Pacific rails.

The Oroville Branch

The line of railroad later known as the Oroville Branch was in actuality the first line of Northern Electric anywhere. The first NE construction took place in Oroville on October 1, 1905, with the ultimate destination of Chico. There was only a stagecoach line connecting Chico with Oroville at that time and service was anything but fast and comfortable.

NE crews reached the Feather River near Oroville by January 29, 1906, and a rather impressive covered bridge was constructed to take the interurban line over the sometimes turbulent waters of the major river. The line was constructed up to steam railroad standards in every respect; and propulsion current was supplied by a direct suspension overhead trolley line.

On April 11, 1906, the first official trip was made between Oroville and Chico, using brand new Niles car 100; on board were Henry A. Butters, Superintendent Frank A. Ross, and other NE officials. However, "Old Maude," otherwise locomotive 701, had the honor of being the first electric car ever to operate, having been used in constructing this line.

The Chico-Oroville Line was 24.74 miles in length, and was supplied with current by substations at Chico and at Substation No. 2, located at MP 10.07.

While finishing touches were being put on the Oroville line, and prior to its official opening, the San Francisco Earthquake and Fire occurred on April 18, 1906---a catastrophe which cast a pall over all business enterprises. Nevertheless, on April 25, 1906, Northern Electric proudly opened its first interurban line to public use, and for the first time the upper Sacramento Valley enjoyed fast, comfortable electric railway service equal to any in the nation.

Opening day saw Niles cars 100 and 101 providing the service, each operating separately; a minor rear end collision between these cars at Durham added spice to the occasion but neither car was injured sufficiently to warrant withdrawal from service. The turnout of curious would-be patrons was so great that NE took open bench cars 50 and 51 from their usual Chico local runs and ran them over the interurban line, following the Niles cars each way. A special introductory fare of 25¢ was set for opening day only. Service soon shook down to eight roundtrips daily with a running time each way of 55 minutes.

NE experienced some misfortune with its Oroville passenger depots. The first and second structures were destroyed by fire; the third turned out to be an unimposing building built of corrugated iron.

A local service was performed by NE in Oroville with cars operating on a loop around town, as follows: From the depot at the corner of High & Meyers Sts., down Meyers as far as Montgomery and there turned left onto Montgomery, follow that street as far as Marysville Road, then over Marysville Road to High St., there connecting with the line from Chico. Cars

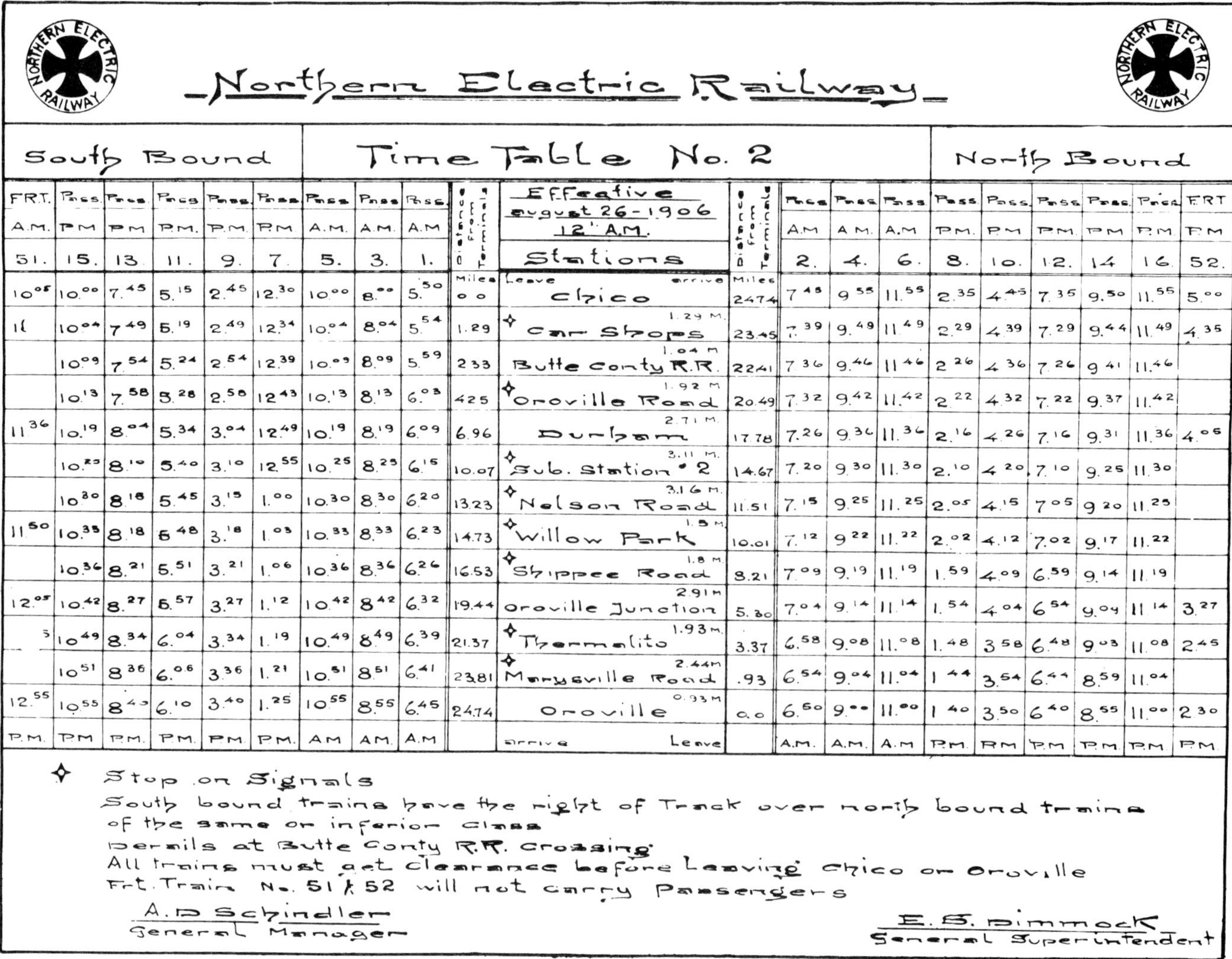

Northern Electric Railway

South Bound — Time Table No. 2 — North Bound

Effective August 26-1906 12 A.M.

51 FRT	15 Pass	13 Pass	11 Pass	9 Pass	7 Pass	5 Pass	3 Pass	1 Pass	Miles	Stations	Miles	2 Pass	4 Pass	6 Pass	8 Pass	10 Pass	12 Pass	14 Pass	16 Pass	52 FRT
A.M.	P.M.	P.M.	P.M.	P.M.	P.M.	A.M.	A.M.	A.M.				A.M.	A.M.	A.M.	P.M.	P.M.	P.M.	P.M.	P.M.	P.M.
10.05	10.00	7.45	5.15	2.45	12.30	10.00	8.00	5.50	0.0	Leave Chico arrive	24.74	7.45	9.55	11.55	2.35	4.45	7.35	9.50	11.55	5.00
11	10.04	7.49	5.19	2.49	12.34	10.04	8.04	5.54	1.29	✧ Car Shops (1.29 M.)	23.45	7.39	9.49	11.49	2.29	4.39	7.29	9.44	11.49	4.35
	10.09	7.54	5.24	2.54	12.39	10.09	8.09	5.59	2.33	Butte Conty R.R. (1.04 M.)	22.41	7.36	9.46	11.46	2.26	4.36	7.26	9.41	11.46	
	10.13	7.58	5.28	2.58	12.43	10.13	8.13	6.03	4.25	✧ Oroville Road (1.92 M.)	20.49	7.32	9.42	11.42	2.22	4.32	7.22	9.37	11.42	
11.36	10.19	8.04	5.34	3.04	12.49	10.19	8.19	6.09	6.96	Durham (2.71 M.)	17.78	7.26	9.36	11.36	2.16	4.26	7.16	9.31	11.36	4.05
	10.25	8.10	5.40	3.10	12.55	10.25	8.25	6.15	10.07	✧ Sub. Station #2 (3.11 M.)	14.67	7.20	9.30	11.30	2.10	4.20	7.10	9.25	11.30	
	10.30	8.18	5.45	3.15	1.00	10.30	8.30	6.20	13.23	✧ Nelson Road (3.16 M.)	11.51	7.15	9.25	11.25	2.05	4.15	7.05	9.20	11.25	
11.50	10.33	8.18	5.48	3.18	1.03	10.33	8.33	6.23	14.73	✧ Willow Park (1.5 M.)	10.01	7.12	9.22	11.22	2.02	4.12	7.02	9.17	11.22	
	10.36	8.21	5.51	3.21	1.06	10.36	8.36	6.26	16.53	✧ Shippee Road (1.8 M.)	8.21	7.09	9.19	11.19	1.59	4.09	6.59	9.14	11.19	
12.05	10.42	8.27	5.57	3.27	1.12	10.42	8.42	6.32	19.44	Oroville Junction (2.91 M.)	5.30	7.04	9.14	11.14	1.54	4.04	6.54	9.04	11.14	3.27
5	10.49	8.34	6.04	3.34	1.19	10.49	8.49	6.39	21.37	✧ Thermalito (1.93 M.)	3.37	6.58	9.08	11.08	1.48	3.58	6.48	9.03	11.08	2.45
	10.51	8.36	6.06	3.36	1.21	10.51	8.51	6.41	23.81	✧ Marysville Road (2.44 M.)	.93	6.54	9.04	11.04	1.44	3.54	6.44	8.59	11.04	
12.55	10.55	8.43	6.10	3.40	1.25	10.55	8.55	6.45	24.74	Oroville (0.93 M.)	0.0	6.50	9.00	11.00	1.40	3.50	6.40	8.55	11.00	2.30
P.M.	P.M.	P.M.	P.M.	P.M.	P.M.	A.M.	A.M.	A.M.		arrive Leave		A.M.	A.M.	A.M.	P.M.	P.M.	P.M.	P.M.	P.M.	P.M.

✧ Stop on Signals

South bound trains have the right of Track over north bound trains of the same or inferior Class

Derails at Butte Conty R.R. crossing

All trains must get clearance before Leaving Chico or Oroville

Frt. Train No. 51 & 52 will not carry Passengers

A. D. Schindler
General Manager

E. S. Dimmock
General Superintendent

operated over this loop and on the Chico line as far as Thermalito, turning back at that point. Eighteen roundtrips daily were provided by this local line, from 6:38 AM to 12:10 AM. One car was sufficient to provide this service.

When the main line of NE was constructed south from the junction at Tres Vias to Marysville, the Oroville Line was demoted to branch line status. Service to Marysville from Chico was inaugurated on December 3, 1906, and thereafter those traveling to and from Oroville had to transfer at Tres Vias.

Oroville Branch trains usually consisted of two cars---a motor and trailer. Cars assigned were usually 103-105 (built by Cincinnati) or 106-109 (St. Louis products), but in certain instances the Niles cars were operated. After the 1928 consolidation, ex-OA&E equipment was pressed into service; one instance of this occurred in 1937 when motor 1008 ran all one Sunday on the Oroville Branch.

NE decided to use third rail between Tres Vias and the Yuba City-Marysville area when it built south from Tres Vias in 1906. Officials liked the third rail, despite its shock hazard and decided to convert the Chico-Oroville segment to third rail operation; despite the action taken by the section gang who resigned en masse in protest over the changeover, NE laid third rail between Speedway and Thermalito in 1909.

The Oroville Branch was noted for its cornfield meets; a good many "derailments" are noted in company records and most of these , it must be confessed, were caused by sudden and unexpected contact with a car moving in the opposite direction.

An interesting highlight, related by the late George I. Turner, former Superintendent of Equipment, pertains to NE's impressive locomotive-baggage car 1010. When a young lad, he was employed by NE in the Chico Shops as leadman electrician; among other duties he supervised the wiring of the 1010. When the big locomotive was completed and turned over to the Transportation Department for its trial run, it was subjected to a series of severe operating tests. The first of these took place on the Oroville Branch, when 1010 was coupled to 22 cars of gravel at the gravel pit between the Marysville Road and the Feather River bridge; needless to add, the big motor walked away with its heavy train with no strain.

Butte County, noted in those days for its gold mining, had several big dredgers working up and down the Feather River. Whenever one of these dredgers moved up or down the stream at the NE Bridge, part of the wooden approach trestle was removed, cutting the rail line. At such times, a motor car operated each side of the cut segment, and passengers had to walk across the gap on boards laid on the river bed; wooden stairs at either end permitted them to descend and ascend to track level. One such instance occurred in 1912.

The junction point of the Oroville Branch and the main line bore three different names in its history. When the main line to Marysville was completed, the junction was known as "Marysville-Oroville Junction," commonly referred to by the operating crews as "M & O Junction." Shortly thereafter the junction was officially named "Tres Vias," meaning "Three Ways." Later this beautiful name was abolished under the cold practicality of SN days, and the junction became simply and unimaginatively "Oroville Junction."

Originally there was a double wye at Tres Vias; there was the "Little Wye" for passenger trains, and the "Big Wye" for freight trains. The double wye was installed in an Oroville to Marysville direction, or southbound.

A substation was installed at Tres Vias and supplied the power for the Oroville Branch and for the main line. A temporary carbarn was located here in construction days to house work motors; it was of corrugated iron construction and contained facilities to maintain NE's three steam locomotives.

The depression of the early 1930s cut patronage severely on the Oroville Branch and a remedy was found in rebuilding car 107 into a one-man car; whenever this car was laid up for repairs, a two-man car had to be substituted.

On December 10, 1937, disastrous floods besieged all Northern California. The Feather River went on a rampage and washed out a portion of the SN bridge on the Oroville Branch. Motor 107 was marooned in Oroville. The bridge was too severely damaged to warrant repair, and SN substituted its own bus service for the rail operation between Oroville and its main line. Motor 107 was moved via WP freight to Marysville, and thus ended rail passenger service by SN into Oroville. Freight service remained at either end---an SN freight motor was kept at Oroville, switching loads to and from the WP interchange in that city; at the other end, freight service between Oroville Jct. and Thermalito remained.

On April 15, 1954, a diesel locomotive took over the Oroville switching chore, and it was discontinued on July 1st, 1957.

Thus ended the Oroville Branch---NE's original line which once figured prominently in Henry Butters' ambitious plan to encircle almost the whole of the Sacramento Valley.

Car 107, as Train No. 82, poses at Oroville Jct. in September, 1937. Note that one-manning this car consisted of turning it around and installing air operated folding doors. (AA-BB)

Above, the original Northern Electric bridge on the Oroville Branch; this unique structure served for many years before being replaced with a larger span. Cars are a Cincinnati motor, 203, and NE home-built combo 129. (CS)

Below we see the NE's Oroville Station as it was about 1910. Train at left appears to be same as in photo above, while at right is a portion of baggage trailer 90. (BS)

Rampaging flood waters of the Feather River proved stronger than SN's steel rails in late 1937. Above we see
the bridge approach swept away by the force of the current. The bridge remained intact, but was dismantled
when surveys proved it would be excessively costly to rebuild its approaches.   (VS)

Below, motor 107 stranded on the Oroville side on December 11, 1937. The car was then tied up between
Marysville Road and the bridge approach. The sandbags were set up in case of a levee break.   (VS)

Engine 701---"Old Maude"---passes through sugar beet fields on Hamilton Branch. (LLS)

The Hamilton City Branch of Northern Electric operated from Chico to Hamilton City, a distance of 11.37 miles. It operated from the Interurban Depot in Chico over the local car line on Main St., down Fifth St. to the Southern Pacific Depot, where it reached its own trackage. Crossing the S.P., the new line entered private right of way, passing through beet fields to the edge of the Sacramento River. Then came the most novel feature of this line---a pontoon bridge; rail was laid on these floating foundations and the opposite shore was reached safely and extremely cheaply. Once on the far shore, cars continued on private way into the town of Hamilton.

Current collection was by means of third rail after passing the S.P. Depot and tracks; once across the pontoon bridge, overhead trolley began, continuing to the end of the line.

The Hamilton City branch opened on September 12th, 1907, using steam locomotives to haul cars. On October 31st, 1907, the first electric operation began, with interurban car 100 being the official car and carrying on board the numerous civic dignitaries, NE officers, and other persons of importance. Regular equipment serving this line were the two Los Angeles type wooden city cars, Nos. 21 and 22.

The sugar beet factory closed temporarily and service was discontinued; in 1913 and 1914, summer service only was provided. In 1915 the rails were torn up and the right of way abandoned beyond the S.P. Station in Chico.

This line was constantly confronted with flood problems and the recurring times of high water often interfered with the operation of streetcars and beet trains. The pontoon bridge was extremely susceptible to high water and replacing it involved a heavy expense. During such time as the bridge was out, a ferry was operated by means of a cable stretched across the river and operated by electricity. At these times one car ran from Chico to the near bank, its passengers then transferred to the ferry, and once on the far side were loaded aboard one of the single truck cars of the 70 Class to conclude their somewhat perilous journey to Hamilton City.

Standard operating schedules called for four roundtrips daily, and Hamilton City runs bore train numbers from 71 to 78.

During summer months NE ran picnic specials to its picnic grounds located on the Chico side of the river at a shady spot known as Chico Riba Grove. These special cars ran from the Chico Interurban Depot every Sunday and a 25¢ roundtrip fare was charged. Chico streetcars carried banners on their sides advertising this special attraction.

The Hamilton City branch was to have played an important role in NE's plans to gridiron the upper Sacramento Valley. The main line which was planned to traverse the West Side of the valley was to have passed through Hamilton City and would have completed the grand encirclement of the valley. However, Hamilton City remained a branch line which was probably NE's least important feeder.

The Hamilton Branch was constructed to transport employees and sugar beets to the sugar beet refinery in Hamilton City. Freight power was picked from second line motors: 1002, 1003, 1004 and 701. Above, the trestle with pontoon draw on the Sacramento River and below, the Shot Over Inn at Hamilton City, with NE track in foreground. (Both, LLS)

A big interurban has Market St., Colusa, almost to itself in 1919; the view looks west. (LS)

Marysville & Colusa car #10 at the original Colusa Station---exact date unknown. (LLS)

107 and "Sacramento" at Colusa Station on special excursion, June 16, 1940. (AA-AH)

The Colusa Branch

The Colusa Branch was constructed by a company with the impressive title of "The Northern Electric Railway Marysville-Colusa Branch." NE owned all capital stock and the line was operated by NE.

This branch line was single track and was operated by third rail from Heyman (Colusa Jct.) to the city limits of Colusa where overhead catenary began. The line traversed Main St., Colusa, with a double track girder rail line. From the junction to the Colusa terminus was 21.71 miles and the line was proud of the large steel bridge crossing the Sacramento River at Meridian.

Colusa trains operated through to Marysville, where they made close connections with main line trains. Six daily round trips were numbered originally in the low 100 series--- beginning with 100 and ending at 112. Under SN, this was changed to the 200 series.

The Marysville-Colusa operation was inaugurated on June 13, 1913 with a gala celebration in Colusa with everyone for miles around on hand, and as usual the town band took a leading part in the festivities. The first train to operate officially consisted of seven cars: 127, 129, 106, 220, 226, 229, and 90 (the baggage trailer). A second train, also carded as an extra, followed; this consisted of two motors: No. 10 of the Marysville & Colusa, and NE 105. Motor 10 was lettered and numbered for the branch line corporation to comply with franchise requirements in Colusa.

Severe floods in the winter of 1914 washed out a large part of this line when the Sacramento River overflowed. Service was suspended between Meridian and Colusa and a motor boat service was operated on the river; this substitute service was supplanted by a bus until rail service could be resumed.

During severe winter floods in 1937 and 1938 service was again interrupted and again in 1939 and 1940 when heavy rains fell and flood conditions prevailed, resulting in a good part of the right of way being washed out between Tarke and Meridian.

The Colusa branch brought NE a fair amount of both passenger and freight business. Southern Pacific's line into Colusa was a branch operation with infrequent service; SP's station was on the west side of town, while NE cars ran down the main street. It was no surprise then when NE took over the bulk of the passenger business. As for freight, the line served rich orchard lands as well as rice country. Freight was interchanged with the narrow gauge Colusa & Lake Railroad which ran from Colusa over to Sites on the west side of the valley; it was necessary to transfer all freight between the two roads due to difference in track gauges.

At one time river boats plied the Sacramento River and served Colusa with both passenger and freight service.

The Colusa branch was intended to serve as one of the rungs on the ladder system originally projected to gridiron the Sacramento Valley with interurban lines. The never built main line on the west side was to have passed through Colusa with a connection at Sycamore (south of Colusa) over to Marysville; its northern terminus would have been Hamilton, and on the south it would have entered Woodland, there to connect with the Vallejo & Northern. This 1906 plan of NE's had merit, but was scrapped along with other plans of "what might have been."

One major accident occurred on the Colusa branch. It involved motor 100 and took place at Harter. The car, bound for Colusa, hit a heavy truck laden with prunes; the speeding car rammed the truck broadside, resulting in the death of the motorman and the demolishing of the entire front end of the car. The 100 was towed to Chico and assigned to the boneyard at Mulberry Shops; it never was repaired.

A colorful operation over this branch in the early days was "The Trolley League Specials," run during baseball season. Towns along the NE sponsored teams, and the interurban trains served as the official transportation for both teams and rooters. Regular rolling stock was supplemented by flatcars, adorned with benches and railings, hauled by electric motors.

The final curtain rang down on the Colusa branch concurrent with passenger service abandonment on the main line: October 31, 1940.

Building the Butte Slough trestle on the Colusa Branch; note temporary track on ground at right. (LLS)

The Butte Slough trestle in service; car 129. This bridge is still in use. (LLS)

Scene at Sutter City on Colusa Branch---about 1914; this was important shipping center. (LLS)

The loop at Colusa with third rail; overhead trolley was installed here in the 1920s. (LLS)

The Suisun-Vacaville Branch of Northern Electric was located on the west side of the lower Sacramento Valley---in Solano County in the heart of a very rich farming area which produced high grade fruits (which were fancy packed and sent to Eastern markets), and considerable other agricultural and dairy products.

NE's isolated branch, completed divorced from any physical connection with the NE system, was originally part of the ill fated Vallejo & Northern project, which was to have operated from tidewater at Vallejo to Sacramento with a branch to Suisun and another to Vacaville.

Grading work on the Suisun-Vacaville Branch began in what was then known as the Suisun Valley District at Willotta, which was the terminal point of the branch southwest of Fairfield. Willotta derived its name from Will and Lotta, the two children of the Pierce family which owned the land over which this branch ran. This portion was constructed in 1911.

Actual laying of ties and rails did not begin until August, 1912. The first piece of rail was inserted at the Plaza in Suisun on August 14, 1912. By August 30th ties had arrived and work progressed up Main St. towards Fairfield, the adjacent town on the opposite side of the Southern Pacific's main line to Sacramento from Oakland. The interurban crossed the SP at grade and apparently there was no crossing "war" on this occasion. By September 26, 1913, rails were complete to Fairfield, and then work began northward to Vacaville.

Prior to this time, back in 1909, terminal facilities, some grading and a cut had been made in Vallejo. This segment of the V&N never materialized beyond this stage and ultimately was leased by The San Francisco, Vallejo & Napa Valley Railway.

The promoters of the V&N were T. C. Gregory of Suisun, President; Melville Dozier Jr., Chief Engineer; and others associated with the project included George C. Lakie, and C. Francis Kinsey, all of Oakland.

Steam operated trains ran over the line from December 1, 1913 from the old docks down at Suisun Slough over to what was called the Willotta Ranch; this service was for the carrying of freight only.

During the construction period between Fairfield and Cement, where this line had to cross the tracks of the Cement, Tolenas & Tidewater Railroad (a privately owned carrier of The Pacific Portland Cement Company), the V&N's track laying forces installed the crossing under cover of night and much to the surprise of CT&T crews the next morning, who found themselves crossing a foreign road unexpectedly. No violence took place, however, because of this bold move and work progressed steadily onward.

Power distribution was by overhead catenary between Suisun and Fairfield. Outside Fairfield, on what was to be the V&N's ;main line, third rail was used in both directions: down to Willotta and north to Vacaville; just before entering that town, overhead wire took over. Trolley voltage was 600 volts and power was purchased from the PG&E.

The only source of information as to the date of the beginning of passenger service on this branch is found in The Sacramento "Bee" under date of Saturday, May 16, 1914:

"Suisun, May 16th: The Northern Electric Railway Company will establish a passenger service between Suisun and Vacaville tomorrow, making four trips as follows: Leave Suisun at 8:00 and 9:35 AM and 2:35 and 7:25 PM. Returning from Vacaville the car will arrive at Suisun at 9:15 and 11:00 AM and 4:00 and 8:30 PM. Fare each way will be 35¢."

"Regular service, both passenger and freight, has already been established between Suisun and the Willotta Ranch in Suisun Valley for the accommodation of the fruit shipping and persons employed harvesting the fruit crop."

The conclusion to be reached from the above is that regular service commenced on Sunday, May 17, 1914.

Passenger trains had their terminus at the Plaza in Suisun, but freights continued down to the docks at Suisun Slough, where small craft had access to warehouses. There was a small depot in Fairfield and another in Vacaville at Ackerly & Elleson's store. All stops en route were made by flagging down the cars.

As of SN's December 27, 1920 Tariff, passengers on the Suisun-Vacaville Branch had to pay the following fares: One way, Suisun-Fairfield to Vacaville, 42¢; Suisun-Fairfield to Vacaville Jct., 30¢; Vacaville Jct. to Vacaville, 18¢. The trip from Suisun-Fairfield to Vacaville required thirty minutes.

No car barn facilities were provided at any town on this branch line. Whenever equipment needed light repairs, shop men from Mulberry were sent down to Suisun; sometimes members of the train crews would assist the mechanical men making these on-the-spot repairs. Major overhauls required equipment being sent to Chico via the Southern Pacific and NE-SN.

NE usually assigned Cincinnati-built passenger interurban cars 103 and 104 to the Suisun-Vacaville Branch. In 1922, California type city car 22 was rebuilt at Mulberry Shops into a three-compartment one-man car for assignment to this line, and it ran until the final abandonment of passenger service.

Whenever SP did not provide a convenient connecting train to Vacaville via its Elmira junction, passengers on SP trains desiring to go to Vacaville found it convenient to detrain at Suisun-Fairfield, board the waiting NE interurban, and continue their trip. There was no agreement between SP and NE to make this connection, but inasmuch as it was much quicker to travel thusly, many SP passengers learned to make this simple transfer.

Freight service on this branch was performed by the famous 701---"Old Maude," a relic of construction days. Later, in the 1920s, interurban car 106 was converted to a freight switcher complete with footboards and was sent down to this line during the summer fruit rush to assist the 701. Freight interchange with SP took place at the crossing between Suisun and Fairfield.

Passenger receipts declined to a point where they did not even cover the wages of the crew, and the last passenger car ran in 1926, concluding a rather forlorn episode on this "orphan" line, once destined for greatness.

The Suisun-Vacaville Branch was finally linked up with the SN system in 1930 when the connection was built from Vacaville Jct. to Creed, on the old OA&E main line. SP objected strenuously, as was to be expected, but after a long series of hearings, SN obtained the necessary permission to build the link. The first train operated from Creed to the Vacaville Jct. connection on July 15, 1930. No passenger service, other than special excursions, was ever operated on this new trackage. SP's main line was crossed by means of an overhead bridge, thus eliminating an interlocking plant.

With the Suisun-Vacaville Branch now a physically integrated part of its system, SN could and did assign any or all of its freight power to the line, and old 701 was honorably succeeded by considerably heavier and more modern power.

See also chapter on Freight.

Construction train, hauled by the 701---"Old Maude"---at work on the main line of the projected Vallejo & Northern in 1912. Note third rail with men working alongside---height of nonchalance? (LLS)

VALLEJO & NORTHERN

(Based on an article appearing in "Electric Traction Weekly," 1913, by Mr. Rudolph W. Van Norden, in VS Collection.)

The Vallejo & Northern system is now engaged in that most tedious but important part of a project of this sort, the acquiring of rights of way, preliminary field work and final location surveys, purchasing land for terminals and stations, contracting for materials, educational campaigns for people who will benefit from the service, financial arrangements, and the thousand and one other steps which take time before much showing is made.

Aside from the surveying, much work has been already accomplished on the right of way. That section of the line which will eventually form two branches and a connecting link of the main line, but which will soon connect the cities of Suisun and Fairfield with Vacaville, is graded and several miles of track have been laid and a service inaugurated thereon. At the Vallejo terminus, a large amount of the fill has been made for wharves and terminal facilities and a very heavy cut through the city is well on toward completion.

Vallejo, which is to be the seaport terminus of the system, is a city of 11,500 population and is situated on the straits which form an arm of San Francisco Bay known as San Pablo Bay and which lies between the city and Mare Island, location of the United States Navy Yard. This channel is about a quarter of a mile wide and is an ideal protected harbor of sufficient depth for ships of all kinds. The city is on several hills, and extends about two miles along the waterfront. Directly opposite the city is the Navy Yard, largest on the coast and principal source of life for the city. Being the logical terminus for interurban lines radiating north thru the fertile Napa Valley and east tapping the entire Sacramen-

to Valley, this city with the assistance of the electric railway systems promises to add greatly to Vallejo's already important place in the commerce of the state.

The connection between Vallejo and San Francisco is necessarily made by means of water transportation, due to the location of the latter city on a peninsula. There is now in service a line of passenger boats, running about every two hours between these cities. These boats make the run of about 28 miles in one and one-half hours. With this connection the total time from Sacramento to San Francisco will be under three hours, which is at least 15 minutes faster than the fastest train service at present.

The seaport terminus has been acquired at Vallejo and tidelands have been filled in. Here wharves will be erected and cars will connect directly with steamers.

Leaving Vallejo, the V&N passes through a low hill, in a deep cut. This cut is about one-half mile in length and its greatest depth is 35 feet. The total excavation will be about 100,000 cubic yards and of this about half have already been removed. This work has been done largely with a Model 40 Marion steam shovel, the excavated dirt being used to fill in the waterfront, which commences at the end of the cut. Two streets will be carried over the cut on plate girder spans; material for these is now on hand, ready for erection. This cut is the heaviest piece of construction work on the line, although there will be a number of cuts and fills where the line passes through Jamison Canyon.

After passing through the cut the V&N takes a northerly course for about ten miles, paralleling the Napa slough, a branch of the Bay, and the Napa Valley Electric Railway, a single phase AC system, and the Napa Branch of the S.P., both on the east. In this section a large pressed brick manufactory and the Standard Portland Cement Works are reached.

The range of hills between the Napa and Sacramento Valleys which extends beyond Vallejo to the Carquinez Straits has two available passes: the Jamison or Cordelia Canyon and the American Canyon. While the latter lies several miles nearer Vallejo, the former, through which a branch of the S. P. now passes, has been found to present the most favorable, having a maximum grade on the V&N survey of 1.56%.

The road will follow the low hills past Cordelia until it emerges onto the flatlands of the Sacramento Valley. This section is highly cultivated and represents much local wealth and gives promise of heavy freight shipments. Rock quarries are also located nearby.

The V&N will next take a northeasterly course on a tangent and almost perfect grade for a distance of 40 miles to Sacramento. The main line will pass about one mile north of the towns of Suisun and Fairfield, the latter being the county seat of Solano County. A branch line will connect these from the main line, running through Fairfield to a depot on the public plaza in Suisun with a connection to wharves and warehouses. This branch is practically completed and has a length of 2.49 miles. After entering the town it passes down one of the main streets which has macadam pavement; standard city practice is followed: ties of split redwood are laid on a bed of crushed rock in a trench. Rails are of heavy girder type, similar to those used in Sacramento and Woodland. Catenary trolley is used, suspended partly from spans and partly from arms. The section of the main line which has been completed is about five miles long and part, including the Suisun-Fairfield branch, has been in operation for several months for local traffic, being operated by steam. This is, of course, only a temporary expedient to accommodate people on the line.

The branch into Vacaville has a length of 5.33

miles. Vacaville is a picturesque town of about 1,200 population, nestled between hills at the southern end of the Vaca Valley. It is the center of a large fruit growing district and is an important shipping point for many agricultural products.

The line from Vacaville to Suisun will be ready for operation early in the spring. It is peculiarly situated to afford a long-needed and desired passenger service, while the salt water connection at Suisun affords an outlet for a heavy freight business in fruits and farm produce. On that section which will eventually become part of the main line are located the two plants of the Pacific Portland Cement Company with a daily capacity of 8,500 barrels.

The long tangent to Sacramento passes through a rich farming country. Its location is suitable for a high speed suburban service.

There are no more unusual features encountered until the West Sacramento storage yard is reached. Here an unusual opportunity for a freight terminal and transfer yard is afforded on the west side of the Sacramento River. On the east side, which is the waterfront of the city of Sacramento, there is no space available. A large section of a fruit ranch abutting on the river was acquired by condemnation procedings, both for a right of way and for a yard. This yard will have a length of three-quarters of a mile and has an average width as planned of 1,100 feet, and contains 101 acres. Wharves are being built along the river levee to form an extensive waterfront where steamers from all inland navigable points will discharge and load. This yard will be sufficient to store a very large number of cars, and will have warehouses and extensive loading platforms. Cars will be loaded here not only for hauling by interurban systems but for foreign roads as well. This yard is a long needed feature at this point and promises not only

Closeup of "Old Maude" at Suisun in 1916. Men are identified only as "Frank" and "Bert." (LLS)

to build up a large freight business for the interurban lines but to rehabilitate and enlarge a commerce which will be of untold help in the growth of the Sacramento Valley.

Track construction will be similar to that employed on the Woodland Branch, namely: 60 lb. rail of ASCE profile on private right of way, and 116 lb. Trilby rail in city streets. Ties are split redwood, 6" x 8" x8 feet and are spaced 15 to a rail length. Rails are bonded with the usual 400,000 c. m. copper bonds, brazed to the rail. At all cattle crossings, pressed steel Kalamazoo cattle guards will be used, along with a standard type of wooden fence. Ballast will be broken rock having about a 9 inch thickness under the ties, and having a width of 14 feet with a total thickness of 14 inches. About 3,000 cubic yards of ballast is used per mile of track.

The system of electric distribution has not yet been definitely decided upon, but indications are that it will be characteristic of the most modern and efficient practice with the highest type of construction for frequent, high speed service.

Only a small segment of the projected Vallejo & Northern ever offered interurban service; below we reproduce Timetable No. 1 of this segment---Vacaville to Suisun. This has been loaned for reproduction herein by Mr James K. Gibson.

At right, a rare photograph of an SN car in passenger service on this segment. It is car 103 at the Plaza Depot on Main Street in Suisun, the end of the Vacaville-Suisun line. Photo was taken in the early Teens. Note car is lettered "Northern Electric."

(LS)

NORTHERN ELECTRIC RAILWAY
SUISUN VACAVILLE BRANCH

SOUTH BOUND — FIRST CLASS					Capacity of sidings in Freight cars	Distance from Vacaville	TIME TABLE No. 1 — May 17-1914 — STATIONS	Distance from Suisun	Telephone Stations Office Hours and Station Numbers	NORTH BOUND — FIRST CLASS				
9 Suisun Passenger	**7** Suisun Passenger	**5** Suisun Passenger	**3** Suisun Passenger	**1** Suisun Passenger						**2** Vacaville Passenger	**4** Vacaville Passenger	**6** Vacaville Passenger	**8** Vacaville Passenger	**10** Vacaville Passenger
Lv. Sat. Only	Lv. Daily	Lv. Daily	Lv. Daily	Lv. Daily						Ar. Daily	Ar. Daily	Ar. Daily	Ar. Daily	Ar. Sat. Only
11.35 pm	8.00 pm	3.30 pm	10.30 am	8.45 am	10	0.00	Vacaville 6.97	11.13		8.30 am	10.00 am	3.05 pm	7.55 pm	11.30 pm
f 11.50 pm	f 8.15	f 3.45	f 10.45	f 9.00	4	6.97	Armijo 3.34	4.16		f 8.15	f 9.45	f 2.50	f 7.40	f 11.15
f 12.01 am	f 8.25	f 3.55	f 10.55	f 9.10	10	10.31	Fairfield 0.82	0.82		f 8.05	f 9.35	f 2.40	f 7.30	f 11.05
12.05 am	8.30 pm	4.00 pm	11.00 am	9.15 am	15	11.13	Suisun	0.00		8.00 am	9.30 am	2.35 pm	7.25 pm	11.00 pm
Ar. Sun. Only	Ar. Daily	Ar. Daily	Ar. Daily	Ar. Daily						Lv. Daily	Lv. Daily	Lv. Daily	Lv. Daily	Lv. Sat. Only

Northbound trains have absolute right over all southbound trains of the same or inferior class

SPECIAL RULES AND REGULATIONS

f Stop on signal.

All trains must come to full stop at Railroad grade crossings and be flagged over by Conductor or flagman

Where only one time is shown it denotes leaving time.

Trains from Suisun to Vacaville are Northbound.

The Suisun-Fairfield yards include all tracks between the wharf at Suisun and the south switch of the wye north of Fairfield.

The Vacaville yards include all tracks north of a point 600 feet south of the south switch at Vacaville

When running within yard limits all trains must be run under full control and be prepared to stop within the limit of vision

J.B. Rowray
Superintendent.

Extra 101 is seen crossing the Southern Pacific main line at Mikon on a warm Sunday afternoon in mid-June, 1940. The joint SN-SP interlocking tower in background was operated by SP and was equipped with G.R.S. electric magnetic equipment. (VDB)

221 and 101 on the Woodland line near Fremont; August 6, 1939. (AA-AH)

Car 1003 was the regularly assigned Woodland car during the last days of passenger service.   Here the 1003 is seen wyeing in front of the Woodland Opera House in 1940. (AL)

The Woodland Branch

The Woodland Branch (as it was referred to in the beginning) was technically not a branch line at all but was part and parcel of Northern Electric's main line. The very first timetable issued by NE and the Sacramento & Woodland Railroad, dated July 15, 1912, proves this fact. That day saw service operated over the Woodland Branch for the first time open to all the public; all main line trains from Chico ran through Sacramento and had their final terminus at Woodland. At the time there were three southbound and four northbound trains daily which confined themselves to the Woodland Branch only, and there were eight trains in each direction daily which operated through between Chico and Woodland. It is difficult to perceive the reasoning behind NE General Manager Schindler's action in making the Woodland Depot the terminus for all Chico trains, when in the past the main line trains laid over at 8th & J Streets, with a convenient storage yard at hand at 17th & D Sts. The Woodland Depot even had sufficient storage yards in its rear to accommodate these main line cars.

Perhaps this method of operation was intended to tie in with the projected Vallejo & Northern line down to tidewater and San Francisco via a ferry from Vallejo; the Woodland to Vallejo trains could have reached the V&N's main line at Winters. Or perhaps NE contemplated running the trains from Woodland back to Chico via the projected west side line through Hamilton City.

In 1914 this through operation ceased, coincidental with the replacing of Mr. Schindler by a new General Manager, Mr. W. A. McGovern.

The opening day of the Woodland Branch was a gala one in every respect. It was July 4th, 1912, and the already holiday-minded populace rode that inaugural train all day long. NE had not intended to open the line yet, but civic officials and organizations persuaded the railway officials to celebrate the day by prematurely placing their

new line in service. To handle the crowds which presented themselves for the free ride, it was necessary to operate an eight car train, hauled in one direction by locomotive 1010 and in the other by the motor cars running in multiple unit. The leading motor car was "Sacramento & Woodland No. 1" which later became NE 108. Following this train was a second motor carrying officials; this was the 107. Regular passenger service started on July 15, 1912.

Woodland trains wyed in each direction---in front of the Woodland Depot at 2nd & Main Sts., and at 8th & I Streets in Sacramento.

After regular branch line type service began, two trains were operated in opposite directions; this continued to the end, the only NE-SN branch line which enjoyed a second set of equipment.

Under NE, Woodland trains were numbered in the 30 and 40 series; under SN, they were numbered in the 40 and 50 series.

Third rail was the method selected to deliver power to cars; trolley wire was used only in Woodland (from just east of the S.P. crossing) and in Sacramento where at first third rail began on the M St. Bridge (which also had catenary overhead); later the changeover point was changed to a point just west of Broderick station.

Chief feature on the new line was the M St. Bridge in Sacramento, built jointly and owned one-third each by the Sacramento & Woodland Railroad, the Vallejo & Northern, and the City of Sacramento.

When OA&E built into Sacramento's hinterland, it reached downtown Sacramento via the Woodland Branch, over which it obtained trackage rights from Broderick to 3rd & M Streets.

In Woodland, a single track was constructed on 2nd St. for a few blocks either side of Main St., providing two legs of the wye at 2nd & Main. Westward, this 2nd St. line was to have been the route out of Woodland over to Winters and into the rich Pleasant Valley district on the west side. This track was built by Vallejo & Northern, but its lengthly pretensions died with the V&N idea, and it ran but a few blocks down 2nd Street.

Original operation called for a one-car train, which at first was, of course, motor No. 1 of The Sacramento & Woodland Railroad; the Niles type motors of NE also served the line. As business grew, two car trains became the order of the day--- usually a motor and a trailer. In the later days, equipment on the Woodland branch was confined to certain cars, such as 101 and 221 or 223; when the second train operated at times of AM and PM rush traffic its consist usually was 127 and 220. There were exceptions to this rule, of course; noted on this line were 107, 1014, 1006, 1004, 1003 and 1009 at various times.

In the early days of joint operation involving the S&W and the OA&E, Woodland trains had rights over OA&E trains between Broderick and 3rd & M Sts. where OA&E trains turned off to their own station. In numerous instances delays to trains of both companies occurred and as a result complaints were passed between the official families. In some instances the crews involved are reported to have come close to blows, so high ran their feelings over delays. Some of these were due to equipment failure, while others were due to Southern Pacific trains blocking Front & M Sts. in switching moves---still others by bridge openings. At such times a serious problem arose concerning interchange of cars and coach passengers between NE and OA&E at 2nd & M Sts.; such meets were victims of these delays and disrupted schedules from Chico to Oakland. To exchange parlor cars and coach passengers with OA&E, NE was obliged to run its trains through from 8th & K to 2nd & M inasmuch as OA&E had no franchise rights on the uptown streets.

In the waning days of Woodland branch operation there was a veteran conductor from NE days by the name of A. C. Baugh; this colorful, kindly gentleman could truly serve as the archetype of all branch line conductors. He wore his tortoise shell glasses down on the tip of his nose; his pencil was stuck in his cap at a rakish angle; an old, worn coat with a hump in the lower back; some kind of flower in his lapel, usually the gift of one of his appreciative passengers. Extremely courteous and helpful to his passengers, Baugh had a good word for one and all. Occasionally he became slightly irritated when handed a through mainline ticket from San Francisco to Woodland, as he was accustomed to Sacramento-Woodland and way station tickets only. He might even punch the main line return portion of the ticket with the customary three punch marks. On one hot Sunday afternoon he was overhead saying: "I always liked the Niles cars better than those others because you can always get a nice cross ventilation inside the car by opening the clerestory windows." How true that was! In spite of his colorful appearance, Baugh was respected and admired by his regular passengers and was greatly missed when service came to an end.

Only one serious accident marred the safety record of the Woodland branch. Motor 1004 in October 1938 collided at speed with a rice truck, jumped the rails and tipped over on its right side. No one was killed and but a few were injured, but it spelled doom for the car which was hauled to Chico and set out in the boneyard of Mulberry Shops, never to run again.

On March 1, 1940 a severe service cut took place which reduced the eight daily roundtrips to but four, with no service whatsoever on Sundays and holidays. The resulting inconvenience and hardship to passengers who depended completely on the interurbans for transportation resulted in the resumption of Sunday and holiday service on May 19, 1940 with three round trips, all carded as Extras. The four weekday round trips were retained until abandonment of passenger service.

Soon afterwards, Woodland found itself bereft forever of the fine interurban trains which had served it faithfully for 28 long years. October 31, 1940 saw the final train leave Woodland Station at 6:30 PM for Sacramento as a deadhead; the car was 1009. The following day Greyhound busses appeared on the scene, operating three daily round trips.

The Woodland storage yard as it appeared about 1914; at extreme right is NE Depot. Cars are 105 at left, 221 in center, and 200 in center distance. (Western Pacific Photo)

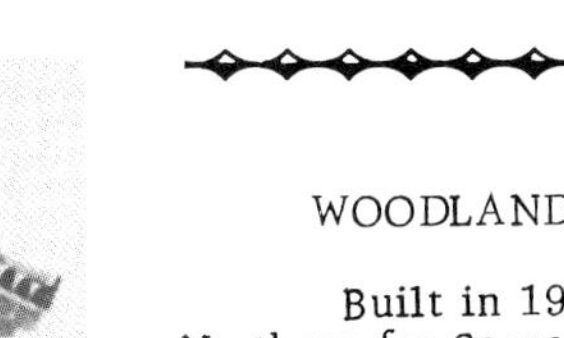

WOODLAND DEPOT

Built in 1912 by Vallejo & Northern for Sacramento & Woodland, this handsome structure was of modified Mission architecture, with gravel stucco finish. Located at Main & 2nd, the property ran along 2nd for 418 feet with width of 113 feet, containing 8 tracks having a capacity of 30 cars.

The main line entered the station at the corner and took a diagonal course through the building in a sweeping curve to the inside property line. To the left as a car entered were the baggage and express rooms, while on the right was the ticket office; behind it and opening on the arcade was a waiting room, with lavatories and store rooms at the extreme rear. This arcade was paved with square red tile.

Sacramento Northern is no longer prominent in Woodland life, but a portion of this attractive depot still stands, remodeled for business use.

In the photo at left, car 129 of NE, its light orange color reflecting the hot sunlight, is seen in the arcade of the Woodland Station.

Cars wyed in the street in front of the station; see map.

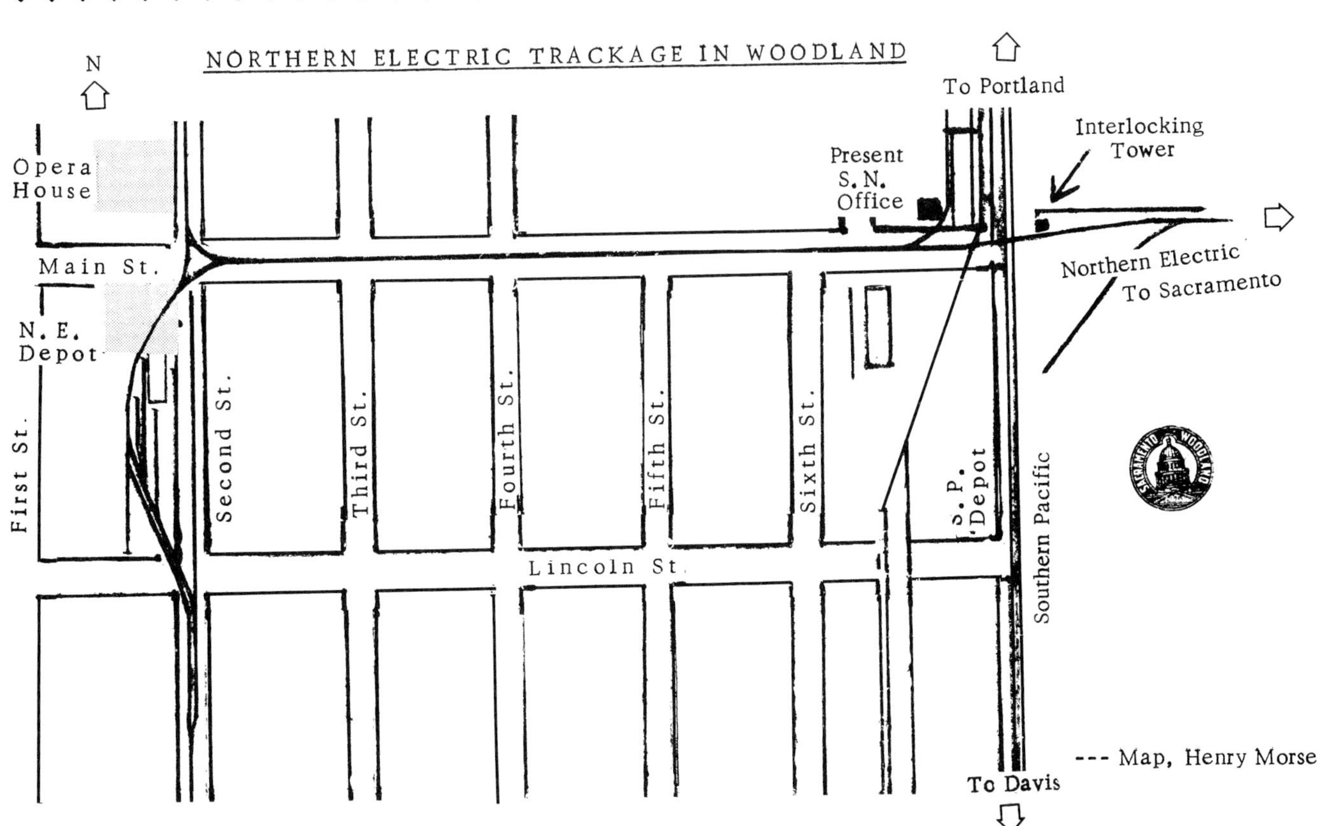

Woodland train No. 13, car 103, is seen in Sacramento outbound on M St. between 7th and 8th Streets about 1914; the California State Capitol looms in background.   (LLS)

(The following description of the Woodland Branch is based on an article appearing in "The Electric Traction Weekly," 1913, by noted author Rudolph W. Van Norden, and supplied by Mr. Vernon J. Sappers.)

The Sacramento & Woodland is the first section built of The Vallejo & Northern Railway and will eventually be a branch of the main line. The road is leased and operated by The Northern Electric Company, and arrangements are contemplated between that company and the Vallejo & Northern to operate in close harmony, the interests behind both roads being thoroughly friendly. Rolling stock, track specifications, etc., of the Sacramento & Woodland follow closely the standards adopted by the Northern Electric and through trains on the latter road are run through to Woodland, making the latter city and the city of Chico the southern and northern terminals at present.

Beginning at the terminus of the NE at the depot at 8th & J Sts., Sacramento, the Woodland line goes south on 8th St. to M St. (Capitol Avenue), thence west on M St. to the river, where after crossing the levee it enters a steel drawbridge and crosses the river.

After crossing the river, this line is carried on a high fill in order to maintain the grade for about one mile, then it curves to the north and crosses the main line of the S. P. at Mikon; it then follows the west bank of the Sacramento River in a general direction to Elkhorn. This part of the line is very picturesque, passing through miles of hop vines and orchards of fruit trees, all with a backdrop of giant cottonwoods and elms.

At Elkhorn the line follows the top of the levee for a mile or so, and then turns to the west, crossing the backland or "overflow" on a pile trestle until the ground grade has reached an altitude which is above the river overflow line. This overflow is the lowest part of the Sacramento Valley and extends a hundred miles north and south; during winter months water over a certain height is spilled over easements built for that purpose and is allowed to flow down this side channel to the delta, thus relieving levees further down the river. During much of the year this overflow land is completely dry.

The line from Elkhorn to Woodland is on a tangent and after the pile trestle is passed there is no other engineering problem, the ground being flat and almost level.

Woodland, the county seat of Yolo County, is entered from the east, and the third rail ends at the edge of town and a catenary trolley is used within the city. The line follows Main St. to the center of the business district and ends in a commodious depot.

Power was supplied by three substations: (1) PG&E's Sacramento substation, PG&E's Woodland substation, and a NE portable substation at Elkhorn, approximately half way. This power is supplied at 600 volts direct current, which will be used for the time being; when the Vallejo & Northern's main line is completed, a decision will be made as to the current pressure to be used by that company. Alternating current at 60,000 volts high tension is supplied to the Woodland substation from two PG&E high tensionlines, and the portable substation at Elkhorn is fed AC current from the Woodland substation at a pressure of 11,000 volts.

As for rolling stock, this road being operated under lease by the NE which sends all of its through trains from Chico and Sacramento over this line has need of but few cars of its own. At present the Woodland line has but one passenger motor and several construction and freight cars. The passenger car was built by NE at its Chico shops, and is similar to the latest cars of this system. It has a length of 50 feet and weighs fully equipped 83,400 lbs. It is divided into baggage, smoking and passenger compartments. The interior finish is inlaid Honduras mahogany, with ebony and white holly trim. The ceiling is veneered, with enclosed tungsten lamps. There are also tungsten side reading lights. Seats are blue plush in the passenger section and leather in the smoker. Ample toilet facilities are provided. Windows are square and large, the whole effect giving an air of restfulness and cheerfulness. A radial draft gear has been used and has been found to be efficient. Trucks are equipped with 36 inch wheels and 90 hp motors. The car body is given a high finish in a light orange color. This car makes runs between the runs of the regular NE trains---making a total of eleven trains daily each way. Scheduled running time is 35 minutes.

The Woodland Branch required some heavy construction in order to maintain sufficiently high grade above possible flooding. As a general rule, NE was unable to build its track atop levees, which follow the Sacramento River for miles, because levees of necessity had to follow the meanderings of the river. Therefore it was necessary to acquire much private right of way generally paralleling the river and build thereon high fills or even long stretches of trestle work.

In the case of the Woodland Branch, after crossing the river at Sacramento, the line ran atop a high fill for about a mile. This fill at some points had a height of 20 feet and served not only to maintain grade but to protect from overflow in case of a levee break and added the extra protection to property through which the line passed. This embankment had a top width of 16 feet, on which rested a ballast of broken rock of about a 9 inch thickness; width of ballast was 14 feet and total thickness was about 14 inches. 3,000 cubic yards were used to the mile. Total volume of fill between the river crossing and the Elkhorn trestle was 1,500,000 cubic yards, entirely earth and done by contract at an average cost of 20¢ per cubic yard.

The long Elkhorn trestle was about 20 feet high and had a length of 8,000 feet; it was supported on 8-pile bents and followed the standard NE trestle design.

The Woodland Branch from the west end of the Elkhorn trestle to Woodland had no engineering problems, and ordinary ditch and fill construction was used.

Photos on this page show well the way NE met the problem of maintaining elevation. Above we see SN 101 & trailer at Marty on June 9, 1940. Note that every tenth tie is 10 feet long to carry the third rail. The third rail is a special 48-lb. section of high carbon steel, its resistance being considerably lower than the running rails. Third rail chairs are similar to those used by NE and were designed by NE's electrical engineer, Mr. J. Paulding Edwards. They consist of a malleable iron clamp seat for the rail which is rested upon an impregnated wood insulator block which in turn is supported by a malleable iron base.   (AA-AH)

At left, 101 is atop the fill at Lovdal on July 4, 1940. (AA-BB)

Woodland train No. 48, cars 101 and 221, prepares to leave M St., Sacramento, for the Tower Bridge and West Sacramento in this September 1937 photo.   (AA-BB)

The same train and same cars passes over the junction with the SN's line to Oakland at Broderick.   Overhead trolley ended a short distance beyond this point.   (CS)

Car 21 at the Swanston terminus, heading back to Sacramento.   Swanston packing house in background.   (Burkett)

The Swanston Branch

This short branch line was built in 1913 by NE after it obtained a franchise originally granted to The Sacramento & Eastern Railroad, incorporated in California on November 28, 1911 with an authorized capital stock of $1,000,000. Due to incomplete records, it is impossible to state whether or not it was this company or The Sacramento-Folsom Electric Railway Company which was intended to construct a branch line from the NE main line at Globe, near Sacramento, to Folsom, 23 miles east. At any rate, NE obtained the rights and franchises of both the above mentioned railway companies on February 26, 1913, and construction of the proposed Folsom branch got no further than Swanston, 4.3 miles from Globe.

The branch was built with overhead catenary and the track construction was to NE standards. This line passed thru North Sacramento which at that time was under development with few houses then erected. The North Sacramento Land Company, developing the area, entered into an agreement with NE whereby passenger service was subsidized by the real estate company in order to attract settlers. This agreement took the form of a firm committment by the developers to re-imburse NE for any deficits incurred by passenger operations.

Service was inaugurated over the Swanston Line some time in 1914, with cars operating from NE's Sacramento Depot at 8th & J Sts. to Swanston, making eight roundtrips per day. These trains were second class on the timetable, and cars 21 and 22, rebuilt for suburban service were on the line during most of the years; however, main line interurbans got onto the Swanston Line in regular service at times. The dispatchers' sheets show that from time to time cars 100, 108, 125, 201 and others were used to Swanston when other cars were unavailable.

In 1932 dwindling traffic reduced passenger trips to six daily, and the following year all passenger service ceased, due to the real estate company's deciding to discontinue all reimbursements.

Several industries had located along this line and were dependable freight producers, so the Swanston Line continued in service and today it sees freight trains rumble over it at regular intervals.

EARLY CARS IN CHICO

Chico Electric Railway Company operated two types of cars: the Los Angeles type of California car---Nos. 21 and 22 (above), and open cross bench cars 50 & 51 (right).   (Both, AA-AH)

Northern Electric bought four single truck California type cars from San Francisco; the 72 (below) illustrates this type.   Two of these were ultimately sold to The Union Traction Company of Santa Cruz and the other two were scrapped at Chico.   In this photo, the car was standing at 5th & Broadway, Chico.
(LLS)

Chapter 6

Street Car Lines

Chico Local Lines

The Chico Electric Railway Company was the first operating electric street railway system to be acquired by The Northern Electric Railway and became the nucleus of NE's interurban operations in the Sacramento Valley.

Chico Electric was incorporated on August 12, 1904, by The Diamond Match Company of Chico. A franchise was granted to Mr. Frank M. Clough who was the manager of the Diamond Match plant, and he served also as manager of the street railway.

Construction began on November 5, 1904, by track maintenance crews of The Butte County Railroad, which was a steam railroad owned and operated by Diamond Match and which ran between Chico and Sterling City hauling lumber. Mr. Charles Moran, in charge of Butte County Railroad's roadway department, directed the track layers.

A line operated from Chico Vecino from "Sandy Gulch" (the Lindo Chennel on the northerly limits of town) down the Esplanade to Main Street, through the heart of Chico on Main Street to Fifth St., which it traversed for one block to Broadway; on Broadway out to Del Norte St. which was later changed to 16th St. It turned off 16th St. easterly onto Del Norte and ran over to Mulberry St., then via Mulberry St. to 22nd St., terminating in an area known as "Chapmantown."

A second line turned off Main St. at 2nd St. and ran down 2nd to Chestnut St., turned onto Chestnut and traversed that thoroughfare to the Diamond Match Company's plant in the Barber Park area.

Still a third line turned off Main St. at Fifth St., running down 5th to the Southern Pacific Depot. There was a turnoff from Fifth onto Broadway, making a physical connection with the Broadway line.

The Diamond Match Company held a franchise on 9th St. from the easterly part of town via 9th St. to the site of its main plant. This was not a part of the streetcar system, but was used to transport logs from the terminus of the company's flume, east of town, through town to the factory. Logs were taken from the forty-mile flume, loaded onto flat cars which were then hauled by horses through Chico. Northern Electric later electrified this line and it became NE's freight transfer line to Southern Pacific. NE then abandoned that portion of the 9th St. line east of Main St.

When Northern Electric acquired Chico Electric Railway, most of the original lines in Chico were abandoned. The line on 2nd St. and Chestnut St. to the Diamond Match plant was abandoned, as was also the line to Chapmantown. However, trackage on Broadway between 5th St. and Del Norte was retained for an undetermined number of years, as was also the line on Del Norte between Broadway and Park Avenue, where a turnout towards Main St. in downtown Chico was installed---this connection being known as "Ashby Junction."

A new line was laid on Main St. from 5th St. to Little Chico Creek, where Main St. became Park Ave. This line then ran on Park Ave. to Mulberry, located at the corner of Park Ave. and 20th St., the location of the car shops. The streetcars then ran from Sandy Gulch down the Esplanade to Main St., to 9th St., over a small bridge crossing Little Chico Creek, Park Ave. to 20th, where it terminated. During morning and evening rush hours, streetcars turned off Park Ave. at 16th St. (Ashby Jct.) and ran down 16th St. to the Diamond Match plant.

Service was also operated from 5th & Main over 5th St. and Broadway to 16th St. to the Barber Baseball Park, at the site of the Diamond Match plant. Service on this line was discontinued at an unknown date. The Chico Vecino line remained in service until the final date of abandonment. Streetcar service from 5th & Main down 5th to the Southern Pacific Depot was discontinued and this line became part of the Hamilton City line and service was provided by cars operating on this line under their carded schedule.

Getting back to The Chico Electric Railway Company: Its carbarn and substation were located at the Diamond Match plant. The lines operated on 600 volts DC, and aggregated about 5.5 miles in length. The first cars were Nos. 21 and 22 which were of the Los Angeles Standard type of California car; they originally had the ratchet type of hand brake. Two more cars were soon purchased, Nos. 50 and 51; these were double truck open bench cars. These four cars comprised the entire roster of The Chico Electric Railway Company. Fare was 5¢, the cars were operated by two man crews with a ten hour day, and service was provided from six AM to eleven PM daily. As its first superintendent, Chico Electric had Mr. E. S. Dimmock and among its first crews were motorman B. R. Kinnicutt, conductor Crum, motorman Black and Motorman W. W. Nelson, a former Pacific Electric man who later became traveling motorman for NE. Night crews in those early days were armed with guns, just in case some bandit might try to take over the company's receipts which were turned in the following morning.

In November, 1905, Northern Electric purchased Chico Electric Railway Company from Diamond Match Company. Alterations were inevitably made under the new ownership: one fourth of the Chico trackage was abandoned and the remainder rebuilt; the line on Main St. was double tracked between First and Ninth Streets; four single truck California type cars were purchased from The United Railroads of San Francisco and were operated in Chico in their original URR paint and numbers until finally shopped, emerging therefrom with new paint and numbers: NE 70, 71, 72 and 73.

From 1906 until 1918 things in Chico remained quiet, but 1918 brought several major changes. First of all, there was a new company name: Sacramento Northern Railroad. Then two new Birneys were purchased and assigned to Chico, numbers 60 and 61. Entering service in October of that year, they brought the one man safety car to Chico, and were given the usual standard Pullman green paint with gold lettering and numbers. With the coming of the Birneys, the bulk of the local lines were abandoned; only the original route from Vecino to Mulberry and the 16th St. branch to Diamond Match Co. were retained; trips to the Diamond Match plant were operated only morning and evening to accommodate workers there.

The new Birneys' debut was spoiled when each in turn tangled at Ashby Junction with interurban car 107; each collision (both occurring within a two week period) required shopping of the little cars.

SN continued operating the Chico local service at a loss for many years. In 1930 the service was cut from fifteen minute headway to thirty. In the 1940s service was reduced even more drastically: on Sundays and holidays the little cars ran for but two hours in the morning and two hours in the afternoon. After the abandonment of interurban passenger service in October, 1940, franchise requirements compelled the company to continue the local streetcar service in order to conduct freight operations through Chico.

Despite the recurring deficits, SN did not increase the traditional 5¢ fare. During World War II, traffic increased greatly for the duration. However, by 1947 SN sought abandonment of the city service and its franchise was amended to permit such action. Very little opposition to the abandonment was voiced by the local citizenry, and approval of the petition was obtained. On December 15, 1947, the last car ran---car 62---which tied up at Mulberry at seven o'clock that evening. The motorman on that occasion was Mr. George C. Rutan, who was a veteran operator and who had previously operated streetcars in Marysville-Yuba City service. Among the Chico citizens making that last ride were Dr. Dan H. Moulton, company physician, who had ridden the first Chico streetcar in 1904, and Mrs. John Maxwell who was also a "first and last" rider.

The abandonment marked the end of Birney operation and the final 5¢ fare in California. The substitute service was offered by another company whose busses subsequently ceased operation due to lack of business.

(Above) Traffic at 5th & Broadway, Chico, was extremely light on the particular day in 1912 on which the above photo was taken. Cars 25 and 21 are seen with identical bodies---but there the resemblance ends. 25 has the St. Louis 47 streetcar trucks, but 21 has been upgraded to Brill 27Es for suburban service---it was then running on the Hamilton City line. (RB)

Below) 'Twas a wintry day, that New Year's Day of 1939, when roller-bearing Birney 60 was snapped at Chico Vecino. (CS)

(Above) SN's original Birney, No. 60, shown on the Esplanade in Chico near the end of the line at Vecino. (VS)

(Right) Birney 62 on Main St. at the City Plaza on the last day of service, December 15, 1947. (VS)

(Below) SN 50, shown in its final condition; the car is in front of Mulberry carbarn in this photo. 50 and 51 were originally open cars with cross benches and in 1910 were partially enclosed; ultimately both were enclosed as seen here. (VS)

Two early views of the Northern Electric's Feather River Bridge. Above, a 1914 scene, with car 50 or 51 crossing. (LS)

Below, a 1912 photo catches a car of the 21 Class at the mid point. (LS)

Perhaps it was the 4th of July---Marysville's D Street was in festive holiday attire back in
1914 when this photo was taken. Right in the foreground was NE's car 21 with a similar car
pulled up right behind. (LS)

Mule cars operated by The Marysville & Yuba City Street Railway provided the first street railway service between the towns of Marysville and Yuba City. This company was incorporated on August 17, 1889, and comprised 3.2 miles of 3'6" gauge track connecting the two towns. There were five cars, numbered 1 to 5. Cars 1 and 2 were of the open bench type with open platforms at each end; cars 3, 4 and 5 were closed with open platforms at each end. All cars were built by Holt Brothers in Stockton, California, in 1889.

The carhouse was located in Marysville on Second St. between C and D Streets and housed two tracks. This barn was vacated and disposed of at an early date; thereafter the cars were stored in the open in the Marysville passenger car yard where a pit track was provided for inspection and light servicing.

Operation commenced in late 1889, operating via the following route: Starting at the Southern Pacific Depot in Marysville, cars ran via 6th & A Streets along Sixth to C St., over C to Second, along Second one block to D St., thence on D to Fifth St., along Fifth to the Feather River which was crossed on an old covered bridge. Entering Yuba City, cars ran along Bridge (later B) St. to Plumas St., turned left on Plumas and thence to the canneries; from here cars turned on to A St. to what is now known as "Old" Yuba City, then the main part of town and the present location of the Sutter County Courthouse and other public buildings. The route then paralleled the levee and up a grade to the top of the levee,

returning to Marysville via the same bridge, located at a considerably lower level than the subsequently constructed Northern Electric bridge.

The entire line was constructed of very light rail--- about thirty pounds.

The fare from one town to the other was five cents, and thirty minute headway was maintained.

The Northern Electric acquired this company on July 12, 1906 and proceeded to rebuild the system for electric operation. Electric trolley cars began operating in 1907. The route remained much the same as before, with the exception that streetcar service was extended out along the main line from Plumas St. along private right of way to Cooper Ave., later known as City Limit, where trolley wire ended and the third rail began. On May 16, 1913, after much bickering with Marysville city officials, the local line was cut back to a new terminus at 5th & C Sts.; service between this point and the Southern Pacific Depot was abandoned due to light patronage.

NE rebuilt the local line to standard gauge with considerably heavier rails. The first type of cars assigned were Nos. 21 and 22, wooden California cars of the Los Angeles type. These were replaced with cars 50 and 51. Cars 25, 26, 27 and 28 also served the line until the coming of Birney safety cars in later years.

On November 18, 1912, a disastrous collision occurred involving a local car, No. 21, and locomotive 1002 midway on the Feather River Bridge. The head-on meet sent the trolley car crashing down into the dry bed of the river, killing several passengers and injuring many more.

In 1924 cars 50 and 51 were taken out of service for rebuilding into one-man cars; they were temporarily replaced by cars 27 and 28, of the Elverta "Scoot" type. Newspapers reported that would-be passengers allowed the Scoots to pass them up because they thought they were interurban cars, not being used to riding closed cars on the local line.

Streetcar service between Marysville and Yuba City outlasted the interurbans. However, on February 16, 1942, SN was permitted to abandon this service---one of the few rail abandonments allowed during World War II. The cars were replaced by busses operated by a local company whose service proved to be inadequate and unreliable. Schedules were drastically cut, and after the war ended the operation passed through the hands of several operators, none of whom could show a profit.

The Marysville-Yuba City local line was the oldest of all lines comprising the Northern Electric, and was the second local system to be abandoned by Sacramento Northern.

(Left) One of the mule cars which served for many years as the chief means of public transportation between Marysville and Yuba City. The year, 1889.   (WP)

(Below) Car 50 crossing the Feather River Bridge; date unknown. (LLS)

A pair of Birneys bid farewell to the Yuba City SN Station on February 15, 1942. Despite the war and its travel emergencies, SN obtained permission to abandon this busy little local line to Marysville. One of the succeeding busses may be seen alongside the station in this last day photo. (JCW)

Birney 68 approaches the 2nd St. stop in Yuba City with a prospective passenger waiting to entrolley. The year was 1941 and the Birney was enjoying the high iron of the main line. (AL)

8th & J Sts., Sacramento, in two eras: Above, as the intersection looked in 1912 when the Northern Electric Depot stood at this location; cars 27 and 228 are seen ready to depart on their respective runs to McKinley Park and Chico. Below, a 1936 view, with an SN Birney drawn up ahead of a CCT car;
(Upper, LLS; lower, CS)

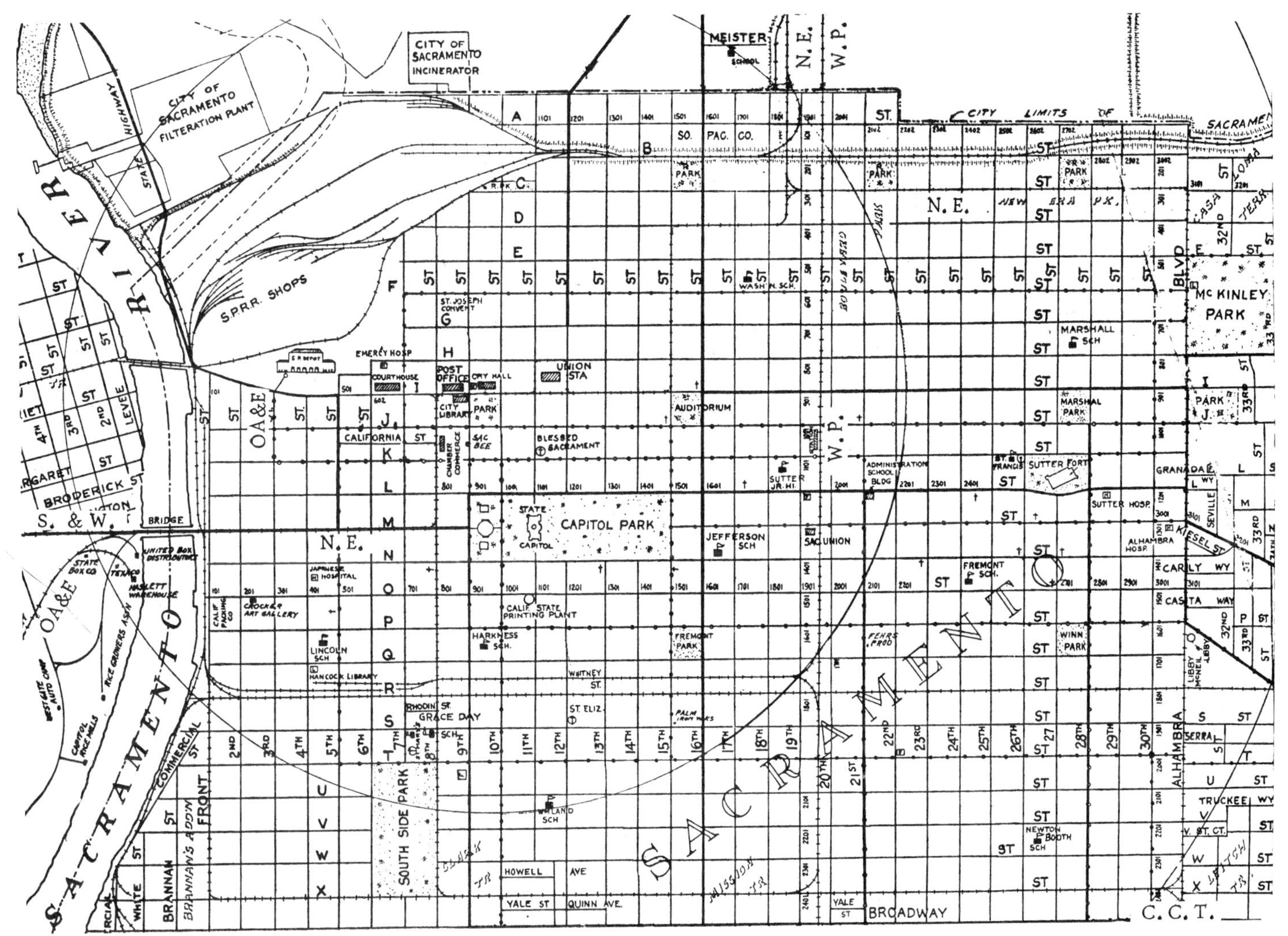

Sacramento Local Lines

Northern Electric applied for a franchise to operate street car service in Sacramento on August 7, 1906 as an amendment to its original franchise which authorized interurban service. The route of this first local line was as follows: Starting at 8th & J Sts., thence via 8th to I St., out I to 14th, over 14th to D, then on private right of way between 18th and 19th to C St., and out C to 30th, the terminus. Subsequently the route was extended out Alhambra Blvd. to McKinley Park, where a new terminus was established at M St. Operation over the original portion of this local line commenced sometime in October of 1907.

Sacramento already had a streetcar system operated by The Sacramento Electric, Gas & Railway Company (later to become The Pacific Gas & Electric Company); this company offered no objections to NE's entering the field of local electric railway operation, probably because NE's line would not serve the part of town wherein the local company was enjoying dominance.

Subsequent to NE's opening its local line The Central California Traction Company (operating the Sacramento-Stockton interurban line) established streetcar service out 8th St. and X St. to Alhambra Blvd., thence over to 2nd Ave., to Stockton Blvd. and out to Colonial Heights. Thus California's capital city had the distinction of being provided electric traction by three separate operating companies.

The first cars NE placed in service on its local line were Nos. 26 and 27 of the Los Angeles Standard type. The local fare was five cents and transfers were issued to the other companies' local routes.

In the meantime The Vallejo & Northern Railroad decided to exercise its franchise in Sacramento and on November 15th, 1911, began its street car service over this route: Starting at the City Wharf at the foot of M St. over M to 8th, on 8th to I, out I to 19th, over 19th to J and ending at the Western Pacific Depot. This was the only passenger service ever to be operated by the Vallejo & Northern, and it also exchanged transfers with the other local streetcar companies. To operate this line, a Los Angeles Standard type car was ordered from St. Louis Car Company; it was lettered "Vallejo & Northern Railroad" and it was No. 1 of that company; it was painted with Pullman green and gold letters. In 1914 the V&N local line was consolidated with NE's local line and the trackage between 14th & I and 19th & J was abandoned; NE cars extended their route beyond 8th & J down to the City Wharf at M & Front Sts. Car No. 1 of V&N was taken into the NE Shops and renumbered NE No. 28 and repainted in the NE orange on December 2, 1914.

In 1924 the L.A. type cars were replaced by Birneys, purchased second hand from The San Diego Electric Railway with numbers from 62 to 68; some of these were assigned also to the Marysville-Yuba City local service. Two additional Birneys were later purchased from The San Jose Railroads and numbered 69 and 70 and used on SN city lines.

Birney operation in Sacramento continued through the intervening years until 1943 when the SN sold its Sacramento local line to Sacramento City Lines, a National City Lines operation which had previously purchased the PG&E local lines. City Lines also purchased the local line of the CCT and this was combined with the former SN local line with CCT cars being used. Final abandonment took place on

THE WEST SIDE RAILROAD COMPANY

THE WEST SACRAMENTO ELECTRIC RAILROAD

The West Side Railroad Company and The West Sacramento Electric Railroad Company were two corporations organized by The West Sacramento Company, which owned 7,000 acres of land on the west side of the Sacramento River; the property was bounded by the Southern Pacific main line on the north, and Broderick on the south and by the river itself, along which the land extended for seven miles along the levee. The land was developed for industrial and agricultural use, with a city subdivision included opposite Sacramento of 240 acres. This development was originally known as "West Sacramento City." To serve its transportation needs, The West Sacramento Company on September 5, 1911, organized an electric street railway company known as "The West Side Railroad Company."

The purpose of The West Side Railroad Company was to provide electric railway service from Sacramento to West Sacramento. The line was built by Northern Electric to its standards and by its crews, and it operated the service. NE also had the privilege of operating freight service and switching over the line. Service commenced on Sunday, December 7, 1913, with NE car No. 26 assigned. Thirty minute service was maintained from 6:30 AM to 9:45 PM daily, and a five cent fare was charged.

The route traversed was as follows: From 8th & J Sts. in Sacramento via 8th, M, over the river on the M St. Bridge, over the line of the Sacramento & Woodland RR. to Broderick where this line switched onto OA&E trackage for several hundred feet before finally arriving onto its own trackage which was on private right of way, proceeding thereon to its terminus in West Sacramento.

In March, 1914, this line was consolidated with NE's own local line with through service provided from West Sacramento to C and 31st.

Operational difficulties soon arose with OA&E on the track jointly operated. The local cars invariably interfered with the OA&E interurban trains, causing delays. NE issued rules which ordered its crews to stop at either end of the joint track, look both ways, and give OA&E trains the right of way if such train were seen approaching.

One accident of note is chalked up against this operation. NE interurban car No. 108---an unusual car to be assigned to this local service and undoubtedly filling in for a streetcar in the shops---split the switch one night at 2nd & M Sts., rolled into the freight depot trackage and collided with OA&E motor No. 106. This occurred on January 21, 1918 and was probably caused by a combination of excessive speed and carelessness in operating over a facing point switch without observing the position of the switch tongue. Apparently there were no injuries except to 108 which could hardly have picked a more formidable opponent than OA&E's mighty passenger and freight locomotive.

Turning now to the second company formed by The West Sacramento Company---The West Side Railroad Company: This company was incorporated on August 31, 1911 and was to operate a belt line running north and south on the west bank of the Sacramento River as far as the town of Rio Vista. This was to be an extension of the West Sacramento street car line. But six hundred feet of track were actually laid beyond West Sacramento Station, and this was ultimately acquired by NE and connected to the OA&E main line. Some grading was done westerly but was given up by the West Side Railroad. This extension possibly could have been doomed by the appearance of the OA&E and the Vallejo & Northern. The West Side Railroad was dissolved as a corporation on March 11, 1936.

The West Side Electric continued under the operation of NE and deficits in conducting the passenger service were met by the West Sacramento Company until 1924, when it was decided to abandon the service. This occurred on March 1st of that year. Legal dissolution of the West Side Electric took place on September 6, 1915, however, and service subsequent to that date was under the aegis of NE-SN.

A fire caused this photo to be taken. A 1918 view of M St., Sacramento, between Front and 2nd Sts., showing car 22 headed for West Sacramento, running on the West Sacramento Electric Ry. Note joint freight station of SN and CCT. (RB)

Looking up M St. from Front St., Sacramento, in 1911, before the opening of the M St. Bridge. A Vallejo & Northern streetcar is seen at its then terminus. (LLS)

Birney 62 on C St., Sacramento, 1940. (VS)

SN Birneys in Sacramento were stored at the 17th St. Yards; here 62 is seen overwhelmed by locomotives in 1940. (CS)

West Sacramento Depot, terminal point in West Sacramento of the streetcar line which operated between West Sacramento and 8th & J Sts. in uptown Sacramento.   Here is car 26, usually used on this run.   This service was subsidized by The West Sacramento Land Company. (VS)

Below, an early day view of the M St. Bridge, Sacramento, over which the West Sacramento streetcar line ran.   This bridge served well for about twenty five years, during which time Sacramento's population expanded from 45,000 to 100,000 and auto traffic increased 700% in volume and 500% in speed, making this bridge with its nine-foot roadways cantilevered out from the trusses on either side not only inadequate but dangerous as well. (WP)

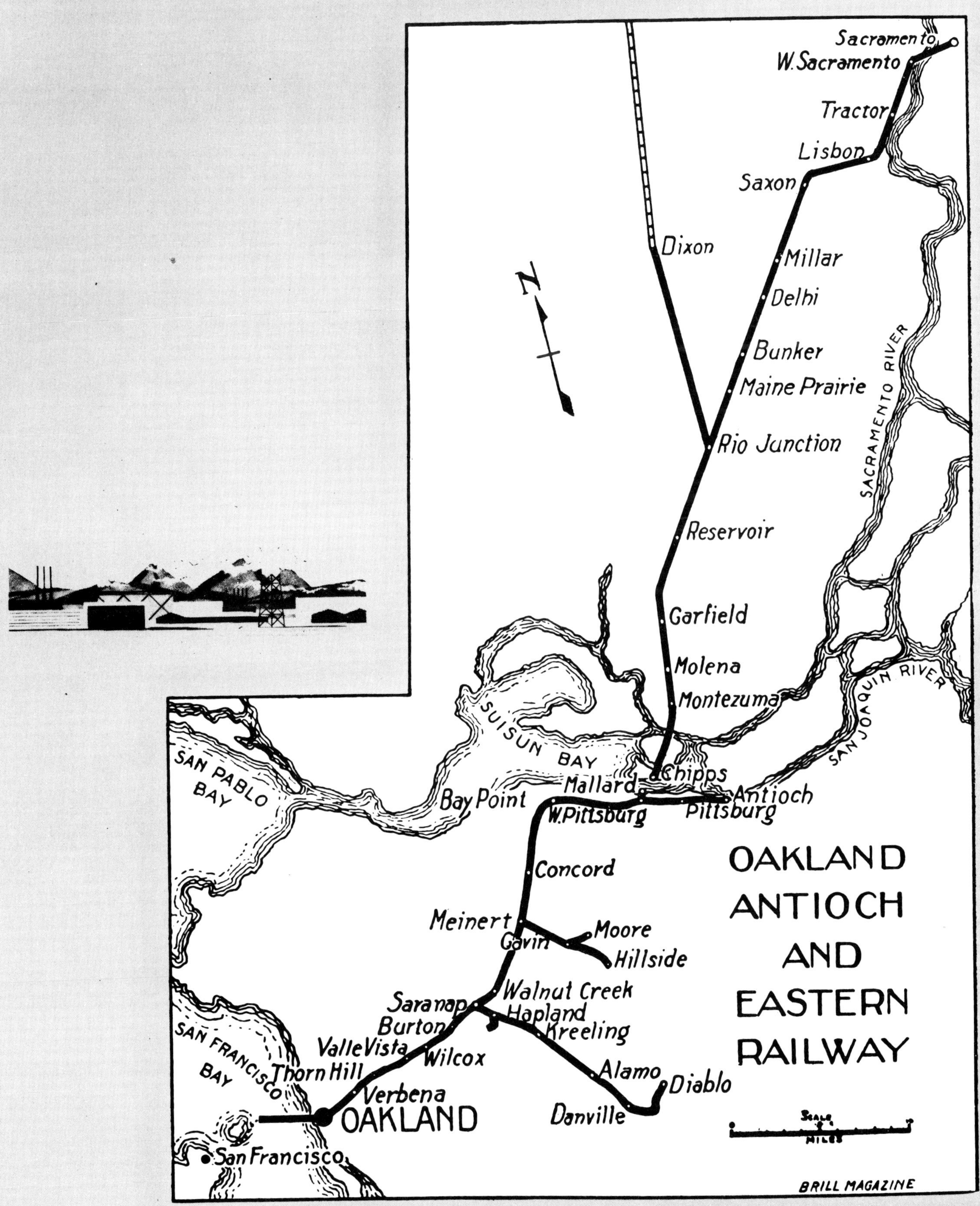
Sacramento
W. Sacramento
Tractor
Lisbon
Saxon
Dixon
Millar
Delhi
Bunker
Maine Prairie
SACRAMENTO RIVER
N
Rio Junction
Reservoir
Garfield
Molena
Montezuma
SAN JOAQUIN RIVER
SUISUN BAY
SAN PABLO BAY
Chipps
Mallard
Bay Point
Antioch
W. Pittsburg
Pittsburg
Concord
Meinert
Moore
Gavin
Hillside
Walnut Creek
Saranap
Hopland
Burton
Kreeling
ValleVista
Wilcox
Thorn Hill
Alamo
Diablo
SAN FRANCISCO BAY
Verbena
OAKLAND
Danville
San Francisco
OAKLAND
ANTIOCH
AND
EASTERN
RAILWAY
SCALE
MILES
BRILL MAGAZINE

JOURNAL OF ELECTRICITY
POWER AND GAS
Devoted to the Conversion, Transmission and Distribution of Energy

VOLUME XXVIII   SAN FRANCISCO, MARCH 9, 1912   NUMBER 10

THE OAKLAND AND ANTIOCH RAILWAY

The census statistics of 1910 gave the population of the Bay Cities of California as 653,449 and that of Sacramento with its tributary district a population of 63,696. It is not surprising, then, that the opportunity to interlink by an electric transportation system these districts, which comprise a population of nearly three-quarters of a million people, should have been developed by local capitalists during the past year.

of 31 miles, that of the extension known as the Oakland, Antioch and Eastern Railway, from Bay Point to Sacramento, comprises a main line distance of approximately 53.5 miles.

From the Key Route junction at Fortieth street and Shafter avenue, the Oakland and Antioch runs for about 1½ miles along Shafter avenue, one of the principal residential streets in Oakland, and continues

Bay Point Station Showing Type of Car.

By reference to the map shown herewith it is seen that the Oakland and Antioch is projected to connect with the Key Route system at Fortieth street and Shafter avenue in Oakland. To the east and north of Oakland the railroad opens up a hitherto secluded but fertile territory, comprising the hamlets of Lafayette, Walnut Creek, Concord and Bay Point. The latter city is the eastern terminus of the Oakland and Antioch Railroad. Recently an extension from Bay Point to Sacramento has been undertaken. While closely affiliated with the Oakland and Antioch, this extension comprises a separate corporation and is known as the Oakland, Antioch and Eastern Railway. The Oakland and Antioch Railway comprises a main line distance

thence for at least another mile through one of the best new villa districts of the city. Between this villa district and the tunnel at the summit of the grade, the line extends for about three miles additional. At the summit in the Contra Costa hills a tunnel 3200 ft. in length is being driven to cut the crest of the ridge. From the eastern portal of the tunnel, the line gradually descends into the wide and fertile Mauraga Valley and then it continues on easy grades to its final terminus at Bay Point. That portion between Bay Point and Walnut Creek was put in commercial operation about six months ago.

The Oakland, Antioch and Eastern Railway proceeds from Bay Point to Sacramento and in doing so extends easterly about 6.6 miles along the south shore of Suisun Bay to a point where a convenient and economical crossing may be effected at an arm on San Francisco Bay. This crossing is made from a point on the south shore about 1½ miles west of Pittsburg, formerly known as Black Diamond. The landing on the north shore is on Chipp's Island. The crossing is a short distance below the confluence of the Sacramento and San Joaquin rivers. The width of the water way is about 3000 ft. The railway trains are to be transferred by ferry. On the north side of Suisun Bay crossing, the Oakland, Antioch and Eastern Railway location lies on tide or marsh lands for about four miles, crossing Chipp's Island and Van Sickle Island to the westerly edge of the Montezuma hills. The two islands are sep-

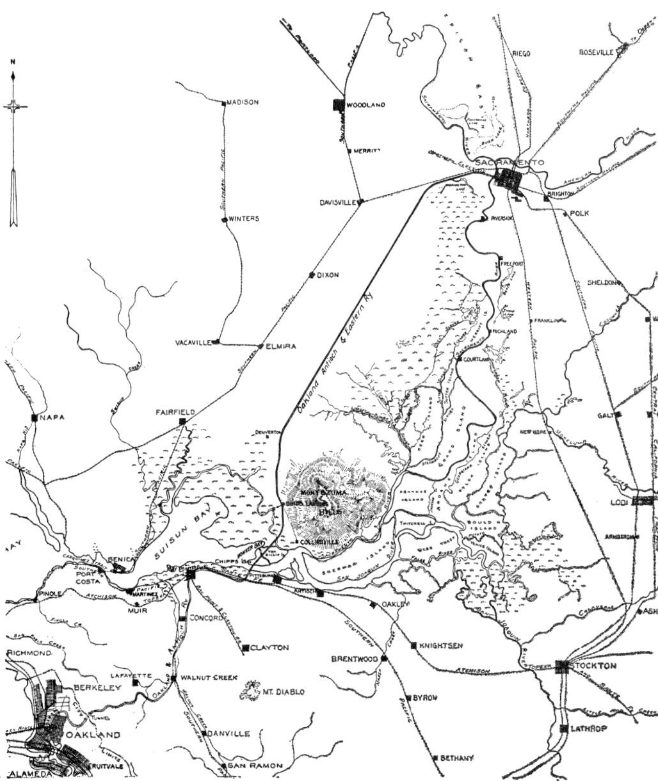

Map of Oakland and Antioch and Oakland, Antioch and Eastern Railways.

arated from each other and from the main land by narrow sloughs, one of which is navigable and over which will be constructed a drawbridge of about 100 ft. span.

The railway location skirts along the westerly edge of the Montezuma hills by means of a grade not exceeding 0.5 per cent to the Montezuma summit. Thence it descends on a gentle grade to a plain at the foot of the hills near Denverton. From this point on, the located line is to finally cross to the east side of the Sacramento River by means of the Northern Electric Railway bridge, and then enter the heart of Sacramento.

Physical Characteristics.

Beginning at the intersection of Fortieth street and Shafter avenue in the city of Oakland, the Oakland and Antioch Railway climbs a continuous grade to the tunnel above mentioned. The sharpest curve in the construction is 12 degs. 30 min., and is at a point in the hills between Oakland and the summit tunnel. This

curve is shown in the heavy cut work illustrated. Aside from this maximum, 10 deg. is the sharpest curve on the first twenty miles and 8 deg. in the valley section below Walnut Creek. For the first 5000 ft. near Shafter avenue the grade is 4.6 per cent compensated, and for the balance of three miles to the summit tunnel, 2.6 per cent compensated. The summit tunnel is 3200 ft. in length and is on a 2 per cent grade descending in the direction of Bay Point. In the descent from the tunnel to the easterly valleys there are also a few short grades, but these are all within the maximum before mentioned, that is, 2.6 per cent compensated for east-bound, and 2 per cent compensated for west-bound traffic.

At the lower end of the valley near Bay Point there is a temporary minor summit with a 3 per cent grade on each side over which trains are now operating. On the 4.6 per cent grade near the Oakland yard a pusher service is to be utilized in the case of the heavier trains, although the lighter trains are expected to operate without pushers, but at slow speed. The topography of the district near Shafter avenue admits of a location having 2.6 per cent grade and at a later date the heavier grade will be eliminated and the latter grade substituted.

All the large culverts on the Oakland and Antioch are of reinforced concrete. In the Walnut Creek section, which is now in operation, there are two plate girded bridges, one of 44½ feet and the other of 54 ft. span. The track is 70-pound rail, rock ballasted. On the 12 miles at the easterly end, 40-pound rails were laid at first, but these are being replaced with 70-pound rails, while this lighter material is being placed in the yard tracks and sidings.

Voltage and Overhead Construction.

The operation is by 1200-volt d.c. overhead trolley, bracket construction, with 0000 trolley wire and the necessary feeders and transmission. Power is bought from the Great Western Power Company, whose lines cross the Oakland and Antioch or pass very closely to it at many points. The substation at Concord is of 600 kw. capacity and in the early future will be increased to 1050 kw. There is another substation at the east portal of the tunnel. Near the Concord station is a temporary carbarn, repair shop and store room. This structure is of wood and is 25 x 60 feet, with one pit and necessary spur and storage tracks.

Oakland, Antioch and Eastern Construction.

The construction on the Oakland, Antioch and Eastern is of the same high class as the Oakland and Antioch with 70-pound rail and rock ballast. It is expected that very high speeds will be attained, especialy on the long tangent between Denverton and Sacramento, and all of the construction and equipment is designed for high speeds and first-class service. On about 30 miles of this section of the line catenary construction is being installed for overhead work with heavy brackets and poles. Track bonds of 0000 capacity are being installed and the line, similar to the Oakland and Antioch, is being operated at 1200 volts d.c., which is to be supplied from the Great Western Power Company; two substations of 750 kw. capacity are being installed.

The standard motor cars for through service are 55 ft. long and have express compartments in addition to a seating capacity for 50. They have an electrical

Roadbed and Cut at Point of Sharpest Curvature.

equipment of four 120 h.p. motors per car. The cars now in use on the Oakland and Antioch, as illustrated, are somewhat shorter and have 75 h.p. motors instead of 120 h.p.

Comparison of Mileage.

As an illustration of the saving in mileage from the cities reached by the Oakland and Antioch, it is interesting to examine the following table, which shows the comparative distance over this line to various stations as compared with those lines already in operation:

	O & A. and connections	So. Pac. Main Line	So. Pac. via Martinez	So. Pac. via Niles	West. Pac.	Santa Fe
S. F. & Key Route Pier	2.6					
Key Route Pier—Shafter Avenue	4.7					
S. F.—So. Pac. Pier		4	4	4		
S. F.—Richmond Pier						10
S. F.—Bay Point	38.1		42			37*
S. F.—Sacramento	91.6	90*	153	140	139	
Oakland—Sacramento	84.3*	85	148	135		
Oakland—Stockton	72.0*		97	87		79
Oakland—Bay Point	30.8*		39			38
Oakland—Martinez	36.8		33*			
Oakland—Concord	25.8*		39			
Oakland—Walnut Creek	19.8*		44			

Note.—In the above table the distances are from the foot of Market street, San Francisco, and from the center of Oakland. The mileage of the San Francisco ferry trip is 2.6 miles for the Oakland & Antioch, 4 miles for the Southern Pacific, about 5 miles for the Western Pacific, and 10 miles for the Santa Fe.

Progress of the Work.

The construction work at the present time is under the supervision of J. G. White & Co., engineers, of New York and San Francisco. The immense cut through which the sharp curve runs passes immediately beneath two towers of the Great Western Power Company. Hence it is necessary that they be removed and actual work is now being undertaken. The tower to the west carries three-phase current at 11,000 and 60,000 volts, while that to the east operates at 110,000 volts, the same being among the highest voltages now in operation.

It is interesting to note the efficient manner in which the yardage in this cut is being handled. A train of four cars, each with a carrying capacity of 1½ cu. yds., is hauled alternately into the tunnel openings shown. Two mules attached to these cars suffice to pull the empty cars to the portal of the tunnel; then by hitching the mules to the wire cable shown on the

ground to the left, the journey of the cars into the tunnel is completed without any lost motion on the part of the mules. The men shown on the embankment above the portals constantly direct the lowering of material through traps until each car is loaded by gravity. When the four cars are completely loaded they are then let down to the fill below by gravity. In a word, the entire process, from the time the train leaves the embankment until its contents arrive in the fill

Tunnel Portal.

below, is accomplished entirely by gravity, as the track itself is laid on a 2.6 per cent grade. By means of an occasional blast in the embankment above sufficient dirt is loosened so that the picks in the hands of the men shown above the traps are usually able to keep a continuous train of these cars in motion.

Continuing up the grade to the summit beyond this heavy cut a picturesque side-hill construction work is encountered. In the main foreground is shown the heavy line work necessitated throughout this construction. For heaviness of cut work and permanency of design this interurban line represents more the appearance of a transcontinental railroad than that of an electric interurban. As can be seen in the figure, all the smaller cuts are being day-lighted, since this can be done much cheaper at this time than at any future period. It also indicates the substantial and permanent character with which the work is being performed.

The tunnel, 3200 ft. in length, is progressing in satisfactory shape, although water with its inevitable slush has had to be summarily dealt with.

The haulage is accomplished by means of a mine type locomotive with Westinghouse controllers, operating at 250 volts, and with a draw bar pull of 1600 lbs. when moving 7½ miles per hour. It weighs 5½ tons and operates by means of two overhead trolley wires. Two lamps in series are located in each end for headlights.

The cars, 18 in all, are made by the Western Wheeled Scraper Company of Aurora, Ill. Power is supplied from the Great Western Power Company's 11,000-volt lines, which pass nearby. In the trans-

Two-Decked Jumbo Used in Tunnel Construction.

former house are to be found three 25 kw. 10,000 to 480 General Electric air-cooled, oil-insulated transformers. There are also three 25 kw., 11,000 to 460 oil-insulated, air-cooled Westinghouse transformers. The station, which is of corrugated iron, is provided with ample lightning protection.

Alternating current at 440 volts is supplied to an induction motor operating at 720 r.p.m., 122 amperes, full load, which drives a General Electric direct-current generator. This generator delivers current at 250 volts when operating at 730 r.p.m. with a full load capacity of 180 amperes. The output is utilized for power in running the tunnel, fan, saw and electric traction locomotive above referred to. A three-phase, 60-cycle, 75-h.p. General Electric induction motor is used to drive, by means of a belt connection, a Sullivan air compressor which has a capacity of 600 cu. ft. of air per minute. A 15-h.p., 230-volt, 1000-r.p.m. General Electric d.c. motor is used to drive a circular cut-off saw. This saw is rigged up with the necessary guides so that the timbers are shaped to exact size for tunnel work with minimum labor.

The electric locomotive, above referred to, seems to have met every requirement put upon it. Not only is it able to handle the load shown in the picture, but also it operates with ease the big two-deck jumbo, which of necessity must climb the two per cent grade in the tunnel.

The tunnel is now, from the east end, completed for the first 450 feet, and is partially completed a total distance of 500 feet. The tunnel cross-section measures 16 x 22 ft. with 20 ft. clearance from the top of the roof. The top is timbered by means of a five-segment arch. The tunnel is well lagged wherever the material encountered necessities. Whenever the ground was such as to require crown bars and the heading was started before the portal was erected, the crown bars

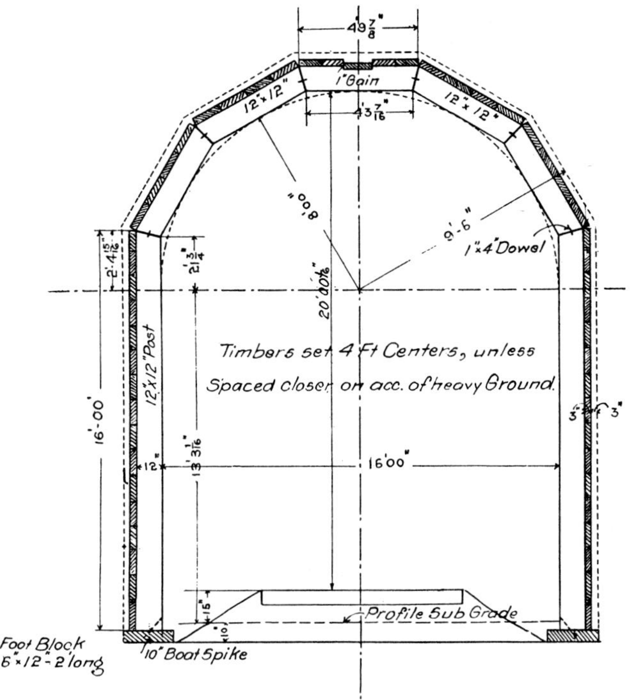

General Plan of Tunnel Timbering.

project out to within six inches of the face of the portal and are thoroughly wedged between the top of the three-inch lagging and the bottom of the three-inch crown bars. The timbers are all 12 x 12 in. The lagging over the segments are always at least 6 inches wide, while the lagging beyond the post is 4 in., or if the character of the ground permitted, it is omitted.

The excavation in the tunnel amounts to 15.3 cu. yds. per lin. ft., 160 ft. of lagging is required per ft. of tunnel and 688 ft. board measure is required per set for timbering. The timbers are set 4 ft. on centers, unless closer space is required on account of heavy ground. The arch of the tunnel, which, as stated above, consists of five segments and is made of 12 x 12 in. timbers carefully sawed to proper angles and have an extreme length of 4 ft. 10 in.

TRANSMISSION POLE EFFICIENCY.

The Joint Pole Commission, representing the public utility corporations of Los Angeles reports the removal of over 120 miles of poles from the streets of the city through combination of duty for poles and removing the superfluous ones. Combinations were obtained for 4586 poles and 6135 were taken out which saved the corporations over $100,000, lowered rates for telephones, light and power and very materially added to the appearance of the streets. Since the commission was organized five years ago 700 miles of poles, representing a saving of $250,000, have been removed.

Central California Traction Company's box motor No. 2 helped build the O&A; here the big motor is seen hauling a train of ballast between Concord and Walnut Creek in 1911.   This car was rented on a per diem basis.   O&A's box motor 102 was also on the line in construction work at this same time; these two box motors were similar then except CCT 2 had two baggage doors, 102 had one.   102 later received an arch roof when OA&E took control. (VS)

Below, busy days at 40th & Shafter; the machine shops were under construction when this photo was taken in 1912.   The camera looks east and a part of Oakland Traction's streetcar No. 52 can be seen at left. (Cook & Cook, VS)

OA&E President Walter Arnstein, explaining a $5 per share assessment on stockholders in 1915, listed the following reasons therefor:

1. The greater cost of terminal properties in Oakland and Sacramento, due to particularly advantageous sites being acquired.

2. Large increase in equipment and operating facilities over original estimate made necessary by rapid development of country served.

3. Installation of Automatic Block Signal system, not originally set.

4. Larger ferry boat and larger slips required to berth it.

5. Concreting the tunnel.

6. Building the line on standard steam railroad specifications.

7. Purchase of bridge site and preliminary work.

Chapter 7

South End History

Winding out of Oakland through the Redwood Canyon, piercing the low hills of Contra Costa County, and crossing the lush agricultural empire of the Sacramento Valley, the swift green electric trains of the "Oakland-Antioch" offered convenient interurban service to California's capital during the pre-automobile era which spurred the development of a myriad of electric railways across the nation.

By the time this line was completed in 1913, the extensive interurban empires of the Southern Pacific in the Eastbay, F. M. "Borax" Smith's Key System, the Northern Electric, the Central California Traction, and John Martin's North Shore (Northwestern Pacific) had virtually reached their zenith in development and operation. The "South End" would be the last major independent interurban railroad to be constructed in California. When completed, it was an outstanding example of that last great burst of electric railway building which was snuffed out by World War I and the automobile.

The South End received its start because of a quirk of geography. Due east of Oakland lie the San Ramon Valley communities of Concord, Walnut Creek and Lafayette. Separating these towns from Oakland is a range of hills (a part of the Coast Range) known locally as the "Oakland Hills." This natural barrier made travel rather slow as a fifty mile jaunt on a steam train was required to traverse the twenty mile distance as the crow flies. Not until 1910 when the O&A appeared on the scene did a glimmer of hope appear for these travellers.

On January 13, 1909 The Oakland & Antioch Railway Company was incorporated in California to construct and operate an electric railway from Oakland to Antioch. The officers of this enterprise were: Walter Arnstein, President; S. L. Naphtaly, Vice President; H. C. Breeden, Vice President; Harry A. Mitchell, Secretary-Treasurer; H. J. Sutherland, Assistant Secretary. The Directors included the officers and H. L. Scott, William Ede, John J. Walker and Burkett Corbett. This was, for the most part, a San Francisco group.

The Key System also had designs on a line to Sacramento out of Oakland, but it died on the drawing boards.

The O&A began building its line between Bay Point and Walnut Creek in 1910. A test run to Concord was made on Feb. 13, 1911, and the entire line opened on May 4, The road was single track, had 48 lb. steel rails, and was standard gauge; trolley pressure was 1200 volts DC, a surprising feature when one considers that the O&A's cars at that time were equipped with type K controllers. Simple overhead trolley wire was hung from brackets attached to a single row of poles. Power was purchased from The Great Western Power Company.

The two interurban cars were built by San Francisco's Holman Car Company and were equipped at O&A's tiny shop in Concord. Not able to operate together in multiple, these little cars, Nos. 1001 and 1002, for heavy passenger movements had rented Santa Fe coaches sandwiched between them, a motorman on each motor car. A small company office was maintained in the Concord station.

Actually, this pioneer segment was the closest the O&A ever got to "trolley standards." A plan was unveiled to build from its line to Martinez, via Pacheco, but the appearance of a new company brought this to naught.

A new company, The Oakland, Antioch & Eastern Ry., was incorporated in California on March 28, 1911. It leased the O&A and immediately set about constructing a through interurban line to the highest standards between Oakland and Sacramento. Its officials were the same O&A group.

The appearance of this new company on the scene, with apparently adequate financing assured, caused certain consternation on the part of established railroads in the area. As Central California Traction crews and equipment were hired in construction days, rumors flew that OA&E would not build to Sacramento but would route its trains to Stockton and then provide a Sacramento connection via CCT. Another report which gained wide credence was to the effect that Santa Fe was behind the OA&E. Neither rumor was true, of course, and OA&E proceeded to build its system oblivious to these guesses.

Gradually the new main line crept east and west from the O&A termini. Rail of 70 lbs. was laid---and it was something new in interurban use, according to "Electric Railway Journal" which described it as being ferro titanium alloy, ASCE standard. Two welding cars installed the rail bonds, supplied by Electric Railway Implement Company. Ties from Oakland to Bay Point were sawn pine, but the remainder of the line used redwood sleepers.

Forty foot poles were used throughout, spaced from 90 to 150 feet apart. Aside from the Bay Point-Lafayette segment, trolley wire was No. 0000 and simple catenary construction was installed. Messenger wire was Siemens-Martin 7/17, hung from steel brackets on a single row of poles. Aluminum 600,000 mil feeders were used and at the river crossing, submarine cables carried the current to the opposite shore. Manually operated substations with Westinghouse equipment were installed at Eastport, Concord, Drawbridge and Glide's Landing; Eastport, at the top of the hill out of Oakland, had double equipment, with single equipments in the other substations. In addition, portable substations were constructed.

Signals were provided by The Union Switch & Signal Company; these were its Model 13 light type signals with continuous AC track circuits. Blade signals were used in Oakland to protect the junction of the OA&E and Key at 40th & Shafter. According to stockholders' reports, the sig-

nals cost the company $101,948.60.

The Coast Range hills behind Oakland had always posed a problem to railroad engineers; both SP and AT&SF had cautiously avoided the direct route, taking a round-about way via Richmond. The interurban, however, went through these hills, running via Redwood and Shephard's Canyons into upper Oakland's Temescal area and down by way of Shafter Ave. to the company's yards and shops at 40th St.

Connecting Redwood and Shephard's Canyons was a tunnel; little trouble was encountered on its eastern half, much of which was dug through solid rock. The western end, however, was a dangerous job due to water and general instability of the earth. Concrete walls outside were necessary, and the tunnel itself through this area was lined with concrete. Even the tunnel floor was concreted, using the form of an inverted arch. When completed, the bore was about 3600 feet in length with a uniform grade of 1.9 percent to the east.

Construction along Shafter Ave., Oakland, was under the name "The Oakland & Bay Shore Railroad," owned by the O&A and incorporated on January 5, 1911. Rails were laid in 1912 amid a heated franchise battle wherein residents on Shafter Ave. sought to prevent the construction of a railroad before their very doors. By that time the city of Oakland had expanded into quite a respectable residential community due, in part, to refugees of the 1906 Earthquake in San Francisco. Shafter Ave. residents tried to influence the Oakland City Council but to no avail. A temporary court order was obtained by the railroad and its rails were quickly laid with the assistance of Key System

line crews. As soon as the trolley wire was completed it was energized at 600 volts and Oakland Traction Company's single truck streetcar 52 was leased and run up and down the street to hold the franchise. The single track was laid off center as it was hoped to someday double track the line; this never came to pass.

At the intersection of 40th St. and Shafter Ave. the company purchased approximately a block and a half of land, adjoining Key's 40th St. car line. Here the shops, offices and yards were established. In a triangular shaped parcel of land a two story depot building was erected with an interlocking tower upstairs. Operated by air, the plant controlled the OA&E's junction with Key Route. A small freight yard was squeezed into the plot of ground, and a wye was available, using Key's 40th St. line as one leg. Property was purchased at Rockridge for eventual development into a shops and yard facility, but this time the protests of the local residents prevailed and the improvement never was built.

Terminal facilities were provided by Key System (see Chapter 7) which through agreement permitted OA&E trains to use Key's 40th St. line to its Key Pier terminal, with connecting ferries to San Francisco's Ferry Building.

Between Chipps Island and Sacramento much of the trackage was on marshy land where ground is constantly sinking. A wooden Howe truss swing bridge was erected across Montezuma Slough, powered by a 1220 volt motor; a substation was located there, and the substation operator doubled as bridge tender. Power to operate the bridge was supplied by submarine cable. The substation was built on top of pilings on a concrete cap above the high water mark.

Two views of 40th & Shafter, Oakland. Above, a 1912 view looking west from Opal Street. Note the early crude connection with Key Route's 40th St. line; this rail was laid hurriedly by OA&E to maintain its franchise which had proved to be difficult to obtain due to protests of residents in area. (Cook, VS)

Below, the same scene as it appeared in 1915. A Key Route Piedmont Line train is approaching. This was the familiar 40th & Shafter remembered fondly by Eastbay commuters. (Cook & Cook, VS)

Crossing the upper arm of Suisun Bay was a major problem which was temporarily met by installing a gasoline powered car ferry, the "Bridgit." Long range plans called for a major bridge, and some foundation work was actually done---but the temporary expedient proved to be permanent.

Near MacAvoy a subway was constructed beneath the tracks of the Southern Pacific and the Santa Fe. At Las Juntas the interurban crossed the S. P. at grade.

At Broderick, near Sacramento, OA&E's route joined that of The Sacramento & Woodland Railway, a subsidiary of the Northern Electric, and entered Sacramento via tracks of that company and of the local streetcar company to OA&E's Station at 3rd & I Sts.

Passenger cars were constructed by several builders to a design worked out by OA&E engineers; the design was to be unique and never repeated by another company. The cars were up to the standards of the times, and were wooden bodied, with steel underframes. Each car had a baggage compartment, a smoking section and a coach section. They were numbered from 1003 to 1018 and were capable of running in multiple unit operation. Eight steel trailers were purchased from the Hall-Scott company of Berkeley; some wooden trailers purchased secondhand for excursion use completed the equipment roster.

On April 7, 1913, OA&E established through service from Oakland to Bay Point when its Timetable No. 1 went into effect on that date. The San Francisco "Examiner" had this to say concerning a preview trip operated by car 1006 on March 29, 1913:

"The first train of the Oakland-Antioch electric line to run from the Key Route Mole through to Bay Point was turned over to the newspaper men of the Bay Cities by General Manager H. A. Mitchell of the traction company yesterday morning...A real country lunch was served at the hotel in Walnut Creek. The train was in charge of Motorman A. B. Hook and P. G. Deyo."

To promote the opening of the line between Oakland and Bay Point, a special timetable was issued and the trains bore names:

Eastbound	Westbound
Ignacio Express	Argonaut
Commuters' Express	Bay Cities Express
Contra Costa Express	Golden Gate Express
San Ramon Express	San Franciscan
Bay Point Express	Oakland Express

These names were typical of the areas served, but these named trains disappeared with the establishing of Sacramento through service.

Before that portion of the line north of the river was opened, special trains were operated from the Key Pier to Solano City; these ran by electricity to Mallard and with steam power north of the ferry as the overhead was not yet in place. The steam locomotives disappeared as soon as the trolley wire was placed in service and never saw regular passenger or freight service.

A parade and celebration commemorated the opening of the Oakland-Bay Point service, but through service to Sacramento passed almost without notice. "Moraga," as a motor car, was out on the line with company officials on August 5, 1913 and operated through to Sacramento. The official opening of through service took place on September 3, 1913, with eight round trips daily listed on the timetable, the largest number of such trips on record. By October 20, 1913, there were 29 main line trains on the timecard with seven round trips to Sacramento.

With the arrival of parlor car "Moraga" and the conversion of car 1016 into an enclosed parlor car named "Sacramento," a round trip "name" train service was established in 1914. Prior to this, "Moraga" had been extensively used as a business car and in regular train service. Northbound, Train No. 8 was "The Capital," while southbound the same cars became "The Metropolitan." In 1915 through service with the Northern Electric was inaugurated with some trailers operating through from Oakland to Chico; these included the "Sacramento" and NE's palatial "Bidwell" on "The Sacramento Valley Limited." The "Comet" offered through cars to Chico from Oakland, but the South End parlor car usually was cut off at Sacramento.

Hardly had through service been well established on OA&E when a disastrous 1914 winter did major damage to the new line. We quote from OA&E's official report to its stockholders, issued in 1915:

"It will be remembered that in January, 1914, one of the heaviest storms on record accompanied by floods occured. Practically all railroad communication out of San Francisco was cut off and the Southern Pacific Company lost parts of its lines paralleling ours in Contra Costa County. Owing largely to this storm, which occurred before our road was in condition to withstand such a deluge and owing also to the installation of various additions, improvements, etc., not originally contemplated, the Company's estimates for completing the road fell short of the amount actually required by approximately $775,000."

As a result of the stormy 1914 winter, OA&E had to rebuild many fills, install 8,000 feet of new trestles, and various waterways had to be installed or enlarged.

On May 17, 1914, the wooden ferry "Bridgit" burned, fortunately with no loss of lives. At once the road was cut in two. From May 18, 1914, to January of 1915 tugs and barges were rented; on January 3, 1915, a new gasoline powered steel ferry, the "Ramon," was placed in service.

Various improvements were made in 1914 to complete the road. Signals were installed from Sacramento to Oakland, twelve passenger depots and shelters were built, extra heaters were installed in the cars, and spring buffers were placed on ends of passenger cars to permit patrons to pass safely from car to car.

OA&E was very considerate of its passengers. Eager to improve its service, it constantly polled patrons on quality of service. Even a crack limited train could be stopped at an obscure depot if requested ahead of time; this was particularly true north of the river where virtually all local passengers consisted of duck hunters. One such hunter stopped all trains one day when he missed his target and instead severed the trolley wire.

Various branch lines were constructed; these are covered in detail in accompanying chapters and will not be duplicated here.

OA&E ceased to exist as an operating company on January 26, 1920, when The San Francisco-Sacramento Railroad Company assumed control. Incorporated in California on January 2, 1920, the SF-S acquired at foreclosure sale on January 26, 1920, all properties of the OA&E, the O&A, and The San Ramon Valley Railroad. From this date to the merger with the North End lines in 1928, SF-S, known as "The Sacramento Short Line," controlled the South End.

In its first report to stockholders in 1920, SF-S had a somewhat optimistic outlook:

"An increase of 20% in passenger rates was granted to the railroad on August 26, 1920. However, we note that passenger earnings had increased before these rates went into effect and it is believed these increased passenger earnings are due to the roadbed's being rebuilt and the increased publicity your railroad is receiving of keeping to scheduled

Building the OA&E---a scene near Molena. The locomotive is the 1369, ex-SP. (RB)

First car ferry was "Bridgit," shown here en route with train No. 21, headed by the 1008. (CS)

time."

The last sentence is noteworthy. The company explained that 99% of its passenger trains were on time in the year 1920. This is interesting in view of the fact that the SF-S was governed by Key ferry schedules and a sometimes temperamental car ferry deep in the wilds of the delta.

This optimism was dimmed in 1922 when the company reported that earnings dipped $39,902.71 to a total of $759,051.37. "This decrease is directly due to an increase of automobiles and paved roads," the company admitted, possibly foreseeing the future. Operating expenses increased $14,331 in 1923 due to track rehabilitation. Again in 1924 passenger revenue dropped 7.55% to $701,762, while freight earnings rose 7.77%.

With some degree of optimism the company gave its stockholders some hard facts concerning passenger business:

"The future of this particular branch of business does not appear encouraging. Passenger earnings decreased from $701,762 in 1924 to $657,851 in 1925, 6.26%. Though this decrease is large, it is less than that averaged by other short line roads. The running time between San Francisco and Sacramento has been shortened fifteen minutes and additional passenger facilities added, in an endeavor to make the road as attractive as possible and to hold the business against increasing competition."

The company continued to improve its passenger service to attract new customers and hold the old ones--- but sales of automobiles steadily increased and the delta region began to be laced with two lane highways of concrete or asphalt, suitable for all weather driving.   The company's prediction that the roads would soon be of insufficient capacity to carry the number of registered automobiles in the state was wishful thinking, indeed.

In 1925, following many years of agitating by Sacramento city officials, railroads, chambers of commerce, and ordinary enraged citizens, a Union Depot was built by the three interurban companies entering that city: the San Francisco-Sacramento, the Sacramento Northern, and Central California Traction. The handsome two story brick and concrete structure covered most of a city block, and its train yard in the rear soon became one of the busiest places in Sacramento. SF-S trains had their running time shaved 15minutes by the new depot. The Sacramento Union Station was placed in service on Sept. 20, 1925.

Meanwhile, events were shaping that would bring the SF-S under Western Pacific control and merger with the North End system. WP and its controlled company, The Sacramento Northern Railroad (successor to Northern Electric) offered to build a branch line from the SF-S main line at Riverview to Oxford (the Holland Branch) in return for the right to use SF-S's main line for freight operation from Sacramento to Walnut Creek. "The result would be this," the South End company told its stockholders, "Your company would either procure the income from freight originating in the Holland district or secure additional income from the use of its tracks."

The Holland Branch did develop into an important feeder, but by the time it was opened on June 29, 1929, the "Short Line" had been merged into the SN. In August, 1927, the Western Pacific through The Sacramento Company (a new holding company incorporated in Delaware on February 1, 1927, with 10,000 shares of capital stock of no par value) acquired control of SF-S by taking over the forty thousand shares of common stock of that company. Another factor leading to WP control was the fact that the steam road had advanced SF-S considerable monies to pay for its share of construction expenses of the Sacramento Union Station.

With the taking over of SF-S control by WP, rumors flew that WP would use South End rails to bring its steam trains into Oakland; on March 10, 1926, President Arthur

Curtis James of WP was quoted as announcing, "The recently acquired Sacramento Short Line, running from Oakland to Sacramento, will be made part of the Western Pacific main line. It will cost money for rebuilding, but it will shorten our main line by fifty miles." However, these plans never materialized, perhaps blighted by the stock market crash of 1929 and the subsequent depression years.

The South End's independent status was brought to a close on December 31, 1928, when The San Francisco-Sacramento Railroad Company conveyed all of its property to a new WP company, The Sacramento Northern Railway Company. This was done under the authority of the U.S. Interstate Commerce Commission's decision rendered October 15, 1928, which authorized the SN Railway to acquire and operate the SF-S in accordance with an agreement between the two roads dated January 14, 1928. The SN Railway also controlled the system of the predecessor North End company, the SN Railroad---so at long last the two systems which had for so many years worked together became a united company.

To recapitulate South End history:

Railroad	Trackage	Mileage	Fate
Oakland & Bay Shore	40th & Shafter to Temescal	3.0	1
O&A Railway	Temescal-Bay Pt.	28.1	2
OA&E	Bay Point-Sacto. W. Pittsburg to Pittsburg	58.3 2.2	2
O&A Ry.	Meinert-Walwood	2.8	2
SRV RR.	Saranap-Diablo	8.6	2
SF-S	Oakland-Sacto.	85.0	3

Fate: 1 - Owned by O&A, absorbed 1912
       2 - Sold to SF-S, 1920
       3 - Sold to SN Ry., 1928

(Above mileage for SF-S corrected for Danville Branch abandonment.)

(Acknowledgments: The author, **Harre W. Demoro**, wishes to thank the following historians and sources for material used in compiling the South End history: Vernon J. Sappers, Frank Rigney, Richard Holmes, James C. Holmes, Donald Olsen, Paul Jacobs, Ralph W. Demoro, George Hademann, L. L. Bonney, Carl L. Germann; Electric Railway Journal, Electric Traction, San Francisco Examiner, and Annual Reports, SF-S RR. Co., and George Hademan.)

●

A notable SF-S special train was "The Riveter," run in World War I days between Danville and Bay Point for the benefit of shipyard workers. As a general rule, "The Riveter" consisted of box motors 101 and 102 on each end with three trailers between. At Saranap the train was broken up with a motor and a trailer running on to Danville in the evening; the other motor and the two trailers remained at Saranap for the night. In the morning, this operation was reversed, with "The Riveter" picking up the motor and trailers left at Saranap the night before. The timetable shows "The Riveter" to have departed from Danville at 6:51 AM, Saranap at 7:21, Concord at 7:43, arriving at Bay Point at 7:58 after its run of 39.2 miles. Returning, "The Riveter" left Bay Point at 5:10 PM, Concord at 5:26, Saranap at 5:48, arriving at Danville at 6:10.

The network of interurban railways in Southern California is largely responsible for the unprecedented growth in that section of our country. The Inland Empire, in and about Spokane, has built up a system of interurban railways during recent years which has brought to the world a second demonstration of the prosperity and development that follow the trail of the interurban.

The severe topography surrounding the bay cities of California has almost made it prohibitive in the past to make electric connection with the great valleys of the interior...

The bay cities, comprising a population of three quarters of a million inhabitants, portray in this fact alone the necessity of having produce markets within easy and rapid reach. Not only, then, is the question of passenger traffic one to be considered in a pliable interurban system, but the enormous movement of fruit & produce from the interior valleys is a problem which must be solved by modern electrical tractive equipment.

It is not surprising, then, that the past few months have seen ample capital subscribed to push immediately to completion an electrical link between Oakland and the city of Sacramento, heart of the valley of the same name... The Coast Range, skirting the suburbs of Oakland and Berkeley, has hitherto been a barrier insurmountable so far as a direct traffic link with the interior Contra Costa drainage is concerned. But now comes The Oakland & Antioch Railroad with its deep cuts, long tunnel and heavy fills and accomplishes with a substantial construction worthy of a transcontinental railroad the piercing of this range and the interlinking of the interior subsidiary valleys hitherto long isolated from nearby cities...

The electric interurban has been known to enter a district where there dwelt but the sage brush and jack rabbit, and to leave in its trail in scarcely a year a row of promising and prosperous hamlets... The thousands of prosperous communities throughout the West bear witness to the early growth and encouragement received from the busy, traffic-giving electric interurban.

(* Reprinted from "Journal of Electricity, Power & Gas," dated March 9, 1912; kindly made available by Mr. Richard Schlaich of San Francisco through Mr. Charles Smallwood.)

RENTAL OF EQUIPMENT: Records transcribed by Thomas R. Bold and others indicate rather intensive rental of rolling stock in the early days:

Auditor's bills collectible:

#865 Nov., 1915   To Tidewater Southern Railway
"To rental of our (OA&E) express motor No. 101 for the month of Nov., 1915. 19 days @ $15.00"

#1735 Nov., 1917   To Northern Electric Railway
"For rental of equipment during month of Nov., 1917; car "Sacramento" Nov. 16 to 28 inclusive. 13 round trips at $2.50 per."

1825 Jan., 1918   To Tidewater & Southern Railway
" $105.00 paid May 1, 1918 for rental of express motor."

957 (SF-S) July, 1921   To Sacramento Valley & Eastern Ry.
"To rental of ballast car 0108 from June 30 to July 31---32 days at $2.00 per day."

961 July, 1921   To Sacramento Valley & Eastern Ry.

"Shipped to G. W. Hark, Bully Hill Station, Four second hand target switch stands @ $10.00."

#4423 Nov., 1926   To Sacramento Northern Railroad
"Service of car 1022, to you on No. 8 of Nov. 24th, returned to us on No. 9 of Nov. 28th, 1926, @ $2.50 per day."

4421 Nov., 1926   To Sacramento Northern Railroad
"For service car 1021, to you on No. 2 of Nov. 23rd, returned to us on No. 9 of Nov. 24th, at $2.50 per day."

#5023 Sept., 1927   To Sacramento Northern Railroad
"Service as follows: Car 1023 to you on No. 8 of Sept. 3rd, returned to us on No. 9 of Sept. 5th, two days at $2.50 per day."

Car 1025 to you on No. 8 of Sept. 5th; returned to us on Sept. 6th; two days at $2.50 per day."

Left: OA&E's original Sacramento Depot was at Third & I Streets; here 1010 and "Moraga" are about to depart for Oakland in 1914. (RB)

OFFICERS OF THE O. A. &E.

President: Walter Arnstein
Vice President: S. L. Naphtaly
Vice President: H. C. Breeden
Secretary-Treasurer: H. A. Mitchell
Asst. Secretary: H. J. Sutherland

DIRECTORS

S. L. Naphtaly	H. A. Mitchell
H. C. Breeden	H. T. Scott
William Ede	Walter Arnstein
John I. Walter	H. J. Sutherland
Burke Corbet	

J. H. Leary: Supt. of Transportation
F. A. Miller: Supt. Power & Eqpt.
M. J. Hynes: Chief Dispatcher
Thomas J. Kearns: Auditor
L. H. Rodebaugh: Genl. Pass Agent
George H. Whybark: Genl. Ft. Agent
George I. Turner: Master Mechanic
John Marshall: Master Car Repairer

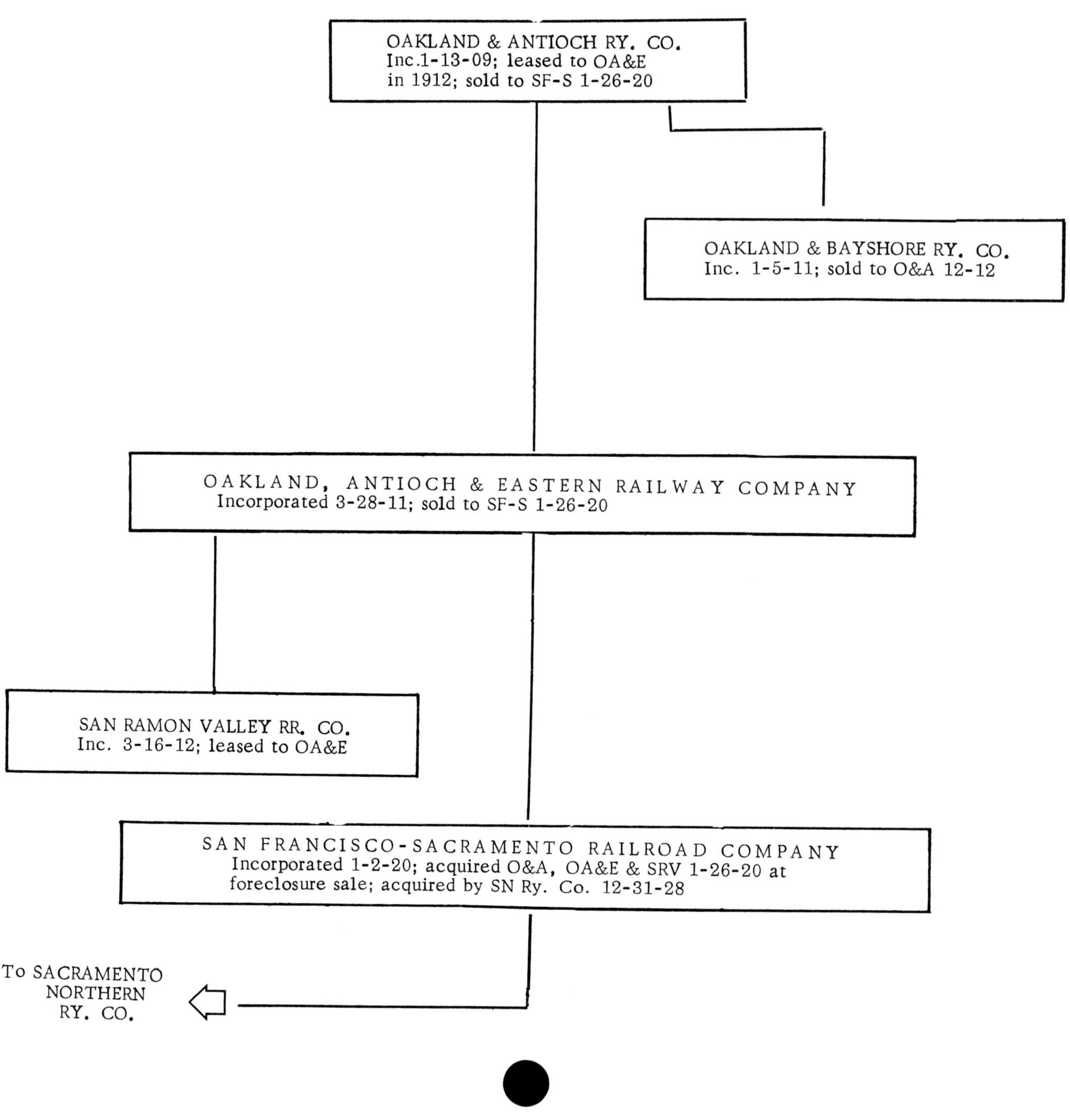

FAMILY TREE, SOUTH END LINES

Note: The Sacramento Valley Electric Railroad was never a part of
the corporate structure of South End companies; its property, the Dixon
Branch, was operated by OA&E but not under lease.

The San Ramon Valley RR. (Saranap-Diablo) was leased to OA&E upon
completion of this branch line, 1914.

The Oakland & Antioch Ry. was leased to OA&E from 1912 to 1920
and was purchased by the SF-S on January 26, 1920.

Chapter 8

The Early Years

<u>"THE EARLY YEARS"</u> --- A compilation of newspaper items reporting the development of the OA&E from inception to maturity, the following excerpts have been made available for publication herein through the gracious cooperation of Mr. Thomas R. Bold of Oakland.

<u>1909</u>

Jan. 13, 1909 --- OAKLAND & ANTIOCH INCORPORATED

The "Oakland & Antioch Railway" was incorporated on this date under the laws of the State of California for the purpose of building and operating an electric interurban railroad from Bay Point (now known as Port Chicago) to Oakland by way of Concord, Walnut Creek and Lafayette, a total distance of 31 miles.

The incorporators were: A. W. Maltby, S. L. Naphtaly, Allan Pollock, Walter Arnstein, F. E. Brooks, H. A. Mitchell, F. W. Smith, and J. Naphtaly. Capital stock of the company was $2,000,000, consisting of 20,000 shares with a par value of $100 each.

---Official Records

March 12, 1909 --- PROMISING OUTLOOK FOR ELECTRIC
ROAD

With the filing of articles of incorporation of The Oakland & Antioch Railway, the announcement is made that the construction work on the new line, which was projected nearly two years ago, will begin within two months and will be pushed to completion rapidly.

At the outset the company met with some obstacles which have been practically overcome. There were hitches over certain rights of way, especially through the Inter-County Tunnel which runs through the hills between Alameda and Contra Costa Counties. The Contra Costa Supervisors were willing to grant the company a temporary right over one-third part which they controlled, but the Alameda County officials were not inclined to grant the concession for the remainder.

At that time, there was some talk of the company overcoming the difficulty by entering into a traffic agreement with the Western Pacific Railroad and building a line through the Moraga Valley by way of Fruitvale (East Oakland). This plan, in the light of other developments, has been abandoned, and it is understood that arrangements are practically completed for the use of the original route, and it is along this that the work will be begun. The connection between Bay Point and Antioch will be made later.

The new road will be about thirty miles in length and it is the expectation of the company to run an hourly service between Oakland and Bay Point and later to Antioch. To the limits of Berkeley the third rail will be used, and from Claremont into Oakland there will be a trolley. The use of the tunnel is said to be only temporary pending the construction of a tunnel of lesser grade by the company. While using the tunnel, the company agrees to have it paved with rock and station a flagman at each end.

--- Contra Costa Gazette

(Note: As mentioned in the preceding article, approximately two years before the incorporation of the Oakland & Antioch various surveys were made (probably by the same men who later were to become backers of the O&A) to find a suitable route for an electric railroad from Contra Costa County to Oakland. However, these plans never progressed beyond the survey stage.

(Also of interest are the original plans of O&A engineers, as outlined herein, to use a third rail from Bay Point to the old Inter County Road Tunnel, change to overhead trolley at the east portal of the tunnel, and come into Oakland along the Key Route's Claremont Avenue line.

(Before construction work actually started, however, it was decided to use an overhead trolley on the entire route, bore a railroad tunnel through the Berkeley Hills, and come into Oakland along Shafter Avenue. --- T.R.B.)

Aug. 17, 1909 --- BOND ISSUE FOR ELECTRIC ROAD

At a meeting of the Board of Directors of the O&A, held today in San Francisco, it was voted to authorize a bonded indebtedness to raise funds with which to construct an electric railroad from Oakland to Antioch by way of Walnut Creek, Concord and Bay Point.

The directors present were Joseph Naphtaly, A. W. Maltby, Walter Arnstein and Allan Pollock. Surveys for the road, which will be 47 miles in length, were reported complete and final locations made. Within sixty days the railroad will be under the course of construction and will be rushed to rapid completion.

Within the past 90 days, a decision by Judge Ellsworth of Oakland declared that the company was a commercial railroad under the state law and had a right to use county roads. Thus ends a delay of nearly two years on account of the inability of the Board of Supervisors to give permission to go through the Inter County Road tunnel between Oakland and Contra Costa County.

---Contra Costa Gazette

The arrival of the first Oakland & Antioch car to run over the line, # 1002, at Concord on February 13, 1911, after completing the first test run from Bay Point to Concord. Though regular service did not begin until the line was completed to Walnut Creek---almost three months later---this did not lessen the enthusiasm of the citizens of Concord who greeted the first electric car "with joy in their hearts." Note that the car has not yet been equipped with pilots or trolley pole hooks and the lack of ballast. (Al H. Lent Photo --- TRB)

What had been merely farm land is transformed almost in a twinkling to an important artery of commerce---(below) O&A construction crew laying the main line in 1911; the scene is near Lafayette. The reader may be excused for asking which came first---the ties or the trolley poles?
(Mrs. Alice Russi --- T.R.B.)

OAKLAND AND ANTIOCH RAILWAY

TIME CARD

LOCAL AND IN CONNECTION WITH SANTA FE RY.

Effective May 28, 1911

NORTH BOUND.

STATION	No.2	No.4	No.6	No.8	No.10	No.12	No.14	No:16
	A.M.	A.M.	A.M.	P.M.	*P.M.	P.M.	P.M.	P.M.
Lv. Walnut Creek	5:45	8:24	10:05	12:15	1:57	4:11	8:06	9:35
Lv. Moore		8:44			2:17	4:31		
Lv. Meinert Junction	5:58	8:51	10:18	12:28	2:24	4:38	8:19	9:48
Lv. Concord	6:05	8:58	10:25	12:35	2:31	4:45	8:26	9:55
Arr. Bay Point	6:18	9:12	10:39	12:49	2:45	4:59	8:40	
Lv. Bay Point	6.23	9:17		12:54		5:05	8:45	
Arr. Richmond	7:19	10:20		1:50		6:05	9:40	
Arr. Berkeley	7:43	10:43		2:08		6:23	9:58	
Arr. Oakland	7:50	10:50		2:15		6:30	10:05	
Arr. San Francisco ..	8:20	11:10		2:45		7:00	10:30	
Lv. Bay Point......			10:45		3:47	5:47	8:45	
Arr. Antioch			11:06		4:08	6:07	9:08	
Arr. Stockton			12:05		5:10	7:10	10:15	
Arr. Sacr. over C. C. T. Co. Lines..			3:37 P.M.		8:40			

SOUTH BOUND.

STATION	No.1	No.3	No.5	No.7	No.9	No.11	No.13	No.15
	A.M.	A.M.	A.M.	A.M.	A.M.	P.M.	P.M.	P.M.
Lv San Francisco...			7:00	9:00			4:00	6:45
Lv. Oakland			6:50	9:20			4:20	6:40
Lv. Berkeley			6:57	9:26			4:26	6:46
Lv. Richmond			7:55	9:55			4:54	7:45
Arr. Bay Point			8:48	10:45			5:47	8:45
Lv. Stockton		5:00	8:00		11:35 P.M.		3:45	7:35
Lv. Antioch		6:00	8:56		12:33		4:43	8:29
Arr. Bay Point		6:23	9:17		12:54		5:05	8:45
Lv. Bay Point		7:15	9:22	10:51	1:00	3:06	6:02	8:50
Arr. Concord	5:20	7:29	9:36	11:05	1:14	3:20	6:15	9:04
Arr. Meinert Junction	5:27	7:36	9:43	11:12	1:21	3:27	6:22	9:11
Arr. Moore					1:28	3:34	6:29	
Arr. Walnut Creek..	5:40	7:49	9:55	11:25	1:47	3:54	6:49	9:24

* Train No. 10 connects at Bay Point with S. P. train for Martinez, Oakland and San Francisco.

L. R. RICHARDS, Agt.   H. H. FULTON, Agt.   G. R. HAMLETT, Agt.
BAY POINT   CONCORD   WALNUT CREEK

R. H. FISH, Traffic Manager, Concord.

O&A Timetable No. 2, effective May 28, 1911, Showing service between Bay Point and Walnut Creek, together with connecting Santa Fe trains at Bay Point to and from San Francisco and Stockton.

The O&A station "Moore" (later renamed "Gavin") was the terminus of the Walwood Branch which left the O&A main line at Meinert Jct.

---TRB Collection

April 20, 1910 --- CONSTRUCTION WORK STARTED

(From the Concord Transcript) At noon today the construction engineers and their gangs of workmen commenced grading for the new electric line which is to connect Concord, Bay Point and Walnut Creek with Oakland. The first shovelfull of earth was turned at Walnut Creek and the work of building the road will be rushed to completion as speedily as it can be done by a large crew of engineers and hundreds of workmen. Fred Brooks, chief engineer in charge of building the road, was in Concord this afternoon and when seen by a Transcript representative both he and A. W. Maltby, one of the foremost promoters of the road, stated that work begun today would only terminate when electric cars are in operation from tidewater in Oakland to tidewater at Bay Point.

--- Contra Costa Gazette

June 23, 1910 --- OAKLAND & ANTIOCH BONDS

The O&A Board of Directors has voted to create a bonded indebtedness of the Oakland & Antioch Railway in the sum of $2,000,000 for the purpose of constructing its railroad and to provide for additions and extensions thereof, and for the purchase of equipment and rolling stock and other property suitable for corporate purposes. The bonds to be issued are to be known as "Oakland & Antioch Railway First Mortgage 5% Sinking Fund 30 Year Gold Bonds."

--- Contra Costa Gazette

Sept. 17, 1910 --- SHIPMENT OF O&A RAILS AT BAY POINT

Any fears that might have existed in the minds of anyone as to whether or not the O&A line is a "paper" road or an actual railway will be allayed when they learn that the first shipment of ties and rails have arrived at Bay Point and that today the engineers for the electric line started over the line, as laid out, determining the center of the roadbed for the laying of the ties and rails. In addition to the shipment of ties which were delivered by the Robert Dollar Company, there are at the present time in the Santa Fe yards at Bay Point three carloads of angle bars and one carload of 60-lb. rails.

Ten tons of heavy copper wire which will form the main power line for the new road are also stored in Ivey's Livery Barn in Concord and as soon as needed will be stretched. The poles for carrying the power wire are also on hand and on many parts of the road have already been raised.

---Contra Costa Gazette

Nov. 22, 1910 --- FIRST RAILS LAID ON O&A

At one o'clock this afternoon the work of laying the rails of the O&A started at Bay Point where the connection was made with the Santa Fe Railroad. There are at the present time one hundred men at work laying the rails and within a few days fully one hundred more will be engaged.

--- Contra Costa Gazette

Dec. 31, 1910 --- O&A CONSTRUCTION WORK

The O&A electric road is being completed as fast as possible. One of Chadwick & Stokes' little steam engines is busy hauling ties and rails from Bay Point toward Concord, and the trolley wire is being put up.

--- Contra Costa Gazette

1911

Jan. 5, 1911 --- SUBSIDIARY TO O&A INCORPORATED

"The Oakland & Bay Shore Railway Company" was incorporated on this date as a subsidiary corporation to the Oakland & Antioch, for the purpose of obtaining a franchise for the O&A in the City of Oakland along Shafter Avenue from a point east of College Avenue to 40th Street. The O&BS owned no equipment and was a railroad "in name only."

--- Official Records

Feb. 13, 1911 --- O&A OPERATES FIRST CAR

Promptly at the hour of three o'clock this afternoon the first electric car of the Oakland & Antioch Railway hove in sight over the Maltby Hill north of Concord and, amid the acclaims of the joyful populace, the tooting of scores of horns, and the tooting of many whistles, the car completed the first run from Bay Point to Concord.

The hour for the arrival of the first car had been originally set for two o'clock but owing to the condition of the roadbed which has not yet been ballasted the running was exceedingly slow and it was an hour later when the first car hove in sight over the hills to the north.

During the afternoon the Concord band discoursed music and the entire population of the town turned out to make "a Concord holiday." Long after the car had arrived at the end of its journey, and although the promoters had announced that because of the soft condition of the track caused by the recent heavy storm that no passengers would be carried over the line, the people stayed near admiring the beautiful car which is to be one of those in which they will soon ride. It was only after the car left on its return to Bay Point that the crowd dispersed.

C. E. Starkweather, general superintendent of construction work, operated the car from Bay Point to the present end of the line. From the moment it started its triumphal journey over the eight short miles, Messrs. Maltby, Arnstein and Naphtaly stood in the power house watching the indicator by whose fluctuations they could judge the progress of the car. In speaking of the run afterwards, Mr. Starkweather stated that not once after he started from Bay Point did he stop the car, which ran along on its own power as though it had been doing so for years. Following close behind the car was the construction engine and crew with a load of ties to be used in further work on the road.

--- Contra Costa Gazette

March 28, 1911 --- O&A IS REORGANIZED

The "Oakland, Antioch & Eastern Railway" is incorporated under the laws of the State of California by the backers of the Oakland & Antioch Railway for the purpose of extending the O&A eastward from Bay Point. The Oakland, Antioch & Eastern has an authorized stock issue of ten million dollars.

--- Official Records

(Note: When first incorporated, it was announced that the line would be extended from Bay Point to Stockton, there to connect with the Stockton-Sacramento line of the Central California Traction Co.; it is interesting to note that the OA&E stock certificates were illustrated with a picture of a CCT train. In December, 1911, however, it was announced that the OA&E would build its line from Bay Point to Sacramento.

(Though both the O&A and the OA&E were, for all practical purposes, one and the same, the Contra Costa County operations (Bay Point to Walnut Creek and later Lafayette) continued to be carried on under the name of O&A, with this name appearing on equipment, timetables, etc. The construction work from Bay Point to Sacramento was done under the name of the OA&E.

(In 1913 when through service commenced from Oakland to Bay Point and later to Sacramento the corporate name, "Oakland, Antioch & Eastern Railway," prevailed along the entire route. --- T. R. B.)

April 1, 1911 --- WORK PROGRESSING ON O&A

The O&A is rapidly building and while the track layers are waiting for the bridge men to finish the steel bridge at Hookston, the graders have completed the roadbed from the Smith Ranch to Castle Rock. (Note: This latter was to be the Meinert Jct.-Walwood Branch, about two miles long.)

Also the branch line to the Martin Ranch (Note: A

short branch of the Walwood Branch.) where the lime quarries
of the Spreckles Company are located is being rushed to completion.

The overhead wire construction on the main line
has been completed to Walnut Creek and as soon as the Hookston Bridge is completed track will be laid down on this last
stretch.

The roadbed along the line from Bay Point to Concord is being leveled as rapidly as possible in preparation for
operation of cars on a regular schedule. However, it will be
some time before the road is built on to Lafayette when the
active competition with the Southern Pacific throughout the
valley can be started.

--- Contra Costa Gazette

April 11, 1911 --- O&A REACHES WALNUT CREEK

The rails of the O&A have at last reached the town
of Walnut Creek. The boosters of that town are planning a big
celebration to be pulled off soon... The schedule for regular
train service has not yet been worked out, but Traffic Manager
Fish has taken the matter up with the Santa Fe company and
trains on the electric line will soon be running to make connection with the Santa Fe trains at Bay Point.

The Concord depot is to be put up at once. The
building will be put up as a freight depot but for the present it
will also be used as a passenger station.

A night ballasting crew was put on the line Thurs-
day night and the roadbed will be put in first class shape at once.
Large numbers of laborers, in fact all the men that can be used
to advantage, are at work on the main and branch lines.
---Oakland Enquirer

May 4, 1911 --- TIME SCHEDULE TAKES EFFECT ON
OAKLAND & ANTI OCH!

Commencing this morning, the regular passenger schedule
went into effect over The Oakland & Antioch Railway. The
schedule, as announced at this time, is only temporary and
may be altered somewhat within a short time.

The electric cars will be operated on a schedule connecting at Bay Point with Santa Fe trains to and from San Francisco.

The first car left Concord this morning at 6:05 AM , arriving at Bay Point fifteen minutes later.

Cars will leave Walnut Creek, bound for Bay Point, at:
5:45, 8:25, and 10:40 AM; 12:18, 2:06, 4:02, 7:00 and 8:25
PM. Returning, cars will leave Bay Point at: 7:15, 9:17 and
11:22 AM; 1:00, 3:03, 6:02, 7:45 and 9:02 PM.

The eleven miles from Walnut Creek to Bay Point will be
covered in a little over 30 minutes.

The above schedule was furnished a Gazette representative
by Manager Fish of the Oakland & Antioch.

---Contra Costa Gazette

May 5, 1911 --- O&A TO CONNECT WITH KEY ROUTE

According to a well founded report in circulation in
realty circles in Oakland, a deal was closed in that city today
whereby the O&A secured possession of a large tract of land at
40th St. and Shafter Ave. for use as a railroad terminal. The
consideration was not made known but it is understood that extensive improvements will be made and that this will be the
connecting point with the Key Route, over which line passenger
service will be handled to San Francisco.

The Oakland & Bay Shore Railway Company, a
sister corporation to the O&A, has filed an application with
the Oakland City Council for a 50 year franchise on Shafter
Ave. from 40th St. to a point beyond College Ave. This

line will form the connecting link between the O&A, which
will come into Oakland over private right of way, and the
Key Route.

--- Contra Costa Gazette

June 13, 1911 --- THREE INJURED IN WRECK ON O&A

Two trainmen were seriously injured and a third
badly bruised and cut when a three car O&A train derailed
this afternoon in the first wreck to occur on the new line.

Scene of the wreck was at the foot of the grade on
the branch line leading to the Spreckles Quarry (Note: the Walwood Branch). The grade is rated at 6%, but the railroad men
claim that it is 7% or over.

A few minutes before two o'clock this afternoon
the train started from the quarry with the first load of rock to
be hauled from that place. The train consisted of one of the
O&A's fine new passenger coaches, a flat car and a large steel
rock car. When the descent began, Motorman Young applied
all the brakes but even with the wheels locked and the rails
heavily sanded, the rock car with its 55 tons was too great for
the passenger car to hold back. The train gradually gained mo-
mentum until the men found that it was running away; at this
point all three men jumped.

The train dashed down the hill with ever increasing
speed until it reached a curve at the bottom where it left the
rails. All three cars were very badly smashed and much repair
work will be necessary before they can be returned to service.

Luckily no one was in the passenger coach at the
time, for he would have been terribly mangled and instantly
killed.

---Contra Costa Gazette

June 26, 1911 --- OAKLAND GRANTS FRANCHISE ON
SHAFTER AVE.

The City of Oakland today granted a 35 year franchise to the Oakland & Bay Shore Ry. (Note: Actually O&A)
for a single track electric railway on Shafter Avenue from 40th
St. to a point several hundred feet east of College Avenue to
connect with the O&A's proposed line.

--- Official Records

July 6, 1911 --- SECOND WRECK ON ELECTRIC LINE

At 3:05 this afternoon the second wreck on the O&A
electric occurred at the same place and in almost the same
manner as the former one about three weeks ago when a train
jumped the track and was badly damaged at the foot of the hill
leading to the Spreckles Quarry.

A few minutes after three o'clock, motor car No.
2 (Note: Believed to be Central California Traction Co. box
motor No. 2 which records indicate was leased to the O&A),
having completed the switching work at the quarry started down
the grade with two empty gondolas. Though the brakes were
set hard and fast and the wheels were dragging on the sanded
rails, the train increased its speed and the crew, realizing that
another wreck was impending, jumped for their lives, escaping
with a few minor cuts.

At the foot of the long grade the motor car crashed
into two empty flat cars. The trucks of the motor car remained
on the rails while the body was hurled into a field.

The loss to the company will be considerable, and
officials are considering installing a drum and cable to ease the
loaded cars down the hill.

--- Contra Costa Gazette

July 22, 1911 --- MONEY SECURED TO COMPLETE O&A

A $2,000,000 bond deal for which negotiations were
started some time ago by the promoters of the O&A has been
closed in New York and the funds are now available for com-

O&A's opening day crowds were so large that the interurban company rented a coach from the Santa Fe; here this makeshift train is seen---a motor at each end, no multiple unit operation, and the outsize coach taxing the light rails sorely.   (CS)

This busy scene was snapped in 1912 near Concord and shows a steam shovel of the period hard at work loading a ballast train, hauled by an ex-SP steam engine of the 4-6-0 type. (Carl German---AEB)

pleting the electric road into Oakland. The Anglo California
Trust Company of San Francisco will act as trustee in the bond
deal and as soon as desired the money will be handed over to
officials of the line.

> --- Contra Costa Gazette

July 22, 1911 --- CABLE BEING INSTALLED AT QUARRY

A great drum is being installed at the Spreckles
Quarry which, with a cable, will be used in easing the loaded
gravel cars down the steep grade in order to prevent a recur-
ence of the costly accidents which have happened at that place
on the O&A line.

> ---Contra Costa Gazette

July 26, 1911 --- GREAT TUNNEL FOR O&A

After many months of preliminary effort, the great
work of tunnelling the Contra Costa hills for the running into
Alameda County of the O&A electric railway has been defini-
itely settled, according to a special message received this afternoon.

The message states that yesterday in San Francisco
in the offices of the O&A the contract for building a tunnel thru
the hills from Redwood Canyon was signed.

> --- Contra Costa Gazette

Aug. 2, 1911 --- O&A TICKETS SOLD BY SANTA FE

Through an arrangement reached by the Santa Fe
and the O&A, one-way or round trip tickets may now be purchased in Oakland for all points touched by the O&A line. Previously it was necessary to buy tickets to Bay Point on the Santa
Fe and make the purchase of another ticket for stations on the
O&A between Bay Point and Walnut Creek.

> --- Oakland Enquirer

Aug. 16, 1911 --- WORK STARTED ON TUNNEL

Work has been started and a force of laborers is
being augmented from day to day by the O&A in Redwood Canyon, where the railroad will start its tunnel leading through the
hills into Alameda County.

The brush has all been cut away from the hillside
about the mouth of the proposed bore and the line of the railway is surveyed and staked out from Walnut Creek to the hill
at the head of Redwood Canyon. A commissary department has
been started and all of the preliminary preparations made for
the working of a big force of men.

> --- Oakland Enquirer

Sept. 28, 1911 --- FIRST O&A RAILS LAID IN OAKLAND

The actual laying of rails on the O&A Ry. in Oakland commenced yesterday when a spur track connecting the
new line with the Key Route was put in at 40th St. and Shafter
Ave. Trolley poles are being set along the route as fast as possible and a big crew of graders is now at work laying the grade
for the trackmen.

This morning work began on the Oakland side of
the 3,200 foot tunnel through the Contra Costa hills. A crew
is already at work on the Contra Costa County side and work
is to be hurried as fast as three shifts can do it.

Yesterday a crew of Key Route track layers put in
a switch connecting the track of the O&A with the Key Route's
40th St. line. O&A laborers cut through the block at Opal and
Shafter Ave. and 40th St. which is to be the Oakland terminal
of the new road. Tracks were laid there today.

The engineering corps on the final survey between
the Oakland terminal and the tunnel, more than three miles,
will have completed their work within a few days. Trolley
poles have already been planted along Shafter Ave. to College
Ave. Grading on Shafter Ave. to the point where the line begins climbing into the hills will be done by the Ransome-Crummy

Co. of Oakland, but the grading from that point to the tunnel
will be done by the Shattuck-Edinger Co. of San Francisco who
have contracts for other work on the road which is now in progress.

Crews of workmen will begin Monday both at the
tunnel and at the end of Shafter Ave. in Oakland cutting the
grade of the new line and as fast as it is made rails will be
laid from the tunnel end and the rock taken from the tunnel
will be carted down the grade for ballast, and rails will be laid
both from the tunnel and from the Oakland ends of the grade.

A big crew of men are rushing work on the line
from Walnut Creek to Lafayette. Another gang of men is at
work in the Moraga Rancho and still another at the north face
of the big tunnel.

> --- Oakland Enquirer

Dec. 1, 1911 --- LAFAYETTE RECEIVES FIRST O&A CAR

The first electric car over the O&A Ry. into Lafayette was operated today and the arrival of the car in that town
from Bay Point, Concord and Walnut Creek with officials of the
road and a large number of passengers from the above towns
marked a new era in the development of the hill region of western Contra Costa.

The road as far as Lafayette will soon be completed. The work of rocking and ballasting the roadbed not being
finished yet, but this will be done shortly.

> --- Contra Costa Gazette

Dec. 19, 1911 --- OA&E SEEKS FRANCHISE IN SACRAMENTO

Application was made to the Sacramento Board of
Trustees last night by a representative of the OA&E Ry. for a
franchise to enter Sacramento.

Speaking of the project today, a representative of
the railroad denied that "Borax" Smith of the Key Route or the
United Properties of San Francisco are interested in the road.
He said the road is completely financed and when finished will
give Sacramento a two and a half hour electric train service to
San Francisco.

The road will enter Sacramento from the west side
over the new Vallejo Northern Bridge, crossing the river at "M"
Street. Application was made for three separate franchises last
night. The route outlined therein was as follows: (1) On "M"
St. from the center of the channel of the Sacramento River to
Fourth St. (2) Along Front St. from "M" St. to "Y" St. (3)
From Fourth & Y along Fourth to "I" St., down I to 3rd St.
This last gives an outlet to the new Southern Pacific Depot as
proposed, while the other lines signify use of the tracks of
other electric railroads in this city.

> --- Sacramento Bee

<u>1912</u>

March 16, 1912 --- SAN RAMON VALLEY RAILROAD
INCORPORATED

The "San Ramon Valley Railroad" was incorporated on this
date under the laws of the State of California as a subsidiary
corporation of the Oakland, Antioch & Eastern for the purpose
of building an electric railroad from Saranap (near Walnut
Creek) to Danville, a distance of eight miles. Capital stock:
$250,000.

When placed in service in 1914, this line was known as the
Danville Branch of the OA&E.

> --- Official Records

April 5, 1912 --- WORK ON O&A TUNNEL PROGRESSING

Although work is progressing on the great tunnel of
the O&A Ry. through the hills from Redwood Canyon to Oakland, there is little possibility of the bore being completed by

the first of July.

Three eight-hour shifts are at work on both the east and west portals of the tunnel but the work is necessarily slow because of the water encountered, the hills seeming to be literally permeated with water which drips from the roof of the tunnel in a steady stream.

The grading for the railroad through Moraga Valley has been completed but the bridges and culverts are not in place and work has been stopped there.

--- Contra Costa Gazette

April 6, 1912 --- STEEL BRIDGE PROPOSED FOR OA&E LINE

An application for permission to build a drawbridge across Suisun Bay from a point west of Pittsburg to Chipps Island has been filed with the War Department by the OA&E Ry. The projected bridge is on the site of the one proposed several years ago by the Santa Fe Railroad, but withdrawn after strenuous objections had been encountered. The proposed bridge of the electric line will clear the high water mark by about ten feet, is of steel construction and will have a passage in the center 300 feet wide with a lift span for the passing of river craft.

--- Contra Costa Gazette

May 21, 1912 --- LAYING RAILS TOWARD REDWOOD CANYON

The work of laying rails along the line of the O&A Ry. from Lafayette, the present terminus of the line, to the Redwood Canyon tunnel was begun today. The roadbed has been entirely completed with the exception of two cuts and labor crews are working at these places now to have the grade established by the time the track men arrive at these points. The ties and rails to be used have been on spur tracks at Walnut Creek and Lafayette for several weeks.

--- Contra Costa Gazette

May 28, 1912 --- ELECTRIC LINE LETS CONTRACT

It was reported locally today that the contract for the building of the OA&E's line from Bay Point to Sacramento has been awarded on a percentage basis to J. G. White & Co., the well known firm of construction engineers. Work is to be commenced early in July or as soon as the right of way are secured from Bay Point eastward and will be rushed with all possible speed.

--- Contra Costa Gazette

June 29, 1912 --- TRAIN FERRY FOR ELECTRIC LINE

That the OA&E Ry. is not carrying all of its fish in one basket is shown by the fact that a contract for a car ferry for transporting electric trains across Suisun Bay from West Pittsburg to Chipps Island has been awarded to an Oakland shipbuilding firm and work has already commenced. The railroad has applied to the War Department for permission to bridge the upper bay, but it is possible that the permit will be refused because of the opposition which has developed among the steamer men on the grounds that the bridge will be an impediment to river traffic. Even though the permission for the bridge is granted, it will be a long time before it is completed and the electric road, which is building into Sacramento as rapidly as possible, is desirous of having the road in operation.

According to company officials, the ferry trip will consume eight minutes and it is believed by them that the work of getting an electric train onto the boat, ferrying it over, disembarking, and getting under way again, will not take more than ten minutes in all. This is less than half the time the Southern Pacific devotes to transporting its trains across Carquinez Straits.

Electric trains three cars long will run directly onto the ferry, and the trip will begin immediately. In a train of six cars, the fourth car will be a motor also, and thus the two sections will pull upon the ferry boat at practically the same time without requiring the services of a switch engine and without the delays incident upon cutting loose the engine and a few cars and then coming back for the others.

--- Contra Costa Gazette

Aug. 3, 1912 --- NEW BRIDGE PLANS SUBMITTED

After numerous conferences with officials representing the various navigation interests on the Sacramento and San Joaquin Rivers, it is reported that the management of the OA&E Ry. has decided to submit to the Federal engineers an amended set of plans for the proposed bridge across Suisun Bay at Chipps Island.

The new plans call for a sloping structure, the highest portion of which would be about 70 feet above high water. Rough sketches of the proposed bridge show three spans each 290 feet long, and a draw span of about the same length, all of which are about 70 feet above high water. From either end of this elevated stretch the bridge begins sloping down to the shore line on a grade of from 1-1/2 % to 2%. The span along the sloping sections of the bridge are narrower than those along the highest stretch and the piers are nearer together as the shores are approached.

It is claimed by the engineers for the railroad that the new plans would permit all river craft, save vessels with very high masts, to pass under the high section and that the width of the spans would minimize the danger of collision with the piers. Vessels carrying high masts would be obliged to pass through the drawbridge.

--- Contra Costa Gazette

Oct. 5, 1912 --- RUSHING WORK NORTH OF BAY

The first grading camp of the OA&E Ry. in Solano County has been established at Bird's Landing and the grading crews with teams, scrapers and plows are being assembled there by the contractors who have charge of the grading thru that territory.

All of the rights of way through eastern Solano and Yolo Counties have been obtained by the electric railroad and the construction work is expected to proceed without delay.

--- Contra Costa Gazette

Oct. 10, 1912 --- SUISUN BAY BRIDGE PERMIT GRANTED

The OA&E Ry. today received permission from the War Department to bridge Suisun Bay. However, the electric line will have to share the bridge with any other railroad company which desires to use it. This is a condition imposed by the War Department.

The terms under which the bridge permit was given are as follows: The draw span must be a vertical lift 200 feet wide and 150 feet high, or a bascule 200 feet wide, or a swing draw with 170 foot openings each side and a center draw pier. The bridge must be commenced within one and completed within three years. The OA&E must furnish and maintain tugs, lights, fog signals and guides to help vessels through the draw, and must make the bridge suitable for steam and electric railroads, highway and pedestrian travel.

The officials and promoters of the OA&E are greatly encouraged now that the desired bridge permit has been issued by the War Department and announce that the road will be completed through to Sacramento as soon as possible. Opposition is still to be encountered from the shipping interests of Stockton, but it is hardly expected that this will prove an obstacle and that all difficulties which may arise will be readily overcome.

--- Contra Costa Gazette

Oct. 19, 1912 --- OAKLAND & ANTIOCH TO RELAY TRACK

Seventy pound rails which are to be laid on the line of the O&A Ry. in Contra Costa County and which will replace the present 48 pound rails in preparation for the handling of through traffic to Sacramento have arrived on the ground and have been distributed along the line from Bay Point to Lafayette. The light rails which are now in service along the

Laying track on upper Shafter Ave. between College Ave. and Rockridge in 1912. This work was conducted by private contractors using manual and animal labor. This part of the line was constructed by
The Oakland & Bayshore Railway, a paper company formed to secure the franchise within the Oakland
city limits and maintain it until 1913 when train operation got underway.   (Cook & Cook, VS)

Finishing touches are being put on track at the corner of Shafter & College Avenues, Oakland, where
the interurban crossed the College Ave. streetcar line. The year: 1912.   (Cook & Cook, VS)

line will be used in building spurs and side tracks. The heavy
rails will make a more substantial and stable roadbed on which
greater speed can be made by the electric trains when the line
is completed through to Sacramento.
--- Contra Costa Gazette

Oct. 21, 1912 --- BEGIN WORK ON OA&E SUBWAY

With several score teams, graders and scrapers at
work near McAvoy, the Palmer, McBryde & Quayle Construction Company this morning began the work of digging OA&E's subway under the tracks of the Southern Pacific and Santa Fe. The
contract for the undergrade crossing was awarded last week and
terms call for the completion of the work within six months.

The work of driving piles for the ferry slips on Chipps
Island has begun and the slips will be finished in record time in
order that the car ferry which will transport the electric trains
across the head of Suisun Bay until such time as the bridge---
permission for which has been granted by the War Department---
will be completed.

The electric line is being built southward from Sacramento with all possible speed and also from Bay Point eastward, and the tracklaying will begin within a short time.
--- Contra Costa Gazette

Nov. 23, 1912 --- CONSTRUCTION OF SUISUN BAY BRIDGE
BEGINS

The actual work of construction of the great drawbridge which is to span Suisun Bay at Chipps Island has been
started by the OA&E Ry. at a point near Pittsburg where the
line swings northward. Three piledrivers are now at work on
the Contra Costa shore driving piles for the slips for the ferry
which is to be operated until such time as the great bridge is
completed. The piledriving crews are also carrying on similar work on the Chipps Island side.

The chief engineer who is in charge of the bridge
construction stated on Thursday that the work will require two
and a half years for completion. Large gangs of men will be
employed for that period. The ferry which is now being built
in Oakland will be rushed to completion in order that it may
be ready for operation when the electric line is completed to
Sacramento and before the bridge is completed.
--- Contra Costa Gazette

Dec. 9, 1912 --- TUNNEL MEN BURIED

Crushed under tons of rock and earth which crashed
through heavy timbers placed in position for their protection,
Tobo Arozich and Luke Paich, Austrian tunnel workers in the
employ of the O&A Ry., were instantly killed in the Redwood
Canyon tunnel this morning.

The accident occurred at 10:10 AM and it was not
until half an hour later that the debris had been sufficiently
cleared to permit the recovery of the bodies of the unfortunate
men. The men were shovelling earth at the face of the heading near the engineers' station about 2,000 feet from the east
portal of the great bore. The cave-in came without warning
and the men were unable to save themselves.
--- Contra Costa Gazette

<u>1913</u>

Jan. 12, 1913 --- GREAT TUNNEL IS REALITY

The OA&E's great tunnel through Redwood Peak at
Shepherd Canyon is a reality. The laborers working from the
two ends finally plowed their way through the last remaining
wall at 9:45 o'clock last night and grasped hands through the
little hole first made.

Samuel L. Naphtaly, president of the railway,
went through the tunnel from end to end this morning in company with the engineers who were in charge of the work. The

bore is 3,400 feet long and will take about thirty days more
to complete with the necessary timbering, etc. The outer
circumference of the two bores made from the opposing ends
met within an inch, according to Naphtaly.
--- Contra Costa Gazette

Jan. 18, 1913 --- SACRAMENTO DEPOT SITE OBTAINED

The OA&E Ry. this week closed a deal whereby it
becomes the owner of property situated on Third St. between
"H" and "I" Streets in Sacramento, which will be used as a
depot site. There was some question as to whether the railroad could obtain the site for its depot without condemnation
proceedings, but the recording of the deed indicates that some
compromise was reached.

The railroad recently filed a petition with the City
Commission asking for permission to lay a spur track at this
point. Two tracks are already laid there and there is little
question but that this property will be the site of the depot, although the company has not officially made any announcement.
--- Sacramento Bee

Feb. 14, 1913 --- FIRST ELECTRIC TRAIN THROUGH OA&E
TUNNEL

The first OA&E electric train passed through the
Redwood Canyon tunnel this morning onto the Oakland side and
ran down the line for a distance of one mile to Lake Temescal,
to which point the rails have been laid. On board the first car
were Vice-president Naphtaly of the railroad, members of the
Board of Supervisors of Contra Costa County, other county officials, and prominent citizens.

At this time the track layers have completed their
work one mile west of the tunnel in Oakland and the railroad's
big rock quarry in Redwood Canyon is working to capacity turning out the rock for the ballasting of the roadbed.
--- Contra Costa Gazette

Feb. 17, 1913 --- PERMIT GRANTED FOR SAN RAMON LINE

Prescribing how and where the tracks shall be built,
how the crossings shall be maintained, and fixing a time limit
for the completion of the work, the Board of Supervisors this
morning granted to the San Ramon Valley Railroad, a subsidiary corporation to the OA&E line, a permit to build its line
through the San Ramon Valley along the county road, said permit to hold for fifty years. The granting of the permit was
hailed with joy by the people of Danville and vicinity who are
anxious to have the road built and who, in order to further the
project, have subscribed large sums in bonds to pay for the construction of the line.
--- Contra Costa Gazette

March 2, 1913 --- GOLDEN SPIKE DRIVEN AT MIDNIGHT

A golden spike driven at midnight by General Manager H. A. Mitchell of the OA&E Ry. marked the completion
of the electric line from Oakland to Bay Point and the first electric train to pass over the line arrived at the Oakland terminal shortly after three o'clock this afternoon.

The contractors agreed that the rails would be laid
by March 1, and to make good their promise it has been necessary to work day and night for some time past. The result
being that it was just 24 minutes after midnight when the last
spike was driven.

The last spike was driven at a point midway between Lake Temescal and the Dingee Ranch in Oakland, and
marked the completion of the first 30 miles of main line track
from Oakland to Sacramento. A regular passenger service has
been offered between Bay Point and Concord and as far as Lafayette for over a year past, but the big tunnel and the difficult
fills on the Oakland side delayed the completion of the line into the Bay city.
--- Contra Costa Gazette

Track aligning on upper Shafter Ave., Oakland, in early 1913; this scene is between College Ave. and Chabot Road, better known as Rockridge. This is part of the Oakland & Bayshore Ry. franchise.   (Cook & Cook, VS)

Right: Car 52 of the Oakland Traction Co. at 40th & Shafter Yard in 1912; this car was leased by Oakland & Bayshore Ry. and operated on Shafter Ave. to hold the franchise until regular service could begin.   In this photo are important OA&E officials: Sam Naphtaly, second from left; W. Arnstein to his left; Harry A. Mitchell, fourth from left on step of car; Note rough roadbed and dirt bank at right; this later became part of storage yard trackage.
    (Cook & Cook, VS)

March 8, 1913 --- OA&E OFFICIALS HOSTS ON EXCURSION

With General Manager H. A. Mitchell acting as motorman of the train, the official opening of the OA&E Ry. from Oakland to Bay Point took place today when members of the Board of Supervisors of Contra Costa and Alameda counties, county officials, representative citizens and newspaper men were the guests of the officials of the electric line on the first tour of inspection.

Another excursion is to be held on April 5th, and regular passenger train service will be inaugurated on April 7th, according to a statement made by Vice-president W. Arnstein.
--- Contra Costa Gazette

March 22, 1913 --- ELECTRIC LINE NEARING COMPLETION

Track laying on the OA&E Ry. in the Sacramento Valley, which began two weeks ago on the Yolo County side of the "M" St. Bridge, has reached Glide's Pumping Station, six miles down the river.

Two hundred men, under the direction of Foreman S. T. Hughes, are steadily engaged in the work and by July 1 it is promised that the remaining 45 miles between Glide's and Montezuma will be laid and the new line connecting Sacramento with Oakland and San Francisco will be complete.

The rails are being made at the Illinois Rolling Mills in Joliet, Illinois, and considerable delay in delivery is being experienced. The grading is completed and the long trestle over the Yolo Basin will soon be finished.
--- Sacramento Bee

March 30, 1913 --- CARS CRASH; EIGHT INJURED

Running down from the tunnel of the OA&E Ry., a distance of two miles, a runaway steel gondola loaded with broken ties today crashed into a northbound College Avenue streetcar at Shafter Ave. crossing, demolished the front of the streetcar, injured eight persons, then hurtled on across College Ave. after leaving the tracks, tore down a eucalyptus tree, clipped off a telephone pole, demolished a vacant real estate office and was brought to rest in a ditch after tearing out the side of Dr. Newell Wilson's home, 5663 Shafter Ave., and deposited the wood in the basement of the home.

The accident was caused by the failure of an attempted coupling of the gondola to an engine, after the car's brakes had been loosened. The coupling pin fell into place without catching the link and the car started down the grade from the tunnel. The conductor on the runaway car tried in vain to stop its progress by setting the hand brakes, but they failed to check the increasing speed of the runaway. Bravely sticking to the swaying car as it lurched around curves on the steep descent, he finally jumped for his life when he saw that there was no hope of stopping it.

The College Ave. car had stopped south of the Shafter Ave. crossing where the railroad makes a sharp curve to the south. The conductor of the streetcar ran ahead and reported the line clear. He could see but a short distance up the track on account of the curvature and because of a drug store at the southeast corner of the intersection. The motorman sent his streetcar ahead and had crossed the intersection when the gondola, in a cloud of dust, bore down at terrific speed. He had only time to stop his car when the gondola struck the first portion of the curve. So terrific was its speed at that point that it left the rails without deviation from the straight line it had pursued down the stretch. It tore across the surface of the street, struck and smashed the front portion of the streetcar, and continued across the street.
--- Oakland Enquirer

April 3, 1913 --- CONTRACT LET FOR SAN RAMON VALLEY
RAILROAD

The contract for the building of the San Ramon Valley branch of the OA&E Ry. by the San Ramon Valley RR., a subsidiary corporation, has been awarded to the firm of Pal-

mer, McBryde & Quayle, and grading work is to begin at once.

The OA&E's ferry slips on Mallard and Chipps Islands have been finished and the new ferry boat, "Bridgit," will be launched within a few days in the Oakland shipyards. The drawbridge across Montezuma Slough has been finished, as has the 13,000 foot trestle across Yolo Basin. The subway under the Santa Fe and Southern Pacific railroads near McAvoy will be finished about the first of May.
--- Contra Costa Gazette

April 7, 1913 --- OA&E OPENS LINE, S. F.-OAKLAND TO
BAY POINT

The OA&E on this date inaugurated regularly scheduled passenger and freight service between San Francisco, Oakland and Bay Point as "OA&E Time Table No. 1," with a schedule of six roundtrips daily between San Francisco, Oakland and Bay Point, and five roundtrips daily on the Walwood Branch from Meinert Jct. to Walwood goes into effect. This timetable succeeded O&A Time Table No. 7 which covered operations between Bay Point and Lafayette, including the Walwood Branch.

Under terms of an agreement worked out between the OA&E and the San Francisco-Oakland Terminal Railways (the Key Route) the OA&E interurbans were operated over the Key Route's 40th St. line between the OA&E Depot at Shafter Ave. and the Key Route Pier which jutted far out into San Francisco Bay, thus enabling OA&E passengers to transfer directly to Key Route ferry boats to San Francisco.
--- T.R.B.

April 23, 1913 --- OA&E BUYS MOUNTAIN LINE

Purchase of the controlling interest in the Nevada County Narrow Gauge Railroad by the OA&E Ry. from Mrs. S. A. Kidder, President and principal owner, was announced in Grass Valley today.

The deal was negotiated by I. Steinhard of the London-Anglo-Paris Bank of San Francisco and involves nearly $500,000.

The Nevada County Narrow Gauge was built from Colfax to Nevada City in 1875 by John Kidder. Upon his death a few years ago, control passed to his widow who since has been at the head of the operating company.
--- Contra Costa Gazette

April 26, 1913 --- CONSTRUCTION OF SAN RAMON BRANCH
BEGINS

With the arrival of the first shipment of timbers and materials required for the construction of the overhead crossing of the San Ramon Valley Railroad over the tracks of the Southern Pacific south of Walnut Creek, the actual construction work has been started on the first main branch of the OA&E.

The material arrived over the OA&E line Tuesday and a large crew is now engaged in the preliminary construction. As soon as the crossing is completed the grading of the roadbed and the laying of the rails will proceed with dispatch.
--- Contra Costa Gazette

May 31, 1913 --- PROGRESS ON SUISUN BAY BRIDGE

A concrete pier which is raising its head above the waters of Suisun Bay off the shore of Mallard Island in Contra Costa County and which is nearly half finished is the initial unit of construction of the highest and longest railroad bridge in the west. The OA&E's span from Contra Costa County to Chipps Island. The bridge, with its approaches, will be about two miles long and it will tower 70 feet above the channel of the bay so that the ordinary river craft may pass under it without delay. It will cost in the neighborhood of $1,500,000.

Waddle & Harrington, engineers of St. Louis, are in charge of the bridge construction.
--- Contra Costa Gazette

Motor 1013, Train No. 10, in the hole between Chipps and Sacramento in October, 1913.
(Frank A. Jay Photo --- TRB)

June 21, 1913 --- LAYING OF RAILS COMPLETED TO CAPITOL

The laying of rails on the line of the OA&E Ry. from Bay Point to Sacramento was completed today and when the power line work, which is being rushed at all possible speed by a large crew of electricians is completed, the line will be ready for traffic. Poles for the trolley line have been erected to a distance of ten miles south of Sacramento.

Engines are being installed this week in the railroad's ferry boat which is under course of construction at Alameda. The vessel will be ready for service by July 1st. It will be christened the "Bridgit," and will carry six standard coaches when loaded to capacity.

The new rolling stock ordered by the company is beginning to arrive. Eight passenger coaches (1007-1014) and a parlor-observation car ("Moraga") are already in the Oakland yards. Eight steel cars (1019-1026) are being built in Berkeley. Four additional cars (1015-1018) are due to be shipped from the east on July 15th, and two 65-ton electric locomotives (105 & 106) will be shipped at the same time.

--- Contra Costa Gazette)

July 2, 1913 --- FIRST OA&E TRAIN FROM CAPITOL TO BAY

The first electric train over the OA&E line from Sacramento to Oakland was operated today when officials and promoters of the road made their first official tour of inspection of the entire line. The ferry boat "Bridgit," which will ferry the electric trains across Suisun Bay pending the building of the big bridge, was delivered to the railroad company last night and carried its first train of cars this morning.

The train left Sacramento at eight o'clock this morning and at West Pittsburg, where the line to Pittsburg connects, the train was run on eastward into that town. This trip being made imperative by the reported threat of interested Pittsburg persons to revoke their grant of land and rights of way if the first car was not run into Pittsburg today.

The line from Bay Point to Sacramento, a distance of 53 miles, was built in eleven months, and among the engineering problems overcome were a two-mile trestle across the Yolo Basin, a concrete subway near McAvoy and the building of a high embankment to cross a great lake on the property of the Solano Irrigated Farms Company.

--- Contra Costa Gazette

July 19, 1913 --- TRACK LAYING BEGINS ON SAN RAMON VALLEY BRANCH

The laying of rails on the San Ramon Valley line of the OA&E Ry. started this morning when a crew of workmen in the employ of the firm of Palmer, McBryde & Quayle began work on the Naphtaly Ranch just south of Walnut Creek.

The bridges between Naphtaly Jct. and Danville have been completed and construction work on the overhead crossing over the Southern Pacific line is also finished. The electricians will follow closely upon the tracklayers.

--- Contra Costa Gazette

Aug. 5, 1913 --- OA&E TRAINS OPERATE TO PITTSBURG

The OA&E Ry. extended through service to Pittsburg a distance of eight miles beyond Bay Point, today and trains will now operate daily from that terminus. The new stations after leaving Bay Point are: Nichols, McAvoy and West Pittsburg on the Sacramento main line, and Pittsburg on a branch line extending from West Pittsburg, a distance of two and one half miles.

Effective today a new timetable was adopted which will have six trains daily in each direction between San Francisco-Oakland and Pittsburg, and one train each way, in addition, which will run between San Francisco-Oakland and Concord.

--- Contra Costa Gazette

Aug. 23, 1913 --- NEW LOCOMOTIVES FOR OA&E ARRIVE

Two electric passenger locomotives (105 & 106), for use by the OA&E for heavy passenger trains, have arrived in Oakland from Pittsburgh, Pa., after a very speedy trip from the east. They were brought "special" by a single steam locomotive. For the "special" transportation the OA&E paid out $2,400.

The new locomotives are guaranteed to draw a 7 car passenger train 75 miles per hour on level track.

--- Contra Costa Gazette

Sept. 3, 1913 --- OPENING OF ELECTRIC LINE LINKS VALLEY AND BAY

The first electric railroad ever built between Sacramento and Oakland and San Francisco was placed in operation today when the Oakland, Antioch & Eastern Railway commenced regular passenger and freight service between the Capitol City and the Golden Gate.

Key Route Ferry Used

Passengers from San Francisco to Sacramento purchase tickets at the Key Route Ferry Depot (the Ferry Building) in San Francisco and take the Key Route boats to the pier on the Oakland side of the Bay (the Key Route Pier), where connections are made with electric trains of the OA&E. The trains run over the Key Route tracks to the corner of 40th St. & Shafter Ave., where the Oakland Depot of the OA&E is located.

The line from Oakland to Bay Point has been in operation since last April. From the Oakland Depot the route passes through the Rock Ridge district and Cape Horn, a deep gorge in the hills, which affords a magnificent panoramic view of Oakland and San Francisco.

Burrows Through Tunnel

At the top of the Berkeley Hills the route burrows through a 3,700 foot tunnel which carries the trains across the border line from Alameda into Contra Costa County, emerging in picturesque Redwood Canyon. Thence the line slopes down through fertile Moraga Valley and Lafayette, Walnut Creek and Concord; the scenery along this section of the route is unsurpassed. Bay Point is reached after a 39 mile ride from San Francisco.

Train Ferry Used

Leaving Bay Point, the line extends to Mallard Island, six miles further on, where---for the present---the cars are being ferried across Suisun Bay to Chipps Island, a distance of 2,200 feet, on the ferry boat "Bridgit." Preliminary work has been commenced upon a monster bridge to span Suisun Bay near this point.

The line runs northeasterly from the Chipps Island ferry slip towards Sacramento, passing Chaplin Station, an old Sacramento River settlement not far from Collinsville, and proceeding to Montezuma Station where the old hamlet, formerly called Bird's Town, is located. Seven miles past this point lies the site of Solano City, the center of a big subdivision known as Solano Irrigated Farms. Passing this station, the line approaches the Sacramento River at Lisbon. The tracks run along the west levee of the Sacramento River for a short distance, pass through the West Sacramento colony and cross the River into the City of Sacramento via the "M" Street Bridge, in which the OA&E owns a part interest. A temporary brick building is being erected at the corner of Third & "I" Streets in Sacramento to serve as a passenger depot pending the construction of a permanent depot. The temporary depot will cost about $3,000.

The Train Service

Beginning today, eight passenger trains are running each way between Sacramento and San Francisco daily. The first trains in the morning will leave each end of the line at 6:30 AM. The last trains will leave at 7:40 PM. On the timetable, all the Sacramento trains will make connections at West Pittsburg with a branch line car into Pittsburg. The six trains each way now running between San Francisco and Bay Point and the commuters' train each way between San Francisco and Concord appear on the new timetable, in addition to the Sacramento trains. Thus making thirty passenger trains daily arriving and departing from Oakland and San Francisco.

Joins Other Lines

Through passenger and freight rates have been established with the connecting electric lines at Sacramento, viz: Northern Electric, Sacramento & Woodland, the Marysville and Colusa branch of the Northern Electric, and the Central California Traction Company. The company has a long lease with the Key Route for the conveyance of passengers across San Francisco Bay.

--- Sacramento Bee

Oct. 29, 1913 --- BLOCK SIGNAL SYSTEM ON OA&E

The OA&E Ry. today put into operation its electric block signal system between Oakland and Chipps Island. Incidentally, it established a national record as the first interurban traction company in America to install a complete safety system of this character. Work is in progress now upon the installation of the block signals between Chipps Island and Sacramento. The full route from San Francisco Bay to the State Capitol will soon be safeguarded by these modern devices.

The A.C. automatic electric light block signal system is operated with a system of powerful electric lights, which are declared to be distinctly visible at a distance of one thousand feet in the stormiest weather or even in a heavy fog. The signals are located at intervals of about a mile along the route, although in some instances the intervals are shorter.

--- Contra Costa Gazette

Nov. 1, 1913 --- THE SAN RAMON VALLEY BRANCH

Construction on the San Ramon Valley Branch of the OA&E Ry. has been rushed within the last few days until the extension is now close to completion. The ground work has been finished to within two or three blocks of Danville but the wires have not yet been strung.

--- Contra Costa Gazette

Chapter 9

Facilities

Facilities on the South End were less pretentious than those of the North End. For instance, OA&E's shops at 40th & Shafter were by no means comparable to Mulberry Shops. Freight stations were smaller, terminal facilities at Oakland were not required as Key provided them, and no bridges of dimensions as great as those needed by NE were needed.

Perhaps of all the facilities OA&E did construct, two rate special attention: the tunnel, and the ferry. The ferry operation is given its own chapter herein, and the tunnel has already been described in previous chapters.

OA&E did take special pride in its automatic block signal system, a product of The Union Switch & Signal Company. Union's Model 13 block signals were familiar sights on South End lines from end to end, and were doubtless contracted for because of certain disastrous wrecks on Western interurban lines in 1913: Pacific Electric's rear end collision of crowded Venice trains at Vineyard, and the Napa Valley's unfortunate head-on meet with resulting damage suits which played an important part in slowing the progress then being made by that road.

To describe the OA&E's block signal system, we turn to a man who perhaps knew it better than anyone, Mr. F. A. Miller, OA&E's Superintendent of Power & Equipment:

"The present signal system was completed in May of 1914, following the extension of the original Oakland & Antioch Railway from Lafayette to Oakland, at which time the service was altered from suburban to interurban type. The original line had no signals whatever. The system now in use was furnished by The Union Switch & Signal Company, both for the section between Oakland and Bay Point and the last extension completed September 1913 to Sacramento. This signal installation is the only AC track-circuit system in the vicinity of San Francisco which uses light signals.

"The system is operated by 60 cycle current which is supplied to the signal mains at 2200 volts at Eastport and Concord for the signals from Oakland to Mallard, and at Dozier or Lisbon for the signals from Chipps to Sacramento.

"At signal locations and cut sections 0.6 kva. transformers supply current at 110 volts for relays and signals. Adjustable core transformers feed the track circuits at the center though about twenty less than 4,000 feet in length are end-fed. All spurs have a light switch indicator to show when a train may enter the main line. Sidings having one set of home signals are provided with light switch indicators at the east ends; sidings having two sets of home signals are provided with light switch indicators at both ends.

"Signals are hung on cedar poles 25 feet long, 7 inch tops, shaved and painted. All wiring is carried down poles and underground in redwood trunking and galvanized conduit. Bonding at switches and frogs and connections to impedance bonds is No. 0000 DBWP stranded copper.

"Track circuit wiring is No. 6 copper, rubber covered and all connections between the line wires and signals and relay boxes are made with No. 12 and No. 14 copper, rubber covered. Spare wires are drawn through all conduits. Distant signals (non-automatic) placed 1000 to 2000 feet in advance repeat the indications of their respective home signals. The overlaps favor west-bound trains; they vary in length from 300 feet to 400 feet.

"The number of miles thus protected is 85; the number of home signals, 117; the number of distant signals, 90; and the number of crossing signals operated in conjunction with the signal system, 14. The greater part of our line is, of course, single track with sidings at intervals varying from two to five miles. Our passenger trains are run up to a maximum speed of 62 mph, although our cars are geared for 55 mph.

"We have approximately 300,000 signal movements per month. Three men are employed exclusively for the maintenance of all signals and telephones. Each man has approximately one-third of the mileage to inspect and maintain. Gasoline cars are used to get over the line quickly. The maintainers must report to the dispatcher every hour, thus furnishing an account of their movements and enabling the dispatcher to reach the maintainers quickly in case of trouble.

"Although we have every confidence in the signal system, we do not feel that we would be justified in having it take the place of regular train order dispatching. Both practices in cooperation appear necessary to secure the greatest degree of safety.

"Fourteen automatic flagman highway crossing signals are operated from the track circuits. They ring a bell, swing an arm and show red and white lights. These were originally operated from the 1200 volt DC trolley circuits, but we found that maintenance costs would be decreased by using alternating current at 110 volts in place of 220 volts DC. The flagmen were furnished by Bell & Jamison, Los Angeles."

SAN FRANCISCO-SACRAMENTO RR.
All Concerned: August 27, 1925
    Please be advised that it is intended to start the new Union Passenger Station at Sacramento, 12th & H Sts., on Sunday, September 20, 1925. Train No. 11 on Saturday, September 19th, will be last to leave 3rd & I St. Station and Train No. 26 same date will be last to enter. Trains No. 8 and 10 on Saturday, September 19th, will operate into new station.
                                    L. H. RODEBAUGH

Concord Station was terminus of commuter trains as well as an important stop for main line trains. The 1916 view above shows motor 1017 next to platform and motor "Moraga" at right. Note "block" sign on roof of depot.

(J. K. Southerland Photo, TRB)

Below is Concord about ten years later. Motor 1017 heads a commuter train at center, while motor 1015 leads Train #17 at right. Note catenary, relocated pole line, and minor changes brought about in ten years.

(TRB Collection)

The wye at Saranap, 1913---during construction of Danville Branch. The main line is in center, with Train No. 13 approaching en route to Oakland. Track on right is the branch line to Danville and to Diablo, while at left a local freight is in the siding. Originally called "Ramon Junction," the station was called "Saranap," obtained by contracting Mrs. Sam Naphtaly's name: Sara-Nap. (Cook-VS)

Drawbridge, in Solano County, with a special, Extra 1014 West, crossing. The building at right was the substation, which remained manually operated to the end of electric operation---because it was necessary to maintain a bridge tender to operate the span; he doubled as substation oper ator. This photograph was taken in 1924. (Estey-VS)

A striking example of the problem of shifting earth faced by OA&E engineers in digging and maintaining the tunnel is shown in these photos, taken in 1914 and 1941.

Above, the west portal is seen as it appeared in 1914; note that earth was removed well down the sides of the retaining walls erected along the approach, strengthened by overhead girders. (DS)

The photo at left, taken on June 23, 1941---last day of passenger service between San Francisco and Pittsburg---reveals that earth had shifted well up on either side and extensions of the retaining walls had been required.   (VDB)

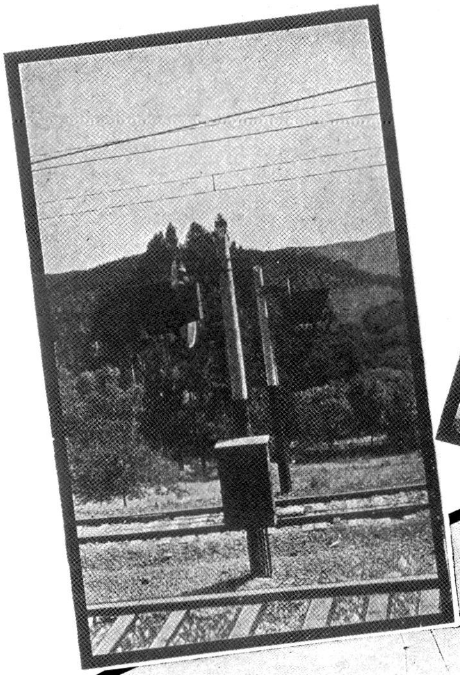

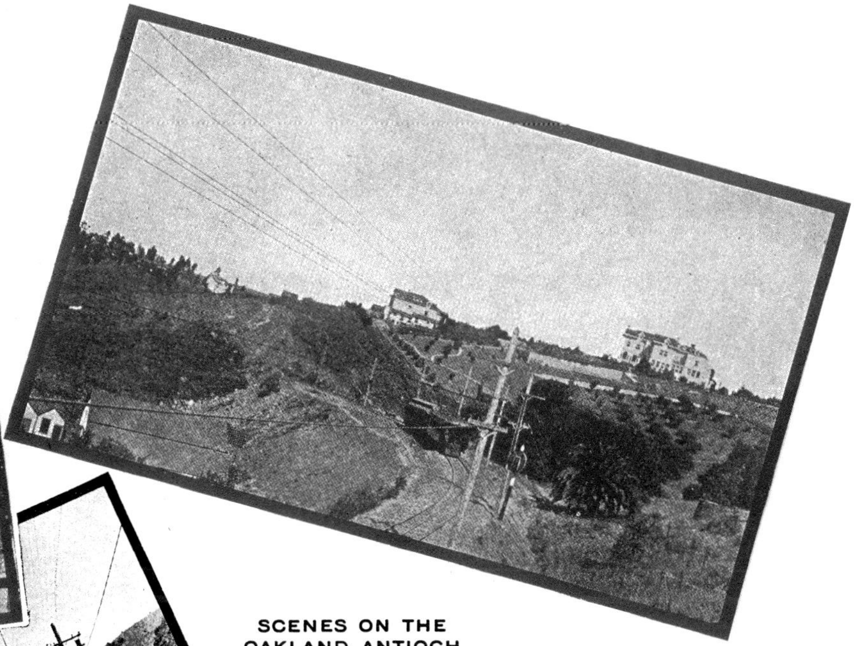

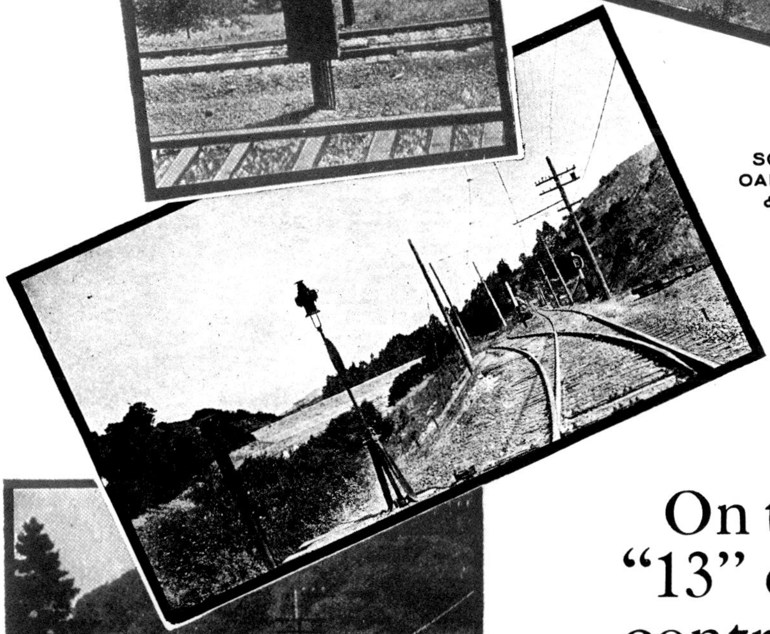

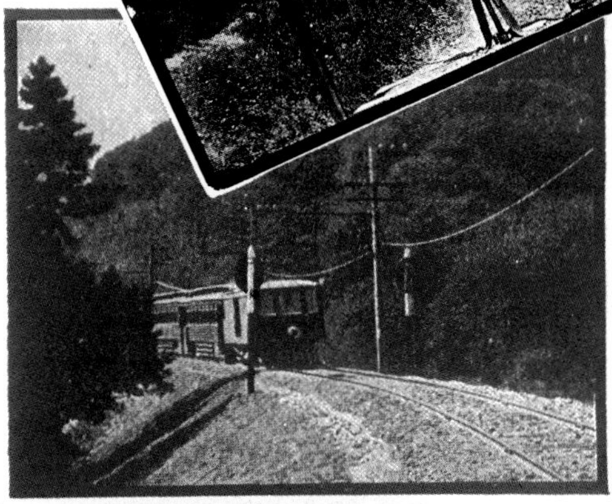

This 1915 ad is notable for the view of a box motor hauling rented Key System trailers in picnic service. (A. E. Barker)

On the O., A. & E., Model "13" electric light signals controlled by continuous A. C. track circuits facilitate traffic and protect trains.

Thus this road eliminates the collision hazard and promotes efficiency in operation.

Nerve center of OA&E was this complex at the intersection of 40th St. and Shafter Ave. in Oakland. Here cars were repaired and rebuilt; a miniature freight yard with interchange activities hummed with a myriad of moves; a busy interlocking plant sorted out hundreds of car movements; train crews reported on and off their runs; officials checked the pulse of this 85 miles of high speed interurban railway.

These photographs show 40th & Shafter as it is fondly remembered; today the site is unrecognizable: all these buildings, tracks and appurtenances have been swept into discard and new glass and steel structures have sprung up. Nothing is left to mark one of the west's interurban jugular veins save a single office door lettered "Western Pacific-Sacramento Northern."

(Top) 40th & Shafter from the west, looking east on 40th St. in 1939. The large building in foreground housed the shops and maintenance facilities.

(Left) 40th & Shafter from the east, looking west on 40th St. in 1939. This was the freight end of the site, with the freight house in center and the yard tracks to its rear. As can be seen, passenger cars were also stored here.

(Both, REM)

(Below) A head-on view of the junction. Repair shops are on the left, the triangular building in the center formerly housed the auditor's office and the accounting department. The first floor was occupied by the baggage room, store room and trainmen's locker room. Here also was the Westinghouse electro-pneumatic interlocking plant with eleven active and twelve spare levers. (AA-AH)

40th & Shafter

<u>PRESIDENT HARRY A. MITCHELL REMINISCES:</u> *

In the matter of not building into Antioch, Mr. Harry A. Mitchell years later gave this insight into the happenings which prevented OA&E's adding that prosperous area:

"It was Mr. Henry L. Lardner, San Francisco manager of J. G. White & Co., noted contractors who built the OA&E, who recommended that the OA&E lease the rails that were to have been used between Pittsburg and Antioch to The Sacramento Valley Electric, then building a proposed line to Red Bluff. Despite my protests, this was done and the short-lived Dixon Branch came into being.

"We had a hard time getting those rails back. When they were finally returned, the franchise to Antioch had lapsed and the right-of-way had reverted back to Mr. Hooper, the original owner. This was one of the early mistakes, and the present status of the country around Dixon and Antioch bears this out. Because of this, the SN today is not able to cash in on the present day development of Antioch."

On the subject of the OA&E's Sacramento extension, Mr. Mitchell had this to say:

"For us to get to Sacramento, it was necessary to outwit both the Southern Pacific and the Northern Electric. At that time, the NE was attempting to reach San Francisco through the means of the projected Vallejo & Northern which would connect Sacramento and Vallejo. At Vallejo, a fast steamer would connect with San Francisco.

"As a trick, we (OA&E) surveyed a line between Antioch and Lodi to give the impression we intended to come to Sacramento over the Central California Traction Company. However, at the same time we quietly surveyed the present route between Chipps and Sacramento. It is a further tribute to the early promoters that they were able to get War Department permission to build a bridge across Suisun Bay; the SP had tried to get this permission but had failed.

"We did the Northern Electric a favor by building the way we did. Had the Vallejo & Northern been completed, the present day Sacramento Northern would have been in a very unfavorable position."

A little known but exhilarating chapter in South End history was next recalled by President Mitchell:

"In 1918 the Key System suffered a strike and their trains were completely tied up. We needed the passenger business, so I arranged with Mr. W. R. Alberger (Key Route General Manager) to have the interlocking lined up so that OA&E trains could run straight to the Pier from 40th & Shafter. At the same time we hired a Crowley launch to run between the Key Pier and the Ferry Building; it carried a banner: 'OA&E.'

" When the strike became effective despite assurances to the contrary, I rode the head end of the first OA&E train to the Pier. The only incident was the explosion of a torpedo at 40th & Grove which sent its fragments in machine gun like fashion against the trap door of the steel trailer which was leading the train. After several days of operation, the Key union warned me that striking shipyard workers who had their headquarters near the subway planned to blow up OA&E Train No. 11 in the subway. Mr. Alberger also phoned me and begged me not to run the train.

"When the day came, we tied down the roof-mounted train trip arms so that the mob could not stop the train that way. As I boarded the head end of No. 11, I asked Motorman Charlie Holmes if he was willing to take that train down to the Pier. He was. As we approached the subway, Holmes put the controller on full and we set a speed record through the subway. As our train flew past, the crowd cheered. They didn't blow up the train, but that was the start of my gray hairs."

* In a talk before The Bay Area Electric Railroad Assn. on December 9, 1949; reported by Addison H. Laflin, Jr.

<u>THE ROCKRIDGE YARD, OAKLAND:</u>

The Rockridge Yard, commonly known as 59th Street Yard, was located in the Rockridge section of Oakland; it was at the point where the interurbans left their private right of way and entered upper Shafter Avenue. A spur led off the main line at the crossing of Chabot Road.

In OA&E's original plans, its main shops were to have been constructed on this site, but major opposition on the part of local residents was successful in preventing construction. A good reason for OA&E's reluctance to press its shop plan could readily be found in the fact that the company already was facing implacable opposition by residents to its operation of cars along Shafter Avenue. To antagonize them further would have been pointless and even dangerous.

The Rockridge property was used for the storage of the 1200 Class trailers, and Section Foreman's equipment and the Bridge & Building Department also used its storage tracks, of which there were many.

During the last ten years of operation by SN, most of the yard trackage disappeared; at the time of final abandonment in 1957, only a small stub track was left and this, of course, disappeared when the line was ripped up shortly thereafter.

The author, Vernon J. Sappers, wishes to acknowledge the kind cooperation of the following for whose aid in preparing this history he is deeply grateful:

Mr. Milton Ziehn, Secretary, S.N. Ry.
Mr. George Hademan, retired SN motorman
Mr. W. W. Nelson, retired Supt. Transportation, SN
Mr. Robert Bell-Booth, retired SN electrician
Mr. Emmett Murphy, retired Shop Foreman, SN
Mr. George Turner, Supt. of Equipment (deceased)
Mrs. Ellen Ruggles, stepdaughter of the late Charles
    Grell, SN brakeman
Mr. Frank Jay, retired OA&E conductor
Mr. O. H. Fischer
Mrs. Ethel Meier, widow of A. H. Meier, Master
    Car Builder, SN
Mr. Richard R. Reynolds, W.P. Public Relations Dept.
Mr. Brian Thompson
Mrs. Myrtle Richards
Miss Selma Prescher
Mr. George A. Alexander

"Ramon" was not beautiful, as this view demonstrates beyond cavil. However, the ferry served faithfully for forty years in all kinds of weather and seas. Here cars 1023 and 1014 were among others hitching a ride on December 24, 1939. (AA-AH)

"Twas so pleasant crossing the bay---" and passengers could hardly overlook the opportunity to stretch their legs during the few moments their train was aboard the "Ramon." Here Train No. 7 crosses on July 4, 1939.   (AA-AH)

Chapter 10

Operation

Train operation on the Oakland, Antioch & Eastern and its successor, San Francisco-Sacramento Railroad, was somewhat different than train operation on the Northern Electric. Unlike NE, OA&E passed through very few intermediate towns and had street running only in its terminal cities. Except for Concord---which was an important operating point and the terminus of several commute runs---there were no operators to speak of between Oakland and Sacramento. In most instances, OA&E train crews had to phone for their orders and take them over the telephone. The line was equipped with telephone jack boxes along the way so that crews could contact the dispatcher by plugging in the phone which was carried on all combination passenger motor cars.

Like Northern Electric, the OA&E used Forms 19 and 31 for train orders and its crews had to register their trains at certain points.

Unlike NE, the OA&E main line was completely equipped with automatic block signals of the track circuit type. Color light signals were used and all siding switches were equipped with switch indicators so crews could tell at a glance whether or not the main line was occupied. While OA&E's automatic block signal system was so complete that trains could be operated safely on signal indications alone, the management firmly believed in train orders and considered the signals to be an additional safeguard for the safe operation of the line.

Like NE, OA&E cars were equipped with air communicating signals, and the steam railroad code was used.

Inasmuch as OA&E's grade out of Oakland was 3% and included a short section of 4.5% grade near Lake Temescal, close attention was paid to brake tests. All OA&E trains were required to make a brake test just after passing Havens, and speed on the downgrade between Havens and Rockridge was restricted; in fact, a bell rang at 40th & Shafter whenever a train entered or left this section. Later the same srrangement was provided on the Lisbon Trestle.

OA&E-SF-S employees' timetables indicated all meeting points by printing meeting times in red instead of the usual bold face type, the usual practice. One OA&E rule which carried over to the end of service out of Oakland in 1957 required a motor to be on the downhill end of every train between Rockridge and Havens. In later years, however, this rule was not applied to passenger trains consisting of a motor car and a trailer.

OA&E train crews consisted of a conductor, motorman and brakeman. However, two man crews were used on the one-car trains which operated on the Danville, Dixon and Pittsburg branches. The short Walwood branch was

an exception, as in its later years one motor car was used and the crew consisted of a motorman, conductor and a brakeman; however, this was due to the fact that Walwood service was provided by the crew of a two-car Concord Local during its layover time at Concord.

OA&E and SF-S trains were under the jurisdiction of Key System officials while operating on rails of that company. It is interesting to note that the agreement between OA&E and Key Route (San Francisco-Oakland Terminal Railways) gave Key Route trainmen operating rights between 40th & Shafter and Havens; there is no record, however, of Key's ever exercising this right although possible operation of Key trains on this section of OA&E trackage was seriously considered in the 1930s and as late as World War II.

Because of the train ferry crossing, OA&E timetables carried certain special instructions. Until the large trolley wheels became standard equipment, trains used to change trolley wheels at the ferry on each trip. OA&E and SF-S used trolley poles exclusively while operating on their own rails; only in the last few months of passenger service was the use of the pantagraph by passenger cars permitted by SN, and then only when switching along the line, as at Concord.

The following eight pages are devoted to the reproduction of OA&E Operating Timetable No. 8, dated January 3, 1915. This has been loaned through the kindness of Mr. Addison H. Laflin, Jr.

OAKLAND, ANTIOCH & EASTERN RY.

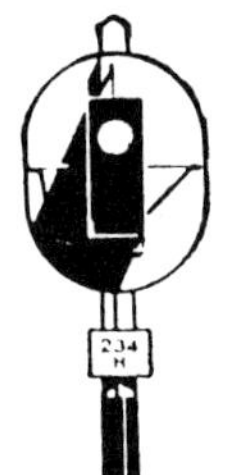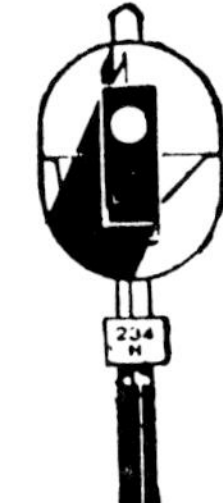

ELECTRIC TRAINS

PROTECTED BY

AUTOMATIC

Block Signals

BETWEEN

SACRAMENTO - SAN FRANCISCO

1006 appears to have been brand new when the above photo was taken at 40th & Shafter; second car is 1004.   (ECH)

OA&E changed Oaklanders' travel habits: Photo below is of an 8-car picnic train, about 1916. (D. Stearns)

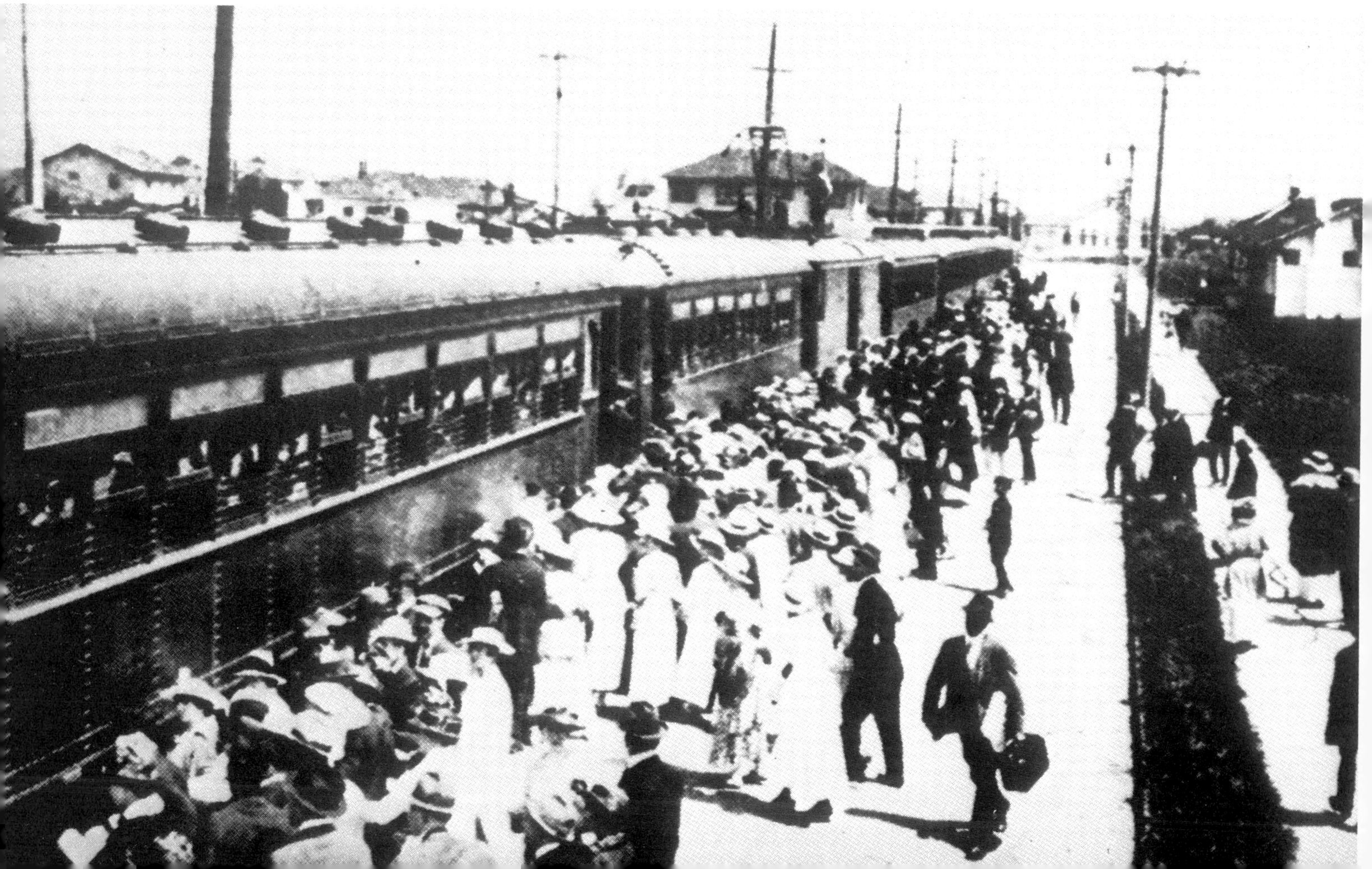

OAKLAND, ANTIOCH AND EASTERN RAILWAY

TIME TABLE

8

TO TAKE EFFECT SUNDAY, JANUARY 3, 1915 at 2 A. M.

PACIFIC STANDARD TIME (120TH MERIDIAN)

For the government and information of employes only and not intended for the use of the Public.
The Company reserves the right to vary from this
time table at pleasure.

H. A. MITCHELL, General Manager,

J. H. LEARY, Superintendent of Transportation.

PITTSBURG BRANCH

TIME TABLE No. 8 — January 3, 1915

WESTWARD — TOWARD SAN FRANCISCO — FIRST CLASS

Stations	Distance from Pittsburg	3	51	53	55	57	59	61	63	65	67	69
Service		Daily Ex. Sun.	Daily	Daily	Daily	Daily	Daily	Daily	Daily	Daily	Daily	Daily
(A.M./P.M.)		A.M.	A.M.	A.M.	A.M.	P.M.	P.M.	P.M.	P.M.	P.M.	P.M.	P.M.
WEST PITTSBURG (Ar.)	2.1	6.55	8.42	9.01	10.31	12.36	2.41	4.21	4.43	6.01	8.31	9.46
PITTSBURG (Lv.)	0.0	6.50	8.35	8.55	10.25	12.30	2.35	4.15	4.37	5.55	8.25	9.40

EASTWARD — FROM SAN FRANCISCO — FIRST CLASS

Stations	Distance from West Pittsburg	50	52	54	56	58	60	62	64	20	66	68
Service		Daily	Daily	Daily	Daily	Daily	Daily	Daily	Daily	Daily Ex. Sun.	Daily	Daily
(A.M./P.M.)		A.M.	A.M.	A.M.	P.M.	P.M.	P.M.	P.M.	P.M.	P.M.	P.M.	P.M.
WEST PITTSBURG (Lv.)	0.0	8.46	9.06	10.45	1.14	2.57	4.25	4.46	6.25	7.12	8.35	9.51
PITTSBURG (Ar.)	2.1	8.52	9.12	10.51	1.20	3.03	4.31	4.52	6.31	7.18	8.41	9.56

WALWOOD BRANCH

TIME TABLE No. 8 — January 3, 1915

WESTWARD — TOWARD SAN FRANCISCO — FIRST CLASS

Stations	Distance from Walwood	81	83
(A.M./P.M.)		P.M.	P.M.
MEINERT (Ar.)	2.8	1.00	6.23
WALWOOD (Lv.)	0.0	12.45	6.10

EASTWARD — FROM SAN FRANCISCO — FIRST CLASS

Stations	Distance from Meinert	80	82
(A.M./P.M.)		P.M.	P.M.
MEINERT (Lv.)	0.0	12.25	5.45
WALWOOD (Ar.)	2.8	12.40	5.58

DANVILLE BRANCH

TIME TABLE No. 8 — January 3, 1915

WESTWARD — TOWARD SAN FRANCISCO — FIRST CLASS

Stations	Distance from Danville	101	103	105	107	109	111
(A.M./P.M.)		A.M.	A.M.	A.M.	P.M.	P.M.	P.M.
SARANAP	8.6	7.30	9.05		1.10	4.05	6.30
ALAMO	4.4	7.17	8.52	10.00	12.54	3.50	6.18
DANVILLE	1.7	7.06	8.45	9.55	12.45	3.40	6.10
DIABLO	0.0	7.00					6.00

EASTWARD — FROM SAN FRANCISCO — FIRST CLASS

Stations	Distance from Saranap	100	102	104	106	108	110
(A.M./P.M.)		A.M.	A.M.	A.M.	P.M.	P.M.	P.M.
SARANAP	0.0		7.35	9.25	2.15	5.20	6.34
ALAMO	4.2		7.47	9.37	2.27	5.32	6.45
DANVILLE	6.9	6.50	8.00	9.45	2.35	5.42	6.55
DIABLO	8.6	6.57		9.52		5.50	

DIXON BRANCH

TIME TABLE No. 8 — January 3, 1915

WESTWARD — TOWARD SAN FRANCISCO — FIRST CLASS

Stations	Distance from Dixon	201	203	205	207	209	211	213	215
(A.M./P.M.)		A.M.	A.M.	A.M.	P.M.	P.M.	P.M.	P.M.	P.M.
DIXON JCT. (Ar.)	11.8	8.00	9.45	11.20	1.50	3.35	5.15	7.00	7.54
DIXON (Lv.)	0.0	7.30	9.15	10.50	1.20	3.05	4.45	6.30	7.29

EASTWARD — FROM SAN FRANCISCO — FIRST CLASS

Stations	Distance from Dixon Jct.	200	202	204	206	208	210	212	214
(A.M./P.M.)		A.M.	A.M.	A.M.	P.M.	P.M.	P.M.	P.M.	P.M.
DIXON JCT. (Lv.)	0.0	8.05	9.55	11.25	2.05	3.42	5.33	7.03	7.55
DIXON (Ar.)	11.8	8.35	10.25	11.55	2.35	4.12	6.03	7.28	8.25

If westbound block signal at Havens shows clear after No. 4 passes, No. 5 may proceed without waiting for indicator to clear.

If westbound block signal at Bay Point shows clear after No. 4 passes, No. 7 may proceed without waiting for indicator to clear.

If westbound block signal at Dozier shows clear after No. 4 passes, No. 9 will back out beyond home signal without waiting for indicator to clear. If home signal shows clear, No. 9 may proceed.

If westbound block signal at Havens shows clear after No. 2 passes, No. 7 may proceed without waiting for indicator to clear.

If eastbound block signal at McAvoy shows clear after No. 9 passes, No. 2 may back out beyond home signal without waiting for indicator to clear, and if home signal is clear they may proceed.

If westbound block signal at Millar shows clear after No. 2 passes, No. 11 will back out beyond home signal without waiting for indicator to clear, and if home signal shows clear they may proceed.

If eastbound block signal at Ohmer shows clear after No. 11 passes, No. 10 may back out beyond home signal without waiting for indicator to clear, and if home signal shows clear they may proceed.

If eastbound block signal at McAvoy shows clear after No. 13 passes, No. 12 may back out beyond home signal without waiting for indicator to clear, and if home signal shows clear they may proceed.

If westbound block signal at Saranap shows clear after No. 14 has passed, No. 15 may back out without waiting for indicator to clear.

If westbound block signal at Havens shows clear after No. 16 passes, No. 15 may proceed without waiting for indicator to clear.

If westbound block signal at Bay Point shows clear after No. 18 has passed, No. 19 may proceed without waiting for indicator to clear.

If westbound block signal at Saxon shows clear after No. 18 has passed, No. 21 will back out beyond home signal without waiting for indicator to clear, and if home signal shows clear they may proceed.

The above applies to trains meeting at their time card meeting points. In case trains meet at other than time card meeting point they will be governed by rule covering switch indicators unless they receive a train order authorizing them to proceed before indicator clears.

FIRST CLASS

TIME TABLE No. 8
JANUARY 3, 1915
STATIONS

22	20	18	16	14	12	10	2	6	4	Distance from San Francisco	Stations
Lv. Daily	Lv. Daily Ex. Sun.	Lv. Daily	Lv. Daily	Lv. Daily	Lv. Daily	Lv. Daily	Lv. Daily	Lv. Daily	Lv. Daily		
P.M.	P.M.	P.M.	P.M.	P.M.	P.M.	A.M.	A.M.	A.M.	A.M.		
8.00	5.15	4.40	4.00	3.00	1.00	11.20	9.00	8.00	7.20	0.0	SAN FRANCISCO — 2.9
8.15	5.29	4.54	4.15	3.15	1.15	11.35	9.15	8.15	7.35	2.9	PIER TERMINAL
8.18	5.35	4.57	4.18	3.18	1.18	11.38	9.18	8.18	7.38	2.9	PIER TERMINAL — 3.3
8.25	5.42	5.04	4.25	3.25	1.25	11.45	9.25	8.25	7.45	6.2	EMERYVILLE JCT. — 0.5
8.26	5.43	5.05	4.26	3.26	1.26	11.46	9.26	8.26	7.46	6.7	SAN PABLO AVE. — 1.2
8.29	5.47	5.08	4.29	3.29	1.29	11.49	9.29	8.29	7.49	7.9	R OAKLAND (40th & Shafter) — 0.0
s 8.30	s 5.50	s 509	s 4.30	s 3.30	s 1.30	s 11.50	s 9.30	s 8.30	s 7.50	7.9	R OAKLAND (40th & Shafter) — 1.8
f 8.36	f 5.56	5.15	f 4.36	3.36	f 1.36	f 11.56	9.36	f 8.37	7.56	9.7	ROCKRIDGE — 2.2
f 8.41	f 6.01	5.20	f 4.41	3.42	f 1.41	f 12.01 P.M.	9.41	f 8.42	8.01	11.9	THORNHILL — 1.5
f 8.45	f 6.04	5.24	f 4.45	3.46	f 1.45	f 12.05	9.46	f 8.46	8.05	13.4	HAVENS — 1.0
f 8.48	f 6.07	5.27	f 4.48	3.50	f 1.48	f 12.07	9.48	f 8.49	8.07	14.4	EASTPORT — 2.3
f 8.53	f 6.12	5.31	f 4.53	3.54	f 1.53	f 12.12	9.52	f 8.54	8.11	16.7	PINEHURST — 0.9
f 8.55	f 6.14	5.33	f 4.55	3.56	f 1.55	f 12.14	9.54	f 8.56	8.13	17.6	VALLE VISTA — 1.2
f 8.59	f 6.18	5.36	f 4.59	3.59	f 1.58	f 12.18	9.57	f 9.00	8.16	18.8	MORAGA — 2.9
f 9.04	f 6.23	5.41	f 5.07	4.04	f 2.03	f 12.23	10.02	f 9.05	8.21	21.7	BURTON — 2.4
f 9.08	f 6.28	5.45	f 5.13	4.07	f 2.08	f 12.27	10.06	f 9.09	8.25	24.1	LAFAYETTE — 1.8
f 9.11	f 6.32	5.48	f 5.18	4.10	f 2.11	f 12.31	10.09	f 9.13	8.28	25.9	SARANAP — 1.5
f 9.15	f 6.35	5.50	f 5.23	4.13	f 2.15	f 12.36	10.12	f 9.20	8.32	27.4	WALNUT CREEK — 2.2
f 9.21	f 6.42	5.54	f 5.28	4.17	f 2.20	f 12.41	10.16	f 9.25	8.36	29.6	LAS JUNTAS (S.P.R.R.Crsg.) Derailer — 1.7
f 9.25	f 6.46	5.57	f 5.32	4.19	f 2.23	f 12.44	10.19	f 9.29	8.39	31.3	MEINERT — 2.4
f 9.30	f 6.51	6.01	s 5.37	4.23	f 2.29	f 12.49	10.23	s 9.35	8.44	33.7	CONCORD — 2.5
f 9.34	f 6.55	6.05	P.M.	4.27	f 2.34	f 12.55	10.27	A.M.	8.48	36.1	OHMER — 1.0
										37.1	B. P. AND C. R. R. Crossing Derailer — 2.1
f 9.40	f 7.01	6.12		f 4.33	f 2.40	f 1.02	10.33		f 8.55	39.2	BAY POINT — 3.2
f 9.45	f 7.07	6.19		f 4.40	f 2.50	f 1.07	10.38		f 9.00	42.4	McAVOY — 2.5
f 9.50	7.12	6.23		f 4.45	f 2.56	f 1.12	10.44		f 9.05	44.9	WEST PITTSBURG — 0.6
s 9.54	P.M.	s 6.26		s 4.48	s 2.59	s 1.15	s 10.47		s 9.08	45.5	MALLARD — 0.6
f 10.03		6.35		f 4.57	s 3.07	f 1.24	10.55		f 9.17	46.1	CHIPPS — 2.3
f 10.09		6.41		f 5.03	f 3.13	f 1.30	11.01		f 9.23	48.4	DUTTON — 3.9
f 10.15		6.47		f 5.09	f 3.19	f 1.36	11.07		f 9.29	52.3	MOLENA — 8.4
f 10.27		6.59		f 5.24	f 3.30	f 1.47	11.18		f 9.41	60.7	RESERVOIR — 2.1
f 10.35		7.03		f 5.31	f 3.35	f 1.52	11.23		f 9.46	63.7	DIXON JUNCTION — 0.8
10.37		7.05		5.33	f 3.38	1.55	11.25		9.48	64.5	DOZIER — 2.9
f 10.41		7.08		f 5.37	f 3.43	f 2.01	11.29		f 9.53	67.4	MAINE PRAIRIE — 2.5
f 10.45		7.12		f 5.42	f 3.47	f 2.06	11.33		f 9.57	70.1	BUNKER — 4.1
f 10.51		7.19		f 5.48	f 3.53	f 2.13	11.40		f 10.03	74.2	MILLAR — 5.4
f 10.58		7.27		f 5.55	f 4.00	f 2.21	11.48		f 10.10	79.6	SAXON — 4.5
f 11.05		7.34		f 6.02	f 4.07	f 2.28	11.55		f 10.17	84.1	LISBON — 2.3
f 11.10		7.39		f 6.07	f 4.12	f 2.33	11.59		f 10.21	86.4	GLIDE LANDING — 4.5
f 11.17		7.45		f 6.14	f 4.18	f 2.40	12.05 P.M.		f 10.27	90.9	HEADQUARTERS — 1.07
f 11.20		7.47		f 6.18	f 4.20	f 2.43	12.08		f 10.30	92.6	SACRAMENTO, Front&M St. — .05 S.P.R.R. Crsg.
11.25		7.55		6.25	4.25	2.48	12.15		10.35	93.1	R SACRAMENTO
P.M.	P.M.	P.M.		P.M.	P.M.	P.M.	P.M.		A.M.		
Ar. Daily	Ar. Daily Ex. Sun.	Ar. Daily	Ar. Daily	Ar. Daily	Ar. Daily	Ar. Daily	Ar. Daily	Ar. Daily	Ar. Daily		

Side annotations: FERRY (San Francisco–Pier Terminal); KEY DIVISION and DOUBLE TRACK (Pier Terminal to R Oakland); AUTOMATIC BLOCK (R Oakland to West Pittsburg); FERRY (Mallard–Chipps); AUTOMATIC BLOCK (Chipps to Sacramento); Dbl Track (Sacramento).

TIME TABLE NO. 8

JANUARY 3, 1915

FIRST CLASS

STATIONS	DISTANCE FROM SACRAMENTO	3	5	7	9	11	13	15	1	19	21
		Ar. Daily Ex. Sun.	Ar. Daily	Ar. Daily	Ar. Daily	Ar. Daily	Ar. Daily	Ar. Daily	Ar. Daily	Ar. Daily	Ar. Daily
		A.M.	A.M.	A.M.	P.M.	P.M.	P.M.	P.M.	P.M.	P.M.	P.M.
SAN FRANCISCO	93.1	7.55	8.55	10.35	12.15 P.M.	2.35	4.35	5.35	6.10	7.55	10.35
PIER TERMINAL	90.2	7.40	8.40	10.20	12.00	2.20	4.20	5.20	5.55	7.40	10.20
PIER TERMINAL	90.2	7.32	8.35	10.15	11.55	2.15	4.15	5.15	5.53	7.35	10.15
EMERYVILLE JCT.	86.9	7.24	8.28	10.07	11.49	2.06	4.08	5.08	5.45	7.28	10.06
SAN PABLO AVE.	86.4	7.23	8.27	10.06	11.48	2.05	4.07	5.07	5.44	7.27	10.05
R OAKLAND (40th & Shafter)	85.2	7.20	8.24	10.03	11.45	2.01	4.04	5.04	5.41	7.24	10.02
R OAKLAND (40th & Shafter)	85.2	s 7.18	s 8.22	s 10.02	s 11.43	s 2.00	s 4.02	s 5.02	s 5.40	s 7.22	s 10.01
ROCKRIDGE	83.4	f 7.11	f 8.16	9.56	11.37	f 1.54	3.56	f 4.55	5.34	f 7.15	f 9.55
THORNHILL	81.2	f 7.05	f 8.10	9.50	11.32	f 1.48	3.50	f 4.49	5.28	f 7.09	f 9.49
HAVENS	79.7	f 7.01	f 8.05	9.46	11.29	f 1.45	3.46	f 4.45	5.24	f 7.05	f 9.45
EASTPORT	78.7	f 6.59	f 8.01	9.44	11.26	f 1.42	3.43	f 4.38	5.21	f 7.02	f 9.42
PINEHURST	76.4	f 6.55	f 7.55	9.40	11.23	f 1.37	3.39	f 4.32	5.17	f 6.57	f 9.37
VALLE VISTA	75.5	f 6.53	f 7.53	9.38	11.21	f 1.34	3.37	f 4.30	5.15	f 6.55	f 9.35
MORAGA	74.3	f 6.50	f 7.49	9.35	11.19	f 1.31	3.34	f 4.26	5.12	f 6.52	f 9.32
BURTON	71.4	f 6.45	f 7.43	9.30	11.14	f 1.25	3.29	f 4.20	5.07	f 6.47	f 9.27
LAFAYETTE	69.0	f 6.40	f 7.38	9.26	11.10	f 1.20	3.24	f 4.15	5.02	f 6.42	f 9.22
SARANAP	67.2	f 6.36	f 7.33	9.23	11.07	f 1.16	3.21	f 4.10	4.59	f 6.38	f 9.18
WALNUT CREEK	65.7	f 6.33	f 7.30	9.20	11.04	f 1.13	3.18	f 4.04	4.56	f 6.35	f 9.15
LAS JUNTAS (S.P.R.R. Crsg.)	63.5	f 6.27	f 7.23	9.14	10.59	f 1.07	3.13	f 3.58	4.51	f 6.30	f 9.07
MEINERT	61.8	f 6.24	f 7.20	9.11	10.56	f 1.04	3.10	f 3.54	4.48	f 6.28	f 9.04
CONCORD	59.4	6.20	f 7.16	9.07	10.52	f 1.00	3.06	3.50	4.44	f 6.24	f 8.59
OHMER	57.0	A.M.	f 7.10	9.02	10.48	f 12.55	3.01	P.M.	4.39	f 6.19	f 8.54
B. P. AND C. R. R. Crossing	56.0										
BAY POINT	53.9		f 7.04	f 8.55	10.42	f 12.49	f 2.55		4.33	f 6.12	f 8.48
McAVOY	50.7		f 6.59	f 8.49	10.38	f 12.44	f 2.50		4.27	f 6.06	f 8.40
WEST PITTSBURG	48.2		6.55	f 8.45	10.32	f 12.40	f 2.45		4.22	f 6.02	f 8.34
MALLARD	47.6		A.M.	s 8.41	10.28	f 12.36	f 2.41		4.18	s 5.58	f 8.30
CHIPPS	47.0			s 8.33	s 10.20	s 12.27	s 2.33		s 4.09	s 5.50	s 8.21
DUTTON	44.7			f 8.27	10.14	f 12.21	f 2.27		4.03	f 5.43	f 8.15
MOLENA	40.8			f 8.21	10.08	f 12.14	f 2.20		3.57	f 5.37	f 8.09
RESERVOIR	33.4			f 8.09	9.57	f 12.02	f 2.08		3.45	f 5.24	f 7.58
DIXON JUNCTION	29.4			f 8.04	9.52	f 11.57 (P.M.)	f 2.03		3.40	f 5.19	f 7.54
DOZIER	28.6			8.02	9.48	11.55	1.55		3.38	5.17	7.50
MAINE PRAIRIE	25.7			f 7.58	9.43	f 11.51	f 1.50		3.34	f 5.13	f 7.46
BUNKER	23.0			f 7.54	9.39	f 11.47	f 1.46		3.30	f 5.10	f 7.42
MILLAR	18.9			f 7.48	9.33	f 11.40	f 1.39		3.25	f 5.05	f 7.36
SAXON	13.5			f 7.41	9.26	f 11.30	f 1.31		3.18	f 4.58	f 7.27
LISBON	9.0			f 7.34	9.20	f 11.23	f 1.24		3.12	f 4.51	f 7.20
GLIDE LANDING	6.7			f 7.29	9.16	f 11.18	f 1.19		3.08	f 4.46	f 7.14
HEADQUARTERS	2.2			f 7.22	9.10	f 11.11	f 1.11		3.02	f 4.40	f 7.07
SACRAMENTO, Front & M St.	0.5			f 7.19	9.07	f 11.08	f 1.09		2.59	f 4.37	f 7.04
R SACRAMENTO	0.0			7.15	9.00	11.05	1.05		2.55	4.30	7.00
				A.M.	A.M.	A.M.	P.M.		P.M.	P.M.	P.M.
		Lv. Daily Ex. Sun.	Lv. Daily	Lv. Daily	Lv. Daily	Lv. Daily	Lv. Daily	Lv. Daily	Lv. Daily	Lv. Daily	Lv. Daily

Intermediate distances between stations (miles): San Francisco 2.9 Pier Terminal 3.3 Emeryville Jct. 0.5 San Pablo Ave. 1.2 R Oakland 0.0 R Oakland 1.8 Rockridge 2.2 Thornhill 1.5 Havens 1.0 Eastport 2.3 Pinehurst 0.9 Valle Vista 1.2 Moraga 2.9 Burton 2.4 Lafayette 1.8 Saranap 1.5 Walnut Creek 2.2 Las Juntas 1.7 Meinert 2.4 Concord 2.5 Ohmer 1.0 B. P. and C. R. R. Crossing 2.1 Bay Point 3.2 McAvoy 2.5 West Pittsburg 0.6 Mallard 0.6 Chipps 2.3 Dutton 3.9 Molena 8.4 Reservoir 2.4 Dixon Junction 0.8 Dozier 2.9 Maine Prairie 2.5 Bunker 4.1 Millar 5.4 Saxon 4.5 Lisbon 2.3 Glide Landing 4.5 Headquarters 1.07 Sacramento, Front & M St. S.P.R.R. Crsg. .05 R Sacramento.

Division/line notes: KEY DIVISION — DOUBLE TRACK — FERRY (Pier Terminal); AUTOMATIC BLOCK. Derailer at Meinert and at Bay Point. FERRY at Mallard. Dbl. Track at Sacramento, S. P. R. R. Crsg.

Schedule meeting points are designated by red figures and must be considered positive meeting points unless otherwise directed by train order.

A train must not leave its initial station or a junction or any station which is a terminal for another train until all trains which are due or overdue have arrived, unless given authority by train order to do so.

Eastward trains will take siding at meeting points for opposing trains of the same class unless otherwise directed by train order or special rule in time table.

Eastward extras will take siding for opposing extras unless otherwise directed by train order.

Trains must obtain clearance card before leaving initial stations.

Freight trains must have motor on down-hill side of train at all times between Havens and Rockridge.

Cars must never be left standing on main track on any grade unless motor is attached to them.

SPEED RESTRICTIONS

Freight or work trains will not exceed 25 miles per hour over any portion of road.

Westward freight or work trains must use ten (10) minutes' actual running time from Havens to the high bridge at Lake Temescal and not less than 10 minutes' actual running time from high bridge at Lake Temescal to Rockridge, bring train to a stop at Rockridge and proceed at speed of not more than ten (10) miles per hour to 40th and Shafter.

Eastward freight and work trains will not exceed speed of 15 miles per hour between Eastport and Moraga.

Freight and work trains will use not less than five (5) minutes between Eastport and Havens in either direction.

Passenger trains must not exceed speed of 25 miles per hours between Eastport and high bridge at Lake Temescal, and 20 miles per hour between high bridge at Lake Temescal and 40th and Shafter.

Passenger trains will not exceed thirty miles per hour over long trestle between Lisbon and Saxon and over all trestles between Chipps and Molena.

Interlocking plant governing switches leading to and from Key Route tracks on 40th Street is located at 40th and Shafter. Movements through these switches must not be made unless proper signal is given by towerman.

AIR TESTS AND TRAIN INSPECTION

Freight or work trains must test air and examine brakes at Havens in each direction. Westward freight trains must test air and examine brakes before descending grade just west of Lake Temescal bridge. Retainers must be used by freight train between Havens and Rockridge.

Note carefully last paragraph on page 87 of book of rules regarding running tests. In addition to points mentioned therein, running test must be made at the Summit at Havens. This test must also be made when approaching meeting points at least one mile from the station.

At meeting points where it is necessary for train which take siding to back in, it must be done under flag. Train will be brought to a stop before it proceeds over the switch, and flagman must precede train at least 500 feet before going over switch to back in.

Trains will come to a stop before crossing over Drawbridge just west of Montezuma, and will not exceed 5 miles per hour over the Drawbridge.

Trains in pulling on boat will come to a stop before going on apron, and after getting a signal from the officer on the boat, will proceed onto the boat, at a speed not exceeding 4 miles per hour. Hand brakes must bet set and wheels blocked on all freight cars. Wheels must be blocked on all passenger cars, and brakes set with air on all passenger trains, all vestibules and traps must be open while train is on boat.

Motorman must never leave his cab while his train is on the boat.

ADDITIONAL STOPS

Trains 3, 5, 11, 15, 19, 21, 6, 10, 12, 16, 20 and 22 will stop on flag at all stations.

Trains 15 and 16 will stop on flag at Heimboldt Property between Rockridge and Verbena.

No. 7 will stop on flag at all stations east of Bay Point and stop at Bay Point to discharge passengers and will pick up passengers at Bay Point for Concord, Walnut Creek, Oakland and San Francisco and points on the Danville Branch. Will also stop at Concord and Walnut Creek to pick up passengers for Oakland and San Francisco.

Nos. 1 and 9 will stop at Dixon Jct. to discharge passengers for Dixon and pick up passengers for Oakland and San Francisco and stop at West Pittsburg to discharge passengers for Pittsburg and pick up passengers for Oakland and San Francisco.

No. 1 will stop at Bay Point to discharge passengers and pick up passengers for Oakland and San Francisco.

No. 13 will stop on flag at all stations east of Ohmer and will stop at Concord and Walnut Creek to discharge passengers from points east of Ohmer. Passengers for points other than Walnut Creek and Concord will be given to No. 15 at Concord or Walnut Creek.

No. 2 will stop at Bay Point to discharge passengers from Oakland and San Francisco and pick up passengers for Pittsburg and Sacramento; also stop at West Pittsburg to discharge passengers for Pittsburg and pick up passengers for Dixon and Sacramento; also stop at Dixon Jct. to discharge passengers for Dixon and pick up passengers for Sacramento.

No. 4 will stop at Walnut Creek and Concord to discharge passengers from Oakland and San Francisco and will pick up passengers at Saranap, Walnut Creek and Concord for points east of Ohmer and will stop on flag at all stations between Ohmer and Sacramento and on school days will stop on flag at Moraga, Lafayette, Saranap, Walnut Creek, Locust, Pleasant Hill, and Meinert to pick up pupils for Concord.

No. 14 will stop on flag at Saranap, Walnut Creek and Concord to pick up passengers for points east of Ohmer and will stop on flag at all points east of Ohmer.

No. 18 will stop at West Pittsburg to discharge passengers from Oakland and San Francisco and pick up passengers for Dixon and Sacramento; also stop at Dixon Jct. to discharge passengers and pick up passengers for Sacramento.

Train No. 5 take siding for No. 4.
Train No. 7 take siding for No. 4.
Train No. 7 take siding for No. 2.
Train No. 9 take siding for No. 4.
Train No. 11 take siding for No. 2.
Train No. 15 take siding for No. 14.
Train No. 15 take siding for No. 16.
Train No. 19 take siding for No. 18.
Train No. 21 take siding for No. 18.

Trains Nos. 3 and 15 will start from Main Street, Concord.

Trains Nos. 6 and 16 will run to Main Street, Concord.

Trains which originate or terminate at Concord will register there. Conductors of westward Sacramento trains will call dispatcher from Mallard and obtain from him a check of this register, by train order. In the absence of such a check, trains must stop and conductor check the register and furnish motorman register check on prescribed form.

Train No. 21 must either receive a train order check on the register at West Pittsburg or stop and check same.

Conductor must ride on front end of passenger train between Havens and Rockridge and take up slack in hand brake and be ready to use same if necessary.

WHEN FLAGGING A BLOCK, FLAG TO FIRST CLEAR HOME SIGNAL.

ALL TRAINS MUST BE PRECEDED BY A FLAGMAN WHEN CROSSING COLLEGE AND SHAFTER AVENUES.

Brakeman must ride on the rear of every train while passing through the tunnel and have lighted Red Lantern ready for immediate use. In addition to Red Lantern, he must have fuses ready for immediate use.

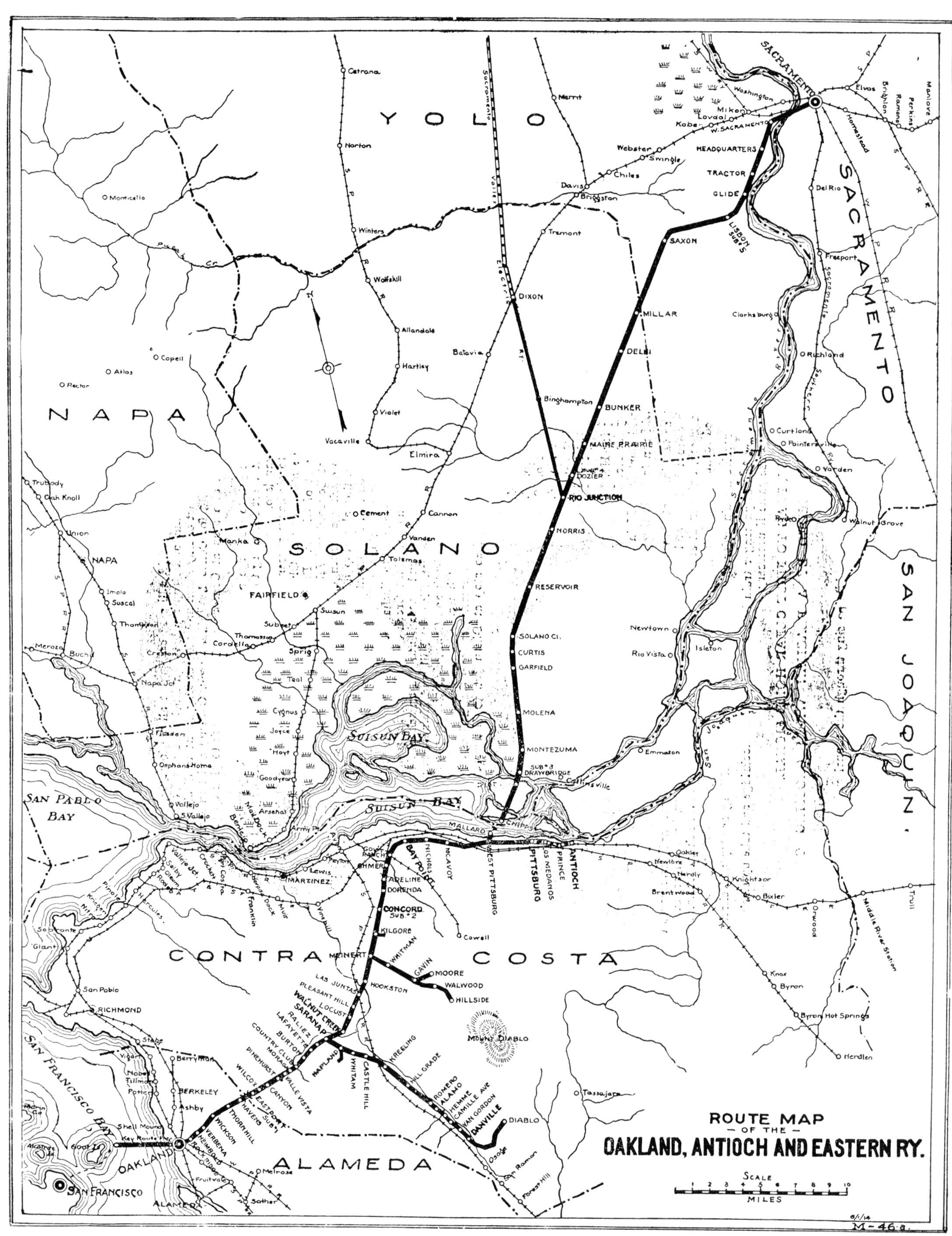

ROUTE MAP
- OF THE -
OAKLAND, ANTIOCH AND EASTERN RY.
SCALE
MILES
YOLO
SACRAMENTO
NAPA
SOLANO
SAN JOAQUIN
CONTRA COSTA
ALAMEDA
SAN PABLO BAY
SUISUN BAY
SAN FRANCISCO BAY
MOUNT DIABLO
M-46.a.

Chapter 11

The Water Barrier

Rail and highway engineers have traditionally found a major barrier to land arteries in the peculiar topography of the Bay area. The broad bays and rivers, a boon to marine commerce, present formidable obstacles to wheeled vehicles. This problem was compounded for the OA&E, which arrived on the scene much later than its railway and roadway rivals. How it solved the dilemma of transporting its trains across a wide water barrier is an engrossing tale, not without its heart-breaks.

Due to the unusual topography of the delta region the OA&E engineers had to decide which crossing of the upper bay or the two great rivers converging thereupon was superior from both a construction and an operating standpoint. Suisun Bay or Carquinez Strait? The Sacramento or the San Joaquin?

Pioneer railroad surveys entered the San Francisco Bay area through Altamont Pass and Niles Canyon, crossing the San Joaquin at a point now called Mossdale. This route was followed by the original Western Pacific in 1869.

In 1878 the Northern Railway built what is today the Southern Pacific main line along the east shore of the San Francisco and San Pablo Bays and the south side of Carquinez Strait to Martinez; the strait was then crossed in two places: Vallejo Junction and Port Costa. From Vallejo Junction a passenger ferry crossed to South Vallejo, there connecting with the California Pacific Railroad. At Port Costa, a car ferry operated to Benicia, carrying through trains. In 1930 this ferry was replaced by the huge Martinez-Benicia bridge.

When the Santa Fe arrived it preempted one more of the practicable entries: from Stockton it traversed the delta region by means of much expensive construction, including three river crossings (the San Joaquin, Old, and Middle rivers). From a point near Oakley to Port Chicago the Santa Fe paralleled the Southern Pacific; from there it diverged, to pass through the foothills to Franklin Ridge and Franklin Canyon, and then to Pinole where it turned south to Richmond.

The present day Western Pacific roughly parallels the pioneer WP route as outlined above.

Thus the OA&E had to find yet another route from Oakland to its ultimate destiny at the edge of the upper bay. Its engineers selected a serpentine route which doubtless was only practicable because of electric operation. The Oakland hills were negotiated with the help of a tunnel nearly a mile long; Shepherd Canyon, Moraga Valley, San Ramon Valley, around Mt. Diablo, and finally out upon the flatlands bordering Suisun Bay and the delta of California's two great rivers was the twisting, climbing route finally selected.

Thus the OA&E arrived at high tide line with a choice of where and how to cross the water barrier: by a bridge, or by ferry---a fateful choice, indeed. The narrowest single crossing was from the Contra Costa shore to Chipps Island--- Suisun Bay at this location is but 2,600 feet wide. Also necessitated by taking this route was a crossing of Spoonbill Creek and Montezuma Slough, but bridges were suitable for the latter. Suisun Bay, however, presented a difficult problem; a low level bridge was out of the question because of the river boats and the War Department. A high level bridge was entirely feasible but prohibitive in cost. Even as OA&E brass toyed with the idea of making the high bridge a reality, a ferry capable of transporting six cars was constructed, even though it was considered at the time to be but a temporary solution, pending construction of the great bridge.

That first ferry, the "Bridgit," was a wooden hulled, double end vessel which was launched in 1913. It lasted a little more than one year, being completely destroyed by fire on May 17, 1914, luckily with no loss of lives.

The ensuing emergency pending the construction of a steel-hulled replacement ferry saw OA&E use various expedients, none with any degree of satisfaction. A passenger launch, the "Laguna," was purchased second hand; it shuttled passengers back and forth between the trains on opposite shores, but the inconvenience of changing cars was not popular with OA&E's patrons.

Next came a single track barge named "Harry," honoring OA&E General Manager Mitchell; the barge was ballasted with car wheels and was thought to be suitable, until the first trial trip. Lashed to the tug "Ida," the "Harry" was taken to Chipps and Train No. 7 with Mitchell aboard was duly run upon the barge. Hardly had the strange consist cast off, however, when it was all too apparent that "Harry" was entirely too narrow; indeed, had the barge not been lashed alongside the "Ida" it would have overturned immediately in the choppy waters. The tug's captain, fearing for the safety of his craft, wanted to cast off and leave the barge & cars to their watery fate but Mitchell insisted that either the barge and tug get across to Mallard together or both go down together. Long minutes later the "Harry" was docked and its two cars trundled onto dry land. The "Harry" was thereupon retired to other duties.

Until the new ferry, named "Ramon," could be put into service, OA&E rented tugs and car floats from Santa Fe and Western Pacific.

Over at the Lanteri Shipyard in nearby Pittsburg a strange, angular craft was taking shape. Because of the all important element, time, the hull of the "Ramon" was built of flat plates---not a single curved plate was used. This resulted in a box-like design which was anything but beautiful. Built about a central girder formed by two longitudinal bulkheads extending the entire length of the boat, the hull had

139

The "Bridgit" leaving Mallard Slip in 1913 with three freight cars aboard. Note that even the framework to support trolley wires was of wood. (Union Gas---VS)

End elevation drawing of ferry "Bridgit." A comparison of this and photo above shows minor changes made in order to simplify construction. (Union Gas Engine--VS)

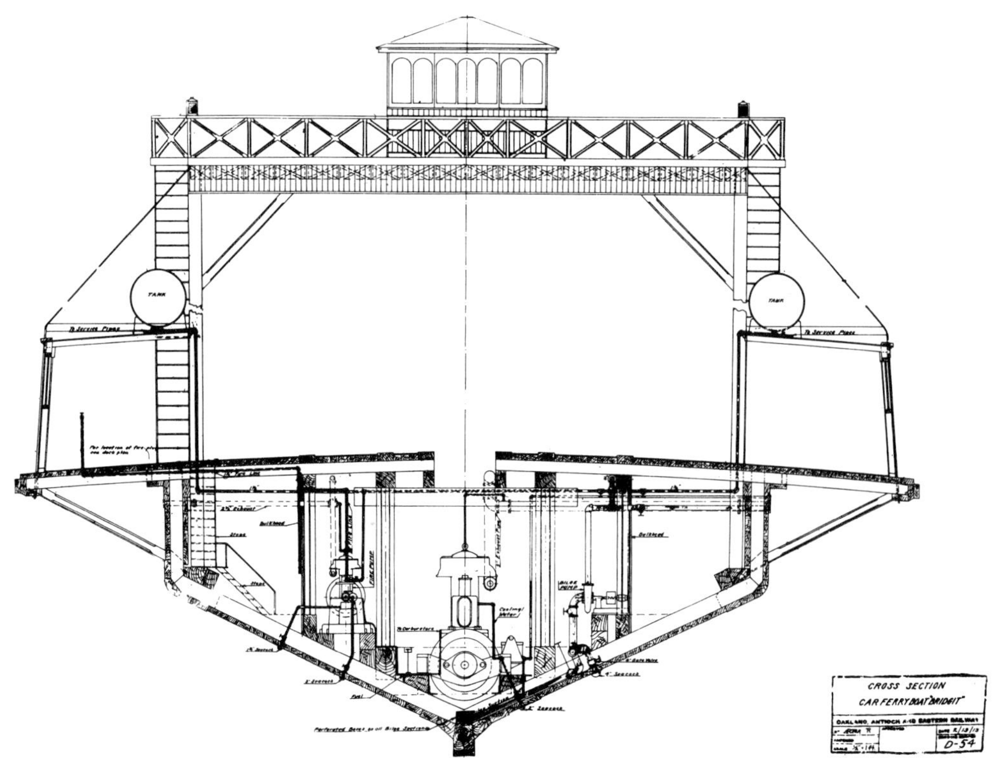

exceptional longitudinal stiffness and rigidity. The engine room was located between these bulkheads, providing a very stiff bed necessitated by the length of the engine. This room was 70 feet long, 13 feet wide and 16 feet deep and was limited fore and aft by two transverse bulkheads extending the entire width of the vessel. Thus the hull was divided into no less than eleven watertight compartments, making it virtually unsinkable. At either end of the engine room was an intermediate deck whereon auxiliary machinery was located.

The engine itself was an eight cylinder distillate type which turned out 600 horsepower. The choice of this engine was also dictated by three standards: reliability, economy, and quickness of delivery. With the schedules of the entire railroad depending upon the unfailing dependability of the "Ramon," careful thought was given to the type of engine to be installed. The internal combustion engine won out, for these reasons: (1) Absence of standby losses between trips; (2) Using distillate as fuel would cut down the size of the vessel and require fewer men to operate it; (3) Quicker delivery could be obtained from the distillate engine people.

The deck was given over to three tracks: one center track for short (3 car) trains, and two side tracks for trains of up to six cars. Along either side were deck houses which formed the base for the pilot's bridge. The deck houses contained a cabin, toilets, and lamp room. Crew's quarters, galley and dining room (seating 45) were below deck; in later years the dining room was moved to the main deck.

Trolley wires were suspended between two steel towers and the pilot's bridge. The trolley wires were energized only when the boat was docked and a switch was thrown in the pilot house after contact was made with the shore trolley wires. While en route, cars aboard the "Ramon" were lighted by means of small battery lights.

Rails (each track was 220 feet long) were laid flush with the wooden deck planks for safety of passengers promenading. These planks were laid over the steel deck plating.

At the time of its installation the distillate engine was the largest internal combustion engine with electric ignition yet constructed on earth. It was about 46 feet long and had a weight of approximately a hundred thousand pounds. It had eight cylinders which developed 600 horsepower at a normal speed of 200 revolutions per minute. It was an open crosshead type engine and was built by the Union Gas Engine Company, San Francisco. The open crosshead in this case was slightly different in design from those obtaining in steam and large diesel engines, and consisted of a water-jacketed extension

on the lower end of the cylinder which acted as a crosshead guide. Pistons were exceptionally long; their lower end, which held the wristpin, acted as a crosshead. There were openings fore and aft in both cylinders and pistons to permit circulation of air about the wristpins. The intake and the exhaust valves were placed on either side of the cylinders in the familiar "T" head arrangement; exhaust valves were cooled by water.

Distillate was used as fuel, as already mentioned. It was vaporized by means of two carburetors used in conjunction with two jacketed inlet manifolds of special construction, heated by exhaust gasses to prevent condensation of the heavy fuel. Each manifold supplied four cylinders. Lubrication of cylinders and bearings was accomplished by force feed lubricators mounted on the back of the engine and driven from the cam shaft. Crankpin bearings were lubricated by a centrifugal ring oiling device mounted on each crank web and connecting with oil holes leading out to the center of the crankpin.

The engine was placed in the center of the hull and was connected to two four-bladed propellers, 72" in diameter---one propeller on each end. As "Ramon" was double ended, propellers were of opposite pitch and were thrown in and out of action by a clutch mounted on each end of the engine. At one end of the engineroom a 20 hp. two cylinder distillate engine was belted to a generator to supply current for lighting the ferry and also cars in transit.

"Ramon" entered service on January 3, 1915 and the first train to board was No. 4, "The Sacramento Valley Limited," the first northbound train of the day. This train consisted of motor 1007 and parlor car "Sacramento." This important event in the history of the OA&E was further commemorated by the establishment of through parlor car service on that date in conjunction with the Northern Electric Railway.

"Ramon" served long and well, being out of service only once each year for inspection and repairs. At those times, the launch "Countess" substituted for her with passengers transferring between turn-back trains. After passenger service was abandoned, freight trains were rerouted over the Western Pacific during these inspection periods.

"Countess" was also used to transport members of duck hunting clubs during hunting seasons, inasmuch as most of these clubs were located along the river banks, far from roads. 1942 saw the sale of "Countess" to The Harbor Tug & Barge Company of Oakland, which company also used her for excursions and fishing trips. "Countess" replaced "Laguna" in 1920.

SACRAMENTO NORTHERN'S NAVY

Item	"Bridgit"	"Ramon"	"Countess"
Official Number:	211,089	212,870	
Year Built:	1913	1914	1912 (Acquired 1920)
Builder:	Schultze, SF	Lanteri, Pittsburg	Unknown, but Sacramento
Type:	Double End Screw Ferry	Double End Screw Ferry	Launch, screw propeller
Hull:	Wood	Steel	Wood
Length:	186'	202.7'	60'
Beam:	57'	39'8"	10.5'
Depth:	14.7'	8.3'	4'
Draft Loaded:	13'	13.5'	
Gross Tonnage:	594	775	21
Net Tonnage:	381	527	16
Engine:	8 Cyl. 500 hp distillate	8 cyl. 600 hp dist.	Atlas 6 cyl.
Full Speed:	200 RPM	210 RPM	
In Service:		January 3, 1915	
Out of Service:	May 17, 1914	April 7, 1954	

In OA&E days, "Ramon" sported a white paint job with the company name emblazoned thereon.   This photo was probably taken in early 1915, for "Moraga" was a motor here. (VS)

Another view of "Ramon" as an OA&E property. It looks as though a full load was aboard, including "Moraga" again as a motor car.   (Peter Gump)

Above: The ferry slip at Mallard, on the Contra Costa side of the bay. Motor 1007 on No. 11, "The Meteor," is ready to roll off the "Ramon" and resume its fast run into Oakland. This was the first through daily train, Chico to Oakland. The siding on the left was used by trains for transferring passengers to the launch, "Countess," which is tied up here. "Countess" was used when "Ramon" was out of service for repairs and annual inspection, made in one of the shipyards in the San Francisco area. Spur on right was used for unloading supplies needed by the Marine Department.   (Estey-VS)

Left: "Ramon" originally had a below-deck restaurant, seen here. Note the rather crude appointments, especially when compared to the lavish interiors of "Alabama" and "Bidwell." Passengers riding non-limited trains were afforded these dining facilities, and one did not dwell in this atmosphere long when crossing the bay on the short running time. In later years the restaurant facilities were moved top deck, making it more convenient for passengers.   (VS)

"Ramon" was removed from service in 1954 for her annual inspection by the Coast Guard; major repairs were indicated
and SN decided that the expenditure required could not be justified and elected to retire the vessel instead. On April 7, 1954
"Ramon" was officially declared "removed from service." The
hull was scrapped in Antioch, marking the end of a most colorful chapter in the saga of American interurbans.

(Top) Launch "Countess," moored at ferry slip, Mallard,
July 1940.   (VDB from VS Collection)

(Below) From "Ramon's" pilot house, the Mallard slip
showed all details of the complicated trackwork necessary to make connection with shore. (AL)

Closeup of "Ramon" under way. No. 3, "The Meteor," is aboard; note its unusual consist: two steel motors and the "Sacramento."   The year, 1938.   (AA-BB)

Another view of "Ramon" hard at work; this one was taken on June 12, 1938 with but two cars on board. Note calmness of the bay (see cover photo).   (AA-AH)

The crew of Train No. 11 (left), motor 1017 with a steel trailer, unloads express for transfer to the Walwood Branch car (right), motor 1014, at Meinert Jct. on April 23, 1916---as a local farmer looks on.   (Charles Gselle Photo --- TRB)

June 13, 1911---and one of O&A's two brand new passenger motors lies crushed and broken at the foot of the steep hill below the quarry on the Walwood Branch. The entire baggage compartment of this car has been torn away.   (RB)

Chapter 12

South End Branch Lines

The Walwood Branch

The original intent motivating the construction of this branch line was a promotional plan to build up tourist passenger business and excursions to Mt. Diablo. The Walwood line was originally projected to run to the base of Mt. Diablo and there transfer passengers to a sightseeing stage for the trip to the summit of the mountain; at the summit was to have been a $50,000 hotel, but it failed to materialize.

From all available accounts and sources of information, the Walwood Branch was built to haul limestone from the Spreckles Quarry, located at a station on the line designated as "Hillside." This quarry line was a branch of a branch, and ran up a steep hill to the quarry site. The limestone was hauled to the Southern Pacific's San Ramon Branch and the transfer was made at a point then known as "Ramon Jct." later called "Las Juntas." From this point the rock was hauled to the sugar refinery down at Spreckles, in the Salinas Valley in Monterey County.

Construction of this branch took place in April, 1911, by the O&A and actual service commenced about June 15, 1911. The Walwood Branch was 2.8 miles long from Meinert Jct. to Walwood. Stations along the branch were Whitman, Gavin, Moore (where the quarry spur branched off), and Walwood. At first this branch extended only as far as Gavin, but on April 1, 1912, service was extended to Walwood. On original time tables this branch was referred to as the "Ignacio Valley Branch."

Timetable No. 6 of the O&A, dated June 20, 1912, indicated three roundtrips daily. This was operated as a side trip made by the main line cars, which at that time were operating between Bay Point and Lafayette. As of November 26, 1912, Employees' Timetable No. 7 showed five roundtrips daily. The one way fare from Meinert Jct. to Walwood and intermediate points was 10¢.

Motor car 1002 was assigned to the Walwood Branch by the OA&E in 1913, with 1051 substituting when needed. The regular crew on this branch was Motorman Gibson and Conductor Hanlin.

An amusing incident occurred in 1912. It seems that the crew was not satisfied with the timetable then in effect, so to change it to meet their own desires they unofficially circulated a petition in the town of Concord (supposedly initiated by merchants) to have the last daily trip moved up an hour earlier so Motorman Gibson could tie up at Concord and go home for supper. General Manager Mitchell somehow got word of the petition and the parts played by his train crew, and both motorman and conductor came very near being discharged; it was said that all that saved them from Mitchell's wrath was his need of them to testify in court in an accident case. They were spared and remained in service for many years.

The volume of passenger traffic was negligible, as is illustrated by a passenger count made in 1916 on trains 82 and 83. During September, train 82 carried 28 passengers and train 83 had but 19 on board. October saw 82 haul 53 while 83 was down to 17. November was even worse: 82 carried only 26 people all month, and 83 had an abysmal 14! Passengers complained that schedules were not convenient, being operated solely to make connections with main line trains--- with through service into Concord being provided only at very awkward times of the day. Rather than accommodate themselves to the unpopular schedule, people either walked into Concord or hitched up old Dobbin to the buggy.

It was readily apparent that continued operation was unprofitable and hopeless. Application to abandon the Walwood Branch was made to the Railroad Commission and on December 20, 1916, trains 82 and 83 were discontinued. The Commission ordered one roundtrip to be operated daily to be performed by a mixed train. Often even this schedule was annulled by the dispatcher when no one at all showed up to ride. One amusing annullment was made on the basis that one of the motors assigned to the line on that particular day had just emerged from the paint shop with a brand new paint job---and the untrimmed trees along the line would inflict severe scratches on the car! Other runs were made by box motors 101 or 102, sometimes hauling a car or two of freight, either rock from the quarry or fruit from the adjacent orchards.

Two accidents occurred on this line which merit notice. One took place on June 13, 1911 when O&A was using one of its brand new passenger motors to haul a steel gondola of limestone down the steep hill from the quarry. The weight was too much for the car's brakes and the train ran away--- its crew jumping for their lives. At the foot of the grade at a sharp curve the train left the rails, and $30,000 damage was caused to the cars---$15,000 to the new passenger car. This was the first movement of rock from the quarry.

The second accident occurred at the same spot under similar circumstances just a few weeks later. On July 6th, leased box motor #2 of the Central California Traction Co. was taking two gondolas of rock from the quarry when again the load proved too heavy and the train ran away. This derailment sent the box motor to the shops for extensive repairs and resulted in the installation of a large drum and a cable by means of which rock cars were eased down the hill to the bottom, where box motors picked them up. OA&E's 102 was usually assigned this job.

The Walwood Branch was officially abandoned in 1920, when the quarry closed down. At that time the quarry provided all of the branch line's revenue. For a short time after the quarry closed down the Concord Locals made side trips over the branch; this continued until final abandonment.

The old and new depots at Pittsburg; above, motor 1010 awaits departure time sometime in the early Twenties; below, Train #6 on July 12, 1941. (RB & DJ)

This branch of the once-longest interurban line in the world might well have been the route of the OA&E's main line into the Sacramento Valley. At the time of the formal announcement of the extension east from Bay Point, it was rumored that the main line would pass through Pittsburg and on to the small town of Antioch, where a mighty bridge would carry the electric trains high across the upper Suisun Bay; OA&E secured permission from the War Department to construct the bridge and actually poured concrete piers on the Contra Costa side. The line was thence to be constructed eastward toward Stockton to connect with the line of the Central California Traction Company and over the CCT main line into Sacramento. Perhaps this proposed route was created out of whole cloth to assuage the fears and avoid the impressive wrath of the Southern Pacific which company could correctly be predicted to raise whatever obstacles it could devise to harrass the building of an interurban railway over a direct route from Oakland to the state capitol.

A franchise was desired by OA&E in November, 1912, to operate trains within the city limits of Pittsburg. The franchise was slow in coming, but when it was issued it included authority to extend the line through Los Mendanos to the industrial district and to terminate in Antioch.

Construction to Pittsburg from Bay Point began at once, and passenger service to Pittsburg began on August 5th, 1913. Actually this service was merely an extension of route of trains which formerly terminated at Bay Point. The first schedule into Pittsburg called for the daily operation of six round trips between the Key's Pier Terminal and Pittsburg.

Pittsburg remained on the main line but a short time; On September 3, 1913, the extension to Sacramento was opened for service, and main line trains thereafter shunned the city, a reduction in status which became permanent. A shuttle car operated from Pittsburg to the junction at West Pittsburg, and at morning and evening rush hours, commuter trains operated between Pittsburg and the Pier Terminal.

The extension from Pittsburg to Antioch never materialized. Although the right of way was secured and graded, and although rails, ties and other necessities were placed on the grade, the decision to construct the Dixon Branch resulted in the track material being put down in that location. The Antioch right of way reverted to its original owners.

At the time of the construction of the Pittsburg Branch, that town had a population of some 5,000 inhabitants and was rapidly becoming an important manufacturing center; later its factories were to provide the interurban with a very important and lucrative freight business. Executives of these firms prevailed upon OA&E to institute passenger service for the convenience of their employees which lived along the route; steam railroads' schedules were most inconvenient, with most trains being too important to handle local business. OA&E's passenger trains not only hauled employees but also many school children. The service was provided by "Extras" six days weekly, and a special commuter rate was placed in effect. The industrial firms partly subsidized the expense of passenger service.

Early Dispatchers' sheets reveal some very interesting facts. The first train to run between Oakland and Pittsburg on August 5, 1913, was Train No. 2, which departed from Oakland at 8:15 A.M. with Motor No. 1005, operated by Motorman C. H. Holmes and Conductor F. E. Stewart. The first scheduled train from Pittsburg to Oakland was composed of two motors, 1003 and 1011, which left Pittsburg at 6:50 A.M., its crew being Motorman Taylor and Conductor Platt. According to a note on the dispatcher's sheet, the first motor assigned to the pioneer run from Oakland to Pittsburg was the 1006, but it was removed from service at 40th & Shafter due to a broken train line and 1005 was substituted. A work train was also operated between Bay Point and Pittsburg that first day, working Extra between 6:40 A.M. and 7:20 P.M.; it was motor 1051, and undoubtedly was used to place the finishing touches to the

new line. During that same month of August parlor car "Moraga" made a test run between Oakland and Pittsburg as a single unit motor car; this was for the benefit of the Mechanical Department upon completion of installing electrical equipment on that car. The dispatcher designated this movement "Extra Moraga."

On September 3, 1913, the first day of operation as a branch line, the Pittsburg run was taken care of by motor 1001 which sometimes alternated with motor 1002.

The Pittsburg Branch depended upon passenger revenue during its early years, for freight business to its points was monopolized by the steam railroads which paralleled it. LCL freight helped some, but the initial construction was only to Pittsburg---not as far as Los Mendanos and the eastern section of Pittsburg where were located the industries. Not until fifteen years later was the Pittsburg Branch extended to tap these lucrative sources of freight.

The story is this: According to contemporary accounts appearing in the daily newspapers, the SF-S (through its parent company, the Western Pacific) applied on November 10, 1927, to extend the Pittsburg Branch from its terminus at Cumberland St. to the industrial district. The WP proposed to reballast and improve the trackage to permit heavy freight operation. However residents along the route raised vociferous objections to the extension, which would be a mile in length, crossing Cumberland, Los Mendanos and East Streets via a right of way one hundred feet wide.

Nor were the competing steam roads sleeping; Santa Fe and Southern Pacific filed their protests against the proposed SF-S extension on December 14, 1927. Only the industries the proposed line would serve were in support of the extension.

Opposition was finally overcome. Construction was undertaken in early 1930 and completed on April 1st of that year. The WP bore the entire cost of construction of the 1.85 miles of new track and in exchange was given trackage rights over the entire SF-S main line (which the WP never exercised). It was considered for a time that WP main line trains could run via the SF-S between Sacramento and Oakland, thereby cutting mileage considerably from the round-about route via Stockton and Niles; apparently the severe grades near Oakland, the short radius curves and the route followed within Oakland precluded operating heavy steam trains over the SF-S.

As a part of being awarded the franchise for the extension, SF-S agreed to erect a new depot (which cost $30,000) in Pittsburg and to widen Eighth St and install curbs and gutters.

Passenger operation on the Pittsburg Branch outlived that of the main line. The new depot was built after the old one was completely destroyed by fire; coincident with this loss, Conductor French, who had served as a branch line conductor on both the Dixon Branch and the Danville Branch, passed away on the same day the depot burned.

Upon abandonment of passenger service on the main line between Oakland and Sacramento in August of 1940, the Pittsburg Branch briefly regained its original status as terminus of main line trains. The remaining passenger service had its easterly terminal at Pittsburg until the following June 30th, when all SN passenger service ended---except for two franchise runs operated a week apart: Saturday, July 5th, with motor 1014; Saturday, July 12, 1941, with the same motor. Thus ended passenger operation over the entire SN system.

THE DANVILLE BRANCH

(Left) Diablo Valley with the rails of the Danville Branch in foreground, 1915. In the background stands Mt. Diablo. The level ground in center became a racetrack, where the wealthy guests of Diablo Country Club held horse races.

(Cook & Cook, VS)

(Below) The grounds of the Diablo Country Club at the end of the Danville Branch, Diablo Park. These guests have just arrived on the special train in background and are about to enter the main building. Cars in the train consist of 1051, a Hall-Scott steel trailer, and combo motor 1003. The 1051 will remain on the branch and 1003 & trailer will return to Oakland as an "Extra West." Note markers on rear of Hall-Scott trailer with "X-1003" in train indicator box.

(Cook & Cook, VS)

The Danville Branch was familiarly known as "The Toonerville Trolley," a term affectionately given this little line by the local citizenry and newspapers---both local and Bay area. In many respects the Toonerville appelation was well deserved, as personnel and operations truly lived up to the comic antics portrayed in Fontaine Fox's daily newspaper cartoons.

Operation on the Danville Branch was conducted strictly on the true interurban branch style---train crews were most informal, and each passenger was treated as a personal friend rather than as a business patron. Operation of this line was undoubtedly more comical and colorful than on any other OA&E trackage. Interwoven were humorous incidents and near tragedies; the latter were rendered innocuous only by the quick and efficient actions of the skilled crews (who were used to such hazards and accepted them as a part of the normal day's work). We will enlarge later on some of these incidents, but let us turn now to factual aspects of this branch's origin and construction.

The Danville Branch was incorporated and constructed under the name of The San Ramon Valley Railroad which began its corporate life on March 16, 1912. Its announced intention was to build an electric interurban line from Saranap to Danville, thence on to Diablo, a distance of 10.15 miles. This company leased the completed line to OA&E. Officers of the San Ramon Valley Railroad were: President S. L. Naphtaly; Vice-president Walter Arnstein; Secretary-Treasurer-General Manager Harry A. Mitchell.

Construction of the new railroad took place between March, 1913, and March, 1914. The contractors were Palmer, McBride & Quayle, and the line was single track, light rail, and direct suspension overhead with 1200 volts DC. Just outside Saranap was a long spur off the branch, designated on maps as the Wine Spur; this ran over property owned by the president of the road, where his home was located, and also served a nearby winery. Stations along the Danville Branch were Saranap, Winehaven, Castle Hill, Krelling, Alamo, Camelle Avenue, Danville, Danville Freight Station, and Diablo Park. Originally this branch was to have terminated in the little town of San Ramon and consideration was given to extending it over into the Tassajara and Sycamore Valleys, eventually terminating in the little town of Livermore; this never came to pass, as instead it was decided to build the line over to Diablo Park, at the foot of Mt. Diablo.

Service to Danville started on March 2, 1914 and on June 27 of the same year was extended to Diablo Park. Branch line cars connected at Saranap with main line OA&E trains. The conductor on the Danville Branch was William French, who had served on the Dixon Branch; motorman was Frank Flautt, who was No. 1 on OA&E's seniority list.

Originally this branch prospered, due to the development of the country in the Mt. Diablo Park area. A company known as the Mt. Diablo Scenic Boulevard Company was formed and it established a residential tract as well as the Mt. Diablo Country Club. Roads were paved and a scenic road constructed to the summit of Mt. Diablo, which could then be reached by private auto or by a sightseeing bus operated by the realty company. In addition to the shuttle branch line service provided by the OA&E, through trains were operated out of the Key Route Pier on regular main line schedules with cars being cut off at Saranap and operated over the branch to the Mt. Diablo Park Country Club. According to an advertising folder published in 1915 by OA&E, trains departed from the Pier Terminal at 8:00 AM, 1:00 PM, and 4:00 PM daily except Sunday; on Sundays they left the Pier at 9:40 AM and 5:15 PM. Trains left Diablo daily at 7:00 AM, 8:35 AM, 12:35 PM, and 3:30 PM; on Sundays, departure from Diablo was at 6:00 PM in addition to the daily schedule. Fare to Diablo one way was $1.20 from San Francisco and $1.10 from Oakland. Round trip fare from either city was $1.50. OA&E as well as the public generally referred to this service as "The Million Dollar Specials." Regular main line equipment was used; on one occasion the private car of William Randolph Hearst was hauled over the branch and spotted at the County Club. This

occurred in the summer of 1916 and the car was pulled by passenger locomotive #106; the Hearst car was picked up from the Santa Fe at Bay Point.

Special trains were operated Sundays and holidays for the R. N. Burgess Company which was also interested in selling land adjacent to the Diablo Country Club---the direct service out of San Francisco and Oakland being an added attraction for their prospective buyers.

Freight service on the branch was usually hauled by car 1051, or if the loads were extra heavy, by box motors 101 & 102. Motor 1051 was the regularly assigned equipment, however, and was a unique car. Formerly a Southern Pacific combine which had run on the Eastbay suburban steam lines, 1051 was an ungainly brute and this perhaps earned for it an unusual nickname, "The Alligator." In an interview with the former conductor's daughter who resides in Danville, it was learned that during the rainy season one was required to open his umbrella and spread newspapers on the seats due to a leaky roof. Passengers could never be sure when departing on their trip whether they would arrive at the junction in time to make connections; derailments were frequent. Conductor French was fond of telling his passengers that 1051 was hinged in the middle to permit it to go around the tight curves. The little windows rattled incessantly and the tiny pot bellied coal stove was capable of heating but one small corner of the baggage compartment and there the 1051's shivering passengers huddled around on winter mornings to exchange country gossip. Under the seats were assorted picks and shovels for use in case of slides or washouts.

Skipper French was known to be superstitious and would never make a trip with thirteen persons aboard. If he were flush he would ring up an extra fare on the Ohmer register; otherwise, someone would have to get off. This was particularly depressing in the later years of operation because there were exactly thirteen regular commuters and unless someone brought a guest home for the night the passengers and the Skipper would spend fifteen or twenty minutes matching coins to see who was going to pay an extra fare or walk; only after this problem was solved did the 1051 begin its homeward trip from Saranap.

When the company decided that train crews would wear service stripes and stars denoting longevity, it was reported that an old lady in Danville inquired of Skipper French,

"Pardon me, Brigadier, but has the government taken over the road?"

The Skipper was sporting so many stars and stripes that he was taken for one of the military.

In its December 14, 1923, issue the San Francisco Call-Bulletin ran the following hilarious account of life on the Danville Branch:

" DANVILLE TROLLEY TO BE EQUIPPED FOR OCEAN

"Danville---Dec. 14: The Toonerville trolley arrived at Danville Jct. today with 65 of its 345 cracks leaking, the coal stove afloat and passengers sitting on the backs of seats.

"There was a concensus of opinion that wet weather was being experienced.

"The Puddle Jumpers Club, formed last year, was called into existence again this morning; J. Sims winning the company's championship wringer by getting soaked to the third vest button---two buttons higher than P. Watkins record for 1922.

"Mrs. James Riley rolled up a 'splat' score by sitting in a blonde puddle before she could be warned.

Poor old 1051---unloved, ridiculed and extremely ungainly---was a fixture on the Danville Branch; here the "Alligator" handles a cut of freight cars in Danville in 1923. (Bear Photo Service)

Old 1001 was almost equally a fixture on the Pittsburg Branch. This car, one of the two interurbans which opened the O&A, is shown here at Mallard, date unknown; the car was used also to transport crews to and from the ferry "Ramon," which is probably its task here. (CS)

"Boat service was established in the car aisle and passengers were ferried between the cash register and the back platform on a car seat rowed by Hank Potter, eminent Contra Costa oarsman.

"When water was drained from the vehicle at Danville, Joe Mills was found asleep on the floor; he had been under two feet of water for eight miles, but declared this was not unusual and was, in fact, exceeded by the freshet of 1920, when the company employed a diver to go down and locate Skipper French under a seat during a stop at Alamo Valley.

"The car was taken off the run today and will be equipped with a keel and gasoline engine.

"T. Watkins, who rows stroke oar on the trolley, declared last night's rain was only a light shower and that rough weather will probably be encountered next week on Saranap bar."

Returning to the serious, the condition of the roadbed, the poor condition of the car and the popularity of the automobile all hastened the death of the Danville Branch. The SF-S RR. filed an application with the California Railroad Commission on July 18, 1923 for the complete abandonment of this line, and at the same time asked permission to replace the service with a bus. Permission was granted in due time, and on the first day of March, 1924, the last passenger train operated. The new bus service connected with main line trains at Walnut Creek and ran all the way out to Diablo.

Contracts for removing the rails were awarded to the Hyman-Michaels Company and by March 31, 1924, the last rail had been removed and finis written to a typical side of the road branch line.

Car 1051 saw some service in switching duties elsewhere, but its days were numbered and it, too, was soon scrapped.

The Dixon Branch

The Dixon Branch, extending some 11.8 miles across the flat lands from Dixon Jct. (originally called Rio Jct.) to the town of Dixon, was unique in at least two respects: (1) It was built by another railroad company, The Sacramento Valley Electric, and leased to the OA&E; and (2) it lasted only three years, which probably assures it of fairly high ranking among short-lived interurban railways.

The Sacramento Valley Electric was organized by prosperous farmers who sought quicker and better ways of getting their products to market. The SV as originally announced was to extend from tidewater up the west side of the Sacramento Valley via Woodland and Hamilton City to a terminal at Red Bluff. Its intentions were to compete directly with other interurbans: SN, OA&E, Vallejo & Northern, as well as with the steam railroads. It proposed to operate its own boats to San Francisco from its tidewater connection. SV's incorporation date was May 4, 1912, and its officers, all of whom were wealthy farmers and land owners, were: President George W. Pierce; First Vice-president H. W. Mann; Second Vice-president Louis L. Janes; Secretary H. R. Timm; Treasurer Arthur C. Huston; General Manager Melville Dozier, Jr.; Financial Agent Vern Dumas. The head office of the SV was located in the Shreve Building, San Francisco.

The right of way traversed a flat non-scenic area, use of which was limited principally to grazing; closer to Dixon the land improved in quality---the so-called "Prairie Lands" giving way to farms, most of which raised alfalfa with the main agricultural activity being dairying, with some orchards situated northwest of town. The major commodities were milk and cream from the dairies, plus cattle which were shipped to slaughter houses in the San Francisco Bay region.

Construction took place in 1913 and 1914 by the firm of Palmer, McBride & Quayle. The OA&E supplied the rail, which had been intended for extending the Pittsburg Branch to Antioch. Equipment used in constructing the line was obtained from OA&E on a daily rental basis. Rail was standard 70 lb. weight and overhead was OA&E's standard catenary. A substation was located on the main line at Dixon Jct., supplying power at 1200 volts DC.

The financial agreement between SV and OA&E was to the effect that all the costs of operating the branch were to be paid by SV to OA&E on a monthly basis; included herein were maintenance of track, crews' salaries, power, rental of cars, dispatchers' services, etc., except that OA&E paid the Dixon station agent's salary. Evidently being way out on the end of the lonely branch line caused OA&E's main office to be forgetful: records indicate that the Dixon agent had to send off numerous letters to get his salary, and was constantly submitting requests for the necessary supplies to carry on the business of his office or making desperate appeals to the Stores Department for sacks of coal to keep his waiting room and office bearable during cold winter months.

But to get back to construction days: The new branch was formally opened on October 10, 1914, with a great public celebration. A special three-car train (cars 1015, 1020 and 1024) arrived at Dixon Jct. to be greeted by the Dixon Town Band. The train then proceeded over the branch line to Dixon, where a major celebration took place, including the inevitable speeches and barbecue. Everyone desiring was then given a free ride over the branch.

As stated before, the new line was 11.8 miles long; it had five sidings: Brown, 3.8 miles from Dixon Jct.; Binghampton, 5.4 miles; Petersen, 7.6; Silver, 9.6; and Mayes, 10.7. At the terminus there were two spurs, one on either side of the main. The Dixon Station was located in a building occupied by the Dixon Auto Service.

The equipment assigned to provide passenger service on the Dixon Branch has aroused discussion. The official dispatchers' sheets, which are the most authentic source of information, reveal that car 1017 opened the line; according to men of OA&E's Mechanical Department, the 1017 had a General Electric type K-36 master controller located in the baggage section against the bulkhead; on either end of the car, a dummy controller was installed and connected to the master controller by means of chains and sprockets. This method of control was devised by Mr. F. A. Miller, Superintendent of Equipment of the OA&E. On November 11, 1914, only a few days after commencement of service, motor 1017 encountered mechanical trouble and was returned to Oakland shops for "heavy repairs." Motor 1015 was then sent out to substitute, this car having a large baggage compartment to accommodate the large milk shipments originating on the branch. Dispatchers' records show other cars assigned--- the unique 1051, 1001, 1002, and 1004. Motor 1017's K-36 control proved unsatisfactory and the car was equipped with OA&E's standard Westinghouse HL type. Motor 1002 became the regular Dixon car, shuttling back and forth over the 12 flat miles. On June 8, 1915, 1002 caught fire at Dixon Jct., but the flames were extinguished by Conductor French and Motorman Davis before too much damage was done. The car was severely smoked up, however, and was returned to Oakland for repairs and painting. Motor 1001 was then assigned to the branch. Motor 1051 played a part in constructing the branch, along with OA&E's steam locomotives; 1051 also hauled freight cars over this line. This car lacked electric heaters, depending upon a pot-bellied coal stove, which at times was most impractical. Motorman George Hademan remembers setting an oil marker on the floor under his stool to keep his feet from freezing. A more or less improvised method of car maintenance was carried on by Mr. Hademan; once he had to borrow a screwdriver from a carpenter working at the Dixon Station when a motor developed trouble. After making the repair, he absent-mindedly put the screwdriver in his pocket and left town. It took the Dixon station agent, working through OA&E's Superintendent of Transportation, Mr. J. H. Leary, several days before Hademan was

Passengers were invited to ride free on the opening day of the Dixon Branch; here is the special train at Dixon Jct. on that happy day. (Dudley A. Westler Collection)

Dixon's town band turned out for the momentous occasion, adding its tootles to the festivities; photo below was taken at Dixon Jct. on opening day. (Dudley A. Westler)

contacted on his main line run in Sacramento; he returned the screwdriver at once, along with his apologies and thanks.

Passenger train operation on the Dixon Branch was quite unsuccessful. From March 1 to June 8, 1915, 56 passengers rode from Dixon Jct. to Dixon, while but 10 rode in the opposite direction during the same fifteen week period. Receipts for passenger traffic from January 1, 1915 to May 31, 1917, were $376.22 while operating expenses were $1,156.25---a deficit of $780.03. OA&E was not in any position to absorb such a deficit, and, inasmuch as there appeared no prospect for improvement in the foreseeable future, the SV applied to the California Railroad Commission for permission to abandon its entire operation. On July 23, 1917 the Commission ordered abandonment, and the last car ran on August 9, 1917.

Abandonment was not caused by auto and truck competition as was the case in most interurban abandonments; there was no paralleling road.

The Dixon Branch rail was torn up to satisfy creditors of the SV, and the overhead was removed and salvaged by the OA&E. The SV was dissolved as a corporation on March 2, 1918---and so died the short lived Sacramento Valley Electric.

A serio-comic incident took place after abandonment.

One day after abandonment, a knock was heard on the door of OA&E's freight agent. A rather buxom elderly lady entered in an obviously dejected mood, informing the surprised gentleman that "she wished to make peace with him and the Lord." Although somewhat taken back and more than a little baffled, the agent, by dint of considerable diplomacy, heard the lady's sad tale. It seemed that in her earlier years the lady had been unable to resist the tempting array of milk and cream cans on express wagons at 40th & Shafter Station waiting to be delivered to Oakland area creameries. She slipped little nips regularly and was never once noticed; indeed, the losses were ascribed to train crews who always stoutly protested their innocence when questioned, as they frequently were. Down through the years the mystery of the disappearing milk persisted, not to be solved until the conscience-stricken lady confessed all, upon the advice of her minister. She offered a sum of money to clear herself, but OA&E had no way of determining the cash value of her thefts, so she was absolved of blame and directed to contribute the money to some deserving charitable organization.

The very idea of there being a Sacramento Valley RR. at all is almost inconceivable. Both SN and V&N and their subsidiary companies were well established in the Upper Sacramento Valley, as was the OA&E in the lower Valley. How could SV's venture prosper? Perhaps it was just as well it succumbed, for all the interurban companies would have been weakened by the duplication of service.

Another view of the special train on opening day of the Dixon Branch. The special was comprised of cars 1015, 1020 and 1024, and operated through from Oakland to Dixon prior to giving free rides on that joyous day. (Dudley A. Westler)

CROSSING THE BAY in pre-bridge days was a delightful journey. SN trains first ran out over the Mole and Pier to the Key Pier Terminal, seen at the left as it appeared in 1930; note the stub of the original Pier is in service to store cars.

Arriving at the Pier Terminal, passengers then boarded one of the big orange Key ferries and were swiftly transported to the famous Ferry Building at the foot of San Francisco's Market Street (seen at lower left as it was in 1915). The double streetcar loop at the Ferry Building was then the greatest local and foreign traffic channel in the world, being served by nine United Railroads lines and four of the Municipal Railway---with an average headway of 15 seconds in rush hours, 30 seconds other times.

Boarding one of these cars, the SN passenger was whisked swiftly to any part of the city.

Pier Terminal Yard, Showing New Construction with 2-Mile Fill

Chapter 13

Operation On Key Division

One of the most difficult construction problems confronting engineers of the OA&E was the route to be followed to tidewater and terminal facilities on the east shore of San Francisco Bay.

Many approaches were considered. Some were quite interesting and worthy of mention herein. One plan was to connect with the Western Pacific in the Melrose district in the eastern part of Oakland, thence by a trackage agreement over WP's rails to that company's ferry terminal. On the face of it, this plan appeared to offer sound economical advantages, but it was finally abandoned because it would entail an excessive amount of street running as well as posing some major engineering and construction problems due to the topography of the hills behind Oakland.

Another suggested solution was to use the Oakland & Bayshore Railway's franchise down Webster St. to 14th & Franklin Streets in downtown Oakland to the depot of the S.P.'s suburban electric trains; OA&E's passengers could there be transferred to SP's Red Electrics to continue their journey to San Francisco via the SP ferries. The alternate route over which the Oakland & Bayshore had a franchise was down 37th St. to Wood St. in West Oakland and then parallel the SP along the shore to a point northeast of the SP Pier (which is now occupied by Albers Brothers Milling Company), at which point they would construct their own ferry terminal and operate their own ferry to San Francisco. Neither of these plans materialized as the railroad was already faced with many financial and construction problems.

Consideration had been given by OA&E officials to connecting with the Key Route's Claremont Line in the Rockridge district. This called for running down Chabot Road instead of Shafter Avenue and joining the Key's line on Claremont Avenue. This would have been a simple solution and nearly came to pass because of certain difficulties attendant upon securing a franchise on Shafter Avenue. However, the difficulties were overcome and terminal facilities were constructed at 40th & Shafter and a junction made with the Key Route at that point.

On January 30, 1911, an agreement was signed with Key for operation of O&A trains over Key's 40th St.-Piedmont Line. This agreement was executed by the San Francisco, Oakland & San Jose Consolidated Railway (Key) and the O&A.

This agreement included certain charges for operating O&A trains over the Key tracks. For movement of equipment (regular, deadhead and switching) a charge of .02¢ per kilowatt hour was made for power. The charge for switching a car was one dollar per car. Handling of baggage to and from the San Francisco Ferry Terminal cost O&A $75.00 per month. For printing joint tickets, 50% of the printing cost of the tickets. Rental of Key Route motors or trailers was put at a flat $5.00 per day per car. Rental of the Brown Diamond Roller Trolleys, $5.00 each per month (and Key required O&A cars to use these while on Key trackage). These are but a few of the expense items agreed upon by the two companies for joint operation over the Key Route.

Included in this agreement also was crew responsibility. All trains were operated under the jurisdiction of and under the supervision of the Key Route's Superintendent. His authority took effect when OA&E trains passed over the derails at 40th & Shafter. OA&E crews were required to break in on Key trains and qualify by written examination before being permitted to operate to the Pier Terminal. They were supplied with a Key Rule Book, Employees' Timetable and Special Bulletins, as well as maintaining a Train Register at the Pier. Conductors were required to turn in all tickets, ferry checks and cash fares collected while operating over the Key Route and were provided with a separate Key Route numbered Ohmer Fare Register Key, which had to be inserted into the register when departing from 40th & Shafter westbound to the Pier. Upon returning to this point from the Pier, the key was removed and a closing impression made. Revenues for tickets sold were allocated on a percentage basis between the two companies.

Equipment was required to measure up to Key standards. Specifically, all motors had to be equipped with Key's Brown Roller Diamond Trolley. In the early days OA&E rented six of these for motors 1001, 1002, 1003, 1004, 1005 and 1006. At a later date four more were added for box motors 101 and 102 and locomotives 103 and 104. The remaining motor cars were equipped with Westinghouse Type 121-A pantagraphs---Key agreeing to a modification of this item.

All motor cars were equipped with the automatic safety trip valve on the roof for use on Key's automatic block signal system. Control trailers also received the trip valves. All windows were equipped with window bars because of the center pole construction on Key's main line to the Pier. The one exception to this was the observation cars.

All power jumpers were removed at 40th & Shafter for westbound operation to the Pier and motors were required to draw their own current through their respective pantagraphs.

The changeover switch on cars had to be reset from 1200 volts to 600, as Key Route operated at the lower pressure. The car inspector at the Oakland Shops was required to meet each train, lower the trolley, reset the changeover switch, raise all pantagraphs (which was performed manually) test the tripper arm on the roof of each car, and make an air brake test before he released the train to proceed on the Key Division.

The junction of the OA&E and Key at 40th & Shafter was officially designated on the timetable as "OA&E Junction;" later when the OA&E became The San Francisco-Sacramento Railroad it became "Short Line Junction." This junction was

(Above) At 40th & San Pablo, SN trains negotiated the busy rail network comprised of a Key System junction point and the car line on San Pablo Ave. Here SN deadheads a train headed by motor 1016 west, while eastbound Key unit 154 on the "C" Line waits for the signal. The time: May, 1941. (VS)

(Left) A westbound Concord Local with motor 1014 on the head end, dives through the Key System subway, carrying the electric railways beneath the Southern Pacific's main line; 1940. (RD)

(Below) Key Route Pier showing junction of old and new trestles. Old trestle went straight ahead and when this 1924 photo was taken it had been cut back for car storage use. It was removed in 1931. SN cars were stored on the old stub.   (HD)

controlled by an interlocking plant located on the second floor of the depot building. It was equipped with Union Switch & Signal Company's electro-pneumatic signal system. Semaphores were of the upper quadrant three position type, which were standard on the Key Division. OA&E paid for the interlocking plant, but its maintenance and towermen's wages were divided equally between the two interurban companies.

Prior to starting the operation of its trains to the Pier, Key and OA&E caused several trial runs to be made, using the OA&E's cars. On December 20, 1912 the first such trip was made using OA&E's 1004 with a crew supplied by Key; this operation lasted 2 hours and 10 minutes and was uneventful except that 1004's pan became entangled in the overhead at 40th & Shafter, resulting in OA&E's being billed for $200 to repair the damage. The cost of the crew for the trip was but $1.82, and $2.00 for the movement to the Pier Terminal and return.

To digress momentarily: On January 26, 1916, OA&E was ordered by Oakland's Mayor John L. Davie (noted for his hostile attitude toward traction companies and railroads) to cease operating its trains over Key Route tracks on 40th St. and instead operate its trains direct to the center of downtown Oakland via Webster St. to the S. P. Depot at 14th & Franklin Streets. The OA&E's original franchise, granted to the Oakland & Bayshore Railway, had expired by this date by failure to exercise rights granted by same. OA&E officials on February 2, 1916, replied to the Mayor that they would be pleased to comply with his order except for the fact that they did not have the necessary funds to construct the line from their depot to downtown Oakland. Davie thereupon ordered Key to cancel its trackage agreement with OA&E to force action. Both Key and OA&E ignored his order as they were not subject to regulation by the city government, they possessed the required franchise and were complying with its provisions. No further action took place and OA&E trains continued to operate over Key tracks to the Pier.

In order to give the reader an idea of the methods used in operating trains to the Pier and handling them there, the following information is given:

OA&E trains usually consisted of a motor and a trailer. However, at times a single motor car sufficed, and at others, as many as six cars were operated in a single train. Named trains usually comprised two motors and a parlor observation. Picnic trains consisted of from five to ten cars---their usual consist being five trailers pulled by the box motors. In some instances Key's locomotive 1001 was used to haul one of these trains to 40th & Shafter, where an OA&E locomotive took the head end.

At this point it should be mentioned that OA&E's four big Baldwin-Westinghouse locomotives: 103, 104, 105 and 106, were not permitted to run to the Pier Terminal because of their weight; the trestle was not designed to bear such loads.

Dispatchers' sheets indicate that OA&E motors not ordinarily operated over the Key Division occasionally did run to the Pier. Motors 1001, 1002 and even 1051 showed up occasionally when equipment shortages existed due to heavy holiday travel or extra heavy business to Redwood Canyon to picnic parks at Madrone Park or Pinehurst. Motor cars of the Northern Electric also ran to the Pier occasionally; NE motors 103 and 201 have been hauled over Key in special trains.

In a move to reduce deadhead movements and power consumption, OA&E equipment was operated to the Pier in a "turn around" movement, usually departing for the north after laying over for just one boat. Where considerable time had to elapse between arrival and departure, OA&E cars were stored at the Pier Terminal on what were known as Yard Tracks 7 and 8, outside of the train shed.

OA&E trains were scheduled first out from the Pier, and usually left on Track 1 with Key's 40th St.-Piedmont trains following. Extra long trains departed from Track 5 or 6. In the event of a mechanical failure, Key trains left the Pier in their usual order and the OA&E train followed, last out. The trains made no stops in either direction between the Pier Terminal and 40th & Shafter.

An OA&E inspector of equipment was stationed at the Pier; he inspected all cars, made emergency repairs and acted as hostler. A car cleaner was also detailed there part time.

As in all large train terminals, problems arose at the Pier. Baggage was left behind, passengers found themselves on the wrong train despite a large train directory board, milk & cream soured due to delays en route, but such difficulties were usually solved to the satisfaction of all concerned. Not so fortunate, however, was one inebriated passenger who attempted to board a moving train from the wrong side and was flung to his death.

Once Train No. 20, consisting of cars 1007, 1026 and "Alabama," was loading passengers at the Pier. The inspector on the roof lowered 1026's pan as 1007 coupled on, then returned 1026's pan to the wire. A short circuit caused the roof to catch fire, filling the car with smoke and causing a near panic inside the crowded car. The flames were quickly extinguished and passengers reboarded, but the scheduled departure times were well snarled by then.

Another instance of a minor delay was caused by a most unusual occurrence. Train #8, The Meteor, was about to depart, but its motorman was nowhere to be found. The Key's Trainmaster appeared and demanded to know what the SF-S conductor had done to his motorman. The poor conductor had no explanation whatsoever to give, and after a further delay it was learned that the motorman had gone over to San Francisco and had missed the return connection. Finally a Key extra motorman who was familiar with the big green trains was called upon to move the train to 40th & Shafter.

OA&E motormen were known to be fast runners and were frequently tripped by the automatic train stops on the Key Division in their attempts to run through the automatic block signal territory, especially when the signal was changing from a stop position to caution. Operating rules strictly forbade this type of operation and any motorman guilty of running a board or being tripped was usually given time off. One in particular who comes to mind was a certain motorman, Mr. "X" of the SF-S; one day he was operating deadhead equipment to the Pier---cars 1014, 1005 and 1018---and was passing Interlocker Tower No. 2 when he ran the board and trailed the crossover switch, only to stop short of the derail. He was placed on report to Superintendent E. E. Thornton of the Key System who in fairness to the individual referred the matter to General Manager Mitchell of the Short Line. Mitchell in turn referred the matter back to Thornton, claiming that Mr. "X" was not under his jurisdiction at the time and whatever discipline Mr. Thornton elected to administer would be carried out. Mr. "X" was given seven days off and Mitchell saw to it that the punishment was also effective on the SF-S.

The inference may be quickly and correctly drawn that this action was used as a precedent when it came time to fix responsibility of crews in event of accidents. This was most strongly stressed in the accident investigation hearing involving the Short Line and Key System at a later date.

To bear out this point further, a minor accident occurred on February 4, 1922 at 40th St. & Telegraph Ave., when SF-S Train No. 5, motor 1020, struck the rear of a standing Key 40th-Piedmont train. Key requested SF-S to bear the cost of repairing the minor damage to its car, but SF-S denied liability, claiming the crews of both trains were under Key jurisdiction and both trains were on a Key line at the time.

The most serious accident of all which occurred on the Key Division took place on December 4, 1924 on the fill. The most accurate and complete account of this tragic collision is that returned by the Interstate Commerce Commission Investigation Report, which we quote verbatim:

"One of the most serious rail accidents in the Bay Area occurred on the Key Division on December 4, 1924, involving trains of the two companies. The results of which caused the death of 8 passengers and 2 employees off duty, injury to 36

The tragic accident of December 4, 1924 was the worst ever to occur involving either a Key or South End train. These photos, taken on that wet grim morning, convey a bit of the shock evident on the faces of the workmen as they sought to clear the line.

Top photo shows SF-S car 1014 deeply embedded in Key System steel center entrance car 665. Note that much of the glass is intact.
(AEB)

Center picture shows the cars separated after the 665 was pulled free of the jacked up 1014.
(VS)

The bottom photo is a closeup of the bettered front end of 1014 with raincoated workmen hard at work cleaning up debris.
(AEB)

(Right) Closeup of type of signal used on Key Pier, 1923. Note tripper arm which would stop a train if it were to pass a "stop" indication. Here the signals are at "proceed."

passengers and 2 employees.

"The accident took place opposite Signal #104, located at a point 1-1/4 mile east of the Pier Terminal on the Key System Fill.

The collision occurred at 7:54 AM, the height of the commuter rush period. Trains involved in the accident were Key System westbound Train No. 729 of the Key System Oakland 12th Street Line, which consisted of four steel center entrance cars Nos. 655, 656, 664 and 665 in the order named. SF-S RR. Train #15 consisted of one single motor combination car #1014.

"The Key train had come to a stop due to stop position of signal at Pole 100. The motorman whistled out a flag and the brakeman of the rear car was on the ground and halfway back of his car when Motor 1014 crashed into the rear end of car 665 and telescoped it for a distance of 18.5 feet. The results were that the rear portion of the Key car was practically demolished. Estimated speed of the Short Line train at the time of the collision was between 35 and 40 miles per hour. It was the opinion of witnesses aboard the Short Line car that its brakes locked the wheels after an emergency application and the car slid forward until the impact of the collision."

The summary and final conclusion of the Director of the Bureau of Safety of the I.C.C. which conducted an investigation of the accident stated as follows:

"This accident was caused by failure of the motorman of the Sacramento Short Line to operate his train in accordance with the requirements of existing rules and to observe and obey automatic block signal indications; also by reason of the fact that trains were operated and were permitted to be operated at speeds which required greater distance in which to bring them to a stop than the minimum braking distance provided by the automatic stop system as installed on this line.

"To provide against a recurrence of an accident of this character, the Key System Transit Company should at once establish a maximum speed restriction for all trains operated over this line which will insure that any train can be stopped in the minimum braking distance provided by the automatic stop system."

This recommendation was signed by W. P. Borland, Director of the I.C.C. in Washington, D.C., under date of January 12, 1925.

Train #15 was a local which originated at Concord and consisted of two wooden motor cars, 1014 on the head end and 1008. 1008 was cut off at 40th & Shafter, while 1014 continued to its fateful rendezvous with destiny. All mechanical devices were checked on the 1014 by the car inspector at 40th & Shafter and the train was released to the motorman (who had traded his regular run with the regular motorman of #15 for the one run only). On that morning a light mist was falling, but visibility was good and signals were clearly visible, as Key's motormen were able to operate their trains without difficulty. There are many rumors in circulation and unauthenticated stories told about the facts and circumstances of this collision, but the facts as related above are true and have been found to be correct by reliable sources.

In October 1919 employees of the San Francisco-Oakland Terminal Railways (Key Route) went out on strike for several days, completely tying up the Key Division. This presented a headache to the OA&E, as its trains would be compelled to tie up at 40th & Shafter Depot. OA&E crews refused to operate the trains to the Pier, so General Manager Mitchell took the controls, despite rumors that he would be dynamited near the subway under the S.P. main line; Mitchell made it to the Pier Terminal without incident and his passengers safely boarded a ferry for San Francisco. This was the only trip made for the duration of the strike, however, as OA&E officials considered the safety of their passengers should not be endangered simply to make ferry connections. OA&E passengers were transferred by bus (thought to be Greyhound or its predecessor company) to the SP Pier and thence to San Francisco by SP ferry.

The next interruption to service to San Francisco occurred in May, 1933 when the Pier caught fire and burned on the night of May 6th. Service had to be suspended for several days; again the facilities of SP were used, with Greyhound busses taking SN passengers to the SP Pier to board the boats. Service to the makeshift Key ferry terminal facilities which offered but limited trackage was resumed several weeks later. Cars were then stored in Key's Yerba Buena Yard between runs and were deadheaded to the ferry terminal to make their scheduled departure times.

Another interruption took place in August, 1938 and was three weeks in duration. The Key's main line was being equipped with Automatic Train Control and the Bridge Yards were being installed preparatory to inaugurating service over the Bay Bridge to San Francisco. SN's motor cars were not then equipped with coded cab signals, hence could not operate to the Pier. The new Key units were so equipped, and they carried SN passengers between the Pier and 40th & Shafter until September 10, 1938, when a sufficient number of SN motors were equipped with train control to permit that company to return to the Pier.

With inauguration of electric train service over the San Francisco-Oakland Bay Bridge on January 15, 1939, service to the Key Pier ended. The last SN train to pull out of the train shed eastbound was No. 10, and the last to arrive was No. 11 from Chico; it returned to 40th & Shafter as a deadhead.

With the exception of a few Exposition Specials which operated to the Key Pier during the World Fair in 1939, service to that storied spot came to an end. SN trains continued to use Key trackage between 40th & Shafter to a point west of the subway where the State property line was located; from that point west into the San Francisco terminal they operated under the authority of the Superintendent of the Bridge Railway.

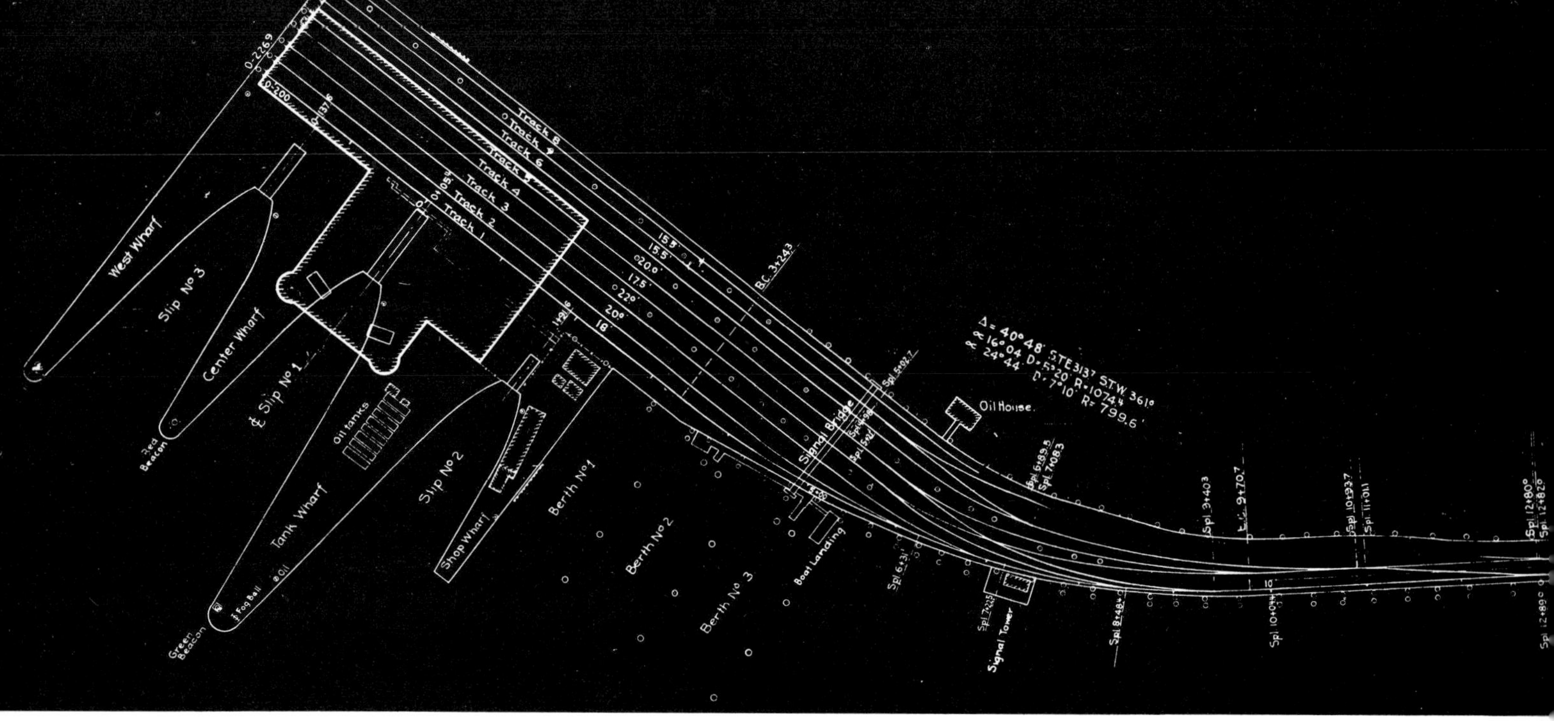

Drawing of Key Pier as it was about 1923; Oakland to right, San Francisco to lower left. (RD)

KEY PIER SIGNAL SYSTEM

By 1924 the Key Pier was handling more than 800 trains daily---more than New York City's Pennsylvania Station. Up to the moment of the wreck on December 4, 1924, more than 3,500,000 trains had been handled through the block signal system without a loss of life. These trains had carried more than 250,000,000 passengers. Key's block signal system on the Pier and its approaches constituted the most densely signalled stretch of track in the world, having 145 signals in 3.87 route miles. None of the signals had ever failed. Such a record merits further attention:

Key not only installed the usual standard block system of semaphore operation but combined it with automatic tripper train stops. This tripper arm which was about four feet below the signal blade was rigidly attached to the blade and moved in synchronization with it. When the blade was at the "stop" or horizontal position, the tripper arm was also horizontal and struck a valve arm on the roof of a passing car; the car's brakes immediately went into emergency stop.

Another safety feature of the busily travelled stretch of track between San Pablo Ave. and the Pier Terminal was the fact that full block overlaps were employed. This meant that instead of a single block separating a caution signal and a stop signal, Key used an intermediate block also. Thus a train encountering a "caution" indication could pass through that block, enter the next block which would display a "stop" indication, pass entirely through that block and into a third block (also displaying a "stop" indication) before encountering any obstruction on the track.

Repeated tests on Key trains showed that deceleration from full speed to complete stop position was at the rate of three miles per hour per second, and signal spacing was more than sufficient to bring an eight-car train to a full stop in less than a single block.

The demands of the train-ferry service were such in 1924-25 that from ten to fourteen trains had to be operated through the Pier Terminal at as near the same time as was consistent with safety, half of them going in each direction. It was the only terminal in the world where trains had to arrive and depart at substantially the same time, or within a 5 minute period, while the ferry with which the trains connected was lying in the slip. Thus the Pier's tracks were alternately jammed and idle.

Signals of the block signal system allowed trains to leave the Pier Terminal at a 30-second headway, gradually spacing them out so that upon reaching maximum speed they were running on a 45-second headway. The system worked out to one train for every 2,376 feet, or a total of 7 trains each way between the Pier Terminal and the subway beneath the Southern Pacific main line. These trains had signals in front of them constantly---at least one every 420 feet---to inform the motorman of the condition of the track ahead; so no matter how foggy or how dark it might be, all motormen were informed of any danger by a caution signal at least 900 feet in advance of any danger, and their emergency brakes would stop them in a maximum distance of 350 feet.

Key's automatic signals were raised to the "clear" position by electricity and dropped to the "stop" position by the infallible source of gravity. Thus any power interruption or any other break, either in the rail itself or in the signal wire, caused the blade to drop to "stop" position.

Interlocking towers protected all junctions. Apparatus in these towers was also a model of efficiency. "Clear" signals could not be displayed to move a train over a switch until trains on conflicting routes had been blocked in predetermined order by displaying signals at "caution" and "stop," derailers set to derail position, and tripper arms set to automatically stop any train approaching the cleared route too closely. Signals of the block signal system were interconnected with signals of the interlocking towers.

What about the safety of the Pier itself? Very substantially constructed, the Pier consisted of a fill and a trestle--- the latter composed of nine-pile bents surmounted by 8" x 8" ties thirty feet long, extending under both tracks and across the entire width of the trestle. Spaced but seven inches apart these ties made it impossible for derailed wheels to break thru or to bunch them together. Tracks were spaced on 17 foot centers. Trolley poles stood between the two tracks and a 3' wide plank walkway extended the entire length of the trestle. The two curves on the trestle were not actually reverse curves although often erroneously called that; there was a stretch of straight track 200 feet long between them. Both curves were four degrees, having a radius of 1432.5 feet with spirals at each end to ease the transition. Outer rails were super-elevated to permit operation at speed. Guarding these curves were three steel guard rails on each track plus an 8" x 8" wood guard rail at outer ends of ties. Rails were 90 lb. and were renewed frequently at the first signs of wear.

CONSOLIDATION

**Direct Service
Between**

SAN FRANCISCO
OAKLAND
PITTSBURG
SACRAMENTO
WOODLAND
MARYSVILLE
COLUSA
OROVILLE
CHICO

Consolidation brought new faces to both North and South Ends.   Above, South End motor 1006 heads Train No.
7 as it meets northbound No. 2 at Manzanita Siding, between Live Oak and East Gridley in October, 1940.
No. 2's second car is a control Niles trailer of the 222 Class, while No. 7 has 129 and 220.   (VS)

Down on the South End, North End car 226 appears right at home training with 1011 near Mallard in May of
1940---a time when North End trailers saw extensive use as the Hall-Scott steel trailers were laid up to
avoid wheel wear; they were being saved for use between San Francisco and Pittsburg local trains after the
abandonment of through service to Sacramento. (VS)

Chapter 14

History

On January 1, 1929, a new interurban railway came into being---the unified Sacramento Northern Railway, stretching from Chico to Oakland and joining North and South Ends under one management with the whole being owned by The Western Pacific Railroad.

Harry A. Mitchell took over as head of the combined interurbans, and with him into top management posts went many South End officers. The end-to-end merger of course obviated major economies, but certain administrative functions were combined, and maintenance and repair of rolling stock was centered at Mulberry Shops, Chico.

Physical changes were few, most evident being renumbering of North End locomotives from the 1000 Class to the 400 Class to avoid conflict with South End passenger equipment. South End cars were taken to Mulberry Shops throughout the following twelve months as their shopping dates occurred and were repainted with the new name. The dark green remained the standard livery for all cars.

Most apparent physical change was the operation of South End passenger motors on the North End. North End passenger motors, of course, could not operate on the South End due to the higher voltage obtaining in trolley wires, but North End trailers 222, 224, 226 and 228 were given the necessary controls, automatic tripper valves, etc., to enable them to operate with South End motors and thereafter were run through to Oakland indiscriminately. North End locomotives which were able to operate on either 600 or 1200 volts also appeared regularly south of Sacramento.

The great depression of the early Thirties made major improvements out of the question, including a proposed re-equipping of main line trains with new all-steel cars patterned after those of the South Shore line out of Chicago. As passenger patronage dwindled, trains were cut on each succeeding timetable; the North End was especially hard hit. Improved highways and the ready availability of low-cost "jallopies" made riding the big green interurbans somewhat of a luxury, especially where family movements were concerned. Reduced fares, advertising and optional ticketing arrangements with Western Pacific failed to reverse the trend.

Freight appeared to be the main hope of the combined companies. In an effort to bolster its service area, SN made two major line additions in 1929-30. On June 29, 1929 (although first appearing in the employees' timetable dated June 9, 1929 and hence possibly occurring that date) the new 13 mile Holland Branch was opened for freight only. This left the South End main line at Riverview and extended in a ;general southwesterly direction roughly paralleling the Sacramento River to the town of Oxford. This line was the first SN operation at 1500 volts---supplied by an automatic mercury-arc rectified substation, located at Greendale.

On July 15, 1930 the hitherto isolated Suisun to Vacaville operation was connected to the remainder of the system by means of a nine mile link between Creed on the old South End main line and Vacaville Jct. This new line was electrified with 1500 volt overhead catenary, and for the first time main line locomotives were able to reach the Suisun-Vacaville area. No passenger service was operated on this branch except for special inspections and excursions. Renamed "The Vacaville-Willotta Branch," plans were on foot to connect this operation with the Napa Valley and the Petaluma & Santa Rosa about 1932 but the opposition of the Southern Pacific and the depression brought these to naught. The huge Fairfield Army Air Base in World War II required relocation of the connection with the main line; the new line was constructed from Dozier to Cordero and it, too, received 1500 volt overhead trolley.

The passing years brought continued retrenching in passenger service. In February of 1936 all dining car service was eliminated, and all parlor cars were discontinued in November, 1938. Heavy floods in 1938 washed out the Feather River bridge near Oroville, and it was not rebuilt; instead, a connecting bus service was inaugurated between Oroville Jct. and Oroville. The remaining stub end in Oroville remained for freight switching moves, although isolated from the remainder of the system.

To protect itself from outside highway competition, SN entered the bus field. On a following page this subject is covered, together with illustrations.

On January 15, 1939 through service to a new terminus in San Francisco via the Bay Bridge was inaugurated with a special six-car train originating at Chico and composed entirely of South End equipment. A separate chapter is devoted to operation over the bridge. In spite of this direct rail connection to San Francisco, passenger business was not stimulated except for special movements to the Golden Gate International Exposition on Treasure Island in San Francisco Bay. It was the old story---Californians, once tasting of individualized transportation as ably represented by the improved automobiles and roads, simply refused to go back to the less flexible mass transportation media of which SN was perhaps the most vulnerable example.

SN management reluctantly came to the conclusion that the company would have to get out of the passenger business and made the necessary applications for abandonment of that service. Its applications were granted with little or no opposition.

First to go was the service between Sacramento and San Francisco; this was ended on August 26, 1940. In service yet on the South End was the commuter service to Concord, extended to Pittsburg coincidentally with the elimination of through trains to Sacramento. Five daily roundtrips were carded between San Francisco and Pittsburg until January 1, 1941 when service was reduced to four daily roundtrips. This timecard remained in effect until final abandonment occurred on June 30, 1941. Greyhound Bus took over the replacing service, SN having sold its paralleling bus operation between Pittsburg and San Francisco to that company. Two franchise roundtrips were run between San Francisco and Pittsburg on July 5th and July 12th, but when DH-27 left on July 12th with car 1014 assigned, that was the absolute finale and South End passenger interurbans entered the pages of history.

It is interesting to note the Train Register entries on the last day of through main line passenger service, August 26, 1940. On that day the following equipment was operated over the Pittsburg Branch: Train #101 consisted of motor 1001; train 102 consisted of motors 1001 and 1019; No. 103 consisted of 1001; then an Extra was operated between West Pittsburg and the ferry slip at Mallard with "Extra 1001" and returned to Pittsburg; train 104 consisted of 1001; train 105 was also the 1001; the 106 consisted of motors 1001 and 1010; train 107 was again motor 1001; 108 had two motors: 1001 and 1011. Motor 1001 was then cut off and placed on the siding at West Pittsburg; thus it was that one of the old O&A's original cars made her last run---she was laid up for good until hauled to the bone yard at Chico. Train 109 was filled by motor 1011, which then ran as Extra 1011 to the slip at Mallard to make the ferry crew relief, then returning to Pittsburg as an extra. Train 110 was served by 1011. Train 117 the final run of the night on the branch, was annulled; it was to have connected with the main line train at West Pittsburg, but the connection was made by an SN bus at McAvoy and passengers carried into Pittsburg by bus on that particular evening.

Employees Timetable No. 21 reveals that a very limited number of trains were operated between Pittsburg and San Francisco between August 26, 1940, and June 30, 1941, when all passenger service on the SN ended. Train No. 32, an eastbound, made the last regular passenger run on that fateful Monday; it consisted of motor 1016 and trailer 1022.

For readers interested in the equipment lineup on that final day, June 30, 1941, the 40th & Shafter Train Register reveals the following: Train No. 15, westbound from Concord to San Francisco, had motor 1015 and trailer 1022; Train 12, eastbound to Pittsburg from San Francisco, had motor 1015 and trailer 1022 when it left S.F., but the 1015 was cut off at 40th & Shafter and the 1016 substituted; Train 1017 west had motors 1005 and 1014; Train No. DH-17 eastbound from S.F. Eastbay Terminal was made up of motors 1005 and 1017; this train was stopped in the Bridge Yards and picked up stored equipment spotted there since the previous September---being out of service for all those months. This train consisted of: motors 1005, 1014, trailer 1021, motors 1008, 1011, 1019 and 1020; this equipment was subsequently hauled to Chico and scrapped. No. 3, westbound from Pittsburg to San Francisco, consisted of 1016 hauling trailer 1022; No. 6 east had the same equipment; Train DH-28 consisted of motor 1012 and trailer 1023, operating as a deadhead movement between 40th & Shafter and the Eastbay Terminal. Train No. 28, east from S.F. to Concord, consisted of the same equipment; No. 27, westbound from Pittsburg to S.F., had 1016 and trailer 1022; Train No. 32, eastbound from S.F. to Pittsburg, also had 1016 and 1022---so these cars made the final passenger run between Oakland and Pittsburg.

Two Extras were operated out of 40th & Shafter on that particular day, one between Oakland and the Bridge Yards consisting of motors 1015, 1010, 1006 and 1005---these being the cars owned by the California Toll Bridge Authority; they were sent down for storage. The other Extra was Extra 661, carrying deadhead passenger equipment which was stored at West Pittsburg pending forwarding to Chico for scrapping: this drag consisted of locomotive 661, and dead motors 1011, 1019, 1008, 1020 and trailer 1021.

The North End saw all of its interurban passenger service terminated on October 31, 1940---including both the Woodland and the Colusa Branches. Streetcars continued in Chico, Marysville-Yuba City and Sacramento for a few years longer, but these, too, were abandoned as follows: Chico, December 15, 1947; Marysville-Yuba City, February 15, 1942; Sacramento, sold 1944 to Pacific City Lines and operated by that company through-routed with the Central California Traction's Colonial Heights Line (also purchased by PCL) with CCT cars until abandoned in 1946.

SN thus ended its career as a passenger hauler, but it continued to serve well as a freight mover. In Many ways the SN served its parent, the Western Pacific, much as Pacific Electric served the Southern Pacific. To cover adequately this phase of the merged lines' history, a separate chapter is included herein, which brings the history of the company up to date at time of writing.

Mulberry Shops next saw a dreary procession of the venerable passenger cars pass through to be scrapped. One by one the cars disappeared---save for a handful saved for MW use and the five which were saved because they were owned by the Toll Bridge Authority; these were sold to Key System and served throughout World War II as the so-called "City of Berkeley," running on the F Line at morning and evening rush hours.

Mulberry Shops was closed down on April 2, 1951, with subsequent maintenance being performed at the Western Pacific's Sacramento Shops. The twenty or so employees of Mulberry Shops were transferred to Sacramento. This change was made possible because both roads at that time were well dieselized---only the three freight motors at Yuba City being required to be hauled to and from Sacramento for servicing.

The South End remained intact as a 1500 volt DC electrified railroad until Tuesday afternoon, July 24, 1951, when a 21 car train of steel proved too heavy for the Lisbon Trestle, which collapsed like a row of dominos beneath the weight of the heavy gondolas bound for Columbia Steel's mill at Pittsburg. Motor 650 and its train came to rest on the ground upright but sadly out of plumb. An emergency rerouting using WP's main line from Sacramento to Stockton and the Santa Fe's main line from Stockton to Pittsburg was arranged, resulting in a permanent trackage rights agreement which obviated the further use of the train ferry "Ramon." That vessel was removed from service on August 31, 1954 and sold for scrapping. In the meantime the ferry had been used to reach points south of the collapsed trestle.

When the Lisbon Trestle was rebuilt it was not electrified and trolley wire was removed between Sacramento and Chipps.

The next emergency occurred at Marysville, when the Christmas Flood of 1955 washed out the approaches to the SN's bridge over the Feather River. A much more imposing structure replaced the old, with concrete pilings being used. The old through truss bridge, dating back to Northern Electric days, was incorporated in the new crossing. Inasmuch as the substation for the Marysville-Yuba City section was located in Marysville, it was decided to electrify the new bridge; today this section remains the sole survivor of SN's many miles of electrification.

The Oakland-Pittsburg segment remained electrified until February 28, 1957 when the last freight train ran uphill and through the tunnel. The main line was then abandoned between Oakland and Lafayette, as a newly constructed line of the Oakland Terminal on Union St., Oakland, served to connect the Western Pacific's main line with those of the Oakland Terminal and Santa Fe. Later that year (1957) the Lafayette-Walnut Creek section was also abandoned; now the once busy Walnut Creek to Pittsburg line which once saw 14 daily electric trains has but a ragtag assortment of five diesel freights weekly.

Up on the North End, the American River bridge at Sacramento was sold and SN trains were diverted to the WP's main line between Haggin Yard and Globe. The same 1955 floods which washed out the Feather River bridge at Marysville also caused the abandonment of the main line of the SN from

East Nicolaus to Marysville; again the WP main line served as the replacement.

1954 saw the end of the 600 volt switching operation at Oroville; this was the last segment of electrification served by a manually operated substation, and with the closing down of that facility and the retirement of its operator, the day of the substation operator was over on the SN. In 1955 the Oroville line itself was abandoned.

By the spring of 1957 electric operation had been restored between Marysville and Yuba City. The return was suitably celebrated on May 18th of that year when Birney 62 made a series of special trips sponsored by a railfan group.

The summer of 1960 saw the Colusa Branch cut back to Meridian---no longer did the SN serve Colusa County.

Additional coverage of SN as it appears today is to be found in a following chapter devoted to Freight.

SUBSTATIONS

The North End had thirteen 600-volt substations; in 1923 three of these were modernized and automatic control placed in two of them. In 1927 another became automatic and in 1929 all the remainder were changed to automatic operation.

The South End's seven substations provided 1200 volt DC current until 1936 when pressure was stepped up to 1500 volts. All except Montezuma were automatic, operating on the line voltage drop principle; the automatic features were installed in 1929. A manually operated portable substation was located at Concord, and a similar portable was located at 40th & Shafter until

removed from its car and permanently installed in one of the shop buildings---it is included in the total above.

Standard equipment of all South End subs except Eastport was one 750 KW 1100 volt, 60 cycle AC-1500 volt DC Westinghouse synchronous motor generator set; Eastport had two such installations and it was at Eastport that PG&E determined the maximum half-hour demand which set the charge for SN power. A 250 KW rectifier unit (automatic) at Greendale fed the 15.77 mile Holland Branch (Riverview to Oxford). The two portables above mentioned were also 250 KW machines of the synchronous motor-generator type.

Last ex-SN passenger cars to remain in service were the five purchased by Key System from the Toll Bridge Authority and used as trippers on the F Line during World War II. Here all five are seen on Shattuck Ave., Berkeley, on June 22, 1943. (H. T. Wolfe)

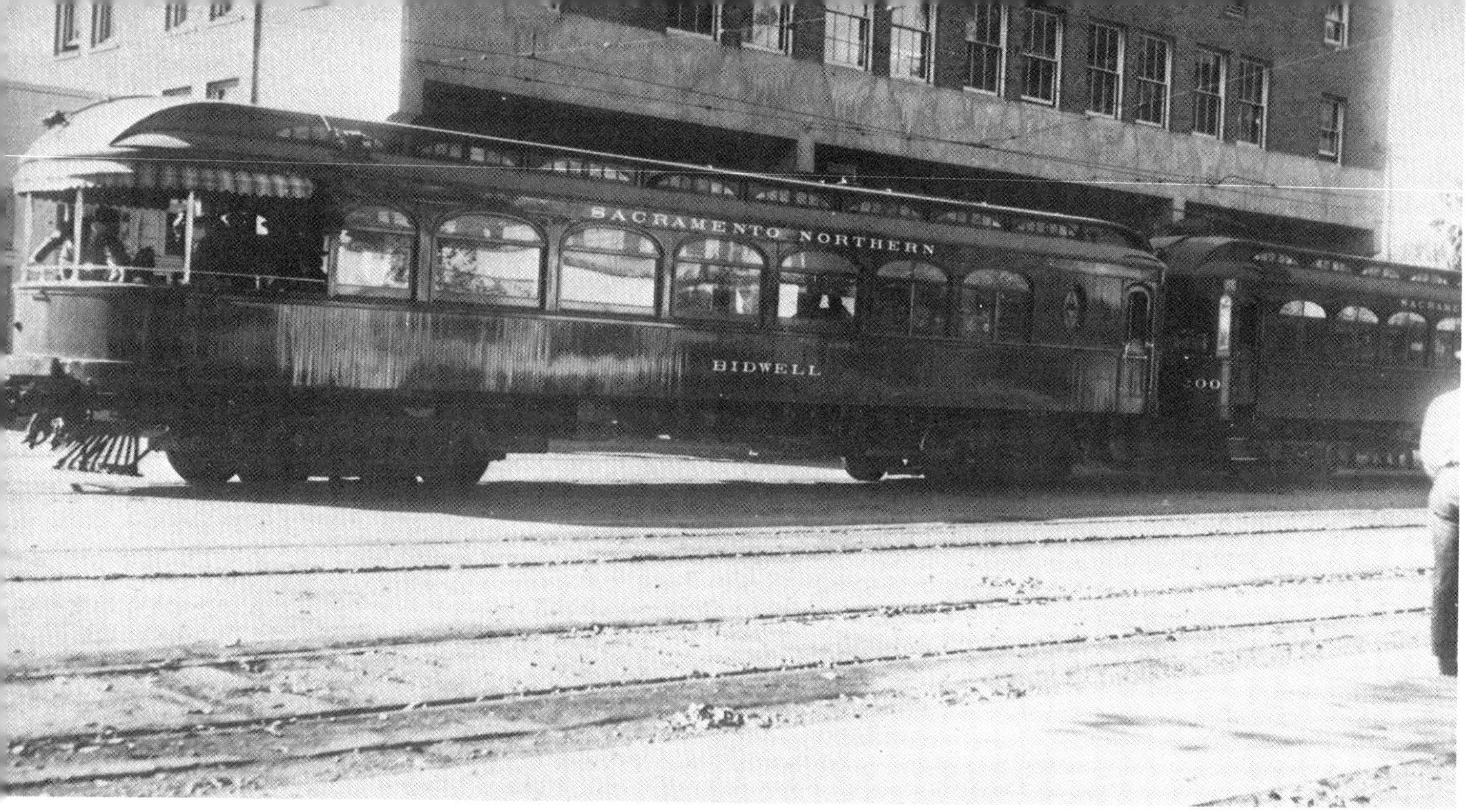

LAST RUNS: On these two pages are shown the final runs of significance as Sacramento Northern bowed out of the passenger business for all time.   Above, "Bidwell" at Sacramento Union Station on last Sunday in October, 1940---the last day an observation car ever ran to that spot. (AL)

Below, the last train to use Union Station, Sacramento. Car 101 was just about the same as it was when passenger service was inaugurated on Northern Electric. October 31, 1940. (AL)

Above, car 1009 heads last No. 10 for Sacramento; at San Francisco on August 26, 1940. (AA-AH)

Below: July 12, 1940 and the last passenger run on the South End. Car 1014 as Train No. 27 passes Sequoia Station for the last time. (Motorman Roy Titler, Conductor S. R. Bowman) (VS)

Sacramento Northern used motor coaches sparingly. The first instance was the Fageol Safety Coach (left) which replaced cars on the Danville Branch; it connected with SF-S trains at Walnut Creek, running from there to Diablo via Danville. This photo was taken in Walnut Creek, 1924. (VS)

Center photo shows one of the ACF coaches at Pittsburg in 1940. Bus service was inaugurated in Contra Costa County in 1936, operating from Pittsburg to San Francisco. (AL)

Below, a similar ACF coach which ran from Oroville to Portola where it con nected with Western Pacific trains, affording an alternate route for WP passengers to and from the east. Bus service was also offered between Oroville and Oroville Jct., and between Sacramento and Chico. The latter service consisted of one round trip daily except Sunday and replaced the early train up and the late train south. (WP)

Chapter 15

Operation

When The San Francisco-Sacramento Railroad was acquired by The Sacramento Northern Railway on December 31, 1928 the two rather different electric railroads were consolidated into one.

A single employees' timetable was issued for both lines. The South End became the First Subdivision, while the North End became the Second Subsidivision. Seniority of crews on each section was maintained. Had this not been done, old timers of the Northern Electric---the older company---could have outbid former OA&E men for choice runs. Little change occurred in operating methods of either section. Men hired after the consolidation enjoyed seniority on both subdivisions. When service on the North End was rather drastically reduced in the 1930s, many of those men bid in runs on the South End which more or less maintained its usual frequency of service until 1935.

After the end of passenger service in 1940, block signals on the South End between Chipps and Sacramento were removed and reinstalled on Western Pacific's main line thru Niles Canyon. Block signals between Oakland and Pittsburg remained in service until February 28, 1957 when the line was abandoned between Oakland and Lafayette.

With the end of passenger service, SN began to call its motormen "engineers." No firemen are used on diesels of the SN today except for the heavy freight train which operates over the Western Pacific and Santa Fe main lines between Sacramento, Stockton and Pittsburg by means of trackage rights. On those rare occasions when a passenger motor operated between Yuba City and Marysville on SN's only remaining electrified segment, a two man crew was assigned. Otherwise, the Sacramento Northern of 1962 is operated very much in the same manner as any other short line devoted solely to freight hauling.

After the consolidation, all train dispatching was done from the Union Station, Sacramento. Today, dispatching is done from the Western Pacific office building, Sacramento.

The following pages are devoted to a reproduction of the Employees' Timetable No. 20, dated April 23, 1939. In it are, in addition to all the carded trains of that era, the special rules which clearly picture the operation of this busy railroad. A locomotive tonnage table and a system map are also included.

LAST SPECIAL TRAIN: MAY 25, 1941. IT RAN FROM SAN FRANCISCO TO CHICO AND RETURN. CONSIST: 1010, 1024, 1005, 1025, 1012 AND "BIDWELL." CAR 1009 WAS ADDED AT SACRAMENTO. (VS)

SACRAMENTO NORTHERN RAILWAY

EXECUTIVE OFFICES—MILLS BUILDING, 220 MONTGOMERY STREET SAN FRANCISCO, CAL.

H. A. MITCHELL . . . . President.

FRED. W. KIESEL, Vice-President . . . . . . Sacramento, Cal.	D. O. DE GRAFF . . . . Auditor.
W. G. BRUEN . . . . Secretary.	THOS. KEARNS . . . . Auditor Freight and Passenger Accounts.
E. O. BATES . . . . Treasurer.	C. F. POST . . . . Purchasing Agent.

PASSENGER — **TRAFFIC DEPARTMENT** — **FREIGHT**

———, Passenger Traffic Manager.
J. L. SCOTT, General Passenger Agent.

JOHN F. BON, Freight Traffic Manager.
H. E. POULTERER, Assistant Freight Traffic Manager

OPERATING DEPARTMENT—UNION STATION SACRAMENTO, CAL.

J. B. ROWRAY, General Manager
H. O. BROWN, Chief Engineer.

C. D. KENADY, Trainmaster, First Subdivision, Oakland, Cal.
W. W. NELSON, Trainmaster, Second Subdivision,

LEGAL DEPARTMENT, MILLS BUILDING SAN FRANCISCO CAL.

Sacramento Northern Railway is also represented by Officers and Agents of the Traffic Department of the Western Pacific named on page 736.

BETWEEN SAN FRANCISCO, SACRAMENTO, MARYSVILLE, COLUSA, OROVILLE AND CHICO. — Total Mileage, 275.

March 15, 1936.

Southbound (read down)

♮40	♮36	16	10	♮32	♮■8	♮28	6	4	♮■2	Mls.	
P M	P M	A M	P M	P M	P M	P M	P M	A M	A M	.....	lv..San Francisco.ar.
§1000	§600	§8 00	*8 00	†5 20	*4 40	†3 40	*2 00	*1040	*7 40	o	*Key System Ferry.*
10 30	6 35	8 33	8 30	5 50	5 10	4 12	2 30	11 10	8 10	7.9	Oakland (40th & Shatter)
10 35	6 40	8 38	8 35	5 55	5 15	4 17	2 35	11 15	8 15	9.1	Oakland {College and Shafter.}
10 59	7 07	9 05	8 57	6 22	— —	4 48	2 55	11 38	a8 33	19.1	.St. Mary's College.
11 12	7 22	9 23	9 10	6 35	— —	5 02	3 06	11 52	b8 43	27.4	**..Walnut Creek..**
11 25	7 35	9 35	9 23	6 50	— —	5 15	3 18	12 04	b8 52	33.7	......Concord.....
11 29	7 39	9 39	9 28	6 54	— —	P M	3 22	12 08	— —	35.8	........Ohmer.....
11 36	7 46	9 46	9 36	7 02	— —	.....	3 29	12 15	b9 00	39.2	**..Port Chicago..**
11 42	7 52	9 52	9 43	7 09	— —	.....	3 35	12 21	— —	43.6	....Shell Point....
11 50	8 02	10 02	9 50	7 19	6 17	.....	3 45	12 30	9 13	47.1	arr. **Pittsburg** lve.
P M	P M	A M	*9 38	P M	*5 55	.....	*3 30	*1230	*9 00	47.1	lve. **Pittsburg** arr.
.....	.....	.....	.....	.....	.....	.....	See	Note	e ⊡	52.1	........Antioch ⊡....
.....	.....	.....	10 18	.....	6 40	.....	4 13	12 57	9 38	57.8	. **Rio Vista Junc** .
.....	.....	.....	11 10	.....	7 30	.....	5 10	1 50	10 25	93.8	ar. **Sacramento** lv.
.....	.....	.....	P M	.....	7 40	.....	5 20	P M	10 35	93.8	lv. **Sacramento** ar.
					7 52		5 32		10 46	97.4	.North Sacramento.
					7 54		5 35		10 50	99.2	.....Del Paso......
					7 56		5 38		10 53	101.1	.......Robla ......
					7 59		5 42		10 57	103.4	.....Rio Linda ....
					8 02		5 45		11 00	104.7	.......Elverta.....
					8 15		5 56		11 14	113.0	..Pleasant Grove..
					8 17		5 59		11 17	115.0	......Catlett......
					8 19		6 01		11 20	116.2	......Striplin.....
					8 23		6 06		11 25	119.2	.. East Nicolaus ..
					8 29		6 12		11 31	122.7	......Rio Oso .....
			210		8 37		6 23	206	11 41	129.2	......Arboga......
			P M		8 38		6 24	P M	11 42	130.0	..Reed Junction ..
			*8 55		8 54		6 41	*1204	12 02	135.7	**Marysville** ...
			9 06		9 04		6 51	12 14	12 12	137.5	**Yuba City** ....
			9 20		9 20		7 08	12 28	12 28	145.0	......Sutter ......
			9 34		9 34		7 22	12 42	12 42	153.4	......Meridian.....
			9 47		9 47		7 35	12 55	12 55	161.5	......**Colusa**......
			P M		P M		P M	P M	P M		ARRIVE] [LEAVE
			9 11				7 03		12 18	141.5	........Pease.....
			9 13				7 05		12 20	142.8	.....Nuestro .....
			9 15				7 07		12 22	143.9	.....Sanders .....
			9 18				7 09		12 24	145.5	.....Stafford .....
			9 22				7 15		12 31	148.8	.....Live Oak.....
			9 30				7 22		12 40	152.9	.... Manzanita ....
			9 32				7 26		12 43	154.7	... East Gridley ⊙ .
			9 34				7 28		12 45	156.3	.....Peachton.....
			9 38				7 32		12 49	159.0	....East Biggs ...
			9 48				7 43		1 00	165.3	ar.. **Oroville Jn.** lv.
			9 56				7 52		1 13	168.3	arr..Thermalito.lve.
			10 05				8 01		1 22	170.4	..... **Oroville**....
			P M				P M		P M		ARRIVE] [LEAVE
			9 50				7 45		1 05	165.3	lv.. **Oroville Jn.** ar.
			9 58				7 53		1 13	171.5	........Blavo.....
			10 02				7 57		1 17	174.5	......Esquon......
			10 07				8 02		1 22	177.5	......Durham .....
			10 25				8 20		1 40	184.6	...... **Chico**......
			P M				P M		P M		ARRIVE] [LEAVE

Northbound (read up)

	17	♮1	♮■3	■7	27	9	11
lv..San Francisco.ar.	A M	A M	P M	P M	P M	P M	P M
Key System Ferry.	8 35	10 15	1 55	5 15	5 35	7 55	10 35
Oakland (40th & Shatter)	7 59	9 42	1 23	4 42	5 04	7 22	9 58
Oakland {College and Shafter.}	7 54	9 37	1 18	4 37	4 59	7 17	9 53
.St. Mary's College.	7 27	9 14	12 55	— —	4 33	6 53	9 31
..Walnut Creek..	7 14	9 03	12 41	— —	4 19	6 42	9 19
......Concord.....	7 01	8 52	12 28	— —	*4 05	6 30	9 07
........Ohmer.....	6 55	8 44	12 22	— —	P M	6 25	9 02
..Port Chicago..	6 49	8 35	12 15	3 48	.....	6 18	8 56
....Shell Point....	6 41	8 28	12 08	— —	.....	6 11	8 48
arr. **Pittsburg** lve.	*6 34	*8 17	*1157	*3 30	.....	*5 55	*8 38
lve. **Pittsburg** arr.	A M	8 30	12 30	3 45	.....	6 17	8 51
........Antioch ⊡....	.....	.....	.....	.....	.....	.....	.....
. **Rio Vista Junc** .	.....	7 51	11 31	3 08	.....	5 37	8 14
ar. **Sacramento** lv.	.....	*7 00	10 40	2 20	.....	*4 45	7 20
lv. **Sacramento** ar.		A M	10 30	2 10		P M	7 00
.North Sacramento.			10 16	1 54			6 45
.....Del Paso......			10 13	1 51			6 42
.......Robla			10 10	1 48			6 39
.....Rio Linda			10 07	1 45			6 36
.......Elverta.....			10 04	1 42			6 33
..Pleasant Grove..			9 53	1 30			6 21
......Catlett......			9 50	1 28			6 18
......Striplin.....			9 48	1 26			6 15
.. East Nicolaus ..			9 44	1 23			6 11
......Rio Oso			9 38	1 15			6 05
......Arboga......	205		9 29	1 07	209		5 55
..Reed Junction ..	A M		9 28	1 05	P M		5 54
Marysville ...		9 05	9 14	12 55		8 40	5 43
Yuba City		8 55	9 02	12 42		8 30	5 28
......Sutter		8 42	8 42			8 17	5 07
......Meridian.....		8 28	8 28			8 03	4 53
......**Colusa**......		*8 15	*8 15			*7 50	*4 40
ARRIVE] [LEAVE		A M	A M			P M	P M
........Pease.....		8 54	12 35				5 19
.....Nuestro		8 52	12 33				5 17
.....Sanders		8 50	12 32				5 15
.....Stafford		8 47	12 30				5 12
.....Live Oak.....		8 42	12 23				5 07
.... Manzanita		8 35	12 16				5 00
... East Gridley ⊙ .		8 32	12 14				4 57
.....Peachton.....		8 30	12 11				4 54
....East Biggs ...		8 26	12 08				4 51
ar.. **Oroville Jn.** lv.		8 16	11 59				4 42
arr..Thermalito.lve.		8 02	11 47				4 27
..... **Oroville**....		*7 55	*1140				*4 20
ARRIVE] [LEAVE		A M	A M				P M
lv.. **Oroville Jn.** ar.		8 13	11 57				4 38
........Blavo.....		8 04	11 48				4 29
......Esquon......		8 00	11 44				4 25
......Durham		7 56	11 40				4 20
...... **Chico**......		*7 40	*1125				*4 05
ARRIVE] [LEAVE		A M	A M				P M

CHICO-OROVILLE.

P M	A M	A M	Mls.	LEAVE	[ARRIVE	P M	P M	P M
*4 05	*1125	*7 40	o	..............Chico..............		1 40	8 20	10 25
4 58	12 16	8 32	24.8	..............Oroville..............		*1242	*7 25	*9 50
P M	P M	A M		ARRIVE	[LEAVE	P M	P M	P M

SACRAMENTO NORTHERN WAS REPRESENTED IN "THE OFFICIAL GUIDE," 1936 ISSUE, BY THIS FULL PAGE TIMETABLE. NOTE THREE ROUNDTRIPS DAILY TO CHICO. (Magna)

NOTICE TO TICKET AGENTS.
In selling tickets to any point on the Sacramento Northern Ry. use one coupon from Salt Lake reading via the Western Pacific R.R.

FREIGHT SERVICE.
Daily freight trains between all points.

TRACK CONNECTIONS.
At Oakland—With railroads diverging.
At Port Chicago—With Atchison, Topeka & Santa Fe Ry.
At McAvoy—With So. Pac. Co.
At Sacramento—With West. Pac. R.R., So. Pac. Co., Cent. Cal. Trac. Co.
At Marysville — With Western Pacific R.R., Southern Pacific Co.
At Oroville—With West. Pac. R.R.
At Chico—With So. Pacific Co.

ROUTING.
Westbound Trans-Continental Freight Shipments in connection with **Western Pacific** to destinations on the Woodland Branch and points west of Sacramento to Oakland, via Sacramento; all other points on main line and branches (except Oroville), via Oroville, when destined to Oroville, via Marysville.
In connection with A. T & S. F. Ry., via Port Chicago or via Stockton, C.C.T.Co. to Sacramento, except to stations west of Sacramento to Oakland.
In connection with Southern Pacific to destinations on Marysville-Colusa Branch and points north of Marysville, also Sacramento, via Marysville; points on Woodland Branch and points north of Sacramento to and including Marysville, via Sacramento; to points west of Sacramento to Oakland, via McAvoy.

Holland Branch.—Riverview to Oxford (15.42 miles). Freight service only.

Vacaville, Suisun-Fairfield Branch.—Creed to Willotta (16.74 miles). Freight service only.

For Map, see pages 734-735.
STANDARD—*Pacific time.*

SAN FRANCISCO-CONCORD.
Leave **San Francisco** for Concord ♮†7 00 a.m., ♮d5 40 p.m. Returning, leave Concord ♮†5 55, ♮†6 30 a.m.

SACRAMENTO-WOODLAND.
Leave **Sacramento** ●7 25, *10 30 a.m., ●12 35, *2 15, ●4 40, *5 20, ●6 15, *11 10 p.m.
Leave **Woodland** ●6 40, *8 15, ●11 30 a.m., *1 20, *3 55, ●5 25, *7 00, ●11 50 p.m.

EXPLANATION OF SIGNS.
* Daily; †daily, except Sunday; § Sunday only; a stops daily, except Saturday, Sunday, holidays and school days; b stops Sunday and holidays to receive passengers for Rio Vista Junction and Sacramento; d daily, except Saturday and Sunday. ■Observation car between San Francisco and Sacramento. ⊙ Stages to and from Gridley connect with all trains. ♮ Holiday schedule; regular Sunday passenger schedule will be operated on account of the following holidays: New Year's Day, Washington's Birthday, Decoration Day, Fourth of July, Labor Day, Thanksgiving and Christmas; for other special or local holidays, announcement will be made through ticket offices. ● Daily, except Sunday and holidays.

Note ⊡—Stages to and from Pittsburg connect with all trains.

SACRAMENTO NORTHERN RAILWAY

TIME 20 TABLE

In Effect 12:01 A. M. "Pacific" Time

SUNDAY, APRIL 23, 1939

This Time Table is for the exclusive use and guidance of the employes concerned.   The Company reserves the right to vary from it at pleasure.

Always have the revised Book of Rules of the Transportation Department at hand for reference.

J. B. ROWRAY,
General Manager

W. W. NELSON,
Superintendent of Transportation

2 Eastward — FIRST SUBDIVISION

Time Table No. 20 — April 23, 1939

Left column heading: *Fone, Scales, Wyes, Bulletin, Register Station, Standard Clocks, Interlocking Plant.* Signal territory (narrow column between Distance and Stations): Double Track San Francisco–Oakland (T.C., N.S.); Automatic Block Signals beyond.

Plant	SECOND CLASS 292	FIRST CLASS 40	DH-11	10	DH-7	36	32	8	28	DH-3	6	18	DH-1	DH-17	16	2	12	Distance from San Francisco	STATIONS
	Sacramento Local Freight	Pittsburg Passenger		Sacramento Passenger		Pittsburg Passenger	Concord Passenger	The Meteor	Concord Passenger		Chico Passenger	Sacramento Passenger			Pittsburg Passenger	The Comet	Concord Passenger		
	Leave Daily EX. SUNDAY	Lv. SUNDAY & HOLIDAYS	Leave Daily	Leave Daily	Leave Daily	Lv. SUNDAY & HOLIDAYS	Leave Daily EX. SUNDAY & HOLIDAYS	Leave Daily	Leave Daily EX. SUNDAY & HOLIDAYS	Leave Daily	Leave Daily	Lv. SUNDAY & HOLIDAYS	Leave Daily EX. SUNDAY & HOLIDAYS	Leave Daily EX. SUNDAY & HOLIDAYS	Lv. SUNDAY & HOLIDAYS	Leave Daily	Leave Daily EX. SUNDAY & HOLIDAYS		
PIK		10.30PM	10.27PM	8.10PM	6.03PM	6.00PM	5.23PM	4.43PM	3.57 PM	1.47PM	1.20PM	10.40AM	10.11AM	8.42AM	8.15AM	8.03AM		0.00	SAN FRANCISCO
I																		6.20	EAST JCT. 1.16
I																		7.36	EMERYVILLE JCT. 0.45
I																		7.81	SAN PABLO AVE. 1.09
PRBKIY	6.30PM	10.51 s 10.54	10.48PM	8.31 s 8.40	6.24PM	6.21 s 6.24	5.45 s 5.48	5.04 s 5.07	4.19 s 4.21	2.08PM	1.41 s 1.47	11.01 s 11.05	10.32AM	9.03AM	8.36 s 8.39	8.24 s 8.26	7.27AM	8.90	2S OAKLAND (40th & Shafter) 1.79
P		11.00		8.46		6.30	5.54	5.13	4.27		1.53	11.11			8.45	8.32	7.34	10.69	ROCKRIDGE 1.21
P		f 11.03		f 8.48		f 6.33	f 5.57	5.15	f 4.30		f 1.56	f 11.14			f 8.47	8.34	f 7.37	11.90	TEMESCAL 2.50
P		f 11.09		f 8.53		f 6.38	f 6.02	5.21 [7]	f 4.36 [27]		f 2.00	f 11.18			f 8.52	8.38	f 7.42	14.40	HAVENS 3.30
P		f 11.15		f 8.59		f 6.45	f 6.09	5.27	f 4.42		f 2.06	f 11.24			f 8.58	8.44	f 7.50 [17]	17.70	PINEHURST 2.13
P		f 11.18		f 9.02		f 6.49	f 6.13	5.30	f 4.46		f 2.10	f 11.27			f 9.02	8.47	f 7.55	19.83	MORAGA 0.91
P		f 11.21		f 9.04		f 6.51	f 6.15	5.32	f 4.49		f 2.13	f 11.29			f 9.05	8.50	f 7.57	20.74	ST. MARYS 1.90
P		f 11.24		f 9.07		f 6.55 [19]	f 6.18	5.35	f 4.52		f 2.16	f 11.32			f 9.09 [1]	8.53	f 8.00	22.64	BURTON 2.45
P		f 11.28		f 9.10		f 6.59	f 6.24	5.38	f 4.56		f 2.19	f 11.36			f 9.14	8.56	f 8.04	25.09	LAFAYETTE 1.62
P		f 11.31		f 9.13		f 7.02	f 6.27	5.40	f 5.00 [7]		f 2.22	f 11.39			f 9.17	8.58	f 8.08	26.71	SARANAP 1.73
P		f 11.34		f 9.19 [11]		f 7.05	f 6.31	5.42	f 5.04		f 2.26	f 11.43			f 9.22	9.00 [1]	f 8.13	28.44	D WALNUT CREEK 2.02
P		11.37		9.22		7.08	6.35	5.45	5.07		2.30	11.47			9.26	9.04	8.18	30.46	SPARKLE 0.10
		f 11.38		f 9.23		f 7.09	f 6.36	5.46	f 5.08		f 2.31	f 11.48			f 9.27	9.05	8.19	30.56	LAS JUNTAS (S.P.R.R. Crsg.) 0.55
P		f 11.39		f 9.24		f 7.11	f 6.37	5.47	f 5.10		f 2.32	f 11.50			f 9.29	9.06	f 8.21	31.11	BANCROFT 0.91
P		f 11.41		f 9.26		f 7.14	f 6.39	5.48	f 5.12		f 2.34	f 11.52			f 9.30	9.08	f 8.24	32.02	MEINERT 2.72
PRBK		f 11.45		f 9.30		f 7.18	s 6.45PM	5.51	s 5.15PM		f 2.39	f 11.56			s 9.35	f 9.12	s 8.30AM	34.74	D CONCORD 2.30
P		f 11.48		f 9.33		f 7.22		5.54			f 2.43	f 11.59AM			f 9.39	9.16		37.04	OHMER 1.17
P		f 11.50		f 9.35		f 7.25		5.56			f 2.46	f 12.03PM			f 9.42	f 9.18		38.21	CLYDE (B.P.&C.R.R. Crsg.) 1.82
P		f 11.54		f 9.38		f 7.29		6.00			f 2.50	f 12.07			f 9.46	f 9.21		40.03	DN PORT CHICAGO 3.43
P		f 11.59PM		s 9.42		f 7.33		6.04			f 2.54	f 12.11 [3]			f 9.51	9.25		43.46	McAVOY 1.13
P		f 12.01AM		f 9.44		f 7.35		6.06			f 2.56	f 12.14			f 9.53	9.26		44.59	SHELL POINT 1.19
FRY		s 12.03AM		f 9.47		s 7.38PM		s 6.09			s 2.59	s 12.17			s 9.55AM	s 9.29		45.78	WEST PITTSBURG 0.81
F	2.00AM			s 9.50PM				s 6.12PM [19]			s 3.02PM	s 12.20PM				s 9.32AM		46.59	Suisun Bay Car Ferry MALLARD
	Arrive Daily Ex. Monday	Arrive See Note	Arrive Daily	Arrive Daily	Arrive Daily	Ar. SUNDAY & HOLIDAYS	Arrive Daily EX. SUNDAY & HOLIDAYS	Arrive Daily	Arrive Daily EX. SUNDAY & HOLIDAYS	Arrive Daily	Arrive Daily	Ar. SUNDAY & HOLIDAYS	Arrive Daily EX. SUNDAY & HOLIDAYS	Arrive Daily EX. SUNDAY & HOLIDAYS	Ar. SUNDAY & HOLIDAYS	Arrive Daily	Arrive Daily EX. SUNDAY & HOLIDAYS	(46.59)	
Time Over District		1.33		1.40		1.38	1.22	1.29	1.18		1.42	1.40			1.40	1.29	1.03		
Average Speed Per Hour		29.5		28.0		28.0	25.4	31.4	26.7		27.4	28.0			27.5	31.4	24.6		

Schedule meeting points are ACTUAL meeting points unless changed by train order. See Rules S-72, 83, S-88 to S-90B, inclusive.

EXCEPTIONS TO—AND ADDITIONAL—FLAG STOPS TO RECEIVE OR DISCHARGE PASSENGERS

TRAINS	STATIONS	Receive or Discharge	Passengers to (or Beyond)
All Trains	College Ave., Oakland	Receive or Discharge	
All Trains	All Stations (Through Tickets only)	Receive	
8	Walnut Creek and Concord	Receive	Rail or Stage Points East of Sacramento. / Stage Points East of Rio Vista Jct. / Sacramento—Revenue Passengers Only
2 Sundays and Holidays	Clyde	Discharge	
2 Sundays and Holidays only	San Francisco and intermediate stations to West Pittsburg	No Local Passengers	Pittsburg
2 Daily	Walnut Creek, Concord, Clyde, Port Chicago and West Pittsburg	Receive	Rio Vista Jct., Sacramento
2 Daily—except Saturday, Sunday, and Holidays	Walnut Creek	Receive	Sacramento—Revenue Passengers Only
12	St. Marys	Receive or Discharge	
6-10-12-16-18-28-32-36-40	Oakland to Concord (Terrace, Thornhill, Montclair, Eastport, Wilcox, Sequoia, Canyon, Vallejo Vista, West Lafayette, Ralies, Walden, Pleasant Hill, Kilgore)	Receive	Concord for No. 2
6-10-16-18-36-40	Adeline, Niebols	Receive or Discharge	
12-28	Heimboldt Crossing	Receive or Discharge	
12-13-28-32—(6 Saturday only)	Glenside	Receive or Discharge	
10 Daily (Except Sundays and Holidays)	McAvoy (Stage Connection)	Receive or Discharge	To or from Pittsburg

Within train control territory time-table schedules are informative only. Trains will enter and operate through train control territory in accordance with applicable Interlocking and Cab Signal Rules, irrespective of time-table superiority or schedules, except that a train must not leave San Francisco in advance of its scheduled leaving time. Eastward trains will not register or receive a clearance card at San Francisco.

All trains must get a clearance card at Oakland.

Nos. 12-28 and 32 only will register at Concord.
Nos. 16-36 and 40 only will register at West Pittsburg.
No. 292 has no time-table superiority.
Nos. 2-18-6-8 must get a clearance card at West Pittsburg.
No. 10 must get a clearance card at West Pittsburg Sundays and Holidays only.
No. 40 arrives Mondays and days following Holidays.
Abbreviations: T.C.—Train Control.   N.S.—Non Signal.

HOLIDAYS INDICATED ARE:
New Year's, Washington's Birthday, Decoration Day, Fourth of July, Labor Day, Thanksgiving Day and Christmas.

FIRST SUBDIVISION — Westward

Time Table No. 20 — April 23, 1939

Left-margin signal territory designations: **T.C.** (Train Control) and **Double Track** from San Francisco to Oakland; **N.S.** (Non Signal) at Oakland; **Automatic Block Signals** from Rockridge southward.

STATIONS	Distance from Mallard	15 San Fran. Passenger Arrive Daily	DH-16 Arrive SUNDAY & HOLIDAYS	17 San Fran. Passenger Arrive Daily EX. SUNDAY & HOLIDAYS	1 San Fran. Passenger Arrive Daily	DH-6 Arrive Daily	3 The Meteor Arrive Daily	29 San Fran. Passenger Arrive Daily EX.SAT.,SUN & HOLIDAYS	DH-8 Arrive Daily	27 San Fran. Passenger Arrive Daily	7 The Comet Arrive Daily	19 San Fran. Passenger Ar. SUNDAY & HOLIDAYS	DH-10 Arrive Daily EX.SUNDAY & HOLIDAYS	11 San Fran. Passenger Arrive Daily	293 Oakland Local Freight (SECOND CLASS) Arrive Daily Ex. Sunday	Capacity of Sidings in Freight Cars
SAN FRANCISCO	46.59	s 7.44 AM	8.08 AM	s 8.37 AM	s 10.06 AM	1.09 PM	s 1.44 PM	s 3.52 PM	4.33 PM	s 5.18 PM	s 5.58 PM	s 7.55 PM	8.04 PM	s 10.25 PM		
— 5.47 — WEST JCT.	41.12															Yard
— 1.89 — EMERYVILLE JCT	39.23															
— 0.45 — SAN PABLO AVE	38.78															
— 1.09 — 2S OAKLAND (40th & Shafter)	37.69	7.22 s 7.20	7.46 AM	8.14 s 8.12	9.43 s 9.39	12.48 PM	1.21 s 1.17	3.28 s 3.26	4.10 PM	4.54 s 4.50	5.36 s 5.33	7.31 s 7.27	7.43 PM	10.01 s 9.58	8.00 AM	Yard
— 1.79 — ROCKRIDGE	35.90	7.14		8.06	9.32		1.11	3.19		4.44	5.27	7.20		9.51		38 (Spurs)
— 1.21 — TEMESCAL	34.69	f 7.11		f 8.03	f 9.30		f 1.08	3.16		f 4.41	5.25	f 7.17		f 9.48		16 (Spur)
— 2.50 — HAVENS	32.19	f 7.07		f 7.57	f 9.26		f 1.04	3.12		f 4.36 [28]	5.21 [8]	f 7.13		f 9.44		10 / 11 (Spur)
— 3.30 — PINEHURST	28.89	f 7.00		f 7.50 [12]	f 9.19		f 12.57	3.06		f 4.29	5.15	f 7.05		f 9.37		17
— 2.13 — MORAGA	26.76	f 6.56		f 7.46	f 9.14		f 12.53	3.02		f 4.24	5.11	f 7.00		f 9.33		7 / 30 (Spurs)
— 0.91 — ST. MARYS	25.85	f 6.53		f 7.44	f 9.12		f 12.51	3.00 PM		f 4.22	5.09	f 6.58		f 9.31		17 (Spur)
— 1.90 — BURTON	23.95	f 6.50		f 7.41	f 9.09 [16]		f 12.48			f 4.19	5 06	f 6.55 [36]		f 9.28		35
— 2.45 — LAFAYETTE	21.50	f 6.46		f 7.36	f 9.05		f 12.44			f 4.14	5.02	f 6.51		f 9.24		11 / 8 (Spur)
— 1.62 — SARANAP	19.88	f 6.42		f 7.32	f 9.03		f 12.41			f 4.10	5.00 [28]	f 6.49		f 9.21		42
— 1.73 — D WALNUT CREEK	18.15	f 6.39		f 7.29	f 9.00 [2]		f 12.38			f 4.06	4.58	f 6.46		f 9.19 [10]		12 / 68 (Spurs)
— 2.02 — SPARKLE	16.13	6.35		7.25	8.54		12.34			4.01	4.54	6.42		9.14		10 (Spur)
— 0.10 — LAS JUNTAS (S.P.R.R. Crsg.)	16.03	f 6.34		f 7.24	f 8.53		f 12.33			f 4.00	4.53	f 6.41		f 9.13		15 (Spur)
— 0.55 — BANCROFT	15.48	f 6.32		f 7.23	f 8.52		f 12.32			f 3.58	4.52	f 6.40		f 9.12		16 (Spurs)
— 0.91 — MEINERT	14.57	f 6.30		f 7.21	f 8.50		f 12.30			f 3.56	4.51	f 6.39		f 9.10		64 / 20 (Spurs)
— 2.72 — D CONCORD	11.85	6.27 AM		7.17 AM	f 8.46		f 12.27			3.52 PM	4.48	f 6.34		f 9.07		6 / 68 (Spurs)
— 2.30 — OHMER	9.55				f 8.38		f 12.22				4.44	f 6.30		f 9.02		7 (Spur)
— 1.17 — CLYDE (B.P. & C.R.R. Crsg.)	8.38				f 8.35		f 12.19				f 4.42	f 6.27		f 9.00		26 (Spurs)
— 1.82 — DN PORT CHICAGO	6.56				f 8.30		f 12.16				f 4.39	f 6.23		f 8.56		50 / 47 (Spurs)
— 3.43 — McAVOY	3.13				f 8.25		f 12.11 [18]				4.35	f 6.18		s 8.51		19 / 16 (Spurs)
— 1.13 — SHELL POINT	2.00				f 8.23		f 12.08				4.33	f 6.16		f 8.48		2 (Spur)
— 1.19 — WEST PITTSBURG	0.81				s 8.20		s 12.05				s 4.31	s 6.14		f 8.46		Yard
— 0.81 — Suisun Bay Car Ferry MALLARD	0.00				f 8.17 AM		f 12.02 PM				4.28 PM	f 6.12 PM [8]		f 8.43 PM	11.30 PM	4 / 13 (Spur)
(46.59)		Leave Daily	Lv. SUNDAY & HOLIDAYS	Leave Daily EX.SUNDAY & HOLIDAYS	Leave Daily	Leave Daily	Leave Daily	Leave Daily EX.SAT.,SUN & HOLIDAYS	Leave Daily	Leave Daily	Leave Daily	Lv. SUNDAY & HOLIDAYS	Leave Daily EX.SUNDAY & HOLIDAYS	Leave Daily	Leave Daily Ex. Saturday	
Time Over District		1.17		1.20	1.49		1.42	0.52		1.26	1.30	1.43		1.42		
Average Speed Per Hour		27.1		26.1	25.6		27.4	23.9		24.2	31.1	27.1		27.4		

Schedule meeting points are ACTUAL meeting points unless changed by train order. See Rules S-72, 83, S-88 to S-90B, inclusive.

EXCEPTIONS TO—AND ADDITIONAL—FLAG STOPS TO RECEIVE OR DISCHARGE PASSENGERS

TRAINS	STATIONS	Receive or Discharge	Passengers from (or Beyond)
All Trains	College Ave., Oakland	Receive or Discharge	
All Trains	All Stations (Through Tickets only)	Discharge	
1-3-11-15-17-19-27	Kilgore, Pleasant Hill, Walden, Ralies, West Lafayette, Valle Vista, Canyon, Sequoia, Wilcox, Eastport, Montclair, Thornhill, Terrace	Receive or Discharge	Rail or Stage Points East of Sacramento. Stage Points East of Rio Vista Jct.
7	Concord and Walnut Creek	Discharge	Sacramento-Revenue Passengers Only
1-3-11-19	Nichols, Adeline	Receive or Discharge	
15-17-19-27	Glenside	Receive or Discharge	
27	Heimboldt Crossing	Discharge	
1 (School Days only)	Bacon St., Concord	Discharge	
11 Daily (Except Sunday and Holidays)	McAvoy (Stage Connection)	Receive or Discharge	To or from Pittsburg

Within train control territory time-table schedules are informative only. Trains will enter and operate through train control territory in accordance with applicable Interlocking and Cab Signal Rules, irrespective of time-table superiority or schedules. Westward trains will not register at San Francisco.

Nos. 15-17-27 only will register at Concord.
No. 293 has no time-table superiority.
Nos. 1-3-7-19 must get a clearance card at West Pittsburg.
No. 11 must get a clearance card at West Pittsburg Sundays and Holidays only.
Westward trains when taking siding at Havens will use the spur.
Abbreviations: T.C.—Train Control. N.S.—Non Signal.

HOLIDAYS INDICATED ARE:
New Year's, Washington's Birthday, Decoration Day, Fourth of July, Labor Day, Thanksgiving Day and Christmas.

FIRST SUBDIVISION

Eastward — FIRST CLASS / SECOND CLASS

Time Table No. 20 — April 23, 1939

STATIONS	Miles	Distance from San Francisco	2 The Comet (Leave Daily)	18 Sacramento Passenger (Lv. SUNDAY & HOLIDAYS)	6 Chico Passenger (Leave Daily)	8 The Meteor (Leave Daily)	10 Sacramento Passenger (Leave Daily)	292 Sacramento Local Freight (Leave Daily Ex. Monday)	Fone, Scales, Wyes, Bulletin, Register Station, Standard Clocks, Interlocking Plant / Block Signals
Suisun Bay Car Ferry		47.03	9.43 AM	f 12.32 PM	f 3.13 PM	6.22 PM	f 10.00 PM	2.30 AM	
CHIPPS	1.06	48.09	9.45	f 12.34	f 3.15	6.24	f 10.02		P
SPOONBILL	1.35	49.44	9.47	f 12.37	f 3.18	6.26	f 10.05		P
DUTTON	1.54	50.98	9.49	f 12.39	f 3.21	6.28	f 10.07		P
MONTEZUMA	1.99	52.97	9.52	f 12.43	f 3.24	6.32	f 10.11		P
MOLENA	4.45	57.42	9.58	f 12.48	f 3.30	6.37	f 10.16		P
GARFIELD	1.36	58.78	s 10.01	f 12.50	f 3.34	s 6.40	f 10.18		P
RIO VISTA JCT.	3.00	61.78	10.04	f 12.54	f 3.38	6.44	f 10.22		P.Y.
CREED	2.91	64.69	10.07	12.57	f 3.42	6.47	10.25		P
OLCOTT	0.86	65.55	10.08	f 12.58	f 3.44	6.48	f 10.26		P
DOZIER	2.94	68.49	10.11	f 1.01	3.50 [7]	6.50	f 10.29		P
VALE	2.61	71.10	10.14	f 1.04	f 3.53	6.53	f 10.32		P
BUNKER	0.94	72.04	10.15	1.05	3.54	6.54	10.33		P
BELLEAIR	3.08	75.12	10.18	f 1.09	f 3.58	6.58	f 10.37		P
LIBFARM	1.11	76.23	10.19	f 1.10	f 4.00	6.59	f 10.38		P
YOLANO	4.48	80.71	10.24	f 1.15	f 4.05	7.04	f 10.43		P
SAXON	4.32	85.03	10.30	f 1.21	f 4.11	7.10	f 10.50		P
ARCADE	2.92	87.95	10.34	f 1.25	f 4.14	7.14	f 10.54		P
RIVERVIEW	1.70	89.65	10.36	f 1.27	f 4.17	7.16	f 10.56		P
JEFFERSON	2.91	92.56	10.39	f 1.30	f 4.20	7.19	f 10.59		P
WESTGATE	0.81	93.37	f 10.40	f 1.33	f 4.24	7.22	f 11.02	9.00 AM	P.I.
BRODERICK	0.30	93.67	10.43 [3]	1.35	4.26	7.24 [11]	11.04		P
Union Station SACRAMENTO	1.22	94.89	s 10.50 AM	s 1.45 PM	s 4.35 PM	s 7.30 PM	s 11.10 PM	Ex. Monday Arrive Daily	P.R.B.K.Y. (DS)
	(47.86)		Arrive Daily	Ar. SUNDAY & HOLIDAYS	Arrive Daily	Arrive Daily	Arrive Daily		
Time Over District			1.07	1.13	1.22	1.08	1.10		
Average Speed Per Hour			42.9	39.3	35.0	42.2	41.0		

SAC. Front & M S.P.R.R. Cross.

(Stations CHIPPS through SACRAMENTO are equipped with Automatic Block Signals.)

FIRST SUBDIVISION—HOLLAND BRANCH

Westward

Time Table No. 20 — April 23, 1939

Standard Clocks, Wyes, Bulletin, Register Station, Fone, Scales	Distance from San Francisco	STATIONS	Miles	Distance from Oxford	Capacity of Sidings in Freight Cars
	87.95	RIVERVIEW	3.92	15.77	28 / 10 (Spur)
P	91.87	ARGENTA	0.81	11.85	20
P	92.68	BERMUDA	1.16	11.04	20
P	93.84	TASCO	0.44	9.88	79
P	94.28	WILLOW POINT	0.90	9.44	16
P	95.18	CONISTON	0.83	8.54	22 / 10 (Spur)
P	96.01	NEWTOWN	0.59	7.71	42
P	96.60	CENTRAL	1.86	7.12	36 / 13 (Spur)
P	98.46	GREENDALE	1.52	5.26	30 / 14 (Spur)
P	99.98	SILVERDALE	1.16	3.74	18 (Spur)
P	101.14	SORROOA	1.06	2.58	28
P	102.20	VALDEZ	1.52	1.52	23 / 12 (Spur)
P	103.72	OXFORD		0.00	16 / 21 (Spur)
		Time Over District	(15.77)		
		Average Speed Per Hour			

Schedule meeting points are ACTUAL meeting points unless changed by train order. See Rules S-72, 83, S-88 to S-90B, inclusive.

EXCEPTIONS TO—AND ADDITIONAL—FLAG STOPS TO RECEIVE OR DISCHARGE PASSENGERS

TRAINS	STATIONS	Receive or Discharge	Passengers to (or Beyond)
All Trains	Third & M St., 8th & K St., Sacramento	Discharge	
All Trains	All Stations (Through Tickets only)	Receive	
2	Spoonbill, Dutton, Molena	Discharge	Stage Points East of Rio Vista Jct. Rail or Stage Points East of Sacramento
2	Montezuma	Receive	Revenue Passengers only
2	Libfarm	Receive or Discharge	Sacramento—Revenue Passengers only
14-6-10	Honker, Denverton, Norris, Delhi, Bevan	Receive or Discharge	Revenue Passengers only

Nos. 292 and 294 have no time table superiority.

Nos. 16-36 and 40 must get a clearance card at West Pittsburg.

No. 40 leaves West Pittsburg and arrives Pittsburg Mondays and days following Holidays.

HOLIDAYS INDICATED ARE:

New Year's, Washington's Birthday, Decoration Day, Fourth of July, Labor Day, Thanksgiving Day and Christmas

---

FIRST SUBDIVISION—PITTSBURG BRANCH

FIRST CLASS

Time Table No. 20 — April 23, 1939

(WEST PITTSBURG — distance from San Francisco 45.78; PITTSBURG — 47.95; Miles between 2.17)

Train	Condition	WEST PITTSBURG (Leave)	PITTSBURG (Arrive)	Condition
102 [1] Pittsburg Passenger	Leave Daily	8.20 AM	s 8.25 AM	Arrive Daily
104 [2] Pittsburg Passenger	Leave Daily	9.30 AM	s 9.35 AM	Arrive Daily
16 Pittsburg Passenger	Lv. SUNDAY & HOLIDAYS	9.56 AM	s 10.01 AM	Ar. SUNDAY & HOLIDAYS
106 [3] Pittsburg Passenger	Leave Daily EX. SUNDAY & HOLIDAYS	12.05 PM	s 12.10 PM	Arrive Daily EX. SUNDAY & HOLIDAYS
108 [18/3] Pittsburg Passenger	Lv. SUNDAY & HOLIDAYS	12.18 PM	s 12.23 PM	Ar. SUNDAY & HOLIDAYS
110 [6] Pittsburg Passenger	Leave Daily	3.00 PM	3.05 PM	Arrive Daily
112 [7] Pittsburg Passenger	Leave Daily	4.31 PM	s 4.36 PM	Arrive Daily
114 [8] Pittsburg Passenger	Leave Daily EX. SUNDAY & HOLIDAYS	6.09 PM	s 6.14 PM	Arrive Daily EX. SUNDAY & HOLIDAYS
116 [19] Pittsburg Passenger	Lv. SUNDAY & HOLIDAYS	6.14 PM	s 6.19 PM	Ar. SUNDAY & HOLIDAYS
36 Pittsburg Passenger	Lv. SUNDAY & HOLIDAYS	7.39 PM	s 7.44 PM	Ar. SUNDAY & HOLIDAYS
118 [11] Pittsburg Passenger	Lv. SUNDAY & HOLIDAYS	8.47 PM	s 8.52 PM	Ar. SUNDAY & HOLIDAYS
120 [10] Pittsburg Passenger	Lv. SUNDAY & HOLIDAYS	9.47 PM	s 9.52 PM	Ar. SUNDAY & HOLIDAYS
40 Pittsburg Passenger	Leave See Note	12.04 AM	s 12.09 AM	Arrive See Note

Eastward — SECOND CLASS

Fone, Scales, Wyes, Bulletin, Register Station, Standard Clocks	Train 294 Pittsburg Local Freight (Leave Daily Ex. Sunday)	STATIONS
P.Y.R.	12.30 AM	PITTSBURG
P.B.R.K.	12.45 AM	WEST PITTSBURG
	Arrive Daily Ex. Sunday	

FIRST SUBDIVISION — Westward

Time Table No. 20 — April 23, 1939

	STATIONS	Distance from Sacramento	FIRST CLASS 1 — San Fran. Passenger — Arrive Daily	3 — The Meteor — Arrive Daily	7 — The Comet — Arrive Daily	19 — San Fran. Passenger — Ar. SUNDAY & HOLIDAYS	11 — San Fran. Passenger — Arrive Daily	SECOND CLASS 293 — Oakland Local Freight — Arrive Daily Ex. Saturday	Capacity of Sidings in Freight Cars
	Suisun Bay Car Ferry CHIPPS	47.86	s 8.05 AM	s 11.50 AM	s 4.16 PM	s 6.00 PM	s 8.32 PM	11.00 PM	43 / 11 (Spur)
	— 1.06 — SPOONBILL	46.80	f 8.02	f 11.48	4.14	f 5.58	f 8.30		5 (Spur)
	— 1.35 — DUTTON	45.45	f 7.59	f 11.44	4.12	f 5.56	f 8.27		10 (Spur)
	— 1.54 — MONTEZUMA	43.91	f 7.57	f 11.42	4.10	f 5.54	f 8.25		26 (Spur)
	— 1.99 — MOLENA	41.92	f 7.53	f 11.38	4.08	f 5.51	f 8.21		69
	— 4.45 — GARFIELD	37.47	7.48	f 11.33	4.02	5.45	f 8.16		9 (Spur)
Signals	— 1.36 — **RIO VISTA JCT.**	36.11	s 7.46	f 11.31	f 4.00	s 5.43	f 8.14		24 (Spur)
	— 3.00 — CREED	33.11	7.43	f 11.28	3.57	5.39	f 8.10		71
	— 2.91 — OLCOTT	30.20	7.40	11.25	3.54	5.36	8.07		13 (Spur)
Block	— 0.86 — DOZIER	29.34	7.39	f 11.24	3.53	5.35	f 8.06		11 (Spur)
	— 2.94 — VALE	26.40	7.36	f 11.21	**3.50** [6]	5.32	f 8.03		16
	— 2.61 — BUNKER	23.79	7.33	f 11.18	3.46	5.29	f 8.00		7 (Spur)
	— 0.94 — BELLEAIR	22.85	7.32	11.17	3.45	5.28	7.59		47
	— 3.08 — LIBFARM	19.77	f 7.28	f 11.13	3.41	5.24	f 7.54		22 / 25 (Spur)
Automatic	— 1.11 — YOLANO	18.66	f 7.27	f 11.12	3.40	5.23	f 7.53		46
	— 4.48 — SAXON	14.18	7.22	f 11.07	3.36	5.18	f 7.48		13 (Spurs)
	— 4.32 — ARCADE	9.86	7.15	f 11.00	3.30	5.11	f 7.41		8 / 15 (Spur)
	— 2.92 — **RIVERVIEW**	6.94	7.11	f 10.56	3.26	5.07	f 7.37		28 / 10 (Spur)
	— 1.70 — JEFFERSON	5.24	7.09	f 10.54	3.24	5.05	f 7.33		15 (Spur)
	— 2.91 — WESTGATE	2.33	f 7.06	f 10.51	3.21	5.02	f 7.30		Yard
	— 0.81 — BRODERICK	1.52	f 7.03	f 10.48	f 3.18	f 4.59	f 7.28		Yard
	— 0.30 — SAC. Front & M (S.P.R.R. Crsg.)	1.22	7.01	**10.46** } [2]	3.16	4.57	**7.26** } [8]	5.15 PM	Yard
DS	— 1.22 — **SACRAMENTO** UNION STATION (D.T.)	0.00	6.55 AM	10.40 } AM	3.10 PM	4.50 PM	7.20 } PM		Yard
	(47.86)		Leave Daily	Leave Daily	Leave Daily	Lv. SUNDAY & HOLIDAYS	Leave Daily	Leave Daily Ex. Saturday	
	Time Over District		1.10	1.10	1.06	1.10	1.12		
	Average Speed Per Hour		41.0	41.0	43.5	41.0	39.9		

Eastward — FIRST SUBDIVISION—VACAVILLE BRANCH — Westward

Time Table No. 20 — April 23, 1939

Fones, Scales, Wyes, Bulletins, Register Stations, Standard Clocks	Distance from San Francisco	STATIONS	Distance from Vacaville	Capacity of Sidings in Freight Cars
Y.P.	69.38	**VACAVILLE JCT.**	4.58	
		— 4.58 —		
	73.96	**VACAVILLE**	0.00	24 (Spurs)
		(4.58)		
		Time Over District		
		Average Speed Per Hour		

Eastward — FIRST SUBDIVISION---WILLOTTA BRANCH — Westward

Time Table No. 20 — April 23, 1939

Fones, Scales, Wyes, Bulletins, Register Stations, Standard Clocks	Distance from San Francisco	STATIONS	Distance from Willotta	Capacity of Sidings in Freight Cars
Y.P	61.78	**CREED**	17.16	71
		— 5.34 —		
P.	67.12	CORDERO	11.82	20
		— 2.26 —		
Y.P.	69.38	**VACAVILLE JCT.**	9.56	
		— 2.60 —		
	71.98	ARMIJO	6.96	18 (Spur)
		— 3.11 —		
	75.09	FAIRFIELD	4.65	9
		— 2.14 —		
	76.43	CLIMA	2.51	18 (Spur)
		— 0.18 —		
	76.61	SUVAL	2.33	12 (Spur)
		— 0.36 —		
	76.97	CHADBOURNE	1.97	21 (Spurs)
		— 0.70 —		
	77.67	RUSSELL	1.27	15 (Spurs)
		— 0.96 —		
	78.63	DANIELSON	0.31	4 / 4 (Spur)
		— 0.31 —		
	78.94	**WILLOTTA**	0.00	21 (Spur)
		(17.16)		
		Time Over District		
		Average Speed Per Hour		

Schedule meeting points are ACTUAL meeting points unless changed by train order. See Rules S-72, 83, S-88 to S-90B, inclusive.

EXCEPTIONS TO—AND ADDITIONAL—FLAG STOPS TO RECEIVE OR DISCHARGE PASSENGERS

TRAINS	STATIONS	Receive or Discharge	Passengers from (or Beyond)
All Trains	Third & M St., 8th & K St., Sacramento	Receive	
All Trains	All Stations (Through Tickets only)	Discharge	Stage Points East of Rio Vista Jct. Rail or Stage Points East of Sacramento
3-11	Bevan, Delhi, Norris, Denverton, Honker	Receive or Discharge	
7	Libfarm	Receive or Discharge	Revenue passengers only

Nos. 293 and 295 have no time table superiority.

HOLIDAYS INDICATED ARE:
New Year's, Washington's Birthday, Decoration Day. Fourth of July, Labor Day, Thanksgiving Day and Christmas

FIRST SUBDIVISION--PITTSBURG BRANCH — Westward

Time Table No. 20 — April 23, 1939

STATIONS	Distance from Pittsburg	FIRST CLASS 101[1] — San Fran. Passenger — Arrive Daily	103[2] — Sacramento Passenger — Arrive Daily	105[3,18] — San Fran. Sacramento Passenger — Arrive Daily	109[6] — Sacramento Passenger — Arrive Daily	111[7] — San Fran. Passenger — Arrive Daily	113[8,19] — San Fran. Sacramento Passenger — Arrive Daily	115[11] — San Fran. Passenger — Ar. SUNDAY & HOLIDAYS	117[10] — Sacramento Passenger — Ar. SUNDAY & HOLIDAYS	SECOND CLASS 295 — Oakland Local Freight — Arrive Daily Ex. Sunday	Capacity of Siding in Freight Cars
WEST PITTSBURG	2.17	s 8.17 AM	s 9.25 AM	s 12.02 PM	s 2.55 PM	s 4.28 PM	s 6.05 PM	s 8.43 PM	s 9.43 PM	12.30 AM	Yard
— 2.17 — D **PITTSBURG**	0.00	8.12 AM	9.20 AM	11.57 AM	2.50 PM	4.23 PM	6.00 PM	8.38 PM	9.38 PM	12.15 AM	Yard
(2.17)		Leave Daily	Leave Daily	Leave Daily	Leave Daily	Leave Daily	Leave Daily	Lv. SUNDAY & HOLIDAYS	Lv. SUNDAY & HOLIDAYS	Leave Daily Ex. Sunday	

Time Table No. 20 — April 23, 1939

Fone, Scales, Wyes, Bulletin, Register Station, Standard Clocks, Interlocking Plant	SECOND CLASS 192 Chico-Oroville Local Freight — Leave Daily Ex. Saturday	8 Chico Passenger (First Class) — Leave Daily	6 Chico Passenger (First Class) — Leave Daily	2 Chico Passenger (First Class) — Leave Daily	Distance from San Francisco	STATIONS (miles between stations)	Distance from Marysville	3 San Francisco Passenger (First Class) — Arrive Daily	7 San Francisco Passenger (First Class) — Arrive Daily	11 San Francisco Passenger (First Class) — Arrive Daily	SECOND CLASS 193 Sacramento Local Freight — Arrive Daily Ex. Monday	Capacity of Sidings in Freight Cars
P.R.B.Y.K.		7.40 PM	4.45 PM	11.00 AM	94.89	DS Union Station **SACRAMENTO** {D.T.	41.63	s 10.30 AM	s 3.00 PM	s 7.00 PM		Yard
						1.07						
P.O.	10.00 PM	f 7.45	f 4.50	f 11.05	95.96	SACRAMENTO, C ST.	40.56	f 10.22	f 2.51	f 6.51	7.00 AM	Yard
						0.60						
P.		7.47	4.52	11.07	96.56	HAGGIN	39.96	10.19	2.49	6.49		Yard
						0.98						
P.		f 7.50	f 4.55	f 11.09	97.54	GLOBE, W.P.R.R. Cross.	38.98	f 10.17	f 2.46	f 6.47		31
						0.48						
P.		f 7.52	f 4.57	f 11.11	98.02	NORTH SACRAMENTO	38.50	f 10.16	f 2.44	f 6.45		6 (Spur)
						2.03						
P.		f 7.54	f 5.00	f 11.14	100.05	DEL PASO	36.47	f 10.13	f 2.41	f 6.42		8 (Spur)
						1.81						
P.		f 7.56	f 5.03	f 11.17	101.86	ROBLA	34.66	f 10.10	f 2.38	f 6.39		8 (Spur)
						2.30						
P.		f 7.59	f 5.07	f 11.21	104.16	**RIO LINDA**	32.36	f 10.07	f 2.35	f 6.36		38
						1.31						
P.		f 8.02	f 5.10	f 11.25	105.47	ELVERTA	31.05	f 10.04	f 2.32	f 6.33		6 (Spur)
						2.94						
P.		f 8.06	f 5.14	f 11.30	108.41	RIEGO	28.11	f 10.00	f 2.28	f 6.29		9 (Spur)
						1.98						
P.I.		f 8.10	f 5.17	f 11.34	110.39	SANKEY, W.P.R.R. Cross.	26.13	f 9.57	f 2.24	f 6.26		27 (Spur)
						3.38						
P.		f 8.15	f 5.21	f 11.39	113.77	PLEASANT GROVE	22.75	f 9.53	f 2.20	f 6.21		34 / 12 (Spur)
						2.05						
P.		f 8.17	f 5.24	f 11.42	115.82	CATLETT	20.70	f 9.50	f 2.18	f 6.18		39 (Spurs)
						1.21						
P.		f 8.19	f 5.26	f 11.44	117.03	STRIPLIN	19.49	f 9.48	f 2.16	f 6.15		12 (Spur)
						2.97						
P.		f 8.23	s 5.31	s 11.49	120.00	D **EAST NICOLAUS**	16.52	s 9.44	s 2.13	s 6.11		19 / 34 (Spurs)
						1.05						
P.		f 8.25	f 5.33	f 11.51	121.05	STOLP	15.47	f 9.42	f 2.09	f 6.09		10 (Spur)
						2.37						
P.		f 8.29	f 5.37	f 11.55	123.42	RIO OSO	13.10	f 9.38	f 2.05	f 6.05		42 (Spurs)
						2.11						
P.		f 8.32	f 5.41	f 11.58 AM	125.53	ALGODON	10.99	f 9.35	f 2.02	f 6.01		14 (Spur)
						1.91						
P.		f 8.34	f 5.43	f 12.01 PM	127.44	LEWIS	9.08	f 9.32	f 2.00	f 5.59		12 (Spur)
						0.96						
P.		f 8.35	f 5.45	f 12.02	128.40	PLUMAS	8.12	f 9.31	f 1.59	f 5.58		6 (Spur)
						1.52						
P.		f 8.37	f 5.47	f 12.05	129.92	ARBOGA	6.60	f 9.29	f 1.57	f 5.56		32 (Spurs)
						0.84						
P.		f 8.38	f 5.48	f 12.06	130.76	REED JCT.	5.76	f 9.28	f 1.55	f 5.55		8 / 66 (Spurs)
						2.66						
P.		f 8.41	f 5.52 [11]	f 12.10	133.42	ALICIA	3.10	f 9.24	f 1.52	f 5.52 [6]		9 (Spur)
						1.58						
P.		8.43	5.54	12.12	135.00	SOUTH YUBA	1.52	9.22	1.50	5.50		52
						0.90						
P.I.		8.45	5.56	12.14	135.90	OLIVER, W.P.R.R. Cross.	0.62	9.20	1.49	5.48		
						0.62						
P.R.B.Y.	1.00 AM	s 8.51 PM	s 6.03 PM	s 12.20 PM	136.52	2S **MARYSVILLE**	0.00	9.14 AM	1.45 PM	5.43 PM	2.00 AM	Yard
	ArriveDaily Ex. Sunday	ArriveDaily	ArriveDaily	ArriveDaily		(41.63)		LeaveDaily	LeaveDaily	LeaveDaily	LeaveDaily Ex. Monday	
		1.11	1.18	1.20		Time Over District		1.16	1.15	1.17		
		35.2	32.0	31.2		Average Speed Per Hour		32.9	33.3	32.4		

Schedule meeting points are ACTUAL meeting points unless changed by train order. See Rules S-72, 83, S-88 to S-90B, inclusive.

Nos. 192 and 193 have no time table superiority.
Nos. 2, 3, 6, 7, 8 and 11 must get a clearance card at Marysville.

EXCEPTIONS TO—AND ADDITIONAL—FLAG STOPS TO RECEIVE OR DISCHARGE PASSENGERS

TRAINS	STATIONS	Receive or Discharge	Passengers from (or Beyond)
All Trains	G. St. Sacramento, Altos, Hagginwood, Brooke, Allison, Ardmore Short, Esmeralda, Bear River, Howard.	Receive or Discharge	

Time Table No. 20 — April 23, 1939

Eastward: **SECOND CLASS** = 190, 192; **FIRST CLASS** = 210, 8, 208, 6, 206, 2.
Westward: **FIRST CLASS** = 205, 3, 7, 207, 11, 209; **SECOND CLASS** = 191, 193.

Eastward

Fons, Scales, Wye, Bulletin, Register Stations, Standard Clocks, Interlocking Plant	190 Colusa Local Freight (Leave Daily Ex. Sundays)	192 Chico Oroville Local Freight (Leave Daily Ex. Sundays)	210 Colusa Passenger (Lv. SUNDAY & HOLIDAYS)	8 Chico Passenger (Leave Daily)	208 Colusa Passenger (Leave Daily)	6 Chico Passenger (Leave Daily)	206 Colusa Passenger (Leave Daily)	2 Chico Passenger (Leave Daily)	Distance from San Francisco	STATIONS
P.R.B.Y.	8.00AM	2.00AM	8.56PM	8.54PM	6.08PM	6.06PM	12.28PM	12.27PM	136.52	2S **MARYSVILLE** (1.81) (D.T.)
P.O.			s 9.06	s 9.04	s 6.18	s 6.16	s 12.38	s 12.36	138.33	**YUBA CITY** S.P.R.R. Cross. (1.29)
									139.62	PALORO (0.72)
P.			f 9.10	f 9.07	f 6.23	f 6.20	f 12.42	f 12.39	140.34	HARTER (0.49)
P.R.Y.	8.30AM		9.11PM	9.08	6.24PM	6.21	12.44PM	12.40	140.83	**COLUSA JUNCTION** (0.35)
P.				f 9.09		f 6.22		f 12.41	141.18	TIERRA BUENA (1.48)
P.				f 9.11		f 6.24		f 12.43	142.66	PEASE (0.71)
P.				f 9.13		f 6.26		f 12.44	143.37	NUESTRO (1.32)
P.				f 9.15		f 6.28		f 12.46	144.69	SANDERS (0.95)
P.				f 9.17		f 6.29		f 12.48	145.64	ENCINAL (0.63)
P.				f 9.18		f 6.30		f 12.50	146.27	STAFFORD (1.74)
P.				f 9.20		f 6.32		f 12.52	148.01	WALTON (1.74)
P. I.				f 9.22		s 6.36		s 12.56	149.75	D **LIVE OAK** S.P.R.R. Cross. (1.75)
P.				f 9.26		f 6.40		f 1.00	151.50	RIVIERA (1.07)
P.				f 9.28		f 6.42		f 1.02	152.57	CHANDON (1.15)
P.				f 9.30		f 6.44		f 1.06 7	153.72	MANZANITA (1.73)
P.				f 9.32		s 6.48		s 1.09	155.45	D **EAST GRIDLEY** (1.68)
P.				f 9.34		f 6.50		f 1.11	157.13	PEACHTON (1.15)
P.				f 9.36		f 6.52		f 1.13	158.28	RICHLAND (1.50)
P.				f 9.38		f 6.54		f 1.15	159.78	EAST BIGGS (0.56)
P.				f 9.39		f 6.56		f 1.17	160.34	RIO BONITO (1.06)
P.				9.40		6.57		1.18	161.40	LOSEE (0.49)
P.				f 9.41		f 6.59		f 1.19	161.89	HASELBUSCH (1.36)
P.				f 9.43		f 7.01		f 1.21	163.25	LORRAINE (2.82)
P.Y.				s 9.49		s 7.07		s 1.30	166.07	**OROVILLE JCT.** (2.80)
P.				f 9.54		f 7.12		f 1.36	168.87	SHIPPEE (1.67)
P.				f 9.56		f 7.14		f 1.38	170.54	RAMADA (1.75)
P.				f 9.58		f 7.16		f 1.40	172.29	BLAVO (3.01)
P.				f 10.02		f 7.20		f 1.44	175.30	ESQUON (3.05)
P.				f 10.07		s 7.25		s 1.49	178.35	D **DURHAM** (4.25)
P.				f 10.15		f 7.32		f 1.55	182.60	SPEEDWAY (0.57)
P.				f		f		f	183.17	STIRLING JCT., S.P.R.R. Cross (0.92)
P.Y.		7.00AM		f 10.19		f 7.36		f 1.59	184.09	**MULBERRY** (0.34)
				f 10.20		f 7.38		f 2.00	184.43	CHICO 16TH ST. (0.98)
P.R.B.Y.K.				s 10.25PM		s 7.45PM		s 2.05PM	185.41	D **CHICO**
	Arrive Daily Ex. Sunday	Arrive Daily Ex. Sunday	Ar. SUNDAY & HOLIDAYS	Arrive Daily	Arrive Daily	Arrive Daily	Arrive Daily	Arrive Daily		
Time Over District			0.15	1.31	0.16	1.39	0.16	1.38		(48.89)
Average Speed Per Hour			17.2	33.2	16.2	29.6	16.2	29.9		

Westward

STATIONS	Distance from Chico	205 Marysville Passenger (Arrive Daily)	3 San Francisco Passenger (Arrive Daily)	7 San Francisco Passenger (Arrive Daily)	207 Marysville Passenger (Arrive Daily)	11 San Francisco Passenger (Arrive Daily)	209 Marysville Passenger (Ar. SUNDAY & HOLIDAYS)	191 Marysville Local Freight (Arrive Daily Ex. Sunday)	193 Sacramento Local Freight (Arrive Daily Ex. Monday)	Capacity of Sidings in Freight Cars
2S **MARYSVILLE**	48.89	s 9.05AM	s 9.12AM	s 1.41PM	s 5.31PM	s 5.36PM	s 8.10PM	3.30PM	1.00AM	Yard
YUBA CITY S.P.R.R. Cross.	47.08	s 8.55	s 9.02	s 1.31	s 5.21	s 5.26	s 8.00			Yard
PALORO	45.79									44 (Spurs)
HARTER	45.07	f 8.51	f 8.58	f 1.28	5.17	f 5.22	f 7.56			31 (Spurs)
COLUSA JUNCTION	44.58	8.50AM	8.57	1.27	5.16PM	5.21	7.55PM	3.00PM		Yard
TIERRA BUENA	44.23		f 8.56	f 1.26		f 5.20				7 (Spur)
PEASE	42.75		f 8.54	f 1.24		f 5.19				24 / 10 (Spur)
NUESTRO	42.04		f 8.52	f 1.23		f 5.17				41
SANDERS	40.72		f 8.50	f 1.21		f 5.15				7 (Spur)
ENCINAL	39.77		f 8.48	f 1.20		f 5.13				25
STAFFORD	39.14		f 8.47	f 1.19		f 5.12				5 (Spur)
WALTON	37.40		f 8.45	f 1.17		f 5.10				8 (Spur)
D **LIVE OAK** S.P.R.R. Cross.	35.66		s 8.42	s 1.14		s 5.07				22 / 26 (Spurs)
RIVIERA	33.91		f 8.38	f 1.09		f 5.03				4 (Spur)
CHANDON	32.84		f 8.37	f 1.08		f 5.02				10 (Spur)
MANZANITA	31.69		f 8.35	f 1.06 2		f 5.00				8 (Spur)
D **EAST GRIDLEY**	29.96		s 8.32	s 1.04		s 4.57				24 / 65 (Spurs)
PEACHTON	28.28		f 8.30	f 1.01		f 4.54				6 (Spur)
RICHLAND	27.13		f 8.28	f 12.59		f 4.52				3 (Spur)
EAST BIGGS	25.63		f 8.26	f 12.58		f 4.51				17 (Spur)
RIO BONITO	25.07		f 8.25	f 12.56		f 4.50				13 (Spur)
LOSEE	24.01		8.23	12.55		4.49				6 (Spur)
HASELBUSCH	23.52		f 8.22	f 12.54		f 4.48				3 (Spur)
LORRAINE	22.16		f 8.20	f 12.53		f 4.46				10 (Spur)
OROVILLE JCT.	19.34		s 8.13	s 12.47		s 4.38				Yard
SHIPPEE	16.54		f 8.09	f 12.42		f 4.34				22 (Spurs)
RAMADA	14.87		f 8.07	f 12.40		f 4.32				20
BLAVO	13.12		f 8.04	f 12.38		f 4.29				27
ESQUON	10.11		f 8.00	f 12.34		f 4.25				25 (Spur)
D **DURHAM**	7.06		s 7.56	s 12.30		s 4.20				27 (Spurs)
SPEEDWAY	2.81		f 7.50	f 12.23		f 4.13				13
STIRLING JCT., S.P.R.R. Cross	2.24		f	f		f				Yard
MULBERRY	1.32		f 7.46	f 12.20		f 4.10			9.00PM	Yard
CHICO 16TH ST.	0.98		f 7.45	f 12.19		f 4.09				
D **CHICO**	0.00		7.40AM	12.15PM		4.05PM				Yard
	Leave Daily	Leave Daily	Leave Daily	Leave Daily	Leave Daily	Lv. SUNDAY & HOLIDAYS	Leave Daily Ex. Sunday	Leave Daily Ex. Sunday	
Time Over District		0.15	1.32	1.26	0.15	1.31	0.15		
Average Speed Per Hour		17.2	31.9	34.1	17.2	32.2	17.2		

Schedule meeting points are ACTUAL meeting points unless changed by train order.

See Rules S-72, 83, S-88 to S-90B, inclusive.

Nos. 2, 3, 6, 7, 8 and 11 must get a clearance card at Marysville.
Nos. 205, 206, 207, 208, 209 and 210 only will register at Colusa Junction.
Nos. 190, 191, 192 and 193 have no time table superiority.

EXCEPTIONS TO—AND ADDITIONAL—FLAG STOPS TO RECEIVE OR DISCHARGE PASSENGERS

TRAINS	STATIONS	Receive or Discharge	Passengers to (or Beyond)
All Trains	Chico, 4th & Main and 9th & Main Sts.; Savona, Yocum's Crossing, Galinda, Bihlman, Tharp, Gomes, Yuba City 2nd St., Marysville WP Depot, Marysville Hotel	Receive or Discharge	
All Trains	Oroville Jct. (Stage Connection)	Receive or Discharge	To or from Oroville

Time Table No. 20 — April 23, 1939

Register	SECOND CLASS 190 Colusa Local Frt. Lv. Daily Ex. Sunday	FIRST CLASS 210^{8} Colusa Passenger Lv. SUNDAY & HOLIDAYS	FIRST CLASS 208^{6}_{11} Colusa Passenger Leave Daily	FIRST CLASS 206^{2} Colusa Passenger Leave Daily	Distance from San Francisco	STATIONS	Distance from Colusa	FIRST CLASS 205^{3} Marysville-Passenger Arrive Daily	FIRST CLASS 207^{6}_{11} Marysville-Passenger Arrive Daily	FIRST CLASS 209^{8} Marysville Passenger Ar. SUNDAY & HOLIDAYS	SECOND CLASS 191 Marysville Local Freight Arrive Daily Ex. Sunday	Capacity of Sidings in Freight Cars
P. R. Y.	8.30 AM	9.13 PM	6.25 PM	12.45 PM	140.83	**COLUSA JUNCTION** 1.53	21.74	8.49 AM	5.15 PM	7.54 PM	3.00 PM	Yard
P.		f 9.15	f 6.28	f 12.48	142.36	ALMENDRA 3.72	20.21	f 8.46	f 5.12	f 7.51		7 (Spur)
P.		s 9.20	s 6.32	s 12.52	146.08	D **SUTTER** 0.46	16.49	s 8.42	s 5.07	s 7.47		15 / 23 (Spurs)
		f	f	f	146.54	NOYES 2.04	16.03	f	f	f		
P.		f 9.24	f 6.36	f 12.56	148.58	SUMMY 1.15	13.99	f 8.38	f 5.03	f 7.43		8 (Spur)
P.		f 9.26	f 6.38	f 12.58	149.73	STOHLMANN 1.38	12.84	f 8.36	f 5.01	f 7.41		18 (Spur)
P.		f 9.28	f 6.40	f 1.00	151.11	TARKE 0.90	11.46	f 8.33	f 4.58	f 7.38		26
P.		f 9.30	f 6.42	f 1.02	152.01	LIRA 1.01	10.56	f 8.31	f 4.56	f 7.36		24 (Spur)
P.		9.31	6.43	1.03	153.02	BEET SPUR 1.33	9.55	8.30	4.55	7.35		38
P. I.		s 9.34	s 6.45	s 1.05	154.35	**MERIDIAN** 1.68	8.22	s 8.28	s 4.53	s 7.33		62 (Spurs)
P.		f 9.37	f 6.48	f 1.08	156.03	SYOAMORE 2.00	6.54	f 8.25	f 4.50	f 7.29		8 (Spur)
P.		f 9.40	f 6.51	f 1.11	158.03	TUTTLE 3.68	4.54	f 8.22	f 4.47	f 7.27		12 (Spur)
P.		9.45	6.55	1.15	161.71	ARBEE 0.86	0.86	8.17	4.42	7.23		17 (Spur)
Y. P. R. B.	12.30 PM	s 9.47 PM	s 7.00 PM	s 1.20 PM	162.57	D **COLUSA**	0.00	8.15 AM	4.40 PM	7.20 PM	1.30 PM	Yard
	Ar. Daily Ex. Sunday	Ar. SUNDAY & HOLIDAYS	Arrive Daily	Arrive Daily		(21.74) Time Over District		Leave Daily	Leave Daily	Lv. SUNDAY & HOLIDAYS	Leave Daily Ex. Sunday	
		0.34	0.35	0.35		Time Over District		0.34	0.35	0.34		
	38.4	38.4	37.3	37.3		Average Speed Per Hour		38.4	37.3	38.4		

Schedule meeting points are **ACTUAL** meeting points unless changed by train order.
See Rules S-72, 83, S-88 to S-90B, inclusive.
Nos. 190, 191, 194 and 195 have no time table superiority.

EXCEPTIONS TO—AND ADDITIONAL—FLAG STOPS TO RECEIVE OR DISCHARGE PASSENGERS

TRAINS	STATIONS	Receive or Discharge	Passengers to (or Beyond)
All Trains—Colusa Branch	Girdner, Cromer Avenue, Humphrey, Rowena, Hooper, Farmlan	Receive or Discharge	

Eastward   SECOND SUBDIVISION—OROVILLE BRANCH   Westward

Time Table No. 20 — April 23, 1939

Register	SECOND CLASS 194 Thermalito Local Freight Leave Daily Ex. Sunday	Distance from San Francisco	STATIONS	Distance from Oroville	SECOND CLASS 195 Sacramento Local Freight Arrive Daily Ex. Sunday	Capacity of Sidings in Freight Cars
P. R. Y.	6.00 AM	166.07	**OROVILLE JCT.** 2.05	5.49	7.40 PM	Yard
P.		168.12	SUMMIT 1.26	3.44		16
P.	7.00 AM	169.38	THERMALITO 1.09	2.18	7.00 PM	14 / 23 (Spurs)
P.		170.47	OROVILLE, Marysville Road 1.09	1.09		Yard
P. R. B. K.		171.56	D **OROVILLE**	0.00		Yard
	Arrive Daily Ex. Sunday		(5.49) Time over District		Leave Daily Ex. Sunday	
			Average Speed per Hour			

"SAFETY FIRST"

SPECIAL RULES

SPEED RESTRICTIONS GENERAL

Oakland, Shafter Avenue......................22 mi. per hr.
Between Temescal and Rockridge—
  Passenger trains..........................22 mi. per hr.
  Freight and work trains...................10 mi. per hr.
Between Walden and Temescal—Passenger trains
  all sharp curves..........................40 mi. per hr.
  Except—Curve Melin Cut..................25 mi. per hr.
  Except—Curve East of Pinehurst..........15 mi. per hr.
  Except—Curve East of Valle Vista........15 mi. per hr.
  Except—Walden Curve.....................30 mi. per hr.
Tunnel No. 1, Passenger Trains...............25 mi. per hr.
  Freight and work trains...................15 mi. per hr.
West Portal Tunnel No. 1 to Rockridge, descend-
  ing grade, Passenger Motors and Freight En-
  gines operated as single unit, unless equipped
  with electric brakes......................10 mi. per hr.
Havens to Rockridge (descending grade), Passen-
  ger Trains use 5 minutes, actual running time.
Walnut Creek—Switch Standard Oil Spur—West-
  ward Trains..............................20 mi. per hr.
Meinert—East Switch—Westward Trains........20 mi. per hr.
Concord—City limits........................20 mi. per hr.
West Pittsburg—Under Pass Curve,
  Passenger Trains.........................30 mi. per hr.
  Freight and work trains...................20 mi. per hr.
Pittsburg—City limits......................15 mi. per hr.
Pittsburg—All street crossings.............10 mi. per hr.
Pittsburg—Columbia St.....................Stop and flag
Mallard—Eastward Trains...................Stop
Ferry Ramon—All movements on and off Ferry..5 mi. per hr.
Chipps—Westward Trains...................Stop
Between Chipps and Montezuma all long trestles.40 mi. per hr.
Drawbridge—Montezuma Slough...............10 mi. per hr.

Highway—State Highway Crossing between
  Armijo and Fairfield......................Stop
Lisbon Trestle (use 3 min. and 30 sec. time).....40 mi. per hr.
  Except—Curve East end...................30 mi. per hr.
Riverview Trestles..........................25 mi. per hr.
Holland Branch.............................30 mi. per hr.
  Except—All curves.......................15 mi. per hr.
M Street Bridge............................15 mi. per hr.
Highway crossing west end M Street Bridge...10 mi. per hr.
Sacramento city limits......................20 mi. per hr.
  Except between 8th & M and 12th & I streets.15 mi. per hr.
  Except—All street intersections...........15 mi. per hr.
  Except—Other points covered by special time
    table instructions.
Sacramento—Arterials—All trains, yard motors,
  deadhead equipment and street cars........Stop
  Exception—No stop need be made when traffic
    thereat is directed or controlled by an officer,
    flagman, semaphore or other traffic signal de-
    vice (when such signal device is in operation).
Sacramento—Traffic Light Signals—All move-
  ments governed by signal indication or traffic
  officer signal.
Sacramento—N. W. corner 12th and I streets....5 mi. per hr.
Sacramento—16th and D streets...............10 mi. per hr.
Sacramento, 19th and C streets, westward trains
  and motors...............................5 mi. per hr.
Marysville city limits......................12 mi. per hr.
Marysville—Highway crossing north end D St.
  Bridge, yard engines.....................Stop and flag
Marysville—Arterials—Trains, yard engines and
  street cars..............................Stop
Marysville, 4th and Orange streets..........Stop and flag
Yuba City, city limits......................12 mi. per hr.
Yuba City—Arterials—Trains, yard engines and
  street cars..............................Stop
NOTE: At Plumas and Bridge Streets stop must
  be made even though a member of the train
  crew acts as a flagman.
Yuba City, Cooper Ave., eastward trains........6 mi. per hr.
Yuba City, Cooper Ave., westward trains.....Stop
Yuba City, Cooper Ave., yard engines.......Slow and flag
Live Oak, city limits.......................15 mi. per hr.
Edgar Slough highway crossing...............20 mi. per hr.
Chico city limits...........................12 mi. per hr.
Woodland city limits........................12 mi. per hr.
Woodland—Arterials—Trains and yard engines..Stop
Road crossing, Shell Oil Plant, Woodland.......6 mi. per hr.
Fremont Trestle............................25 mi. per hr.
Rose Orchard—When no stop is to be made for
  passengers, trains must reduce speed to 20
  m.p.h. 300 feet from the road crossing and
  speed must not exceed 15 m.p.h. when head
  end of train moves over the crossing.......15 mi. per hr.
Oroville city limits........................10 mi. per hr.
Highway crossing, Thermalito................10 mi. per hr.
Meridian Bridge............................6 mi. per hr.
Rowena road crossing........................20 mi. per hr.
Colusa city limits..........................12 mi. per hr.
Approaching spring switches.................6 mi. per hr.
Passenger trains and light motors splitting spring
  switches, except oil buffer switches........6 mi. per hr.
All trains splitting oil buffer switches.......10 mi. per hr.
Birney cars—between Sacramento and Mulbery..20 mi. per hr.
Freight engines, running light—Maximum speed..30 mi. per hr.
Speed restriction signs indicating speed of passenger and freight
trains are located at various places where speed should be reduced.
Maximum speeds permitted under city ordinance do not dis-
pense with the observance of Rule 93.

SECOND SUBDIVISION—WOODLAND BRANCH

Time Table No. 20 — April 23, 1939

Leftmost column (Eastward) header, read vertically: "Foine, Scales, Wyes, Bulletin, Register, Standard Clocks, Interlocking Plant." Rightmost column (Westward): "Capacity of Sidings in Freight Cars." Column reference number "9" appears at the top of each side.

EASTWARD (trains read downward, Sacramento to Woodland)

Reg.	SECOND CLASS 196 Woodland Local Freight	FIRST CLASS 56 Woodland Passenger	54 Woodland Passenger	52 Woodland Passenger	50 Woodland Passenger	48 Woodland Passenger	46 Woodland Passenger	44 Woodland Passenger	42 Woodland Passenger	Distance from San Francisco	STATIONS Union Station	Distance from Woodland
	Leave Daily Ex. Sunday	Leave Daily	Leave Daily EX. SUNDAY & HOLIDAYS	Leave Daily	Lv. Daily EX. SUN. & HOLIDAYS	Leave Daily	Leave Daily EX. SUNDAY & HOLIDAYS	Leave Daily	Leave Daily EX. SUN. & HOLIDAYS			
P.R.B.Y.K.		11.10PM	6.15PM	5.20PM	4.40PM	2.15PM	12.35PM	10.30AM	7.20AM	94.89	DS SACRAMENTO {D,T} 1.22	18.48
L.		11.17	6.23	5.28	4.48	2.22	12.42	10.38	7.28	93.67	Sacr., Front & M Sts., S.P.R.R. Cross. 0.30	17.26
P.	9.00AM	f11.18	f 6.25	f5.30	f4.50	f2.24	f12.43	f10.40	f7.30	93.37	BRODERICK 1.52	16.96
L.		11.20	6.27	5.32	4.52	2.26	12.45	10.42	7.32	94.89	MIKON, S.P.R.R. Cross. 0.63	15.44
P.		f11.21	f 6.28	f5.34	f4.53	f2.27	f12.46	f10.43	f7.33	95.52	ROSE ORCHARD 0.41	14.81
P.		f11.22	f 6.29	f5.35	f4.54	f2.28	f12.47	f10.44	f7.34	95.93	LOVDAL 1.98	14.40
P.		f11.24	f 6.31	f5.38	f4.56	f2.30	f12.49	f10.46	f7.36	97.91	FOURNESS 0.63	12.42
P.		f11.25	f 6.32	f5.39	f4.57	f2.31	f12.50	f10.47	f7.37	98.54	MARTY 1.08	11.79
P.		f11.26	f 6.34	f5.41	f4.59	f2.33	f12.51	f10.49	f7.39	99.62	BEATRICE 0.75	10.71
P.		f11.27	f 6.35	f5.42 [51]	f5.00	f2.34	f12.52	f10.50	f7.40	100.37	VIN 1.05	9.96
P.		f11.29	f 6.37	f5.44	f5.02	f2.36	f12.54	f10.52	f7.42	101.42	KIESEL 1.47	8.91
P.		f11.31	f 6.40	f5.46	f5.05	f2.38	f12.56	f10.55	f7.45	102.89	FREMONT 2.13	7.44
P.		f11.36	f 6.45	f5.51	f5.10	f2.43	f1.01	f11.00	f7.50	105.02	CONAWAY 2.99	5.31
P.		f11.40	f 6.49	f5.55	f5.14	f2.46	f1.05	f11.04	f7.54	108.01	HEBRON 1.96	2.32
L.		f	f	f	f	f	f	f	f	109.96	Woodland, S.P.R.R. Cross. 0.37	0.37
P.R.Y.	11.50AM	s11.45PM	s 6.55PM	s6.00PM	s5.20PM	s2.50PM	s1.10PM	s11.10AM	s8.00AM	110.33	D WOODLAND (18.48)	0.00
	Arrive Daily Ex. Sunday	Arrive Daily	Arrive Daily EX. SUNDAY & HOLIDAYS	Arrive Daily	Ar. Daily EX. SUN. & HOLIDAYS	Arrive Daily	Arrive Daily EX. SUNDAY & HOLIDAYS	Arrive Daily	Arrive Daily EX. SUN. & HOLIDAYS		Time Over District	
		0.35	0.40	0.40	0.40	0.35	0.35	0.40	0.40		Time Over District	
		31.7	27.7	27.7	27.7	31.7	31.7	27.7	27.7		Average Speed Per Hour	

WESTWARD (trains read downward, Sacramento to Woodland)

STATIONS	FIRST CLASS 41 Sacramento Passenger	43 Sacramento Passenger	45 Sacramento Passenger	47 Sacramento Passenger	49 Sacramento Passenger	51 Sacramento Passenger	53 Sacramento Passenger	55 Sacramento Passenger	SECOND CLASS 197 Sacramento Local Freight	Capacity of Sidings in Freight Cars
	Arrive Daily EX. SUN. & HOLIDAYS	Arrive Daily	Arrive Daily EX. SUNDAY & HOLIDAYS	Arrive Daily	Arrive Daily	Ar. Daily EX. SUN. & HOLIDAYS	Arrive Daily	Arrive See Note	Ar. Daily Ex. Sunday	
SACRAMENTO	s7.15AM	s8.55AM	s12.05PM	s1.55PM	s4.35PM	s6.05PM	s7.35PM	s12.25AM		Yard
Sacr., Front & M Sts., Cross.	7.06	8.46	11.58AM	1.48	4.26	5.57	7.28	12.18		
BRODERICK	f7.03	f8.44	f11.56	f1.47	f4.24	f5.55	f7.26	f12.16	4.00PM	Yard
MIKON, Cross.	7.01	8.41	11.54	1.45	4.21	5.53	7.24	12.14		8 (Spur)
ROSE ORCHARD	f6.59	f8.39	f11.53	f1.43	f4.19	f5.52	f7.23	f12.13		7 (Spur)
LOVDAL	f6.58	f8.38	f11.52	f1.42	f4.18	f5.51	f7.22	f12.12		17
FOURNESS	f6.56	f8.36	f11.50	f1.40	f4.16	f5.49	f7.20	f12.10		17 (Spur)
MARTY	f6.55	f8.35	f11.49	f1.39	f4.15	f5.47	f7.19	f12.09		9 (Spur)
BEATRICE	f6.53	f8.33	f11.47	f1.37	f4.13	f5.45	f7.17	f12.07		33 (Spurs)
VIN	f6.52	f8.32	f11.46	f1.36	f4.12	f5.42 [52]	f7.16	f12.06		8 (Spur)
KIESEL	f6.50	f8.30	f11.45	f1.35	f4.10	f5.40	f7.15	f12.05		22 (Spur)
FREMONT	f6.48	f8.28	f11.43	f1.33	f4.08	f5.38	f7.13	f12.03AM		17
CONAWAY	f6.43	f8.23	f11.38	f1.28	f4.03	f5.33	f7.08	f11.58PM		28 (Spur)
HEBRON	f6.39	f8.19	f11.34	f1.24	f3.59	f5.29	f7.04	f11.54		6 (Spur)
Woodland, S.P.R.R. Cross.	f	f	f	f	f	f	f	f		
WOODLAND	6.35AM	8.15AM	11.30AM	1.20PM	3.55PM	5.25PM	7.00PM	11.50PM	1.30PM	Yard
(Leave designation)	Leave Daily EX. SUN. & HOLIDAYS	Leave Daily	Leave Daily EX. SUNDAY & HOLIDAYS	Leave Daily	Leave Daily	Lv. Daily EX. SUN. & HOLIDAYS	Leave Daily	Leave Daily EX. SUNDAY & HOLIDAYS	Lv. Daily Ex. Sunday	
Time Over District	0.40	0.40	0.35	0.35	0.40	0.40	0.35	0.35		
Average Speed Per Hour	27.7	27.7	31.7	31.7	27.7	27.7	31.7	31.7		

Schedule meeting points are ACTUAL meeting points unless changed by train order. See Rules S-72, 83, S-88 to S-90B, inclusive.

Nos. 196 and 197 have no time table superiority.

No. 51 will take siding at Vin for No. 52.

No. 55 arrives daily except Monday and days following Holidays.

HOLIDAYS INDICATED ARE:

New Year's, Washington's Birthday, Decoration Day, Fourth of July, Labor Day, Thanksgiving Day and Christmas

EXCEPTIONS TO—AND ADDITIONAL—FLAG STOPS TO RECEIVE OR DISCHARGE PASSENGERS

Trains	Stations	Receive or Discharge
All Trains	Bryte, Silva, Crossing, Beardslee, Leeman, Birch, Harbinson, Deaner, 3rd & M., 8th & K Sts., Sacramento	Receive or Discharge.

RULES AND REGULATIONS GOVERNING OPERATION OVER OR JOINTLY OPERATED TRACKS OF THE KEY SYSTEM AND BRIDGE RAILWAY

Except as the Rules and Regulations of the Transportation Department effective January 1, 1929 and the Rules and Instructions for Continuous Cab Signal and Speed Control Operation effective August 21, 1938 may be modified, amended or superseded, those rules, regulations and instructions remain in full force and effect, and govern the operation over jointly operated tracks of the Key System and Bridge Railway.

The operation of that portion of the railroad comprising the Westward main track from West Junction to San Francisco, the Eastward main track from San Francisco to East Junction, crossovers between main tracks within those limits, and all tracks within San Francisco Terminal is assigned to the supervision of the Superintendent, Bridge Railway, at San Francisco.

Main Tracks: Main tracks on Key System are numbering from the North, No. 1 Westward track and No. 2 Eastward track.

(a) Main tracks between catenary bridge No. 52 and San Francisco are lettered and used as follows:

Track "A-1"—Westward trains catenary bridge No. 52 to switch No. 19 East switch of Westbound set-out tracks. Used jointly with Key System.

Track "C"—Westward trains switch No. 19 to West Junction thence to West switch of Interurban set-out tracks. Used jointly with Interurban and Key System.

Track "A"—Westward trains West switch of Interurban Westbound set-out tracks to San Francisco. Used jointly with Interurban and Key System.

Track "B"—Eastward trains San Francisco to East Junction. Used jointly with Interurban and Key System.

Track "M"—Eastward trains East Junction to catenary bridge No. 52. Used jointly with Key System.

(b) Tracks in San Francisco Terminal, numbering from the North (Mission Street) are designated 1, 2, 3, 4, 5 and 6. Nos. 1, 2 and 3—tracks of Interurban Electric Railway Co. Nos. 4, 5 and 6—tracks of Key System and Sacramento Northern Railway.

Set-out Tracks:

Set-out Track—a track auxiliary to the main track for the purpose of pick-up or set-out over which schedule trains may be operated as directed.

(a) Westbound set-out tracks lettered and from the North are designated "A-1" and "G".

(b) Eastbound set-out tracks lettered and from the South are designated "L" and "K".

Cross-overs on the San Francisco-Oakland Bay Bridge:

There are five pair of emergency cross-overs on the Bridge structure. Each pair consists of one left and one right hand turn-out. They are identified and located as follows:

(a) Rincon — Located at the West end of the Bridge where it passes over Rincon Hill.

(b) Anchorage — Located immediately East and West of the center anchorage.

(c) Island — Located on Yerba Buena Island.

(d) Cantilever — Located on the East bay crossing approximately 1500 feet East of the Cantilever span.

(e) Mole — Located on the East end of bridge.

Switches of these cross-overs are manually operated and must not be thrown or the cross-over used except under direction of the proper official.

If it becomes necessary to use these cross-overs, the switch taking out of the track, upon which the train to be crossed over is standing, must be thrown first and at least one minute must elapse before switch in the opposite track is thrown and cross-over movement commenced.

Special Signals:

Two indication dwarf signals are located between main tracks at each end of each pair of cross-overs comprising Rincon, Island and Cantilever cross-overs, and at each end of each cross-over comprising the Anchorage and Mole cross-overs. The signals indicate the position of cross-over switches.

A green indication will be displayed when all switches in both main tracks and located between each pair of signals are lined for movement on main track.

A red indication will be displayed when one or more switches in either or both main tracks is lined for cross-over movement, or some other condition exists which might affect safe movement on main track.

A train operating either with or against the current of traffic and finding a signal displaying a red indication, unless otherwise provided, must stop before passing the signal and careful inspection made of the cross-over switches. It must be known that they are lined for proper route before proceeding.

When light fails in signal, train may proceed without stopping, provided Cab Signal indication is more favorable than "Red 11", but report must be made from first convenient point of communication. If Cab Signal indication is "Red 11" the special signal must be regarded as displaying its most restrictive indication.

Train Control Territory:

Limits of Train Control Territory on Westward main tracks extend from fixed Signal No. 199 near San Pablo Avenue and from fixed Signal No. 40 at Tower 2, thence via Tracks "A-1", "C" and "A" to San Francisco.

Limits of Train Control Territory on Eastward main track extend from San Francisco via Tracks "B" and "M" to Signal No. 200 near San Pablo Avenue, and to Signal No. 2 at Tower 2.

Limits of Train Control Territory include all tracks in San Francisco Terminal, Westbound yard track "G" to first switch, and Westbound set-out tracks "A-1" and "G", and Eastbound set-out tracks "K" and "L".

Interlocking:

San Francisco Tower: Limits extend from Signal No. 80, located to the right of Westward track at initial switch at San Francisco, through all tracks in Terminal to Signal No. 72 governing movements on reverse traffic route on Eastward track midway between Folsom and Harrison Street viaducts. Equipped with Klaxon.

Bridge Yard Tower: Limits extend from catenary bridge No. 52 to Signal No. 124 governing movement on reverse traffic route on Westward track located to the left of that track at West switch of Westbound Interurban set-out track and from Signal No. 98 located to the right of Eastbound track at switch of Eastbound Interurban set-out tracks to catenary bridge No. 52. Equipped with Klaxon.

Tower No. 2: Emeryville Junction. Limits extend from Signal No. 3, 60 feet west of subway, to Louise Street and to Hollis Street. Equipped with siren.

Tower No. 3: Adeline and Spring Street: Limits extend from San Pablo Avenue to 42nd Street and to 40th Street. Equipped with siren.

Sacramento Northern Tower: 40th Street and Shafter Avenue Junction with Key System. Limits extend from Webster Street to 41st Street and Piedmont Avenue.

Klaxon and Siren Signals:

Sound	Indication
———	All trains stop immediately.
———	All trains resume normal movement after receiving proper signal or permission from the signalman.
— — —	Trains back up.
— — —	Call Maintainer.
———	Horn or whistle test.

When "STOP" siren is sounded, all trains within Interlocking limits must stop immediately and await proper signal.

Eastward trains shall use the following whistle signals in the event the route is not properly lined:

0 — 0	East Junction
0 0 —	Towers 2 and 3

Yerba Buena Yard:

Tracks numbered from North at Subway are 10A, 10B, 10C, 10D, 3, 6, 7, 8, 9, Lower 11, 12, 13 and 14. At Yard Office 4, 10, 11, 13, 5, (Lead) 14, 15, 16, 17, 18, 19, 19A and 20.

Between Tower 2 and Hollis Street Santa Fe Transfer, Main Tracks 1 and 2, Shop Track 1A, 2A, 3A, 5 (Lead) team track, house track, 16L and 16. Shop track extends from Hollis Street to Line E Main Track No. 2 North of Tower 3 and may be used in either direction with caution.

Derail must not be lined for movement from 10A, 10B, 10C, 10D or Track 3 until Interlocking signal governing the route indicates other than stop. Immediately after such movement, derail shall be lined to derail. Derail No. 28 on Track 10 is operated from Tower 2. The switch to 16L must be unlocked by Towerman and then operated manually. Normal position for 16L.

Rule 93:

All tracks between 42nd and Shafter Avenue, Oakland, and San Francisco Terminal are within Yard Limits.

First paragraph of Rule 93 reading "Within Yard Limits the main track may be used, protecting against first-class trains", will not apply to main tracks between Oakland and San Francisco.

Speed Restrictions:

(a) Within train control limits governed by T. C. Rule 108.
(b) Through subway................................20 m.p.h.
(c) Through Interlocking—outside Train Control.20 m.p.h.
(d) Through cross-overs and turn-outs............10 m.p.h.
(e) Splitting spring switches..................10 m.p.h.
(f) Street railway crossings: approaching Sacramento Northern trains must reduce speed to 15 m.p.h. 60 feet from crossing and speed must not exceed 8 m.p.h. when head end of train moves upon or over the crossing....................8 m.p.h.
(g) Short radius curves......................5 m.p.h.
(h) Rounding all curves (unless restricted to less)..25 m.p.h.
(i) City of Oakland (ordinance)...............22 m.p.h.
    40th and Market Streets.................8 m.p.h.

Interconnected Traffic Signals are located at:

40th and Grove Street.
40th and Telegraph.

Traffic signals are controlled by trains in either direction. Track circuits extend approximately 400 feet each way and trains entering the approach circuit set traffic signals to Green (proceed) for the approaching train and Red (stop) for transverse traffic at the intersection.

Upon display of green signals, trains will proceed—being governed by speed restrictions.

If traffic signal does not display green signal indication with train in approach circuit, train must make a safety stop before entering the intersection.

Rule 103 (a) (Amended):

In general, highway crossing signals are so designed that they will not operate for trains or cars making a reverse movement after having passed over the crossing or when running against the current of traffic on double track. Trains or cars making such movements must protect the crossing, unless it is known that signals are operating.

Telephones:

Telephones are located in Bridge Railway Superintendent's Office at San Francisco, at each set of cross-overs on Bridge, at both ends of Eastbound and Westbound set-out tracks, Inspector's Shed in Bridge Yard, YB Yard Office, in Towers 2 and 3, and Sacramento Northern Tower.

Impaired Clearances:

San Francisco-Oakland Bay Bridge.....Overhead and side
(Trolley 19 ft. 7 in.)

All concerned are warned that insufficient clearance exists on the San Francisco-Oakland Bay Bridge to clear a man between the side of the train on Westward track and the collision wall separating the railroad right-of-way from vehicular roadway. Under no condition should a person attempt to stand between the collision wall and the Westward track to permit passage of train on that track. Motormen operating Westward trains and observing a person standing between collision wall and the westward track must bring train to stop before reaching the point where the person is standing. Persons whose duties require their working on or about the railroad or attendant facilities on the Bridge must take position on planked walk at the south side of the Bridge, standing close against girders during the passage of train on either track.

Key System Subway.....................Overhead and side
(Maximum clearance—15 ft. 2 in.)

Yerba Buena Yard:

Span pole on north side of track leading into Store No. 3	7' 11½"
Span poles on south side of Track No. 3	6' 5¼"
Office building on north side of Track No. 4	6' 11½"
Fence east of office, Track No. 4	7' 10½"
Poles for Track No. 5	7' 0"
Poles for Track No. 10-B	6' 3¼"
Poles for Track No. 10-C	6' 6¼"
Signal box, Track No. 10-A	6' 7¾"
Poles between Tracks Nos. 16 and 17	7' 0"
Poles north of Track No. 10	7' 6" to 8' 6"
Pole, Track No. 16L—2nd east of P. S.	7' 3¼"
Pole, 1st track north of No. 20	7' 9"

Employees must guard against coming in contact with overhead wires or their connections, or when riding on side or top of cars, against striking automatic or interlocking signals.

Third Rail Territory:

Jointly operated portions of the railroad in Bridge Yard, on the San Francisco-Oakland Bay Bridge and Tracks 1 to 6 in San Francisco Terminal are equipped with power rail. Employees must exercise care to avoid contacting it. Should a train become disabled within power rail limits and, in order to proceed, require motorman or trainmen to go beneath car, great care must be exercised to avoid contacting the power rail.

When, in the judgment of motorman or trainmen the situation respecting proximity of power rail precludes the possibility of his going beneath car with safety to himself, he must not go beneath it or attempt to do so. In such circumstances, conductor must immediately report to proper official from nearest point of communication.

When anyone suffers from electric shock, the Prone method of resuscitation should be started at once, as any delay in starting may prove fatal. Get the mouth open, remove false teeth or anything in the mouth, pull the tongue out. Support the patient's head on one of his arms, turn face down and start artificial respiration using about 12 to 15 movements per minute. Send for a doctor at once, but keep up treatment for hours, if necessary.

Detraining on Bay Bridge:

Doors on all equipment must be closed at all times while train is moving on San Francisco-Oakland Bay Bridge. If, for any reason it becomes necessary to open doors while train is standing on the Bridge, they must be opened only by the conductor or under his direction and the following will govern:

(a) Doors must not be opened to permit detraining between tracks, except in case of accident or other cause which would make it impossible to do otherwise. Should it become necessary to permit detraining between tracks, flag protection must first be provided and train movements on the opposite track stopped short of the point of detraining.

(b) Under all other conditions, except as specified in Paragraph (a), doors on trains standing on Eastward track must be opened on the South side only and, when standing on Westward track, on the North side only. In the case of a train standing on either track, employees may detrain over the end of the car at head end or rear end of the train, but in doing so must alight on the track upon which train is standing.

(c) If door is opened to detrain an employee, it must be closed promptly after he has alighted to prevent detraining of passengers.

Telephone Report of Delays or Accidents:

In case of serious delays or accidents, conductors should when possible, notify the office of the proper official by telephone.

In cases involving movement on joint track between West Junction and San Francisco and between San Francisco and East Junction, communicate with Superintendent, Bridge Railway, at San Francisco.

MISCELLANEOUS RULES

Rule 11 (Amended):

Within Train Control limits, a train finding an unattended fusee burning on or near its track may proceed without stopping, but must run with caution not exceeding 11 m.p.h. for a distance of 1,000 feet.

Rule 14 (Amended)—Motor Whistle Signals:

Signal	Indication
— 0	When running against the current of traffic where view may be obscured.
— 0 — 0 0 0	Flagman protect rear of train on both tracks.
— 0 0 0 0 —	Flagman protect front of train on opposite track.
— 0 — — — — —	Flagman discontinue protection of rear on Eastward track, but continue protection on Westward track.
— 0 — — — — — —	Flagman discontinue protection of rear on Westward track, but continue protection on Eastward track.
————	Approaching stations, junctions, railroad crossings at grade and subways.

Rule 17 (c) (Amended):

Electric headlights will be dimmed when approaching stations where other trains are receiving or discharging passengers, except when nearing street or highway crossings.

Rule 30 (Amended):

The gong must be sounded before equipment is moved. Motormen must at all times place themselves in a position which will assure them the best vision of the track ahead and of the approach of pedestrians and vehicles.

Rule 99 (Modified):

Rule 99 will not apply to trains moving with the current of traffic within Train Control Territory, except:

(a) Before a train crosses over to or obstructs another track, unless otherwise provided, it must first be protected, as prescribed by Rule 99, in both directions on that track (Rule D-152).

(b) In event of derailment within Train Control Territory, the train must be protected in accordance with Rule 99.

(c) That, motors or engines not equipped with Cab Signal and Speed Control Apparatus must be protected in accordance with Rule 99 at all times, while operating within limits of Train Control Territory and will enter and operate through Train Control Territory with caution, not exceeding 11 m.p.h.

Rule 108 (Cab Signal Rules):

Movement against current of traffic within that portion of train control territory assigned to supervision of Superintendent—Bridge Railway must not be made except on receipt of written instructions, on prescribed form, issued by authority and over the signature of Superintendent—Bridge Railway; this form to be made in triplicate, copy to be given to conductor and motorman of each train so authorized to move against current of traffic, third copy to be returned to Superintendent—Bridge Railway by the employe issuing same.

Rule 108 (A) (Cab Signal Rules):

In that portion of Train Control Territory between the easterly interlocking limits of San Francisco Tower and westerly limits of Bridge Yard Tower Rule 108 (A) is modified as follows:

Red 11—After required speed reduction and after acknowledgment, train may proceed at or under 11 m.p.h. prepared to stop at least 400 feet back of the rear end of a standing preceding train but must stop before passing the entrance switch to a crossover even though the distance be greater than 400 feet, so that a movement against the current of traffic could be made if necessary. A train so stopped by a preceding train may proceed upon receipt of a Yellow 17 Cab Signal Indication or upon receipt of proper hand signal.

Consolidation of Trains:

When required by schedule or by proper authority, trains will be consolidated.

On all consolidated trains, conductor on leading section is in charge, and must know that train is at all times protected in accordance with Rule 99.

Conductors of all trains will advise the dispatcher from the first convenient point of communication, time of arrival at and departure from San Francisco Terminal.

Trainmen will note if all motor cars in service in their train are operating, and notify motorman in case of failure.

Except in emergency or foggy weather, torpedoes must not be placed on improved public streets.

Trains leaving San Francisco Terminal:

A clock equipped with sweephand registering seconds, a push button type electric switch, and a telephone, all mounted together are located at the west end of each platform and at approximately midpoint of each platform in the train shed at San Francisco. These facilities are for the purpose of starting trains from the Terminal and will be referred to as "Starting Stations". The push button switches, when depressed, illuminate an indicator light in the Interlocking Tower and those at the west end only simultaneously illuminate a yellow starting light located above the platform at the west end of the train shed. On platform serving Tracks 4 and 5, there are two push button switches at each location—the one nearest Track 4 applying to trains on that track, the one nearest Track 5 applying to trains on that track. On platform serving Track 6 there is one push button switch at each location. The telephone is for communicating with the Interlocking Tower.

At least one minute before schedule departure time of a train, conductor will station himself at starting station nearest the head end of his train and, when the sweephand on the clock at that location indicates fifteen seconds in advance of departure time, he will depress the proper push button switch and at the same time raise his hand vertically over his head. Brakemen will station themselves on station platform immediately adjacent to door of car to which assigned being alert to observe yellow starting light or hand signal and, when that light becomes illuminated or hand signal given, brakeman nearest him will repeat the signal which will be relayed by each succeeding brakeman toward the rear of train. Immediately the signal has been relayed, each succeeding brakeman will board the train and close train doors, excepting the doors of cars to which conductor is assigned. After doors have once been closed, they must not again be opened except on direction of conductor. After having depressed push button switch, conductor will board train at his car and close the doors. Upon receipt of proceed signal from conductor, the train shall start to move out of train shed, being governed by signal indication of the first interlocking signal. Lamp signal given by holding lamp at arms' length above the head, may be used instead of corresponding hand signal, if necessary.

Exceptions: Only between the hours of 7:30 A.M. and 9:00 A.M. daily except Sun. and Holi. and between the hours of 4:30 P.M. and 6:30 P. M. daily except Sat., Sun. and Holi., conductors of regular trains shall operate the starting buttons.

Success of the operation on close headways out of San Francisco during peak periods depends on utmost alertness of all concerned.

Every effort must be made to depart from San Francisco exactly on time.

When trains or cars are moved into or out of set-out tracks, an employee must be stationed on the front end of leading car in direction of movement and remain there until the movement is completed.

Motormen and trainmen must observe Rule 122 of "Rules and Instructions for Continuous Cab Signal and Speed Control Operation" before leaving Bridge Yard on deadhead equipment originating at that point.

Running air brake test must be made on Westward trains and deadhead equipment immediately after leaving 40th and Shafter Avenue, Oakland. Eastward trains and deadhead equipment from San Francisco must make running test immediately after passing Rincon cross-overs on the San Francisco-Oakland Bay Bridge. Deadhead equipment originating at Bridge Yard must make running test while moving on set-out tracks and before entering the main track.

In Non-Signal Territory trains in the same direction shall keep not less than 1200 feet apart, except when closing up at stations.

To reduce automobile accidents, special care should be used when approaching grade crossings known to be obscured or hazardous. Where vehicles are moving in public streets in the same direction as the train and are not clear of the track on which train is operating, speed should be so controlled as to permit train being stopped in case vehicle makes a sudden or unexpected stop or turn. When about to pass a vehicle moving in the same direction as train, the motorman should satisfy himself that the driver is aware of approach of the train.

When opposing trains approach on double track located in a public street, speed of both trains must be reduced and gongs must be sounded until the head end of each passes the rear end of the other.

Under normal conditions, yard cuts and extra trains may operage on double track with the current of traffic without orders.

Work extras may operate on single track, clearing regular trains and protecting against other extras.

Trains entering terminals must move with caution, as tracks may be occupied. Responsibility for accident rests with train entering terminal.

When necessary to barge freight cars on the Ferry with passenger trains, not more than four (4) freight cars or one (1) locomotive and three (3) freight cars will be permitted on the Ferry at the same time with a passenger train. The freight cars must be loaded on the Ferry so that there will be room at each end for passengers to walk around the freight cars in order to get to the life-boats in case of an emergency.

Blocks must not be removed until Ferry is against apron.

Motorman must observe Rule 1006 and remain in cab while train is on Ferry.

Motormen must move slowly and watch to the rear until entire train is moved off the Ferry.

Cars containing explosives or inflammables must not be handled on Ferry Ramon with cars carrying passengers.

The spur track which serves the packing house at Chadbourne crosses a State Highway. All trains, engines, motors or cars must come to a stop and no movement made over the crossing until a member of the train crew or other competent employee shall protect the traffic on the highway.

The siding at Cordero and the siding at Belleair are crossed by County Roads. At such times as cars are allowed to stand on these sidings within a distance of one hundred (100) feet of either side of these county roads, a member of the train crew or other competent employee shall protect the traffic on said roads by acting as a human flagman for all trains, engines, motors or cars operating over the adjacent main line track. Cars which are stored on these sidings must not be left standing within 100 feet of either side of the road crossing.

Inside switches of both crossovers at Riverview must be left lined and locked for Holland Branch.

East switch of crossover, located just west of Westgate crossing, must be left lined and locked for storage track.

The W. P. tracks on Front and R Streets leading to the C. P. C. Plant and P Street Dock may be used by S. N. yard crews under yard rules. W. P. yard engines have preference on these tracks.

The three way switch in the eastward track at C Street is lined for the street car track and must be thrown by all trains.

All switches serving the Union Station are spring switches and must be lined as follows: Switch on 11th Street leading to I Street lined as last used. Switches on I Street leading to 12th Street lined for I St. All inside yard switches lined as last used.

Yard Engines, Street Cars, and dead head equipment moving east on I Street, must come to a stop before crossing 11th Street. All trains and dead head equipment moving out of the Union Station and going east on I Street must stop before reaching I Street. Trains moving east on I Street have the preference at 11th Street junction. Westward trains have the preference at 12th Street junction. Eastward trains must not cross 12th Street junction while westward trains are moving over switch leading to 12th Street.

Trains, dead head equipment, yard engines, and street cars making continuous westward movements on I Street must stop 75 feet from the curb line at 11th Street. Westward trains leaving Union Station at 11th Street, have the preference.

Should two trains leave the Union Station simultaneously, the train on the right hand track will have the preference.

All switching movements at the Union Station, Sacramento, must be made in west end of yard. No switching movements are to be made from the yard on to 12th Street.

City Ordinances require all street cars, trains and yard engines within one hundred feet of an intersection to stop immediately on the approach of any police, ambulance, or fire apparatus sounding siren or signal gong except they be at the time on, or crossing an intersection, in which event crossing must be cleared and then stop.

Civil, Military or Funeral processions must not be obstructed.

When trains, street cars, yard engines or dead head equipment approach a street intersection simultaneously, except where traffic is controlled by traffic signals in service or traffic officer, the train, car, yard engine, or dead head equipment moving eastward must reduce speed, stopping if necessary, and must not enter the intersection until the train, car, yard engine, or dead head equipment, moving in the westward direction has passed entirely out of the intersection and the motorman has a clear and unobstructed view; except that regular scheduled trains moving in either direction will have the preference at all times.

Motormen of Eastward trains approaching Walnut Creek will sound signal 14 (L) for the Main Highway crossing and use signal 14 (J) for the second crossing and train-order signal, combined, and omit signal 14 (G) when operator is on duty. When train order office is closed use signal 14 (L) for the second crossing.

High cars when placed on the old Ice House spur at Concord must be left west of the sand bins, so that motorman will have a clear view of the highway crossing, switches and signals.

Cars must not be left standing on Willow Pass road crossing just east of Concord station.

Cars set out at Clyde for loading or unloading must be spotted back from the West Road crossing as far as possible. Not more than six cars are to be spotted on the delivery track for the B. P. & C. R. R. at any one time.

Controls operated by selectors in the dispatcher's office have been installed on block signals 218-H and 219-H at Burton and block signals 646-H and 647-H at Dozier and are used to stop trains for train orders. After the train has been cleared by the dispatcher, the conductor shall clear the signals by pressing a button which is located by the side of the telephone and must see that the signals are clear before leaving the station.

Signs reading—Cars must not be switched beyond this point by S. P. Co.-S. N. Ry.—are located on tracks 1 and 7 at the Shell Chemical Plant, Shell Point. A derail is located 30 feet east of the cement house on track 7 and is locked with a Shell Chemical Co. lock. When necessary to spot cars beyond the derail secure the key from the Yardmaster at the Plant.

Trains approaching West Pittsburg must not stop foul of Branch track unless Branch train has arrived.

Cars must not be stored on wye at West Pittsburg.

The yard limits of Pittsburg include all tracks in Pittsburg, and between Pittsburg and West Pittsburg, and between Pittsburg and Mallard. All movements between Pittsburg and West Pittsburg will be made in accordance with Rule 93. Scheduled and Extra trains must receive a clearance from the Dispatcher for all movements between West Pittsburg and Pittsburg, and in the reverse direction.

All switching movements at any point must be made with caution.

In case of power interruption, signal operator may display "S" sign in which case trains must not exceed series position of controller. When signs are removed, normal speed may be resumed.

When necessary to lower pantagraphs to coast under line breaks, etc., the following procedure should be followed:

ascertain if in proper working order. On trains of three cars or less leave all pantagraphs down except on car with control. If lowering valve is located at other than in cab from which motorman is operating, a trainman must be stationed at valve and when signalled by one long blast of the alarm whistle, lowering valve must be held down until train has again been brought to a stop and motorman sounds two long blasts of the alarm whistle.

In raising pantagraphs, care must be taken to see that they are not directly under trolley cross-arms and they must not be raised until train has stopped.

Care should be used while operating electric equipment during hot weather to observe the condition of trolley wires, especially in the vicinity of curves and cross-overs. When there is any unusual amount of slack in the trolley wire, speed of train should be reduced to a point where pantagraphs or overhead structure will not be damaged. Any unsafe condition should be promptly reported.

In power rail territory, the catenary carries 1200 volts.

When the power leaves the line, the controller should be thrown to "off" position and the train stopped clear of all crossings, if possible. Light circuit switch should be turned on and the train should not be started until lights burn brightly. Westward trains will start first and Eastward trains, after waiting thirty seconds, may proceed if lights continue to burn brightly.

Towermen and switchtenders will notify each other of regular trains passing their stations late or out of regular place and of extra trains or freight movements, giving their destination. Towermen and switchtenders will let all extras and freight movements out onto main tracks to proceed to any point, when such movements can be made without delay to regular trains. Responsibility for delay to regular trains, after clearing interlocker or district under switchtenders' control, rests with the conductor in charge of such movement.

Crossing Watchmen:

When crossing watchman is not on duty or is absent from his post (as indicated by a yellow flag displayed on the front of his cabin), if required by rule or if such crossing is an arterial stop, make safety stop and proceed with caution.

Where required by law or police regulations, all trains must stop.

Crossing watchmen will provide themselves with a red flag, a yellow lantern, a red lantern and a disc "Stop" sign.

Flags and disc shall be used by day and lights of prescribed color by night. When weather conditions obscure day signals, night signals must be used.

The disc signal by day and the red light by night shall be used to stop vehicular and pedestrian traffic when a train is approaching. If necessary to stop a train, red signals must be used. The yellow flag by day and the yellow light by night shall be used, when no trains are approaching, to give proceed signals to street cars and motor coaches of other companies, after such cars or coaches have come to a complete stop.

Under no circumstances may proceed signals be given to vehicles or pedestrians.

Upon approach of trains, crossing watchmen must station themselves near the crossing, in a position to obtain an unobstructed view of the intersection with disc stop sign or red lantern displayed against vehicular and pedestrian traffic. Care should be exercised to so display the red lantern that it may not be accepted as a stop signal by the train motorman.

When crossing watchmen are compelled to leave their post for a short time, a yellow flag by day and a yellow light by night shall be displayed on the front corner of their cabin to indicate that the crossing is unprotected.

MISCELLANEOUS

Westward freight and work trains must make air brake inspection and test at Pinehurst before train is moved over any portion of descending grade between Havens and Rockridge, comply with instructions on Test Card Form 182, and be governed by tonnage rating and car limit as shown in schedule of locomotive ratings. Stop must be made at Havens for the purpose of turning up the retainers on all cars and placing the test card in the box.

Locomotives 603 and 604 are equipped with transfer valves, power and control connections so that these two locomotives when coupled can be handled as a single unit by one Motorman. Locomotives 660 and 661 are equipped with transfer valves but no power nor control connections so that these two locomotives when coupled will require two motormen for power operation but the motorman on the head locomotive will control the air brakes. This same method of operation will apply to locomotives 603 and 660 coupled, 604 and 660 coupled, 603 and 661 coupled and 604 and 661 coupled.

When two locomotives coupled are used in handling trains, not less than 3 air compressors must be in service.

When single locomotives are used both compressors must be in service.

Ninety (90) pounds brake pipe pressure must be carried at all times with main reservoir pressure setting of 110-130 pounds.

The A. A. R. recommended practice for air brake test and inspection must be observed, namely: that the cylinder condition and retaining valve be such that the brake would remain applied at least three minutes and that the piston travel on all cars be adjusted to nominally 7 inches.

Havens to Temescal.—Rock, Sand and Construction Material Service:

Trains not in excess of 10 cars with an average gross load not in excess of 85 tons per car may be handled by two locomotives coupled and equipped with transfer valves. Speed must not exceed 10 miles per hour, and the brake on each car in the train must be properly adjusted and in operative condition.

No attempt should be made to handle any cars down this grade in these heavy tonnage trains with the brake inoperative, either from the air brake failure or foundation rigging failure.

Retaining valves must be in service on all cars.

Havens to Rockridge:

Trains having not less than 85% of the air brakes operative and whose total tonnage does not exceed 50 tons per operative brake may be handled by either two locomotives coupled or by one locomotive, provided they do not exceed the car limit. Speed must not exceed 20 miles per hour, Havens to Temescal, and 10 miles per hour, Temescal to Rockridge. Retaining valves must be used on all cars having operative brakes.

Trainmen on all westward freight and work trains, between Havens and Rockridge, must ride the cars when leaving Havens until it is known that the Motorman has control of the train, and when leaving Temescal must ride the front platform of the caboose and the rear end of the motor and be ready with their brake clubs to set hand brakes in case of an emergency.

No westward freight nor work train heavier than 50 tons per operative air brake will operate between Temescal and Rockridge unless permission is obtained from the proper officer.

Helper engine must be used on rear of all eastward freight and work trains between Oakland Yard and the summit of the grade east of Havens, except that when no helper is provided the Conductor must, after pulling out of the siding, see that the east switch of the siding is left open until rear of train passes the spur switch when it must be opened before lining the east switch of the siding back for the main track. The spur switch will then be left open until the rear of the train passes the summit of the grade. Motorman must then stop and sound the required whistle signal calling his flagman in from the west. The brakeman will then line the spur track switch for the main track and return to his train.

The same rule will apply when pulling off the spur instead of the siding.

Work trains in this territory not originating at Havens must not go east of the summit of the grade unless the locomotive is on the west end of the train.

The trolley or pantograph must be down before removing any jumpers, handling 600-1200 volt switches, when picking up or setting out passenger equipment, when cutting trains at the Ferry or when the motorman is repairing electrical equipment.

The old type whistle must be blown approaching each street intersection in Oakland and blasts must be so spaced that the last blast will continue to the intersection. The air gong may be used, but the engine bell should be used only in an emergency. The use of the pneuphonic air horn between Terrace and Hollis Street, Oakland, and San Francisco when needed.

Within the city limits of Pittsburg the use of the pneuphonic air horn is prohibited. The old type whistle must be used and, if inoperative, the air gong shall be used.

Conductor or Brakeman must ride in cab with the Motorman on all westward trains between Rockridge and College Ave., and all eastward trains between 40th and Shafter and College Ave., to assist in checking clearances between trains and parked automobiles.

Loaded cars in excess of 169,000 pounds, gross weight, must not be accepted from connecting lines nor handled in trains, unless permission is obtained from the proper officer.

Motormen shall sound signal 14 (m) while approaching and before passing the Train Ferry Signs located one-half mile on either side of the ferry at Chipps and Mallard, and shall immediately reduce to 25 miles per hour preparatory to making the stop before moving onto the Ferry.

Should the motorman fail to give signal 14 (m) and reduce as herein prescribed, the conductor must take immediate action to stop the train.

All freight engine pantographs should be lowered and mechanical lever left in down position before going on apron of boat and kept in that position during any operation over aprons at the Chipps and Mallard slips. When tying up freight engine the pantograph must be securely locked in the down position.

Motormen must shut off power at all sectional insulators both in trolley and third rail except at places where insulators have been designed for pantograph operation.

The Captain, or his pilot, will have direct charge of train crews in loading and unloading the Ferry, and movements must be made in accordance with his instructions. 700 gross tons is the maximum load limit. Heavy and light cars must be placed on the Ferry so as to keep the load well balanced. Each track on the Ferry is approximately 220 feet long, but, only 210 track feet may be used. When shoving cars on to the Ferry ahead of Motor, no cars are to be coupled on to, or handled behind the motor.

Hand and air brakes must be set on all freight cars—air brakes set on freight engines; wheels must be blocked on passenger cars (using 4 blocks to each track)—air brakes set and all vestibule and trap doors of passenger cars must be opened while train is on Ferry Ramon except that when it is necessary to cut a passenger train and move it on the Ferry in two cuts, then the vestibule doors facing the opposite track shall be left closed. At night, all marker and classification lamps must be removed.

Rule 838. Cars must not be left standing on any spur or siding within 200 ft. of any highway crossing, if possible to avoid it.

Rule 890 is amended as follows:

A member of the train crew must ride in the last car of each passenger train at all times when his duty does not require his presence elsewhere, when such train consists of two or more cars, except on trains carrying parlor cars, in which case the trainman will ride in the next car ahead.

When passing over long trestles in third rail territory conductor or brakeman must observe trestle from rear of train and be on lookout for fires which may start from third rail arcs.

When approaching and while passing over facing point spring switches on either a passenger or freight train, trainmen must be distributed over the train so as to observe the movement of the entire train over the spring switch and be prepared to stop it promptly in event of derailment.

The Conductor and Motorman are jointly responsible for the speed of trains which must not exceed six miles per hour during the movement of the entire train over a facing point spring switch.

Motormen must not apply any power while going over spring switches unless it be to maintain the speed allowed.

Rule 970 must be observed by train crews before passing through tunnel No. 1, over ferry slips, and all long trestles and bridges.

Rule 1011. When wigwags or bells are found inoperative, train or engine must stop and be preceded over the crossing by a flagman. When a reverse movement is made on Main track or on siding or spur which is not in wigwag circuit a flagman must protect the crossing before the movement is made.

Some wigwag signals are set into operation by third rail shoe contacts and others by trolley contacts. Motormen must slow down at points where trolley and third rail overlap, and where wigwags are operated by trolley contacts so that the trolley can be put on the wire before reaching the "Brush Contacts."

When one train is following another closely in yard limits or closing up at stations where wigwag circuits are maintained the train in the rear must not enter the wigwag circuit before the leading train has passed the wigwag cutout when such circuit is not a track circuit.

Flasher signals which operate in conjunction with wigwag signals are installed in advance of all wigwags which swing parallel with the tracks.

Rule 1070. Applies to two or more freight motors coupled and operated as one unit. Air-brake test must be made before the unit is moved and when motorman changes his operating position from one motor to the other.

Rule 1072 must be observed, air cut in all cars on all yard or train movements over City streets, "M" St. bridge and when switching on any track on a heavy grade.

Rule 1089—Amended. In case of power or air brake failure and there exists the possibility of not being able to hold the train with the air brakes, sufficient hand brakes must be set to hold the train.

INTERLOCKING AND BLOCK SIGNALS

The Interlocking Plant at 40th and Shafter, governs all movements to and from the Key System tracks on 40th Street. Dwarf semaphore signals govern movements from tracks in Oakland Yards to 40th Street.

The standard color of the masts supporting home signals is white, and the masts supporting distant signals is yellow.

Trains finding a Home Block Signal Dark will make a test and if the Red Signal is working may proceed. In making this test train must be backed out of circuit after getting "Red" indication before proceeding.

At meeting points, the train taking the siding, may back out after the train has been met without waiting for the switch indicator to clear and if the facing Home Block Signal is clear may proceed.

Key System crossing College Avenue.

All cars, trains and yard engines must stop at College Avenue and no car, train or yard engine of either line shall proceed over this crossing if there is a car or train approaching on the other line at a distance, from same, that would not permit of safe passage.

Southern Pacific Crossing at Las Juntas is protected by Stop Boards. All trains, engines, motors and cars must stop at stop boards and signal 14-B sounded before proceeding over the crossing, providing that there is no locomotive, motor, train or

---

Rule S-90A.—When a trainman of the opposing train opens a switch he should stay there, signal to the motorman of the other train with a slow down signal and then a slow proceed signal to apprise the motorman of the fact that the switch has been opened and also receive answer from the motorman that his signal is understood before he leaves the switch.

Rule 93. Second paragraph of Rule 93 is abrogated, and the following will govern:

Second and inferior class trains, extra trains and engines must approach and move with caution within yard limits.

When not protected by block signals or when moving against the current of traffic, first-class trains must approach and move with caution within yard limits.

Rule 99-A. The interpretation of this rule is that when a flagman is either sent to hold a train or is left, at a point to hold a train, that his instructions must be in writing on Flagman's Hold Order, form 27.

Rule 104 (C). The interpretation of this rule is that the switch must be locked after a train takes siding when meeting another train or when train is standing on the main track and the switch is lined for the passing track for the opposing train to take siding.

After the train to be met has passed and it is necessary to back the train on the siding in returning to the main track there must be a man in the rear, either on the ground preceding the movement, or on the rear step or platform, stationing himself in such a position that the motorman will be able to see him and his signals at all times. The signal to back the train shall not be given until the switch has cleared the switch point and his signals at all times. The signal to back the train shall has determined the train that has passed has cleared the switch a sufficient length so that there will be no possibility of a collision between the train backing out of the siding and train that has passed in the event the latter train would come to a sudden stop. If the train on the siding consisted of three cars no signal should be given to the motorman of that train to back out of the siding until the train that has passed is five car lengths past the switch point.

Rule 219—Amended. A Conductor taking a train order over the telephone circuit must not repeat or give the "X" response to a train order if the train has been cleared or of which the engine has passed the telephone booth or other point where the order is being received until he has obtained the signature of the Motorman.

Rule 609—Amended. On single track when a preceding train is seen in the block in which the signals are actuated by track circuits, and the intervening track is seen to be clear, train after stopping, will proceed at once with caution not exceeding 12 miles per hour.

Rule 609. The sending of a flagman ahead as prescribed by this rule does not apply to the operators of one-man street cars.

Back-up hose must be used by yard crews in Sacramento yard and Pittsburg yard when shoving cars ahead of motor over city streets.

Yard crews must be cleared by Dispatcher for movements between Haggin and Globe, and between Mulberry and Stirling Jct.

Cars of gasoline when spotted for unloading at any oil spur must be left between the insulated joints and the end of the spur. No cars are to be left standing over the insulated joints or coupled to cars spotted between the insulated joints and end of spur.

Where power switches are installed on gasoline unloading tracks, they must not be closed until it has first been ascertained by a member of the crew that all cars have been disconnected and are ready to move. The power switches must be left open after switching has been completed.

There is no third rail on the Diamond Match Spur at Live Oak, therefore when spotting or picking up cars it will be necessary to hold on to several cars so that the motor will not lose contact with the third rail on the main track.

Freight trains are limited to engine and three cars on Main Street, Chico.

Freight motors, but not freight cars may be moved around the North leg of the wye at 1st and Main Sts., Chico.

Passenger trains will discharge passengers at First and Main Streets, Chico, before going around the wye.

Color light signals which indicate red are installed on the train order masts at East Nicolaus and East Gridley, and are used for stopping trains for train orders when no operator is on duty. After receiving train order Conductor will clear the signal by pressing a button located near the telephone.

Rule 10 (H). When a yellow signal is required it will be displayed to the right of track in the direction of approach, one-quarter mile from structure or track over which speed of trains must be restricted. Where two or more main tracks are affected the signal will be displayed on each track the same as if it were a single track.

A green signal will be displayed similarly on each track immediately beyond the structure or track affected.

Trains must not exceed the speed specified by train order or bulletin, or fifteen miles an hour if no different speed is specified, while passing over the structure or track affected, until the rear of train clears the limit, which shall be indicated by a green signal.

Slow boards, where used, will be similarly placed and observed.

Rule 14-L. Motormen will sound signal 14 (L) in such a manner so as to prolong the last blast of the whistle until the train enters the road crossing. On slow speed movements the signal 14 (L) should be repeated if necessary.

Rule 17 amended. The headlight will be displayed at the front of every train when the visibility is such that a dark object as large as a man of average size can not be seen at a distance of 1500 feet. The headlight must be concealed when a train turns out to meet another and has stopped clear of main track, or is standing to meet trains at the end of two or more tracks or at junctions.

Rule 17-C. Head lights must be dimmed while moving within city limits of Sacramento.

Rule 18—Modified. Yard engines when making a continuous movement along city streets will not display the headlight at the rear by night. A red light must be displayed to the rear.

Rule 84—Amended. A passenger train must not be started from its initial station or any intermediate station, where trucks or mail carts are used in the handling of Baggage, Express or Mail or where destination signs are displayed, until the truck, mail cart, or destination sign has been moved at least six feet away from the train on the side used to receive or discharge passengers.

Rule S-88—Fourth paragraph modified as follows: At meeting point when it is necessary for train which takes siding to back in, train will be brought to a stop before it proceeds over the switch, and in obscure places, or when other conditions require, flagman must prceded train at least 350 feet, or a sufficient distance to insure full protection before going over the switch to back in.

Rule S-88. At following stations the designated switches and tracks are the points where trains take siding. Train holding main track will remain clear until opposing train shall have cleared.

Havens—Eastward trains use the siding. Westward trains use the spur.

Meinert—Siding.

Concord—Westward trains use the field track. Eastward trains use sub-station spur.

Westgate—All trains use west end long siding.

Woodland—All trains use wye switch passenger depot.

Sacramento—
Eastward passenger trains use switch west end double track "M" Street.
Eastward freight trains use switch leading to Front Street.
Westward freight trains use Haggin switch west of American River Bridge.
Westward passenger trains use switch east end double track under subway.

North Sacramento—Siding.

Arboga—West spur.

Marysville—
Eastward passenger trains use switch west switch joint track siding.
Westward trains use switch east end double track Yuba City passenger depot.
Eastward freight trains use switch west switch east and double track Yuba City.

Colusa Jct.—West switch of wye.

Colusa—All trains use switch west end double track.

Live-Oak—Siding west of depot.

Oroville Jct.—West switch of big wye.

Mulberry—Shop siding.

Chico—Eastward passenger trains use switch west end double track Main Street.

---

street intersections over street cars, yard engines, and dead head equipment.

Street Cars of the C. C. T. Co. operating over the tracks used jointly between 8th and J and 8th and M Sts. have the same time table directions as S. N. trains.

Trains and Yard Engines operating on X St. will assume time table directions of C. C. T. Co. trains as follows:

Eastward—Alhambra Blvd. to Front St.
Westward—Front St. to Alhambra Blvd.

Interurban trains, yard engines and street cars operated on tracks in Sacramento running Easterly and Westerly have precedence in the use of the crossing over other interurban trains, yard engines and street cars operated on tracks running Northerly and Southerly except that trains or yard engines in whatever direction they may be running, have the precedence in the use of such crossings over street cars operated in street railway service.

Street Cars of the P. G. & E. Co. after stopping at any crossing with the S. N. Ry. will not move over the crossing if a train or yard engine of the S. N. Ry. is approaching within the distance of one city block, but as soon as the train or yard engine comes to a stop at the crossing the train or cars of the P. G. & E. Co. may start to move over the crossing until such time as the motorman on the train or yard engine sounds his gong or whistle indicating that his train is to move over the crossing.

Motormen must not give a proceed signal to street car men to cross ahead of their trains while the train is standing to receive or discharge passengers or stopped at the street car crossing for other reasons.

At crossings protected by traffic light signals or traffic officers all movements will be governed by signal indication or traffic officer signal.

The tracks in Haggin Yard are used by Western Pacific yard engines and crews when switching their cars to and from the Southern Pacific interchange. Crew must obtain a lineup of the main track S. N. trains from the S. N. dispatcher before using the main track and obey yardmaster's instructions.

Yard engines when switching at Plant 11, C. P. C., must avoid delay to trains and street cars.

Freight trains must not go west of 15th and D Sts., Sacramento.

Spring Switches, except tongue switches, are indicated by yellow lenses and targets on Sacramento Northern tracks. On the joint track at Marysville, all inside switches on the Western Pacific have yellow lenses and targets, but are not spring switches.

The tracks on "X" Street, Sacramento, are operated jointly with the C. C. T. Company.

Street cars of the C. C. T. Company have preference over Sacramento Northern yard engines.

Trains entering or leaving the Swanston Branch, at Globe, must not stand on the Western Pacific crossing.

Switch point locking devices are installed on switch leading to American Packing Shed Meinert, switch leading to Standard Oil Plant Walnut Creek, west switch old siding Westgate, west switch siding at Pease and east switch siding at Encinal. To operate these devices, push down on footlever when throwing the switch.

When throwing oil Buffer switches by hand, sufficient time must be allowed for the point to fit the traffic rail before movement is made over the switch.

Freight trains must not go west of 5th and G Streets, Marysville.

Opposing trains must not move around the double track curve at Fifth and "D" Streets, Marysville, at the same time as the clearance between the two trains is not sufficient. Westward trains have the preference at this curve.

Trains and yard engines must not block Plumas Street, Yuba City.

Back up movements from the west end of the yard at Yuba City on to Bridge Street must be protected by a member of the train or yard crew acting as a flagman. Back up movements over other street intersections or around sharp curves in switching service where the motorman's view is obstructed must be protected in the same manner. The conductor or foreman on the crew is jointly responsible with the motorman for this protection being given.

car of the Southern Pacific approaching the crossing from either direction.

When view is obscured by fog or inclement weather, a member of the crew must go forward to the crossing and ascertain that no train is approaching on the Southern Pacific Railway before proceeding over the crossing.

Bay Point & Clayton Railroad crossing at Clyde, no signals. All trains, engines, motors, and cars, must stop at stop boards and signal 14 (b) sounded before proceeding over the crossing.

When view is obscured by fog or inclement weather a member of the crew must go forward to the crossing and ascertain that no train is approaching on the B. P. & C. R. R. before proceeding over the crossing.

When trains, engines, motors, or cars of both companies approach the crossing simultaneously the train, engine, motor, or car of the B. P. & C. R. R. will have the right to pass first over the crossing.

The tracks at the Shell Chemical Company's plant at Shell Point are used jointly by the Sacramento Northern and Southern Pacific. All movements over these tracks must be made with caution. The tracks leading from the Sacramento Northern and from the Southern Pacific cross at grade. All trains, motors, engines or cars of the Sacramento Northern shall stop at the "STOP" signs located at each approach to the crossing, and shall not proceed over the crossing until it has been ascertained that it is safe to do so. Several derails, properly signed, are installed on the various tracks.

A. T. & S. Fe R. R., crossing at Pittsburg is protected by stop boards. All engines, trains, motors and cars must come to a stop at the "STOP" boards located on either side of the crossing and no movement made over this crossing until a flagman has preceded over the crossing and ascertained that it is safe to proceed. A. T. & S. Fe R. R. have the preference at this crossing.

Southern Pacific Railroad crossing at Front and M Streets, Sacramento, is protected by flagman.

Southern Pacific trains moving on Front Street, Sacramento, and yard engines switching on Front Street, shall stop before reaching the crossing at Front, and M Streets, and will proceed on hand signals from flagman on the ground at the crossing, flagman using a green flag by day and green light by night.

Sacramento Northern trains and yard engines moving over the crossing shall stop before reaching the crossing at Front and M Streets, and will proceed on hand signals from the flagman stationed on the platform of Watchman's Shelter, flagman using a yellow flag by day and a yellow light by night.

All single track curves at 19th and C, 15th and D, 15th and I, 8th and I and 8th and M Streets are protected by block signals operated by trolley contacts. The block signals are located on poles in advance of the curves. The normal indication of the signals is dark. Trains entering the block limit will receive a yellow signal and will be protected by a red signal on the opposite end. Trains entering the block simultaneously will cause the signals to indicate both yellow and red, in which case both trains must stop and the train or car moving in the westward direction will proceed.

Track between 30th and C Sts., and Alhambra Blvd. and F Sts., Sacramento, is protected by block signals. All yard engine and street car movements must be governed by signal indication.

AUTOMATIC INTERLOCKER C & X STREETS, SACRAMENTO

Automatic Interlocking Color Light Signals governing movements of Western Pacific trains and Sacramento Northern trains are located at the crossings on "C" and "X" Streets, Sacramento.

MOVEMENT OF TRAINS OVER "C" STREET CROSSING, SACRAMENTO

WESTERN PACIFIC—Home signal located 480 feet east of crossing governs movement of trains over the crossing westward; Home signal located 450 feet west of crossing governs movement of trains over the crossing eastward. No distant signals.

MOVEMENT OF TRAINS OVER "X" STREET CROSSING, SACRAMENTO

WESTERN PACIFIC—Home signal located 450 feet east of crossing governs movement of trains over the crossing westward; Home signal located 450 feet west of crossing governs movement of trains over the crossing eastward. One distant signal 1480 feet west of home signal.

MOVEMENT OF TRAINS OVER "C" STREET CROSSING, SACRAMENTO

SACRAMENTO NORTHERN—Home signals governing movement of trains with the current of traffic over the crossing located at the curb line 72.5 feet on either side of crossing. Back-up signals governing reverse train movements over the crossing are located at the curb line 72.5 feet on either side of crossing. No distant signals.

Operators of street cars after passing the signal in PROCEED position will make a safety stop 25 feet from the crossing before moving over it. Cars must not be left standing between the home signals unless coupled to another car or an engine which is standing outside of the home signals.

MOVEMENT OF TRAINS OVER "X" STREET CROSSING, SACRAMENTO

CENTRAL CALIFORNIA TRACTION COMPANY - SACRAMENTO NORTHERN—Home signals governing movement of trains with the current of traffic over the crossing located at the curb line 72.5 feet on either side of crossing; back-up signals governing reverse train movements over the crossing are located at the curb line 72.5 feet on either side of crossing. No distant signals.

Cars must not be left standing between the home signals unless coupled to another car or an engine which is standing outside of the home signals.

Cars or trains finding the home signals at "STOP," will stop clear of signal to permit it to change to "PROCEED" position when train on the Western Pacific has passed out of home signal limits.

CLOCK WORK TIME RELEASE

If no cause for signals being at "STOP" is seen, or if there is a train on the Western Pacific tracks standing outside of the home signals with no indication that it is to immediately proceed, operator must be sent ahead to operate a release located in a wooden box attached to the outside of signals governing reverse train movements, one release for each track. Box is provided with standard switch locks. Instructions for the operation of release are posted inside box. The instructions follow:

To operate clock work time release, turn knob to right about one-quarter (¼) turn; hold knob to right about two (2) seconds, and then let go of knob, allowing release mechanism to run down, which will require sixty (60) seconds at "C" Street and forty-five (45) seconds at "X" Street.

After release has run down, a red pilot light located inside of the release box should light up. This pilot light indicates home signals on intersecting tracks are in "STOP" position. Sacramento Northern signal should then change to "PROCEED."

The release must not be operated when Western Pacific trains or engines are between the home signals, or seen to be approaching.

In case the operation of the release does not clear the signal, the car or train will then proceed slowly to a point within fifteen (15) feet of the crossing, and, after stopping, operator must again proceed, on foot, to the center of the crossing, and, after making sure that no Western Pacific trains are approaching within the limits of the home signals, may then proceed over the crossing.

Speed of cars or trains over automatic interlocker must not exceed ten (10) miles per hour.

AUTOMATIC INTERLOCKER, SANKEY

Sankey automatic interlocking plant crossing the Western Pacific tracks is located one-half mile west of Sankey.

Interlocking limits on the W. P. track extend from home light signal 600 feet east of crossing to home light signal 600 feet west of crossing, and on S. N. Ry. track between home light signals located 600 feet on both sides of crossing.

The distant signals are located 3000 feet in advance of the home signals, and the preliminary circuits extend 3000 feet in advance of the distant signals.

The instructions governing the operation of signals and the movement of trains through the interlocking plant at Live Oak will apply at Sankey interlocker.

AUTOMATIC INTERLOCKER, LIVE OAK

Live Oak automatic interlocking plant crossing the Southern Pacific tracks is located one-half mile east of Live Oak.

Interlocking limits on the S. P. track extend from home light signal SA-1522, 517 feet east of crossing, to home light signal SA-1523, 523 feet east of crossing, and on S. N. Railway track between home light signals located 600 feet on both sides of crossing.

The westbound distant signal is located 3000 feet in advance of the home signal and the preliminary circuit begins at a point 4800 feet east of the home signal. The eastbound distant signal is located 1300 feet in advance of the home signal, and the preliminary circuit begins at a point 2500 feet west of the home signal.

Normal Indication of Interlocking Home Signals—"STOP":

When train approaches the crossing and enters approach circuit, the home and distant signals should change to "PROCEED."

Motormen operating single truck Birney cars, after receiving clear indication at home signal will bring the car to a stop not closer than 30 feet from the crossing. The Conductor will then close the Shunt Switch located in a box on the west side of the crossing. Closing this switch holds the signals on the intersecting track at stop. After the movement over the crossing has been made the Conductor will open the Shunt Switch and leave it open. The box must be left locked.

When home signal indicates "PROCEED" or "PROCEED WITH CAUTION" the speed of engine must not exceed thirty (30) miles per hour between the home signal and the crossing.

If no cause for signals being at "STOP" is seen or if there is a train on intersecting tracks standing outside of the home signals, with no indication that it is to immediately proceed, flagman must be sent ahead to operate a release located in box at the crossing. Box is provided with standard switch lock. Instructions for the operation of release will be posted inside box. The instructions follow:

CLOCK WORK TIME RELEASE

To Operate Clockwork Time Release:

(a) The release must not be operated when trains or engines are between the home signals or seen to be approaching on the intersecting tracks.

(b) To operate clockwork time release, turn knob to right to extreme position about one-quarter turn, then let go of knob and allow automatic release mechanism to run down, which will require four minutes. When knob is turned to extreme position and release mechanism has completed its operation, a red indicator light located near this clock release should light up immediately indicating that home signals on intersecting track are in "STOP" position. The home signal on S. N. Ry. should then change from "STOP" to "PROCEED WITH CAUTION."

Note: Where home signals are involved in automatic block signal territory, flagman, upon receiving a red indicator light, must lock box and proceed in accordance with automatic block system rules and where no automatic block signals are involved, flagman will remain at the crossing until train arrives.

In case indicator light fails to appear, the movement must be protected in each direction on the intersecting line.

(c) In case operation of release does not change the home signal indication from "STOP" to "PROCEED WITH CAUTION" after predetermined time has elapsed, a repeater red indicator light located at home signal should then light up, indicating that home signals on intersecting line are in "STOP" position.

JOINT TRACK MARYSVILLE

Sacramento Northern trains operate over Western Pacific track between Sacramento Northern connection with Western Pacific main track, located 356 feet east and 355 feet west of bridge 178.18, Yuba River, Marysville. Sacramento Northern freight trains operate over Western Pacific passing siding between the west switch and the switch leading to the Sacramento Northern track opposite the Western Pacific passenger station at Marysville. These tracks are designated as Joint Tracks.

AUTOMATIC INTERLOCKING Signals governing the Joint Track are located as follows:

THE WESTERN PACIFIC RAILROAD COMPANY

EASTWARD—Home Signal 789 feet west of bridge 178.18; Normal position stop.

Distant Signal 2,500 feet west of Home Signal; Normal position caution.

Home Signal 724 feet east of bridge 178.18; Normal position clear.

Distant Signal 789 feet west of bridge 178.18; Normal position caution.

WESTWARD—Home Signal east end of bridge 178.79; Normal position clear.

Home Signal 724 feet east of bridge 178.18; Normal position stop.

Eastward Signal located 789 feet west of bridge 178.18, will give clear indication when approaching train reaches a point within 3,500 feet from the signal, provided the block is clear, and will go to stop position when the forward wheels of an engine or car pass the signal.

Westward Signal located 724 feet east of bridge 178.18, will give a clear indication when approaching train reaches a point within 500 feet from the signal, provided the block is clear, and will go to stop position when the forward wheels of an engine or car pass the signal.

SWITCH INDICATORS are located as follows:

Switch west end of passing siding.

West end of main track switch leading to interchange tracks.

East end of main track switch leading to interchange tracks.

West end of cross-over leading from main track to passing siding.

Switch east end of High Line Track, located 1,400 feet west of Mile Post 180.

SACRAMENTO NORTHERN RAILWAY

EASTWARD—Home Signal 542 feet west of bridge 178.18, located at left of track; Normal position stop.

WESTWARD—Home Signal 525 feet east of bridge 178.18; Normal position stop.

Home Signals located 542 feet west of bridge 178.18, and 525 feet east of bridge 178.18, will go to clear position when the junction switch and derails are lined up for the Sacramento Northern track, provided the block is clear, and will go to stop position when the forward wheels of an engine or car pass the signal.

SWITCH INDICATORS are located as follows:

Main track junction switches east and west of Bridge 178.18.

All trains and engines must have a clear indication by switch indicator before throwing the switch to enter the W. P. main track.

No engine, car or train of the Western Pacific or Sacramento Northern shall be operated over the railroad crossing located 752 feet east of bridge 178.18 where the Western Pacific house track crosses the Sacramento Northern track, without being brought to a stop at the stop board and preceded over the crossing by a member of its crew who shall determine first that it is safe to proceed. The Stop Boards are located on each side of this crossing 100 feet from the crossing. Sacramento Northern trains and yard engines must approach this crossing with caution and not move onto or over the crossing until it shall be determined first that it is safe to proceed.

DERAILS: Derailing switches, pipe connected and operated with the main track switches are located as follows:

On Western Pacific passing siding 193 feet east of west switch.

On Sacramento Northern track 182 feet west of Junction Switch west of bridge 178.18 and 157 feet east of Junction Switch east of bridge 178.18.

Care must be used in the handling of switches which are pipe connected to the derails to avoid a derailment. Employe opening main track switch that is pipe connected to derails, must lock the switch open and it must remain locked until train has cleared derailing switch.

Motorman must not start his train until home signal clears and brakeman has crossed over track to opposite side of switch stand.

NORMAL POSITION OF SWITCHES—Junction switches must be locked for Western Pacific main track when not in use.

MOVEMENT OF TRAINS—Movement of trains over the Joint Track will be made in accordance with the indication of signals, regardless of right or class. All trains of both companies must approach and pass through the limits of the Joint Track with caution, not exceeding a speed of fifteen (15) miles per hour.

If no cause for signals being at stop is seen or if there is a train on W. P. track outside of home signals with no indication that it is to immediately proceed, be governed by Rule 663.

In using the Joint Track, freight trains should avoid delays to other trains of either company.

Note: WITH CAUTION, means—To run at restricted speed, according to conditions, prepared to stop short of a train, engine, car, misplaced switch or other obstruction, or before reaching a stop signal. Where circumstances require, train must be preceded by a flagman.

W. P.-S. P. crossing 9th Street, Marysville, interlocked. All movements over this crossing will be made in accordance with the rules in Western Pacific current time table.

The single track between Marysville and Yuba City is protected by Automatic Block Signals. Movement of Trains, Yard Engines, Deadhead equipment, and street cars will be made over this track in accordance with the indication of signals regardless of right or class.

The single track between 9th Street, Chico, and Mulberry is protected by block signals operated as follows: Light signals are installed on poles at 9th Street, 16th Street and at Mulberry, the color indications being yellow and red. The track between 9th Street and 16th Street is protected by one set of signals and the track between 16th St. and Mulberry is protected by another set of signals. When the blocks are not occupied the signals will indicate dark. Trains entering the block will receive a yellow signal and will be protected by a red signal on the opposite end. Only one train is permitted within the block limits at a time.

S. P. Crossing—Mikon. Interlocked. Home signals and derails 300 feet east and west of crossing. No distant signals.

S. P. Crossing—Woodland. Interlocked. Home signals and derails 300 feet east and west of crossing. No distant signals.

DRAWBRIDGE SIGNALS

Montezuma Slough Drawbridge has train stop arms. Home Signals located 659 feet east and 840 feet west indicate position of draw. Distant Signals 2119 feet east and 1740 feet west of Home Signals.

M STREET BRIDGE

Bridge Interlocking Signals and Derails:

Note: Directions used are those applicable to the Main Track to Oakland.

Signals and derails are located 413 feet east of Bridge on M Street, 285 feet east of Bridge on Front Street, and 350 feet west of Bridge. Back up derail is located in east bound track on M Street. The switch leading to the River Spur serves as a derail west of the Bridge.

The interlocking home signal at River Spur derailing switch is a three-unit signal; the upper signal governs movements to M Street, the middle signal governs movements to Front Street, and the lower signal governs movements to the River Spur.

Signal No. 2 located at the east end of the Bridge governing eastward movements is a three-indication light signal. Green indication governs movements to M Street. Yellow indication governs movements to Front Street. The red indication is a stop signal.

The switch at the east end of the Bridge is electrically operated from the tower.

Broderick Junction Interlocking Plant:

Interlocking home signals are located 163 feet east of Junction switch on Woodland Branch, 712 feet west of Junction Switch on main track, and 13 feet east of Junction Switch on main track. The interlocking home signal located 13 feet east of Junction Switch is a two-unit light signal. The upper signal governs movements to Oakland main track, and the lower signal governs movements to Woodland Branch. These interlocking signals are operated by remote control from the tower.

Dual Control Switch:

The dual control switch at Broderick Junction is operated by remote control from the tower and is so equipped that it may be operated by trainmen, when authorized to do so by the towerman. When trainmen are authorized by towerman to operate this dual control switch by hand, the selector lever must be kept in hand-throw position until all movements over the switch have been completed. All movements within the working limits must be made with caution and upon completion notify towerman.

Trainmen must notify motorman when the selector lever is in hand-throw position, and also notify him when it is returned to motor position, so he may know when to be governed by the interlocking signals governing movements over the switch.

The selector and hand-throw levers must not be forced. They will move easily when properly in mesh, although some manipulation of first one and then the other may be necessary to get them in proper mesh. If the switch was lined for Woodland Branch when dual control use was started it must be again lined for Woodland Branch before selector lever is restored to motor position.

Block Signal System:

The automatic block signal system on the First Subdivision begins and ends at the home block signal located 350 feet west of the M Street Bridge.

Switch Indicators:

The switches leading into the main track from Westside Spur and the drill track are protected by switch indicators. The switch leading from the River Spur to the main track is protected by light signals operated from the tower.

Movements of Trains and Yard Motors:

Movements through and between these two interlocking plants shall be made in accordance with signal indication. In case of signal failure at M Street Bridge Interlocking Plant, be governed by Rule 663 and failure at Broderick Junction Interlocking Plant, be governed by Rules 663 and 509.

Trains and yard motors must not exceed a speed of 15 miles per hour over the bridge and 10 miles per hour over the highway crossing west of the bridge.

Eastward trains and yard motors entering the main track from the drill track at east switch Westgate must have clear indication by switch indicator before opening the switch.

When the switch is opened an indicator light in the tower will light, indicating to the towerman that a train is approaching. When the interlocking home signal clears, train or yard motor may proceed.

When the interlocking home signal at east switch Westgate indicates "STOP" eastward trains of more than three cars on either the main track or drill track shall remain back of the County Road crossing until the signal clears.

Telephones:

Telephones are installed in the tower, at Interlocking Home Signal on M Street, Front Street, in the shelter house at Broderick Junction, and on a post half way between River Spur and Westside Spur for trainmen to communicate with the towerman. The telephones on Front Street and Broderick Junction have a double-throw switch to connect the phone on the dispatcher's line.

Whenever there is switching to be done on the River Spur or Westside Spur, which requires several movements from the main track to these spurs, or movements on the main track through or into the limits of the Interlocking Plant at Broderick Junction, the conductor shall communicate with the towerman and advise him so that there shall be no delay in the operation of signals or switches.

There is a signal box located on the interlocking home signal on Front Street which is operated by using a switch key. Operation of this signal box gives the towerman an indication in the tower that a train is on Front Street, and ready to move through the plant. This signal box is to be used when whistle signal cannot be heard.

Route Whistle Signals:

From M or Front Street to Oakland . . . . o

From M or Front Street to Woodland . . . . o ——— o

From M to Front or in reverse direction . . . . o o o o

From Oakland or Woodland to M Street. . . . . o

From Oakland or Woodland to Front Street. . . . . o o o

From Oakland or Woodland to River Spur . . . . o o

From River Spur to Main Track . . o o

From Oakland to Woodland or in reverse direction . . . . o o o o

From main track between interlocking plants to Oakland . . . . . o

From main track between interlocking plants to Woodland. . . o ——— o

Regular passenger trains leaving Sacramento will not sound the route whistle signals if the interlocking signals are clear, indicating that the route desired is lined.

Meridian Bridge. Interlocked. Home signals and derails 300 feet east and west of the bridge.

HOSPITALS

Chico	Enloe Hospital
Oroville	Oroville-Curran Hospital
Marysville	Rideout Hospital
Colusa	Pay ward at County Hospital
Sacramento	Sisters Hospital
Pittsburg	Pittsburg Emergency Hospital
Oakland	Providence Hospital
San Francisco	St. Joseph's Hospital
Suisun	Pay ward at County Hospital

FIRST AID STATIONS

(Supplied with First Aid Cabinets and Stretchers)

Oakland Baggage Room	Riverview
Eastport	Sacramento Baggage Room
Concord	East Nicolaus
Ferry Ramon	Vacaville Jct.
Drawbridge	Colusa Jct.
Dozier	Oroville Jct.

The following is a list of all Steam and Electric Railroad crossings and Junctions, protection provided for movements over them, and the name of the Railroad having prior right in the use of the crossing or Junction not protected by signals or flagman:

LOCATION	NAME OF RR.	PROTECTION	RESTRICTION	RIGHT
Oakland—40th & Shafter	Key System	Interlocking Signals	5 mi. per hr.	Governed by Signal
Oakland—College Ave.	Key System	Crossing Signals	Stop	S. N. Ry.
Las Juntas	S. P. Co.	No Signals	Stop	S. P. Co.
Clyde	B. P. & C. R. R.	No Signals	Stop	B. P. & C. R. R.
Shell Point				
Shell Chem. Co.	S. P. Co.	No Signals	Stop	S. N. Ry.
Sacramento:				
Front & "M" Sts.	S. P. Co.	Flagman	Stop	Governed by Flagman
7th & "M" Sts.	P. G. & E.	No Signals	5 mi. per hr.	S. N. Ry.
8th & "M" Sts.	C. C. T. Co.	Block Signals	5 mi. per hr.	Governed by Signal
8th & "K" Sts.	P. G. & E.	Traffic Signals	Trains—Yd. Motors DH Equip. 5 mi. per hr. / Street Cars—Stop	S. N. Ry. / P. G. & E.
8th & "J" Sts.	P. G. & E.	Traffic Signals	Trains—Yd. Motors DH Equip. 5 mi. per hr. / Street Cars—Stop	S. N. Ry. / P. G. & E.
Globe	W. P. R. R.	No Signals	Stop	W. P. R. R.
Sankey	W. P. R. R.	Automatic Interlocking Signals	30 mi. per hr.	Governed by Signal
Marysville—Joint Track	W. P. R. R.	Interlocking Signals	15 mi. per hr.	Governed by Signal
Marysville—House Track	W. P. R. R.	No Signals	5 mi. per hr.	S. N. Ry.
Yuba City	S. P. Co.	No Signals	Stop—Except when proceed signal is received from flagman	S. P. Co.
Live Oak	S. P. Co.	Automatic Interlocking Signals	30 mi. per hr.	Governed by Signal
Stirling Jct.	S. P. Co.	No Signals	Stop	S. P. Co.
PITTSBURG BRANCH				
Pittsburg	A. T. & S. F. R. R.	No Signals	Stop and Flag	A. T. & S. F. R. R.
SACRAMENTO BELT LINE				
Sacramento:				
Front St. N. to "Q" Inc.	S.P.Co.&W.P.R.R. Industrial Tracks	No Signals	Caution	S. P. Co. & W. P. R. R.
Front & "R" Sts.	S.P.Co. & W.P.R.R.	No Signals	Stop and Flag—Except when proceed signal is received from flagman.	S. P. Co. & W. P. R. R.
Front & "X" Sts.	C. C. T. Co.	No Signals	Caution	Caution
8th & "X" Sts. Jct. Joint Track	C. C. T. Co.	No Signals	Stop	C. C. T. Co.
10th & "X" Sts.	P. G. & E.	No Signals	5 mi. per hr.	S. N. Ry.
19th & "X" Sts.	W. P. R. R.	Automatic Interlocking Signals	10 mi. per hr.	Governed by Signal
21st & "X" Sts.	P. G. & E.	Arterial Stop Sign	Stop—5 mi. per hr.	S. N. Ry.
28th & "X" Sts.	P. G. & E.	No Signals	5 mi. per hr.	S. N. Ry.
Alhambra Blvd. & "X" St. Jct. Joint Track	C. C. T. Co.	No Signals	Stop	C. C. T. Co.
Alhambra Blvd. & "R" St.	S. P. Co.	No Signals	Stop and Flag—Except when proceed signal is received from flagman.	S. P. Co.
Alhambra Blvd. & "J" St.	P. G. & E.	No Signals	5 mi. per hr.	S. N. Ry.
19th & "C" Sts.	W. P. R. R.	Automatic Interlocking Signals	10 mi. per hr.	Governed by Signal
WOODLAND BRANCH				
Mikon	S. P. Co.	Interlocking Signals	20 mi. per hr.	Governed by Signal
Woodland	S. P. Co.	Interlocking Signals	10 mi. per hr.	Governed by Signal
OROVILLE YARD				
Swayne Lumber Co.	W. P. R. R.	No Signals	Stop	W. P. R. R.
CHICO YARD				
9th & Orange Sts.	S. P. Co.	No Signals	Stop and Flag	S. P. Co.
D. M. Yard, all crossings	D. M. Co.	No Signals	Stop	D. M. Co.

LOCOMOTIVE RATING IN TONS

Engine	Working Voltage	Sacramento Yard	Car Limit	Tons Per Operative Brake	Oakland to Temescal	Temescal to Havens	Havens to Concord	Concord to Las Juntas
402	600	300	Havens to Oakland	Havens to Oakland	—	—	—	—
403	600	300			—	—	—	—
404	600	300			—	—	—	—
405	600	300			—	—	—	—
410	600	700			—	—	—	—
420	600	700			—	—	—	—
430	600	600			—	—	—	—
440	600	425			—	—	—	—
441	600	630			—	—	—	—
442	600	600			—	—	—	—
601	600 / 1200	225	6	50	75	75	225	450
602	600 / 1200	225	6	50	75	75	225	450
603	600 / 1200	500	10	50	150	200	500	1000
604	600 / 1200	500	10	50	150	200	500	1000
605	600 / 1200	500	8	50	200	200	500	1000
606	600 / 1200	400	8	50	170	170	400	800
607	600 / 1200	225	6	50	75	75	225	450
650	600 / 1200	750	10	50	300	400	750	1650
651	600 / 1200	750	10	50	300	400	750	1650
652	600 / 1200	750	10	50	300	400	750	1650
653	600 / 1200	750	10	50	300	400	750	1650
654	600 / 1200	750	10	50	300	400	750	1650
660	600 / 1200	750	10	50	300	400	750	1650
661	600 / 1200	750	10	50	300	400	750	1650

Engine	Las Juntas to Havens	Concord and P. Chicago	P. Chicago and Sacramento	W. Pitts. to Pittsburg	Pittsburg to W. Pitts.	Riverview and Oxford	Front St. to Broderick	Creed and Cordero	Cordero and Vaca Jct.
402	—	—	—	—	—	—	—	—	—
403	—	—	—	—	—	—	—	—	—
404	—	—	—	—	—	—	—	—	—
405	—	—	—	—	—	—	—	—	—
410	—	—	—	—	—	—	—	—	—
420	—	—	—	—	—	—	—	—	—
430	—	—	—	—	—	—	—	—	—
440	—	—	—	—	—	—	—	—	—
441	—	—	—	—	—	—	—	—	—
442	—	—	—	—	—	—	—	—	—
601	150	150	450	225	150	450	150	450	225
602	150	150	450	225	150	450	150	450	225
603	340	340	1000	500	340	1000	340	1000	500
604	340	340	1000	500	340	1000	340	1000	500
605	340	340	1000	500	340	1000	340	1000	500
606	275	275	800	400	275	800	275	800	400
607	150	150	450	225	150	450	150	450	225
650	540	450	1650	750	480	1650	450	1650	750
651	540	450	1650	750	480	1650	450	1650	750
652	540	450	1650	750	480	1650	450	1650	750
653	540	450	1650	750	480	1650	450	1650	750
654	540	450	1650	750	480	1650	450	1650	750
660	540	450	1650	750	480	1650	450	1650	750
661	540	450	1650	750	480	1650	450	1650	750

Engine	Vacaville and Willotta	Sacramento to Chico	Chico to Yuba City	Yuba City to Alicia	Alicia to Sacramento	Summit to Oro. Jct.	Oro. Jct. to Oroville	Colusa Branch	Sycamore and Beet Spur
402	450	720	720	360	720	720	720	720	300
403	450	720	720	360	720	720	720	720	300
404	450	720	720	360	720	720	720	720	300
405	450	720	720	360	720	720	720	720	300
410	900	1400	1400	780	1400	1400	1400	1200	700
420	900	1400	1400	780	1400	1400	1400	1200	700
430	850	1300	1300	680	1300	1300	1300	1100	600
440	620	950	950	475	950	950	950	850	425
441	900	1365	1365	715	1365	1365	1365	1155	630
442	850	1300	1300	680	1300	1300	1300	1100	600
601	400	450	450	225	450	450	450	360	225
602	400	450	450	225	450	450	450	360	225
603	670	1000	1000	500	1000	1000	1000	800	500
604	670	1000	1000	500	1000	1000	1000	800	500
605	670	1000	1000	500	1000	1000	1000	800	500
606	540	800	800	400	800	800	800	640	400
607	400	—	—	—	—	—	—	—	—
650	1065	1650	1650	880	1650	1650	1650	1300	750
651	1065	1650	1650	880	1650	1650	1650	1300	750
652	1065	1650	1650	880	1650	1650	1650	1300	750
653	1065	1650	1650	880	1650	1650	1650	1300	750
654	1065	1650	1650	880	1650	1650	1650	1300	750
660	1065	1650	1650	880	1650	1650	1650	1300	750
661	1065	1650	1650	880	1650	1650	1650	1300	750

NOTE: Between Havens and Oakland Engines 603 & 604 coupled, and Engines 660 & 661 coupled, car limit 20 cars. Engines 601 & 602 or 607 coupled, car limit 12 cars.

YARD LIMITS DEFINED BY YARD LIMIT SIGNS

Oakland	South Yuba	
Walnut Creek	Marysville	
Concord	Yuba City	} Marysville Yard
Port Chicago	Paloro	
	Harter	
Pittsburg		
West Pittsburg	} Pittsburg Yard	Colusa Jct.
Mallard		Colusa } Colusa Yard
		Arbee
Chipps	Live Oak	
Creed	East Gridley	
Riverview	Oroville Jct.	
Woodland	Oroville	} Oroville Yard
	Marysville Road	
Westgate	Stirling Jct.	
Broderick	Mulberry	} Chico Yard
Sacramento	} Sacramento Yard Chico	
Haggin		
Globe		
N. Sacramento		

STOCK CORRALS

Moraga	Molena	Olcott
Concord	Garfield	Vale
Dutton	Rio Vista Jct.	Bunker
Montezuma	Saxon	Libfarm
Cordero		
Woodland	Meridian	Durham
Sankey	Colusa	Chico
Arboga	Sutter	Shippee
Sycamore	Peethill	Swanston

SIDE AND OVERHEAD OBSTRUCTIONS

(Not Standard Clearance)

Tunnel No. 1—Side and overhead. Protected by Signal Bell Tell Tale.
Walnut Creek—Field track—warehouse—sides.
Meinert—Pole. Stewart Spur—Side.
Concord—Hay Warehouse side and overhead.
Clyde—Building—side.
Ferry Ramon—End towers outside tracks—side and overhead.
General—All loading platforms—side.
Chico—Chico Vecino, Trees, side.
Crane Spur—Marysville Road.
All Stock Corrals—side.
Marysville—Westn. Sts. Groc. Co. Warehouse, side and overhead.
" Sand Bunkers Yuba River—side.
Haggin—Sand Bunkers.
Sacramento—Subway, side and overhead.
" Tracks serving Freight House, 2nd and M Sts.—Side (when cars are standing on tracks which are adjacent.)
Woodland—West Valley Lumber Spur, side.
Trainmen will at all times look out for low hanging trolley and span wires.

SPURS AND COMMERCIAL TRACKS

Stations	Distance from San Francisco	Capacity in Freight Cars
Greenspot	43.54	2
Peethill	93.90	15
Swanston	99.06	9
Pearson	131.44	38
Reed	132.15	26

INTERCHANGE TRACKS

Oakland —Key System.—40th and Shafter.
Las Juntas —S. P. R. R.
Clyde —B. P. & C. R. R.
Port Chicago—A. T. & S. Fe R. R.
McAvoy —S. P. R. R.
Sacramento —W. P. R. R., Haggin, and 19th & X Streets.
S. P. R. R., B Street, and Front & X Streets.
C. C. T. Co., Front & X Streets.
Chico —S. P. R. R., 9th & Orange Streets.
Oroville —W. P. R. R.
Marysville —W. P. R. R.
S. P. R. R.

SPEED TABLE

Time per Mile	Miles per Hour	Time per Mile	Miles per Hour
0 min. 50 sec.	72.00	1 min. 26 sec.	41.86
0 " 51 "	70.56	1 " 27 "	41.38
0 " 52 "	69.24	1 " 28 "	40.91
0 " 53 "	67.92	1 " 29 "	40.45
0 " 54 "	66.60	1 " 30 "	40.00
0 " 55 "	65.40	1 " 31 "	39.56
0 " 56 "	64.20	1 " 32 "	39.13
0 " 57 "	63.12	1 " 33 "	38.71
0 " 58 "	62.04	1 " 34 "	38.30
0 " 59 "	60.96	1 " 35 "	37.89
1 " 0 "	60.00	1 " 36 "	37.50
1 " 1 "	59.02	1 " 37 "	37.11
1 " 2 "	58.06	1 " 38 "	36.73
1 " 3 "	57.14	1 " 39 "	36.36
1 " 4 "	56.25	1 " 40 "	36.00
1 " 5 "	55.38	1 " 41 "	35.64
1 " 6 "	54.55	1 " 42 "	35.29
1 " 7 "	53.73	1 " 43 "	34.95
1 " 8 "	52.94	1 " 44 "	34.62
1 " 9 "	52.17	1 " 45 "	34.29
1 " 10 "	51.43	1 " 46 "	33.96
1 " 11 "	50.70	1 " 47 "	33.64
1 " 12 "	50.00	1 " 48 "	33.33
1 " 13 "	49.31	1 " 49 "	33.03
1 " 14 "	48.65	1 " 50 "	32.73
1 " 15 "	48.00	1 " 51 "	32.43
1 " 16 "	47.37	1 " 52 "	32.14
1 " 17 "	46.75	1 " 53 "	31.86
1 " 18 "	46.15	1 " 54 "	31.58
1 " 19 "	45.57	1 " 55 "	31.30
1 " 20 "	45.00	1 " 56 "	31.03
1 " 21 "	44.44	1 " 57 "	30.77
1 " 22 "	43.90	1 " 58 "	30.51
1 " 23 "	43.37	1 " 59 "	30.25
1 " 24 "	42.86	2 " 0 "	30.00
1 " 25 "	42.35		

Map of Sacramento Northern Railway and Connections

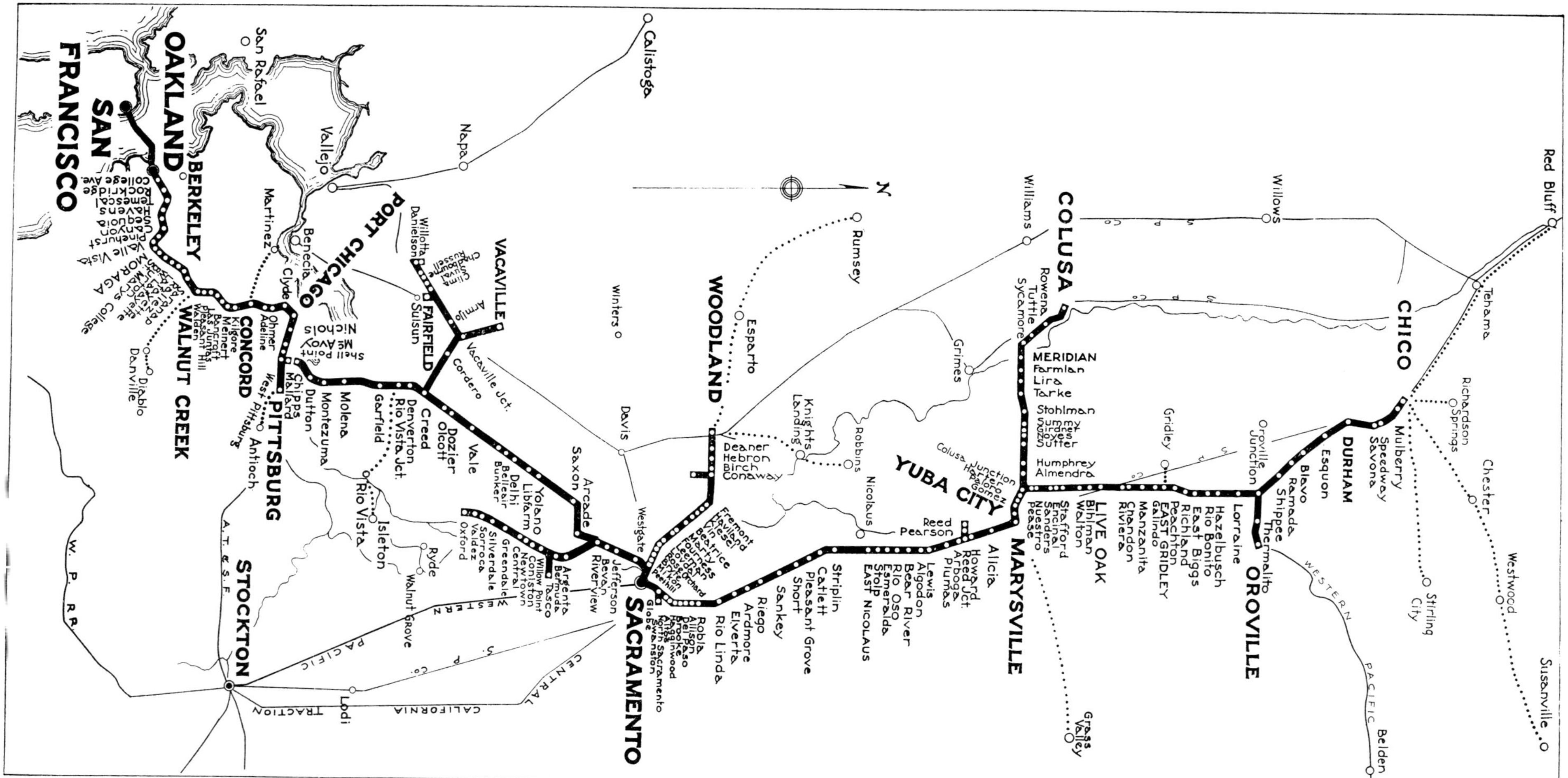

RAILROAD SURGEONS

DR. D. H. MOULTON, Chief Surgeon	Chico
DR. N. T. ENLOE, Consultant, Assistant Surgeon	Chico
DR. P. L. HAMILTON, Assistant Surgeon	Chico
DR. I. O. CHIAPELLA, Eye, Ear, Nose and Throat	Chico
DR. V. E. GREER, Assistant Surgeon	Chico
DR. EUGENE KILGORE, Consultant	San Francisco
DR. ALSON R. KILGORE, Consultant	San Francisco
DR. C. E. SMITH, Consultant	San Francisco
DR. E. GIBSON, Consultant	San Francisco
DR. E. C. BULL, Consultant	San Francisco
DR. EDWARD FLEMMING, Consultant	San Francisco
DR. V. B. PALAMOUNTAIN, Assistant Surgeon	Oakland
DR. L. C. LAWSON, Assistant Surgeon	Oakland
DR. ALBERT BOLES, Assistant Surgeon, Eye, Ear, Nose and Throat	Oakland
DR. EDWARD B. RADFORD, Assistant Surgeon	Walnut Creek
DR. ARTHUR H. BEEDE, Assistant Surgeon	Walnut Creek
DR. H. W. STIREWALT, Assistant Surgeon	Concord
DR. E. B. TODD, Consultant, Eye, Ear, Nose and Throat	Concord
DR. H. D. NEUFELD, Assistant Surgeon	Concord
DR. H. B. FLANDERS, Assistant Surgeon	Port Chicago
DR. L. C. GREGORY, Assistant Surgeon	Pittsburg
DR. DAVID C. WISE, Assistant Surgeon	Pittsburg
DR. M. P. STANSBURY, Assistant Surgeon	Vacaville
DR. A. P. FINAN, Assistant Surgeon	Suisun
DR. C. H. McDONNELL, Assistant Surgeon	Sacramento
DR. BERT S. THOMAS, Assistant Surgeon	Sacramento
DR. MAX C. ISOARD, Assistant Surgeon	Sacramento
DR. GUSTAVE WILSON, Assistant Surgeon	Sacramento
DR. G. A. SPENCER, Consultant, Eye, Ear, Nose and Throat	Sacramento
DR. MICHAEL J. LIPP, Assistant Surgeon	Sacramento
DR. HARRY H. BEAUCHAMP, Assistant Surgeon	Sacramento
DR. JOHN L. FANNING, Consultant, Skin Diseases	Sacramento
DR. FRED FAIRCHILD, Assistant Surgeon	Woodland
DR. W. J. BLEVINS, Assistant Surgeon	Woodland
DR. W. J. BLEVINS, Jr., Assistant Surgeon	Woodland
DR. HOMER WOOLSEY, Assistant Surgeon	Woodland
DR. JOHN SCOTT, Assistant Surgeon	Colusa
DR. E. V. JACOBS, Assistant Surgeon	Meridian
DR. W. L. STEPHENS, Assistant Surgeon	Meridian
DR. G. W. STRATTON, Consultant	Marysville
DR. WM. L. CRUTCHETT, Assistant Surgeon	Marysville
DR. E. E. GRAY, Assistant Surgeon	Marysville
DR. PHILLIP B. HOFFMAN, Assistant Surgeon	Marysville
DR. STANLEY R. PARKINSON, Assistant Surgeon	Marysville
DR. F. B. LAWTON, Assistant Surgeon	Marysville
DR. B. F. MILLER, Assistant Surgeon	Marysville
DR. E. A. KUSEL, Assistant Surgeon	Yuba City
DR. F. M. WHITING, Assistant Surgeon	Oroville
DR. G. A. FROST, Assistant Surgeon	Oroville
DR. I. W. HIGGINS, Assistant Surgeon	Oroville
DR. J. D. COULTER, Assistant Surgeon	Live Oak
DR. W. B. McKNIGHT, Assistant Surgeon	Portola
DR. JOHN W. MOORE, Assistant Surgeon	Portola
	Quincy

WATCH INSPECTORS

S. A. POPE, Manager of Time Service, San Francisco

J. R. CHILDRESS	Oakland
A. C. GRIFFIN	Walnut Creek
H. A. MINASIAN	Pittsburg
H. T. HARGER	Sacramento
T. B. MONK	Sacramento

JAS. R. DUPEN..........Chico
O. D. PAYNE..........Woodland
J. D. POOLE..........Marysville
R. A. WILLIAMS..........Oroville
J. A. McMILLAN..........Colusa
C. J. WIENER..........Fairfield

TRAIN DISPATCHERS

G. A. Rogers   T. C. Morebeck   W. M. Bugbey

Relief Dispatcher: J. E. Chapman

Chief Dispatcher: H. J. Prickett

TRAINMASTER

W. R. PARKS..........Sacramento

SUPT. BRIDGE RAILWAY

F. E. SULLIVAN..........San Francisco

Chapter 16

The Great Bridge

On January 15, 1939 the Sacramento Northern began operating its passenger trains over the Bay Bridge to San Francisco. This new service came at the same time that the SP "Red Trains" and the Key System abandoned their ferry service and rerouted their trains over the span.

For the first time, Sacramento, the capital of California, was directly linked by rail with San Francisco---but it was a link not long destined to endure. An agreement was entered into between the Key System and SP in March 1936 with the State Toll Bridge Authority for the use of the rails to be built on the lower deck of the Bay Bridge. An important part of this agreement was that ferry service would be abandoned when bridge service began. SN was a tenant road on the Key system subject to the latter's rules and regulations, so SN was bound to concur in any Key agreement.

Construction of the transit facilities on the bridge and its approaches cost $18 millions. This included the tracks, the yards, the coded cab signals, the San Francisco terminal, interlocking plants, substations, trolley wire and third rail. The state constructed at First & Mission Sts., San Francisco, a 3-level interurban-streetcar-motor coach depot; the structure is in use today by buses of the Alameda-Contra Costa Transit District, Greyhound, and San Francisco Municipal Railway's cars and buses.

SN installed coded cab signals and automatic speed control equipment on its First Subdivision motor cars. The cost of equipping the cars was $80,690. The Authority paid the bill, receiving in return title to five of the cars.

Of the 32 miles of track constructed, 20 were main line and 12 were for setout and storage. Two impressive yards were built on the fill opposite the auto toll gates on the Oakland end. SN occupied the 600-volt Key System yards where it had a small building and inspection pit. The 1200-volt SP cars used the west yards.

Three substations were built or acquired; the old Key mole substation (built in 1926) was enlarged with 1200 volt equipment added and it served the eastern end of the bridge and its approaches; new substations were constructed at Yerba Buena Island and at Rincon Hill in San Francisco.

Key's 600 volt DC articulated units drew their power on the bridge from a third rail; the 1200 volt SP and SN trains used pantagraphs and overhead trolley for current collection.

SN's trains normally used 1500 volts on their main line and changed over to 600 volts at 40th & Shafter for operation on Key System to the pier. But with the sophisticated automatic pantagraph-third rail changeover system used on Key's bridge units, the Northern Electric-style third rail shoes used by SN had to be removed for bridge operation. So the SN trains ran on half voltage from 40th & Shafter to West Junction, located between Bridge Yard Tower and Mole Substation. Here SN came under 1200 volt wire and Key changed to third rail.

On December 21, 1936 workmen began demolishing buildings in San Francisco for the transit terminal. On November 29, 1937 the first tie was put in place on Span E-22 on the bridge. Workmen began erecting the steel girders for the elevated loop in San Francisco on January 12, 1938. The first spike was driven at Span E-22 on February 1, 1938, and on September 23 of that year a Key System test train, drawing 600 volts from the overhead trolley wire, ventured westbound out on the bridge as far as span W-1. On December 14, 1938, the first Key test train ran from Oakland through to the bridge terminal in San Francisco, using a pantagraph.

Three days later the trolley voltage was upped to 1200 and the first SP test train rumbled into San Francisco. First SN test train, car 1015, ran across the bridge to the terminal on December 20, 1938.

The 600 volt third rail was energized on January 5, 1939 and night tests over the bridge were conducted to familiarize the train crews until regular service commenced on January 15th.

On January 14, 1939 two seven-unit Key trains ran from downtown Oakland to the San Francisco terminal to formally dedicate the new transit facilities. SN ran a six-car special from Chico to the ceremonies; this was headed by car 1011 with car "Moraga" on the rear. SP did not provide a special train.

This first trip, sounding the death-knell to the train-ferry system, was described by the San Francisco "Examiner" reporter as follows:

"Shiny new signal lights flashed from red to green and two 14-car streamliners of orange and silver roared across San Francisco Bay and into the huge new Union Terminal at First and Mission Streets.

"These inaugural trains symbolized San Francisco's dream of decades---an uninterrupted rail link with the East Bay and the East---a pathway of rails and ties high above the bay by the San Francisco-Oakland Bay Bridge."

The Oakland "Tribune's" correspondent had this to say:

"Three blasts of steam from the whistle of a squat bay ferry rose toward the Bay Bridge yesterday, where a long yellow electric train wound its way to San Francisco and marked the end of one era of transportation and the start of a new.

"It was the greeting of the commuter ferry, the nautical hello to the first passenger train over the bridge. And it

The San Francisco-Oakland Bay Bridge links Oakland (upper right) and San Francisco via Yerba Buena Island. Total length of the bridge is 8.25 miles, of which 4.5 miles is over water. Its width is 66 feet, and its total cost was $77,200,000 back between 1933 and 1936 when it was built. Its longest single span is 2,310 feet, and its towers vary in height from 474 to 519 feet. Its piers are embedded to a depth (average) of 235 feet. 200,000 tons of steel were used, plus 18,500 tons of cable wire, one million cubic yards of concrete, 200,000 gallons of paint. Its giant cables are 28.75 inches in diameter and exert a pull at anchorages of 80,000,000 pounds. The San Francisco Terminal is at lower left, and the elevated loop can be seen clearly The old Key Pier is at upper center. (Magna)

Before & After:

    Above, SN train on the old Key System Pier with the Bay Bridge looming ominously in background. (AA-BB)

    Below: The bridge has swallowed up interurban trains and the old Key Pier faces demolition after a few more days of service carrying visitors to the Exposition. The train shown here is the opening day inaugural train from Chico, January 14th, 1939. (AA-BB)

was answered by three blasts from the train, the message of farewell."

While the "Tribune's" reporter meant the train was orange---not yellow---the impact of the bridge rails is evident in his account, and in that of the "Examiner's."

SN's first revenue train clicked across the bridge from Concord at 7:46 AM on January 15, 1939. The first train into San Francisco from Sacramento was train No. 1. The first northbound train to leave the San Francisco terminal was "The Comet" which pulled out at 8:03-3/4 AM.

The first employees' timetable issued by SN for bridge operation, dated January 15m 1939 carded some of the trains to depart from San Francisco at the half and three-quarters minute. Similar fractionated schedules plagued Key and SP. So unsuccessful was this timetable that it was replaced on April 23, 1939. The new timetable mercifully dispensed with 1/2 and 3/4 minute departure times.

Certain SN trains originated at Bridge Yards on the mole between January 15 and April 23. These were deadhead equipment moves which operated as "deadhead movements" to San Francisco to become regular trains. They carried the letters "DH" as prefixes to the train number they were to assume when they reached San Francisco. This practice ceased on April 23, 1939.

Trains of the three interurban companies were governed by the automatic train control system. Cab signals prevented a motorman's getting lost in the dense fog which was so often a menace to ferryboat skippers.

The Superintendent of the Bridge Railway was in charge of all trains. F. E. Sullivan, who was trainmaster of the SP system, was the Bridge Railway's first superintendent, but he died within sixty days of the beginning of service. Paul Stapp then became superintendent.

Ten minutes were saved over the ferry service by the bridge rails---if slow Key System trains didn't get in the way. The SN motors were easily the fastest cars to use the bridge rails.

Despite the time saving, the Bridge Railway failed to halt the declining passenger business of the SN, which gave up in mid-1941 along with SP's red trains. Thus Key was in possession of a monopoly of the Bridge Railway. The five ex-SN cars purchased by Key operated over the bridge from 1943 to 1949 and were the only non-standard Key System passenger equipment to run over the bridge after 1941.

Key System abandoned rail service over the bridge on April 20, 1958 at 3:30 AM. Since then, the San Francisco terminal has been paved for buses and the track area on the bridge has been repaved as part of the reconstruction of the span to "freeway standards."

If ever there are transbay trains again, they will run in the tube proposed by the Bay Area Rapid Transit District--- far in the future, if at all.

TO OUR PATRONS:

Due to a re-arrangement of tracks and equipment necessary in order to prepare for operation of trains direct into San Francisco over the Bridge, trains of the Sacramento Northern will not be able to operate, commencing August 21, for a period of approximately three weeks, between 40th and Shafter Streets, Oakland, and the Key System Pier.

In order not to cause any unnecessary delays or inconvenience to our passengers, arrangements have been completed for the operation of special Key System trains between the two above-mentioned points, making a direct connection with our trains at 40th and Shafter.

It is contemplated that our trains will again be operating direct to the Key System Pier about September 10, and, upon opening of the rail service over the Bridge, will operate direct into the new terminal now being constructed at First and Mission Streets, San Francisco.

SACRAMENTO NORTHERN RAILWAY

In 1938, SN was not as fast as Key in equipping its motor cars with automatic train stop equipment and cab signals, so it was necessary to use a shuttle train between 40th & Shafter and the Key Pier. Photos on this page show this unusual operation.

At the left is reproduced the card distributed to SN patrons advising them of of this change.

(Right) Key Unit 187 waits at the Pier for SN passengers. Note the disc signs telling all it is a "Sacramento Northern Train."

(Below) Key unit 127 transfers passengers to "The Comet" at 40th & Shafter.

(Both, WCW)

The first official SN train to operate over the Bay Bridge is shown here midway on the structure on the opening day, January 14, 1939. This train originated at Chico and picked up invited city and company officials and other guests along the line---arriving in San Francisco in late morning in time to participate in the opening ceremonies of the Terminal at noon. This train operated as Extra 1011 and consisted in order of 1011, 1021, 1018, 1023, 1020 and "Moraga." (VS)

Below, this same train is seen as it pulled into San Francisco on Track 6; note new Key unit at left. (ECH)

Twins 603 and 604 as helpers on Train No. 293, May 16, 1940. The freight is on the main line
near Havens. (AA-AH)

In April of 1951 "turn around" freight operation was the order of the day; locomotives did not
cross on the ferry to save room for an extra car; the motors then returned to their respective
terminals with the train received from the opposite shore. Motor 670 was the former Tidewater Southern No. 106, purchased by SN when TS dieselized.   (VS)

Chapter 17

Freight Operation

I --- THE SOUTH END

The promoters of the OA&E originally expected to confine the traffic of their railway to passenger business, but as soon as the line opened (1913) they quickly realized that a lucrative freight business was theirs for the taking. Tapping rich farm and orchard lands in the Moraga, Ignacio, and Sacramento Valleys which were noted for their excellent fruits, walnuts, vegetables and dairy products, the new electric railway was provided with a splendid opportunity to provide rapid, efficient and dependable freight service.

The OA&E therefore quickly established a Freight Traffic & Information Bureau under the management of Mr. L. H. Rodebaugh, who was assisted by soliciting agents in local areas and in the Sacramento Valley. Interchange agreements were reached with the three transcontinental steam railroads: Southern Pacific, Santa Fe and Western Pacific, and freight was also interchanged with the three connecting interurban companies: Northern Electric, Central California Traction, and the Key Route.

OA&E's Information Bureau made it easy for prospective farmers, settlers and industrialists to locate sites conducive to successful businesses, farms and homes in its serviced areas.

With the construction of warehouses of considerable size, a very lucrative freight business in the Sacramento Valley developed; instead of the farmers' shipping by river boats and barges down the Sacramento River, they routed their shipments by rail.

Vast new acreages were planted in the Moraga, Burton, Walnut Creek, Danville and Concord areas. Pears, grapes and dried fruits were harvested. Walnuts became a major industry in the Walnut Creek section, and in the Sacramento Valley large acreages of Asparagus and celery were planted in Solano and Sacramento counties and especially in the rich Holland district.

Cattle proved to be a substantial source of freight revenue in the lower Sacramento Valley. In Contra Costa County between Bay Point and Pittsburg several large industrial firms were served despite the immediate presence of two transcontinental steam railroads.

As time progressed, OA&E improved its freight service. From the one overnight train first carded, service was expanded to include both local and expedited freight trains. A fast through freight known as "The Cannon Ball" was established , operating between Oakland and Sacramento; departing from Sacramento at 6:00 PM, it arrived at Oakland at 3:00 AM the following morning, in ample time

for delivery to produce areas and warehouses. Motors 101 and 102 were used in this service.

A local service was also operated which conducted all of the switching along the main line. This was a turn-around operation: one train originated at Oakland and ran to Bay Point, picking up and setting out en route. The other train ran out of Sacramento and operated to Bay Point, also doing local switching. In conjunction with the Cannon Ball, which picked up all the through cars destined for off-line locations and which also collected cars accumulated by the locals along the line at Bay Point, OA&E offered its shippers a truly fast freight service.

Transfer with the Southern Pacific was made at Mc Avoy and Las Juntas, and with the Santa Fe at Bay Point; interchange with the Western Pacific took place in Sacramento.

With this stepped up service, all four of the Baldwin-Westinghouse locomotives were being utilized: 103 and 104 were assigned to the local run between Oakland and Bay Point where their multiple-unit controls enabled them to handle the grades, 105 was used between Sacramento and Bay Point, and 106 was used on the Red Ball. This is another reason why 105 and 106 were not used in passenger service after 1913.

Service was not operated on the Cannon Ball eastbound or westbound on Saturday evenings, which made the heavy locomotives available for special passengers trains on Sundays during the picnic season in Redwood Canyon. Local freight service between Oakland and Bay Point was operated on Saturday evenings with 103 and 104, returning to Oakland during the night hours.

OA&E owned and operated its own quarry at Valle Vista where it produced all of its ballast; it also sold rock products to construction companies, thus providing additional revenue.

The Key Route (San Francisco-Oakland Terminal Railways) through its freight department in Oakland interchanged freight with OA&E at 40th & Shafter. Its electric locomotives would trundle up 40th in the early mornings to connect with the Cannon Ball when it arrived, then taking their cars down to their freight terminal or transferring them to the Santa Fe or SP through their interchange tracks.

OA&E very possibly could have utilized additional freight power, but its finances did not permit such an expenditure. Northern Electric, on the other hand, had more capital available and purchased and built a sizeable fleet of freight locomotives.

When the consolidation took place on the last day of

Right: Pride of NE and its heaviest freight power for years was combination locomotive-express car 1010, shown here at Chico Shops when brand new.   (VS)

Center: Motor 1030 and train on Sacramento Terminal trackage at the junction of SN and CCT, 31st (now Alhambra Blvd.) & X Sts., about 1920.   The CCT carbarn is seen at extreme right.   (VS)

Below: NE's Sacramento Freight Station stood at Second & M Sts. and is seen here about 1915 with a 1002 Class motor at right.   This station was knocked down by a runaway freight car in 1917.
(LLS)

1928 both the SN and the SF-S were able to pool their locomotives, as most were equipped for 600/1200 volt operation.
In the case of the SN, this would be its 650 and 660 Classes.
However, SF-S's 103-106 engines were never equipped with
third rail shoes and thus never got north of Sacramento. It
was necessary to haul them dead in freight trains whenever
they needed shopping at Chico.

Even after the consolidation, through freights were
not operated between Oakland and Chico; all trains were
broken up at Sacramento. This was standard practice right
up to the end of operation out of Oakland.

<u>II --- THE NORTH END</u>

Most electric railways depended upon their freight
revenues to offset losses incurred by their passenger trains.
Such was not the case on Northern Electric. From its opening day (April 25, 1906) until the end of 1918, its passenger
revenues exceeded monies obtained from freight; however,
1918's figures showed freight to be responsible for 52% of all
revenue.

Unlike the men who brought the OA&E into being,
NE's promoters realized freight business to be an important
source of revenue and were eager to do all possible to establish and maintain such a business. They had already built
a motor flat for construction service, No. 701 ("Old Maude")
and when construction days were slow, she was able to haul
freight cars in limited number due to her light weight and
small motors.

Immediately NE set about constructing in Mulberry
Shops two large steel locomotives of the steeple cab type,
modeled after Pacific Electric's famous 1600. The bodies
were constructed at the Diamond Match plant in Chico and
electrical equipment was installed at the shops. They were
numbered 1000 and 1001 and were the heaviest rolling stock
on the roster until the advent of engine 1010 in 1910. Other
wooden bodied motors were built---1002, 1003, 1004, and
1005---but these were wooden cabs on flat cars, suitable
for light operation only, having the same 90 hp. motors
as NE's interurban cars, although geared down.

Officials and the Engineering Department considered
this freight motive power to be inadequate and unsuited for
the type of service they desired to operate. They explored
the idea of purchasing locomotives from major manufacturers
but found costs to be prohibitive, so they undertook the construction of heavy steel electric locomotives in the shops at
Mulberry (Chico). Their efforts were successful, as judged
by the two fine locomotives they turned out: 1010, built in
1910, and 1020 in 1915. There was to have been a twin to
1010 which was a combination locomotive and express car,
but it was decided to abandon the idea of a combination express motor and locomotive and 1010 was later cut down to
locomotive size. Then followed locomotives 1030, 1040,
1041 and 1042, all purchased new by the Sacramento Northern Railroad. In addition to these high capacity engines,
which appeared at a most fortuitous time since length of SN
freight trains was steadily increasing, locomotives of the
650 Class were added to the fleet.

On the Sacramento Northern Railroad freight traffic
movements consisted of two heavy freight trains daily north
from Sacramento to Chico and Oroville, and two heavy
trains south from Chico-Oroville to Sacramento. These
trains usually ran from 1,000 to 1,200 tons and required the
heavier type of motive power; 1020 and 1030 were used in
this service.

In addition, one freight motor was kept busy on the
Colusa Branch and another on the Woodland Branch. Small
wooden body motor 701 was employed on the isolated Vaca-
ville-Suisun-Fairfield-Willota Branch in the Suisun Valley
where freight business moved only a few months of the year
when orchard products were being moved.

Two locomotives and at times three were assigned to

(Below) Unusual switching move is shown in this 1937
photo. The scene is N St., Sacramento, between 2nd
and Front Streets, and the stars are SN 650 and Central
California Traction's box motor 6. Probable reason:
No. 6 was in the way of a desired switching movement
so it was shunted onto an adjacent track. (AA-AH)

the Sacramento Yard and Belt Line, switching cars to various industries. This Belt Line encircled the business district and served many industries including the river carriers along the waterfront. The Sacramento Yard, named "Haggin Yard," was located adjacent to the main line between the Southern Pacific underpass and the American River bridge; it contained about ten miles of trackage and between 150 and 200 cars were switched daily in the early Twenties. Freight for Chico and points north were made up in this yard, and interchange with the Western Pacific was made at this point also.

Another yard was located at Front & X Sts. where trains were made up and broken down from the South End; cars were also switched from here to various industries, terminals and warehouses. Extensive switching to the Wharf and to the joint SN-CCT freight depot and team tracks at 2nd & M Sts. was conducted along Front Street.

The third yard in the Sacramento area was located across the Sacramento River at Westgate where trains for and from the South End were made up and broken down. It was also from Westgate that switching moves to the wharves on the west bank of the river were supervised.

Sacramento did not permit freight trains to be hauled through its downtown area, route of the passenger trains. So a belt line had to be constructed around the city center and it was a long, round about route indeed. When necessary to move a cut of cars around the belt line, freight crews had their own colorful descriptive term for it: "Going around Cape Horn." The belt line'sroute was from the riverfront via X St., Alhambra Blvd. (formerly 31st St.), and thence down C St. to 17th where a freight shed was located at D St. Locomotives were stored, inspected and serviced in this 17th & D St. yard, which contained three tracks and a pit.

Freight engines also tied up at the freight sheds at 2nd & M Sts. and on the tracks serving the freight depot on M St. Such was the case also of CCT locomotives and switch engines of SN.

On the Sacramento River Wharf freight interchange was conducted with The California Transportation Company which operated the river steamers and barges up and down the river. For switching the waterfront, locomotive 1040 was usually the assigned engine.

Freight was hauled at night when the bulk of the passenger trains was off the main line; an operating rule was that when a freight train went into a siding for a passenger train, the freight had to wait for five minutes after the departure of the passenger car before starting so that the passenger train would have ample voltage to get it up to speed and safely on its way.

A large part of the countryside tributary to NE north of Sacramento was planted to rice, beans, grain, barley and oats. Fruits and olives were also produced in quantity. In the Marysville and Oroville areas, there was much rock, sand and gravel freight.

Company owned warehouses were maintained and leased to store produce. On the west side of the Sacramento River between Broderick and West Sacramento a great many grain and rice warehouses were located, as well as rice milling plants.

Interchanges were numerous. In Sacramento, connection with the Southern Pacific was made at Front & X Sts.; with the Western Pacific at Front & R, 19th & X and at Haggin Yard; with CCT at X St. & Alhambra Blvd. In the pre-1929 days, OA&E freight was interchanged at West Sacramento and at 2nd & M Sts.   In Marysville NE-SN had connections with both SP and WP; in Chico with SP; in Fairfield-Suisun with SP; this was later changed to Cordeiro on the Willota-Vacaville Branch; at Woodland with SP; and in Colusa with SP.

NE-SN constructed warehouses along its lines at the following locations; Sankey, Live Oak and Esquon in 1916; Woodland, Colusa and Shippee in 1918; these were partly owned by community concerns. In Blava a company owned warehouse was constructed in 1918, also. Over in West Sacramento in 1917 and 1918; Durham in 1918; Tarke (Colusa Branch) in 1918 and this one was also owned in part by the local community.

What might have been a major improvement insofar as additional freight business was concerned was proposed in 1928 under Western Pacific ownership; this would have seen the old Vallejo & Northern idea come to life in a big way: the isolated Suisun-Vacaville Branch would have been extended to connect with the Petaluma & Santa Rosa Railroad entailing a line from Willotta over through Jamison Canyon and across the Napa Valley to Petaluma. This project did not occur, chiefly because the P&SR chose that particular time to sell out to SP.

III --- CONSOLIDATION

On June 9, 1929 freight service commenced on a major new branch: the Holland Branch, which left the main line of the South End at Riverview and extended down the riverbank to Oxford, with a spur to the beet plant at Clarksburg. SN Railroad entered into a trackage agreement with the SF-S between Westgate and Riverview; this agreement was made with the SN and WP jointly to the extent that SN leased the line to SF-S on a 6% cost basis, in return for which SF-S would assume a portion of the operating expenses. This method of operation never came to pass, for on December 31, 1928, the North and South Ends were merged into one railroad. To operate the new Holland Branch, two new Baldwin-Westinghouse steel steeple cab locomotives were purchased, numbers 1060 and 1061 (later 660 and 661); these were SN's heaviest electric locomotives. At first these motors operated on 600 volts between Oxford and Riverview, then 1200 volts into Westgate; Holland Branch voltage was stepped up to 1200 after the consolidation.

After consolidation, also, a physical connection was constructed between the South End main line at Creed and the hitherto isolated Suisun-Vacaville Branch. This link opened for service on July 15, 1930. Overhead catenary with 1200 volts was installed from Creed to Vacaville Jct., where third rail operation on 600 volts began. This made it mandatory to equip all 600-1200 volt engines with third rail shoes if they were to operate on this line; it worked out that South End locomotives 603-606 did not get the shoes, but South End box motors 601, 602 and 607 did.

With the coming of the depression of the early 1930s, business fell off badly all over the nation, and SN felt the effect along with all other roads. Freight service at that time consisted of one roundtrip daily between Oakland and Sacramento and between Sacramento and Chico.

When construction of the Broadway Lower Level Tunnel in the Contra Costa Hills near Lake Temescal took place in 1935, SN was given the business of hauling construction materials. Special sidings were installed at Temescal and extra trains shuttled back and forth to the Oakland Yards where they were interchanged with Key's Oakland Terminal Railroad. At the conclusion of this job, this extra hauling ended, and so did the two rock quarries at Valle Vista.

Hard roads and a multiplicity of trucks also affected SN's freight business drastically from the mid-Twenties on.

The outbreak of the Second World War stimulated SN freight business greatly, and the road prospered for a time. A heavy movement of war materials destined to the Oakland-San Francisco Army and Navy Bases moved over the main line from Sacramento where it was received from WP and given to the Oakland Terminal at 40th & Shafter. To meet the need for additional motive power, SN leased from CCT that company's GE steeple cab steel locomotive 106, similar to its own 650 Class. Diesels were also used, leased from WP. A WP steam locomotive was leased to operate on the Vacaville Branch one summer to handle the fruit shipments.

Business returned to normal at the end of World War II, and then gradually receded, not again turning upward until the outbreak of the trouble in Korea in 1950. Tonnages and trains then grew greatly, especially on the South End. Extras were numerous and it was often necessary to "double" trains over the sharp grades out of Oakland, with cuts placed on sidings at Temescal, Havens and Pinehurst. The direct connection with the Oakland Terminal Railroad proved most advantageous to both WP and Santa Fe, which then turned the cars over to the Army and Navy bases in the Oakland area.

Again business dropped with the termination of hostilities in Korea, and an average tonnage was hauled over the line. The steel business to the Columbia plant in Pittsburg held up well and today the SN still hauls heavy trains between the steel plant and Sacramento.

Then came a period of drastic changes in motive power. The North End converted to diesel operation in 1946 between Sacramento and Marysville. Operation on branches remained electrified, and the conversions occurred gradually. At first, diesels were leased from WP, but then SN began to purchase its own. The Woodland Branch was converted in 1947, followed by the Vacaville Branch. Next came the Colusa Branch, then the second part of the main line between Yuba City and the Chico city limits. Chico itself, including

AT LEFT, A SACRAMENTO NORTHERN LOCOMOTIVE IN SERVICE ON CENTRAL CALIFORNIA TRACTION. SN 651 HEADS A CCT FREIGHT NEAR COLONIAL ACRES ON SEPTEMBER 10, 1939. DURING THE HEAVY PART OF THE GRAPE SEASON CCT RENTED LOCOS FROM SN.   (AA-AH)

● Oakland-Sacramento freight on trestle near Arcade. This shows the reason for the trestle, as heavy winter runoff of Sacramento River floods the lowlands of the delta region. Motor 661 heads this train.   (Fred Fellow)

Mulberry Shops, remained electrified, as did Marysville-Yuba City within city limits. When Mulberry Shops were abandoned in 1951, trolley wire in Chico came down. On April 15, 1954 the Oroville switching operation was dieselized. Switching operations with electric power continued in and around Sacramento until November 28, 1953.

With the conversion of the entire North End to diesel operation (except Marysville-Yuba City), ample electric locomotives were available for the South End. The 650 Class, assisted by the 660 and 661 performed most of the work. The 605 and 606 served as helpers over the hill out of Oakland on the 4.6% grade. However, there were instances when diesel power was used to haul some of the extra long steel trains between Sacramento and Chipps. The heavier motive power and the longer trains were responsible for the collapse of the Arcade Trestle beneath the weight of one such train on July 24, 1951.

On July 1, 1953, electric operation was dieselized between Westgate and Riverview, including the Holland Line---and also on that part of the main line between the west end of the Arcade Trestle and Dutton. When the Arcade Trestle was rebuilt, electric overhead was not installed; hence diesel power took over all operations between Westgate and the ferry at Chipps.

This left the main line between Mallard and Oakland, including the Pittsburg Branch and the Columbia Steel Extension, operated by electric locomotives. At this time, locomotives 605 and 606 were tied up and used only in emergencies.

SN finally abandoned its electric freight operation between Oakland and West Lafayette on March 1, 1957 and the rails between these points were removed. A new connection in Oakland on Union St. permitted WP interchange with the Oakland Terminal.

Service between West Lafayette and Pittsburg was converted to diesel operation next, and remains today; all catenary was removed when the line was abandoned out of Oakland.

On August 10, 1958 the line between West Lafayette and Walnut Creek was abandoned, with a secondary highway being subsequently constructed over a part of the roadbed.

Other abandonments occurred as follows: The Woodland Branch was cut back from the former passenger depot at 2nd & Main Sts. to the Southern Pacific crossing on January 31, 1953; this leaves this branch operating just up to the SP main line to Portland. Then the main line between Haggin Yard and Globe was abandoned; at Haggin the SN today merges with WP and uses that railway's bridge to cross the American River---this taking place on March 26, 1954. The main line between East Nicolaus and Alicia was abandoned on October 15, 1958. That part of the main line between Oliver (Marysville) south to Alicia was abandoned on July 30, 1956. SN trains were given trackage rights on the paralleling WP main line, making these main line abandonments possible.

As of the date of writing (June 25, 1962) the following segments of the SN are being operated:

Walnut Creek to Pittsburg and Columbia Steel Extension.

Westgate to Montezuma.
Dozier to Vacaville and Willotta (Vacaville Branch)
Riverview to Oxford (Holland Branch)
Broderick to Woodland (Woodland Branch)
Globe to Swanston (Swanston Branch)
Globe to Sankey (main line)

Operation from Sankey north is by means of joint operation with WP over the latter company's main line as far as Marysville. SN rebuilt its former Reed Branch (always freight only) to connect with WP's main line at WP milepost 175.63, sometimes called "Cleveland." Instead of calling this the Reed Branch, however, it is now known as the Pearson Branch.

Marysville to Chico, including the Airport Extension northeast of Chico.
Colusa Jct. to Meridian (Colusa Branch)

Joint operation with WP between Sacramento and

Freight interchange between SN and Key System's
Oakland Terminal Railway took place at 40th &
Shafter. In the photo above, motor 1001 of Key
drops off boxcars and then either deadheads back
to Emeryville Yards or takes a cut of cars turned
over by SN to the same location. Two blocks of
SN main line and these yards on Shafter Ave.
were operated at 600 volts, permitting Key's use
of this facility. SN's wrecker may be seen coupled to caboose at extreme left. Photo taken in
the fall of 1941.

(VS)

At right, a westbound freight traverses Melin Cut,
between Havens and Montclair Stations, Oakland.
Locomotives 603 and 604 head this 1948 move.
In 1913 Melin Cut caved in, blocking the main
line, after a severe downpour.

(DLO)

Stockton and with Santa Fe between Stockton and Pittsburg
enable today's SN trains to reach Pittsburg from Sacramento.

At time of writing, negotiations are being considered
whereby SN will operate via trackage rights over the SP main
line between Vacaville ;Jct. and probably Mikon, permitting
abandonment of the main line from Riverview to Libfarm.

The above comprises the SN as of today. The freight
is moving, and SN still remains a progressive and important
factor in the economic life of the Sacramento Valley, as well
as being a highly important feeder for its parent, Western Pacific.

Diesel locomotives 301 and 302 are the largest locomotives owned today by Sacramento Northern.   Their color scheme follows that used by the parent Western Pacific: silver body, orange striping, black lettering.   These units are used on main line freights over Western Pacific and Santa Fe between Sacramento, Stockton and Pittsburg.   (Fred L. Hust)

Sacramento Northern's box cars of today are fully up to the standard of the railroad industry, as witness car 2458, below. Western Pacific is not hesitant about placing its own name on newer SN freight cars to derive certain publicity benefits therefrom.   (WP Photo)

Railroad Link Ends 44-Year Career

Oakland "Tribune"
March 1, 1957
TRB Collection

Last Run Made By Sacramento Northern Here

By JACK RYAN

The old Sacramento Northern Railway made the last run of its 44-year career from Oakland yesterday as the slanting rain beat a soft requiem on the venerable cars.

Only a handful of mourners were on hand to say goodbye too, as the train ground out of the ancient depot at 40th St. and Shafter Ave.

And as the train inched its way up Shafter, few passersby stopped to look. Most of them kept their heads bowed against the rain as though they were searching for a grave for the old equipment.

It was a quiet and disspirited Shafter Avenue office yesterday morning as yard crews and dispatchers went about the job of making up the last train out of Oakland. And as if they hated to part with their old friend, the 8:30 a.m. departure was put over until 11 a.m.

But it wasn't until 11:35 a.m. that Conductor Walter Butterfield, 59, reluctantly called "all board" and the two tiny electric engines began straining to move the nine cars.

FAREWELL TO SHAFTER

In the lead engine, Engineer Les Paul, 60, moved the controller ahead slowly and remarked: "Well, I guess the people on Shafter are having their prayers answered this morning."

In the engine at the rear, Engineer O. H. Schinder, 62, called out to a yard man. "Well goodbye Johnny. Don't get into any trouble in San Leandro."

The old train maintained its funeral pace up Shafter until it crossed College Avenue and then picked up a little speed.

In the cab of the lead engine with Paul, Butterfield chatted quietly with the brakeman, Charles Dowd, 51. The three men had worked together for a number of years.

"Well, I'll make $15.08 for this eight hours," Dowd said. "But it will be the saddest

money I ever got from this railroad."

Butterfield nodded.

STALLS ON GRADE

And as if the train had taken a cue from the men in the cab, it stopped on the steep grade between the old Rockridge and Temescal commuter stations.

The rain hal slickened the rails and the two engines couldn't move the load until four cars were uncoupled. They were shunted into a siding at the Temescal station and the rest of the cars were then brought up. It was only a 10 minute delay. Then it moved on again.

As the little train moved briskly over roadbed, past the ghosts of the former commuter stations of Thornhill, Havens, Canyon, Redwood, Pinehurst, Valle Vista, etc., scores of homeowners nearby the right-of-way turned out to wave goodbye to their old neighbor.

NEIGHBORLY TOUCH

"These people are genuinely sorry to see us go," Paul said, adding with a trace of bitterness in his voice: "Not like those on Shafter Avenue. It was the new people moving in on Shafter that caused the trouble."

The attitudes of the three men brightened even more when a long line of little children and their mothers lined the side of the tracks as the train moved out of the Shepherd Canyon Tunnel.

"Those kids are sure going to miss us," the brakeman observed. "They used to stop playing at school recesses when we'd pass by. Yup, they're sure going to miss us."

Trainmen explained that the heavy steel doors at the mouth of the timber-lined tunnel were installed to close off draft in case of fire. However, there is no record that they were ever used.

A dozen or so cars were parked on a bridge over the tracks as the train approached the Moraga Valley and more well-wishers were waving the train good luck.

FRIENDS TO LAST

"Yeah," said Butterfield, waving heartily from the open window of the cab, "they're all our friends and we're leaving them behind."

Then he turned to a newsman and said:

"Son. This won't be your last story like this. Railroading is dead and I predict you'll write the obituary of all of them."

It was the last run on the railroad between Oakland and West Lafayette. Service on the ine will be continued with diesel engines from there to Chico by

MOVEMENT ORDERS — Conductor Walter Butterfield hands orders for final freight run to Engineer Les Paul.

A steady rain falling from a slate gray sky sets an appropriate mood as SN 652 pulls the last SN train from Oakland to Lafayette on February 28, 1957. We see here the last train at Collego & Shafter. 653 was pusher locomotive.   (TRB)

(LEFT) DIESEL LOCOMOTIVE 201 IS A 1955 PRODUCT OF GENERAL ELECTRIC.   (WP)

The Sacramento Northern Railway of mid-1962 is a far cry indeed from the familiar system of yore. Now segmented into four parts, connected via trackage rights on adjoining major railroads, SN today functions as a feeder for its parent company, Western Pacific.

These main subdivisions and their respective branch lines are:

First Subdivision---East Pittsburg to Walnut Creek, 21.02 miles. Freight to and from this line operates via WP from Sacramento to Stockton and via the Santa Fe, Stockton to East Pittsburg.

Also: Sacramento to Vacaville, 41.24 miles via the old OA&E main line to Dozier and then to Vacaville; at time of going to press, this line is due for a major change in operation---trackage rights over SP from Canon (near Vacaville Jct.) to Sacramento are impending, which means that the OA&E main line from Libfarm to Riverview will be abandoned; this change has been indicated in the accompanying map.

Holland Branch: From Riverview to Oxford, 15.77 miles.

Willota Branch: From Vacaville Jct. to Willota, 9.42 miles.

Montezuma Branch: From Dozier to Montezuma, 14.57 miles.

One daily roundtrip is operated between Pittsburg and Walnut Creek, two between Vacaville and Westgate (Sacramento), two between Riverview and Oxford. Movements on the Willota and Montezuma Branches are not timecarded and train order authority is not required on them but all trains are operated at yard speed.

Second Subdivision: Sacramento to Yuba City, 41.02 miles. Trains originate at B St., Sacramento (junction with WP) and operate via joint track (WP-SN) to Globe, thence to Sankey where WP track is used as far as Marysville, thence to Yuba City.

Also: East Nicolaus Branch: From East Nicolaus to Sankey, 9.83 miles.

Pearson Branch: From a junction with WP at its MP 175.63 to Pearson, 4.70 miles.

Yuba City to Chico, 47.08 miles; this is the old NE main line.

Woodland Branch: Broderick (Sacramento) to Woodland, 16.57 miles.

Meridian Branch: Colusa Jct. to Meridian, 13.64.

SN Timetable 27, effective January 8, 1961, shows two daily roundtrips between Sacramento and Yuba City and between Yuba City and Chico. The East Nicolaus, Pearson, Woodland and Meridian Branches have no scheduled trains, and movement over them is at yard speed with train order authority not being required.

The above lines are governed by dispatchers at Sacramento. SN trains on WP, AT&SF and SP tracks are governed by those railroads' operating rules and special instructions.

Interlocking plants and signals are located as follows: At Clyde (Naval Ammunition Depot Ry.); X St., Sacramento (WP); Sankey (WP); Live Oak (SP); Mikon, Woodland Branch (SP); Tower Bridge, Sacramento (bridge).

All movements are by diesel locomotive power except that electric locomotives are in use between Marysville and Yuba City.

Shop facilities are provided by the WP at Sacramento. President R. T. Kearney, Superintendent H. J. Mulford, Trainmaster-Road Foreman of Engines E. G. Ratcliffe, Chief Dispatcher F. R. Justis and four dispatchers also make their headquarters at Sacramento. At Yuba City is Trainmaster J. E. Kenady.

ROSTER: S. N. LOCOMOTIVES, 1962 By Richard R. Reynolds

Number	Builder	Date	Tractive Effort	Horsepower	Units
142-146	Gen. El.	1946	26,400 Lbs.	380	5
147	Gen. El.	1942	26,400 Lbs.	380	1
201	Gen. El.	1955	41,300 Lbs.	600	1
202	Gen. El.	1956	41,300 Lbs.	720	1
301-303	EMD	1948	59,000 Lbs.	1,500	3

Notes: Nos. 301-303 acquired from The New York, Ontario & Western Ry. when that road ceased operation. 303 is leased to Western Pacific and is 801-D on that road.

In addition, electric locomotives 652, 653 and 654 remain in operation at Yuba City and Marysville.

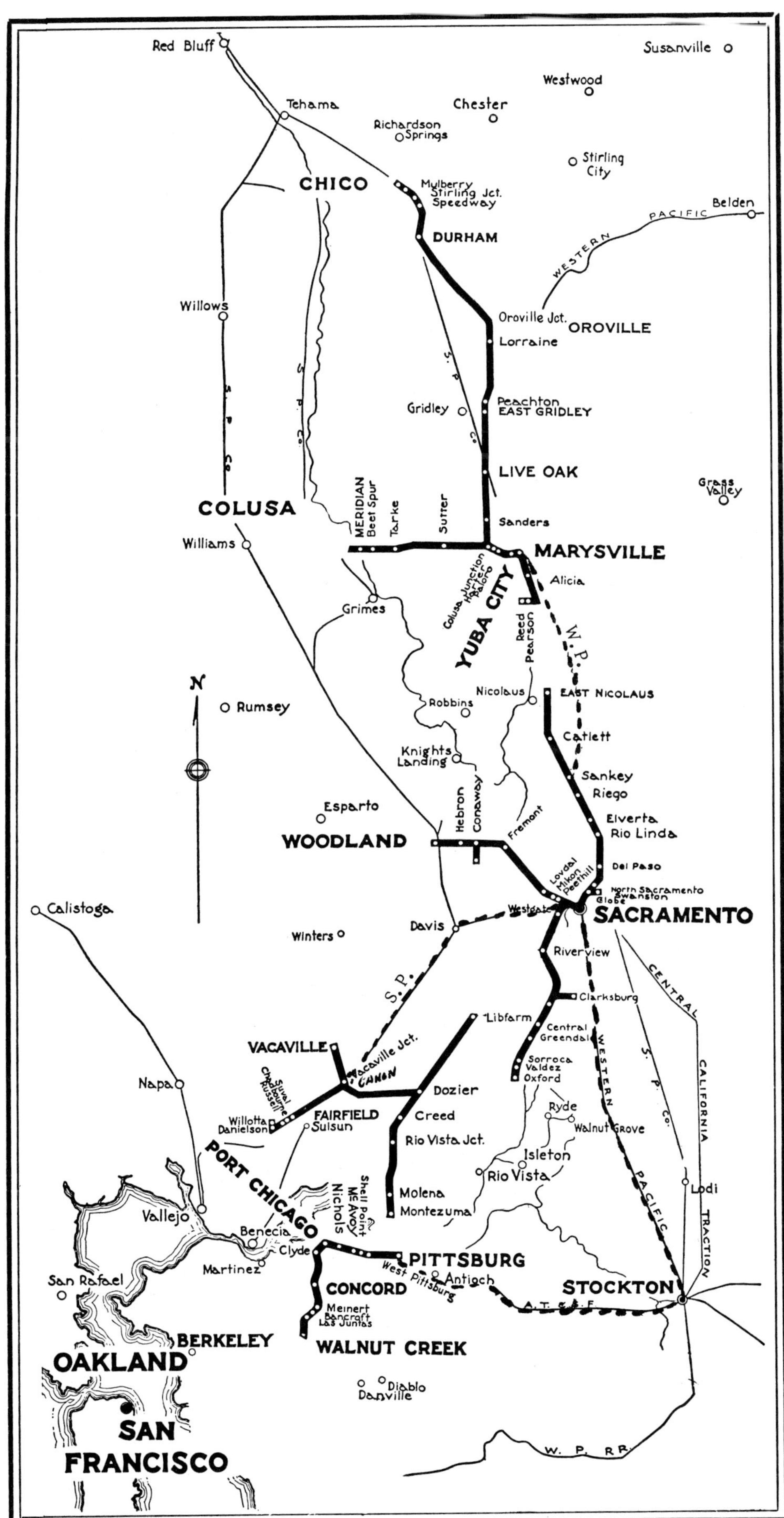

SACRAMENTO NORTHERN, 1962

The map at left shows SN as it exists today (or, rather, as it will appear when trackage rights on Southern Pacific are obtained from Canon (Vacaville Jct.) to Sacramento).

Note that SN consists of four separated systems, connected only by trackage rights on major railroads. Each has been tailored so as best to carry the Western Pacific flag into foreign areas.

The most northerly segment feeds the WP at Marysville, and consists of the old main line from Yuba City to Chico with the remains of the Colusa Branch.

The next segment centers around Sacramento, and feeds WP at that point. Included herein are the Woodland Branch, Oxford Branch, and remnants of the main line north to East Nicolaus.

The Vacaville Branch is now on the main line of the Second Subdivision; from it as branch lines radiate the Willota and Montezuma Branches.

Reached by the most round-about route of all is the old OA&E main line from Pittsburg to Walnut Creek; both the WP and AT&SF main lines must be covered from Sacramento before an SN train rolls on its own rails again.

That condition of track has deteriorated to freight-only requirements is indicated by the fact that maximum speed of all trains is but 30 mph, with 10 mph permitted over turnouts and crossovers.

JOINT TRACK

Santa Fe: Stockton-Pittsburg.
CCT: X St., Front St., Sacto.
WP: South Sacramento-Stockton;
  R St., Sacramento;
  MP 138.2-Globe;
  Sankey-Marysville.

Haggin Yard, Sacramento, is used by WP under trackage rights to enable it to reach its SP interchange.

SP has trackage rights over SN in Sacramento between Sacramento Yolo Port Railroad connection east of Washington underpass and connection to Sacramento Yolo Port Railroad east of county road crossing at Broderick; these tracks are used jointly by SN and SP trains.

The SP crossing at Front St. & Capitol Ave., Sacramento, is protected by a flagman. All SN and SP trains come to a full stop and are governed by flagman's signals before crossing.

S.N. 1981 by Jim Walker

SN in 1981 is an even smaller version of the 1962 railroad described on page 204. Abandonments have created even more isolated segments, reached through trackage rights over WP and SP rails. Many portions of trackage are not in use due to poor condition (this is detailed in the review of lines). Except for a few locations, such as Yuba City, Chico and Pittsubrg, SN has only a handful of customers.

Why, then, does SN exist as a separate entity? It is to the advantage of parent Western Pacific to continue SN as a subsidiary because of tariff rules. As the originating carrier, SN receives a percentage of the revenue for the movement. WP then receives an additional percentage when the shipment is interchanged to its rails from SN. An additional 7% to 9% often accrues to SN/WP account their separate identities.

SN crews man all SN movements, but dispatching of crews and other supervising is handled by WP. The officers of WP hold the same positions on the SN (R.G. Flannery is President and Chief Executive Officer, R.C. Marquis is Senior Vice-President/Operation, and WP Western District Superintendent C. Aadnesen is responsible for all SN operation). All SN movements are handled as within yard limits except the Chico and Yuba City Locals and the Pittsburg steel train.

THE SYSTEM- June 1981

Pittsburg Branch: Clyde to Santa Fe interchange east of Pittsburg. 10.85 miles.

Vacaville Branch: Cannon (S.P. interchange) to Vacaville. 7.87 miles. Track out of service beyond Vacaville Junction (located 2.34 miles from Cannon).

Dozier Branch: Cannon to Saxon. 22.1 miles. Track out of service beyond Dozier (6.94 from Cannon) and track between Libfarm and Saxon may soon be abandoned.

Montezuma Branch: Dozier to Montezuma. 14.75 miles. All trackage presently out of service. Kept intact primarily as potential line to industry proposed as various times at Montezuma.

Holland Branch: Broderick to Oxford. 21.12 miles. Except for spur to Clarksburg, trackage beyond Riverview is out of service and abandonment seems likely.

Woodland Branch: Broderick to Woodland. 16.67 miles.

Rio Linda Branch: Sankey to Rio Linda. 6.11 miles.

Chico Branch: Marysville (W.P. interchange) to Live Oak (13.0 miles) then via trackage rights on S.P. to Durham (27.98 miles) then via SN to Chico (6.62 miles further).

Tarke (formerly Colusa) Branch: Colusa Junction to Tarke. 10.28 miles. Track out of service west of Sutter (5.24 miles from Colusa Junction).

Pearson Branch: From Cleveland Junction (on W.P. near Marysville) to Pearson. 4.70 miles.

Swanston Spur: From Globe to Swanston. 1.8 miles. Out of service.

FREIGHT EQUIPMENT

Box cars bearing the name SACRAMENTO NORTHERN were purchased as late as the 1950s, but only four pieces of revenue freight rolling stock are known to be so lettered in mid-1981. Most have reached the end of their serviceable lives, but the survivors (except for the four noted) have been re-numbered and re-lettered into Western Pacific's series.

ONLY THREE LOCOMOTIVES BEAR SN'S NAME IN 1981. #711 IS SEEN AT YUBA CITY IN JUNE 1981.   Jim Walker

ROSTER: S.N. LOCOMOTIVES- 1981

Number	Builder	Date	Serial	Model	Tractive Effort	Weight	Notes
607	EMC	1939	889	NW2	62,000	248,000	1
711	EMD	1953	18167	GP7	61,700	246,800	2
712	EMD	1953	19168	GP7	61,700	246,800	2

Notes: 1. Purchased new by Stockton Terminal & Eastern (ST&E 1000) and traded to W.P. in 1968. Sent to SN in May 1973. 2. Ex-W.P. 711 and 712. Received in trade for SN 301A and 301D (shown as 301 and 302 in the roster on page 204). S.N. crews also use additional W.P. locomotives.

END OF ELECTRIC FREIGHT OPERATION

The final trolley freight operation on SN, in the Yuba City-Marysville area, was converted to diesel in Spring 1965. After a final excursion on April 10, 1965, power was shut down. Locomotive 654 (and partially dismantled #652) were donated to the California Railway Museum at Rio Vista Junction, and #653 was given to the Orange Empire Railway Museum, Perris, Calif.

UPDATE OF 1962 LOCOMOTIVE ROSTER (on page 204)

None of the units shown on the 1962 roster on page 204 is still in use on the SN. Disposition is as follows:

Number	Mfrs. Model	Date Retired	Sold to
142	44 ton	11/20/70	Chrome Crankshaft Co.
143	44 ton	3/7/69	Associated Metals
144	44 ton	7/30/71	Chrome Crankshaft Co.
145	44 ton	7/30/71	Chrome Crankshaft Co.
146	44 ton	9/21/71	Chrome Crankshaft Co.
147	44 ton	12/4/70	Chrome Crankshaft Co.
201	70 ton	2/9/68	Preston W Duffy & Son
202	70 ton	6/26/67	Prescott & Northeastern RR
301A	F-3	6/18/71	Trade in to EMD
301D	F-3	9/3/71	Trade in to EMD*
303	F-3	7/27/70	Trade in to EMD

*- 301D shown in error as 302 in 1962 roster.

CONTRIBUTORS TO 1981 UPDATE

We thank the following for assistance in gathering information about today's SN: Dick Bridges, Thomas R. Green, Ken Jackson and Pete Norgaard (all of Western Pacific Railroad), and Virgil Staff.

S.N. 1981

REVISED MAP AS OF JULY 1981

The principal change to the SN system is additional use of SP trackage to reach isolated segments of the line between Sacramento and Chico (see list of abandonment dates below).

SACRAMENTO INSET MAP

SN trains to the Woodland and Holland branches originate at Haggin Yard (A.) at 19th & B Sts., then use the WP main and the WP-SP connection, then roll west on SP main to a switch near 5th & Washington in Broderick.

Other locations: B. Western Pacific interchange yard (to SP and also to CCT which uses SP trackage rights to this point). C. S.P. (Amtrak) depot. D. M St. bridge, formerly used by SN to enter Sacramento. E. Swanston branch (not in service).

ABANDONMENT OF TRACK SINCE 1962

Sacramento to Chico: Oroville Junction to Peachton in 1966. Oroville Junction to Durham and Peachton to Live Oak in 1971. (SP trackage rights now used.) East Nicolaus to Carlett in 1965, and Catlett to Sankey in 1971. Globe to Rio Linda in 1971 (also rights over WP between Haggin and Sankey obtained). Operation through Sacramento ceased in March 1962, after which trackage rights on SP used (see inset map above).

Meridian Branch: Meridian to Tarke in 1964.

Willota Branch: Entire line abandoned in 1971.

Pittsburg Branch: From Walnut Creek to Concord in 1-64. Concord to Clyde in 1974.

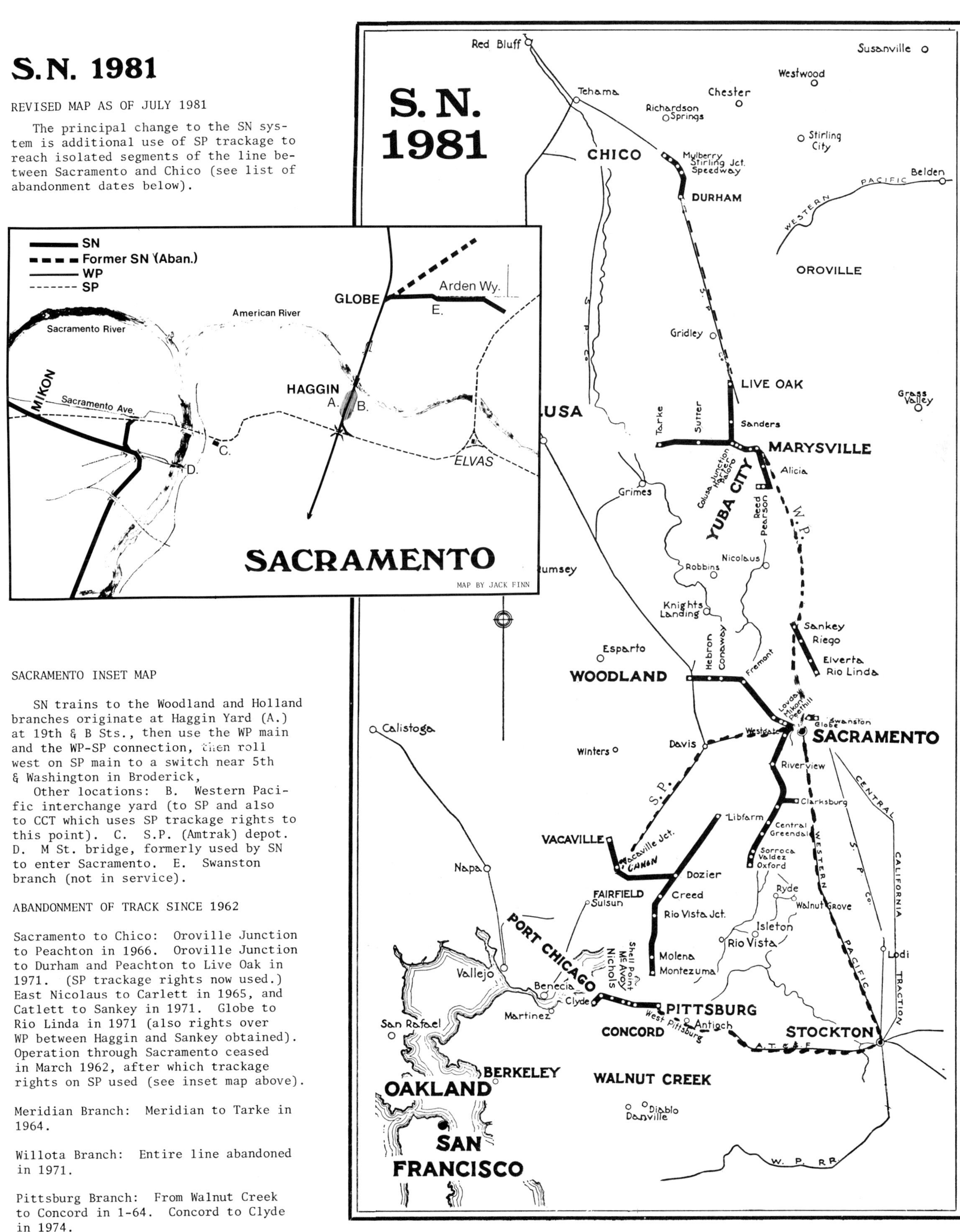

(ABOVE)   Ferry "Ramon" crossing with No. 3 on board.   April 14, 1940.   (AA-BB)

(BELOW)   A typical North End scene.   Train No. 11 at Marysville in May of 1940. (CS)

NOTE: The photographs on pages 208 and 209 were on the front and back covers of
          earlier printings of this book.